Atomic Narratives and American Youth

Atomic Narratives and American Youth

Coming of Age with the Atom, 1945–1955

Michael Scheibach

McFarland & Company, Inc., Publishers

Jefferson, North Carolina, and London

Library of Congress Cataloguing-in-Publication Data

Scheibach, Michael, 1949–
    Atomic narratives and American youth: coming of age with
the atom, 1945–1955 / Michael Scheibach.
        p.   cm.
    Includes bibliographical references and index.

    ISBN 0-7864-1566-5 (softcover : 50# alkaline paper)

    1. Youth — United States.   2. Atomic bomb — Social aspects—
United States.   3. Atomic bomb — Moral and ethical aspects—
United States.   4. Young adult literature — History and
criticism.   5. Atomic bomb in literature.   I. Title.
HQ796.S4117   2003
305.235'0973 — dc21   2003001970

British Library cataloguing data are available

Cover photograph ©2003 PhotoSpin

Manufactured in the United States of America

McFarland & Company, Inc., Publishers
    Box 611, Jefferson, North Carolina 28640
    www.mcfarlandpub.com

For Jamie,
whose unwavering love and confidence
made this book possible

Table of Contents

Prologue:
Sunday, August 5, 1945

For Satchel Paige, it was just another day at the ballpark. The 39-year-old pitching ace of the Kansas City Monarchs notched seven strikeouts in a 6–0 victory over the Sherman Field Flyers, a semi-pro team. In the big leagues, more than 170,000 fans filtered through the turnstiles to root for the likes of the Brooklyn Dodgers' Goody Rosen, Detroit's Hal Newhouser, the Chicago Cubs' Phil Cavarretta, and the Boston Braves' Tommy Holmes, who would finish the season with a league-high 28 homers.

Doubleheaders dominated the schedule. Nearly 30,000 watched the Washington Senators beat the Boston Red Sox 5–4 in fourteen innings, then sweep the doubleheader by winning the nightcap 5–1 for their ninth victory in ten games. In Cincinnati, 17,000 fans suffered through two more dismal games in the club's first losing season in seven years, as Cavarretta and the Cubs subdued the Reds, 12–5 and 2–1. The Philadelphia A's defeated the New York Yankees, 6–3 and 4–3, and the Chicago White Sox took two from the Detroit Tigers, ultimate winners of the 1945 World Series.

That morning, Americans across the country began the day by reading about the seemingly endless and devastating conflict with the Japanese. Troops returning from Europe prepared to ship out immediately to fight on in the Pacific. Troops already there, including the battle-hardened survivors of Okinawa, the war's costliest battle, prepared for the final invasion of the Japanese homeland. General Douglas MacArthur assumed control of conquered Japanese soil for the first time, extending his Army command to the Ryukyu Islands. MacArthur planned to use the islands as the base for the force that would drive "on to Tokyo."

Thousands of B-29 bombers, the famed "Superfortresses," continued to wreak havoc and death on Japan's cities. The previous week alone, ten

1

major metropolitan centers had been incinerated by some 1,400 Super-forts. Another twelve cities, with a combined population of 1.4 million, had been added to the "death list," as one reporter wrote, to be "eliminated" with fire bombs. Planes had dropped nearly a million "evacuate or die" leaflets on Japanese cities during the past few days, warning civilians of the impending destruction. The war was coming to an end. But when?

More than one million New Yorkers jammed the beach and board-walk at Coney Island on the first clear Sunday since July 8. Families in Kansas City, Missouri, enjoyed the warm afternoon at Fairyland Park's swimming pool, featuring "filtered" water. Amusement centers, beaches, swimming pools, and parks around the country were crowded with families enjoying a day off from work. Others stayed home, sitting in the shade on the front porch or in the back yard. They listened to the radio, shared lazy conversations, read the latest magazines. Women looking for a good book turned to Ayn Rand's *The Fountainhead* or Taylor Caldwell's *The Wide House*. For the man of the house, Ernie Pyle's *Brave Men* and Bill Mauldin's *Up Front* provided battle-scarred views of the war.

In Washington, D.C., the *S.S. Potomac* offered free dancing on a special four-hour daytime river cruise to Indianhead, Maryland. Tickets cost $1.00 for adults and 50 cents for children. Later that evening in New York City, civilians, including thirteen members of Congress, joined military personnel on board the *Queen Mary* for an early Monday morning departure across the Atlantic, now that the war in Europe had ended. Patrons in Chicago escaped the daily reminders of war — if only for a few hours — by letting loose at the Parkway Ballroom to the rhythms of the Sultans of Swing.

An infantile paralysis quarantine began in Trenton, New Jersey. Children under the age of sixteen were barred from attending Sunday schools, theaters, stores, playgrounds, parks, and gatherings of any kind. Twelve hundred miles west, in Omaha, Nebraska, rowdy teens in the balcony threw lighted matches on first-floor customers and slashed fire hoses, forcing theater owners to enlist the help of extra security guards. For most theater owners, however, the weekend meant overflowing crowds seeking a comfortable haven from the heat of war as well as the day's temperature.

Sunday afternoon found millions of grandparents, parents, teenagers, and children crowded into "air-cooled" movie theaters to catch the latest newsreels and cartoons, followed by their favorite movies: Van Johnson and Esther Williams in *Thrill of a Romance;* Jennifer Jones in *Song of Bernadette;* Betty Hutton in the comedy *Incendiary Blonde;* the Technicolor hit *Anchors Aweigh,* with Frank Sinatra, Kathryn Grayson, and Gene Kelly; or *A Bell for Adano,* with Gene Tierney and John Hodiak starring in the story based on John Hersey's best-seller. The entertainment sparkled and the price was right. Kids with 14 cents could buy a ticket at the Coed Theatre in Topeka, Kansas, and watch a double feature: Mickey Rooney and Elizabeth Taylor in *National Velvet*, followed by Dale Evans in *Hoosier Holiday*. Their parents joined them at the matinee for just 30 cents. At the local soda shop, high schoolers wondered if officials would once again let them have a prom, a tradition suspended by many schools because of the war.

As the afternoon lingered on, families gathered for the traditional Sunday dinner: a rib roast or fried chicken with mashed potatoes and corn and fresh apple pie for dessert. Over small talk at the table could be heard the sounds of their favorite radio programs: *Your America, Nick Carter, The Family Hour, Blondie, Men of Vision, Lucky Strike Hit Parade*, and *Leave It to Mike*. For the latest news, they turned on evening reports by William Shirer and Drew Pearson.

After dinner, teenage girls, anxious to look good for the upcoming school year, scanned the newspaper ads for back-to-school fashions. The ballerina influence dominated the fall look, with ads showcasing panung-draped ballet tights of red and green check, worn with a dull green skirt, both in wool jersey, with ballerina slippers. Others went for T-square blouses; chambray "shirt 'n' skirts" in aqua with white stripes; horse-blanket plaid wraparound skirts; or gray wool shorts worn with Buffalo plaid lumber jackets. Some girls cut out ads for a $1.25 package of Toni cold wave permanent; others dreamed of a day at the beauty parlor, where they could get a "Duchess" cold wave permanent for as low as $10.00. Teens able to get out of the house for the evening dropped some coins in the local jukebox to listen to Bing Crosby's "You Belong to My Heart," Les Brown's "Sentimental Journey," Louis Prima's "Bell Bottom Trousers," or Louis Jordan's jumpin' rendition of "Caldonia."

Another summer day, more than three-and-a-half years after the surprise attack on the U.S. Naval Base at Pearl Harbor, was coming to an end.

In the Pacific, half a world away, a new day was dawning. The temperature in the Japanese city of Hiroshima had already reached 80 degrees by 8 A.M. that Monday. The wind was calm; the humidity was a sticky 80 percent. Eight thousand schoolgirls worked outside, helping to raze houses to clear firebreaks against a possible incendiary attack. Men and women going to work packed streetcars and jammed streets with their bicycles. Toshiko Sasaki, a young female clerk, had just arrived for another day's work at the East Asia Tin Works. Mrs. Hatsuyo Nakamura and thousands of other women worked in their kitchens, looking out on the rising sun. Military spotters saw three American bombers approaching high on the horizon, just as an announcer for Radio Hiroshima arrived at the studio and prepared to issue an all-too-familiar air-raid warning.

Then, at 8:15 A.M. (Japanese time), while millions of American adults sat around the radio, children prepared for bed, and teenagers played the latest records, the *Enola Gay*, a specially equipped American Superfortress, dropped the first atomic bomb on some 300,000 residents of Hiroshima. The bomb, known as "Little Boy," unleashed the destructive power of 12,500 tons of TNT — more than 1,000 times the explosiveness of what had been the world's most devastating bomb: the 11-ton British "grand slam" bomb.

In a blinding, penetrating explosion that rocked the *Enola Gay* as it pulled away from the drop, more than 70,000 Japanese were killed instantly, many completely vaporized as the temperature at ground zero hit 5,400 degrees Fahrenheit. Thousands more would die later from radiation and flashburns.

The bomb annihilated 4.1 miles, or 60 percent, of the city, with the blast wave traveling at two miles per second. Seventy thousand of the city's 76,000 buildings were damaged or destroyed, 48,000 totally. The destructive cloud rose more than 40,000 feet into the air. Fire consumed a waking population, conditioned by news of American bomb raids over other Japanese cities but unprepared for the most horrific weapon in history hitting their own city.

When Americans gathered for breakfast on Monday morning, they opened their newspapers to read of the continuing bloodletting in the Pacific. Mustang fighter planes had "punished" Tokyo on Sunday afternoon. That night, nearly 600 Superforts of the Twentieth Air Force had hit cities with nearly 4,000 tons of explosives. Hundreds of fighters and bombers also attacked targets in the Kyushu region of Japan. Yet despite this overwhelming destruction, General MacArthur warned that Japan would not surrender to air bombardment alone. Troops on Luzon, Mindanao, New Guinea, Borneo, and other islands battled pockets of Japanese refusing to lay down their arms. Troops struggled against more than 85,000 Japanese on New Britain and New Ireland alone. According to MacArthur and other military leaders, more than forty divisions would be needed in the final assault of Japan, with an estimated one million American casualties. Looking ahead to the final invasion, war correspondent Frank L. Kluckhorn of *The New York Times* wrote that day: "[T]he American people must be prepared to take having losses and suffer continued privations for the victory and peace. It looks more and more as though a war of extermination must be fought."

Americans on the homefront were well conditioned to war. Finishing breakfast, millions of men and women began another week of work, mobilized to support those still fighting in the far Pacific. Then, as suddenly and without warning as the events of December 7, 1941, the news flashed across the nation's radio stations. At 10:45 A.M. (Eastern War Time) on Monday, August 6, President Harry Truman announced that an atomic bomb had been dropped on the Japanese city of Hiroshima sixteen hours earlier.

The following morning, *The New York Times* proclaimed: "First Atomic Bomb Dropped on Japan; Missile Is Equal to 20,000 Tons of TNT; Truman Warns Foe of a 'Rain of Ruin.'" In Topeka, Kansas, *The Daily Capital* emblazoned its front page with a one-line all-caps head that read, "DEMON OF DOOM BOMB BLASTS JAPS." The *Chicago Daily News* stated the blunt truth: "New Weapon Stuns Enemy." Wrote reporter Kenneth McCaleb in *The Washington Post*: "Equal in destructive power to an attack by 2,000 B-29s normally loaded with high explosive and incendiary bombs, the first single atomic bomb dropped on Japan dissolved the city of Hiroshima in a vast cloud of dust." Three days later, an American bomber repeated the mass destruction by flattening Nagasaki.

The Second World War had taken its final breath. On Tuesday, August 14, President Truman announced that the Japanese had accepted the Allies' terms of surrender. The war was over. Japan's conquering sun fell in darkness and Americans celebrated another V-day. The news brought instantaneous response in a country exhausted from nearly four years of war. Americans were overwhelmed with emotion, but not all could celebrate. For many, the moment of victory brought prayers and the uncontrollable release of pent-up feelings. In Seattle, Viola Lander paused on the steps of the city's memorial pylon in Victory Square and wept for her 19-year-old son, a Marine killed a few months earlier on Okinawa — his first combat mission. In Chicago, Mrs. Frances Evans Dyke, a 45-year-old mother of eleven servicemen from ages 19 to 30 (including triplets and three sets of twins), said simply, "Oh, thank God."

Even as the country felt the clear air of victory, however, the threatening cloud of a new, potentially apocalyptic, war slowly rose above them. The generation too young for war — America's children returning to school in September 1945 — soon came to understand the implications of this new threat, a threat encased in the atomic bomb.

Less than two weeks after the bombing of Nagasaki, *The New Yorker* wrote in its August 18 issue: "No matter about grown-ups; the children are already at home in the atomic world. For years the playground in Washington Square has resounded to the high-strung anh-anh-anh of machine guns and the long-drawn-out whine of high-velocity shells. Last Sunday morning a great advance was made. We watched a military man of seven or eight climb onto a seesaw, gather a number of his staff around him, and explain the changed situation. 'Look,' he said. 'I'm an atomic bomb. I just go "boom." Once. Like this.' He raised his arms, puffed out his cheeks, jumped down from the seesaw, and went 'Boom!' Then he led his army away, leaving Manhattan in ruins behind him."

Preface

Hearing an explosion one evening, the father rushed downstairs to check the furnace, while his twelve-year-old son hurried to the window and looked out. "No mushroom cloud," the boy said calmly, returning to his homework with a sigh of relief and reassuring smile for his mother. This anecdote, shared by a school psychologist in 1951, illustrated an important point at the time: Well-adjusted and informed youth will not panic in an atomic attack.[1]

America faced an imposing challenge in the years immediately following the bombings of Hiroshima and Nagasaki. As the Atomic Age expanded, eventually moving into the war against communism, educators, government officials, and parents realized the necessity, even the urgency, of preparing the country's youth for a new, more precarious, world. This required information about both the atomic bomb itself and its political and social implications.

This book is an examination of postwar adolescents' exposure to "atomic narratives"—narratives containing explicit textual or visual images of the atomic bomb, atomic energy, or the Atomic Age, as well as those narratives containing implied or subtextual references to the same images. These fictional and factual narratives encompassed the full breadth of American postwar culture: in the movies; on radio and television; in newspapers, magazines, and books; and, of course, in the classroom and school corridors.

On a larger scale, what Peter Schwenger has called "the polyphony of narrative voices" fused to create the *social narrative of the atom*: the collective array of visual and written narratives, including articles written for and by teachers and school administrators appearing in educational journals and government publications; discussions and other social discourse; values, mores, and attitudes; and sociocultural trends and artifacts relating to the perils and the promise of the atom. This social narrative became, simply, the larger drama of atomic awareness and anxiety that imbued American society between 1945 and the mid–1950s.[2]

The generation born between 1928 (graduating from high school in 1946) and 1942 (graduating in 1960) was inundated, even indoctrinated, with images and messages about its unique and consequential placement in history. Its members matured during complex and contradictory times, hearing messages of impending doom and the absolute necessity to protect democracy against world-threatening totalitarianism, as well as messages about the unlimited potential of the atom in science, medicine, agriculture, and industry.

My intent is to chronicle the wide array of atomic narratives not only accessible to youth or aimed at them but those narratives emanating from youth as well; and to trace the social fallout of the bomb, including the emphasis on safeguarding democracy, practicing civil defense, and fighting communism. I also want to suggest that the broader social narrative of the atom contributed to the creation of a social reality salient to this generation and thus indirectly helped to cultivate a well-defined adolescent culture.[3]

This is not to suggest that the concept of an adolescent, or youth, culture was new in postwar America. Adolescence as an age-segregated subculture with its own self-identity and distinct value system can actually be traced to colonial America. In the early 1800s, adolescent culture existed in community pockets, emerging in mid-century with the expanding school system as well as revival and reform movements. By the Progressive Era (1890–1920), an age-graded adolescent culture had formed around the rapid expansion of public high schools and youth organizations, as a more work-centered youth culture emerged in the country's urban cities, particularly in the industrialized Northeast. A school-based adolescent culture continued to expand through the 1920s, only to be shaken by the Great Depression of the 1930s, which forced many adolescents out of school and into the workplace. During World War II, adolescent males found their moratorium on adulthood replaced with the realities of battle. Even with this disruption of adolescence, though, a younger teenage culture continued to flourish during the early 1940s. In a case study of Indianapolis during the war, for example, Richard Ugland found a thriving and expanding teenage culture with its own distinct identity. Ugland has suggested that this culture developed primarily because teens were forgotten by an adult society focusing on war. Teens turned to the peer group for identification and support. In addition, the lack of employment for teenagers resulted in an increased emphasis on the school experience.[4]

As the country entered the Cold War, a new generation would finish laying the foundation for the ultimate cultural boundaries separating adolescence and adulthood. Exposure to atomic narratives—in school, at home, and within the community—contextualized by the broader social narrative, did not create postwar youth culture. Nonetheless, it unquestionably helped to shape youth's style, attitudes, and underlying concerns more closely associated with the Sixties Generation: those born between 1942 and 1954 and coming of age in a world already numb to the notion of atomic destruction, firmly entrenched in Cold War realities, and undergoing significant social ferment.

In the 1960s, student radicals (largely college-based political activists of the New Left) and members of the street-based, communal-oriented counterculture—*flower children* and *hippies*—differed in their approach to social action. Yet they agreed that something was wrong with America and that each individual could do something positive to make it better. Social psychologist Kenneth Keniston, writing in 1968, at the height of social unrest in America, described young radicals as committed youth who rejected central organizational control, opposed dogma and doctrine, and emphasized participatory democracy; on the other hand, he argued that alienated youth identified more closely with the counterculture and were committed primarily to self-discovery and change through aesthetic, expressive, artistic, and subjective endeavors.[5] Timothy Miller, in his book, *The Hippies and American Values*, also points out that radicals stressed democratic reform, while hippies created a generational community. Radicals attempted to change the political structure; hippies emphasized the need for individuality, creativity, and personal freedom. Radicals and hippies alike endorsed the need for peace and brotherhood while opposing war and destruction; moreover, both expressed dire warnings about the fate of humankind unless society began protecting the earth from people's self-destructive nature.[6]

These themes did not appear suddenly, without warning, when the thirty-fifth president of the United States announced that the country was entering a new frontier. Ten years earlier, General Omar Bradley, chairman of the Joint Chiefs of Staff, adumbrated John Kennedy's inaugural comments when he said, "The time has come for all of us to stop saying, 'What can I get out of this,' and to begin saying, 'What can I give to my country.'"[7]

Bradley directed his message to an America that, in 1951, still reeled not only from the repercussions of Hiroshima and Nagasaki but from the Soviet Union's explosion of its own atomic bomb and the fall of China to the communists two years earlier. His comments also addressed a new generation coming of age literally and figuratively with the atom: a generation bequeathed the heavy burden of safeguarding the country and, lo, life itself. Commenting on the significance of this generation, Philip A. Knowlton, educational director of the Macmillan Co., wrote in 1948:

> How can we live in harmony with an age of such wild confusion? No past generation had a problem approaching this in complexity or challenge. There have been more difficult times, yes. War, slavery, disease, want, and fear have again and again preyed upon the human race. The ravages of disease and war were greater when man had poorer resources with which to resist them. But never before have threats to man's happiness seemed to hold him so powerless when he had prosperity almost within his grasp. Never before has mankind been so frustrated by fear and anxiety.[8]

The ubiquitous atomic bomb, with its multifarious social and political fallout, permeated the lives of postwar adolescents, as the Depression of the 1930s had done to an earlier generation and the Vietnam War would do to a later one.

The narratives to which this generation was exposed did not contain a monolithic viewpoint or tone. Quite the contrary. Many narratives were serious, often espousing the end of civilization, while others took a more lighthearted or optimistic view of the atom. Narratives often encompassed various discourses or ideas representing distinct and often contestable approaches to the wide-ranging implications of the atomic bomb. For example, a single atomic narrative might contain a scientific discourse (on the destructive power of the atomic bomb), a medical discourse (on ways to combat the bomb's effects), a psychological discourse (on how to deal mentally or emotionally with a possible attack), a religious discourse (on the future prospects for humankind), and a political discourse (on efforts to control the atom's development).

Many texts were an amalgamation of themes accentuating the central reality that life in the Atomic Age was ambiguous at best and potentially fatal. Gunther Kress, writing in *Language and the Nuclear Arms Debate: Nukespeak Today*, addresses this process as the politics of discourse, or the marshalling of various discourses into a specific alignment "in the cause of larger political aims." Thus, not only are the multiple discourses within the narrative of importance but so too are the aims of its originator.[9]

For the generation coming of age with the atom, the messages emanating from atomic narratives formed an integral part of its socialization. As a result, the thematic content must be examined as well as the objectives of the narratives' originators (e.g., educators, government officials, the media, and parents). In addition, as historian Lawrence Levine suggests, it is equally important to examine the participant interaction in the cultural expressions of these narratives. "We forget too easily," Levine writes, "that going to a movie or listening to the radio are in and of themselves events and that we may have as much to learn from the process, the ritual, surrounding expressive culture as from the content of the culture itself."[10] Understanding both the audience and the audience's role in the popular culture is essential to historical inquiry.

The narrative, therefore, constitutes a historical metacode. In the words of author Hayden White, this metacode is "a human universal on the basis of which transcultural messages about the nature of a shared reality can be transmitted." Narrative is the mechanism by which knowledge is translated from one generation to the next. Without narrative, argues White, there is no history.[11] Paul Chilton, as editor of *Language and the Nuclear Arms Debate*, amplifies this point by suggesting that production and reception of "text-meanings" depend upon the distribution of power in society at a particular historical time. Text, he argues, is the crucial unit connecting individuals within social formations.[12] Even topics as diverse and seemingly mundane as those dealing with gender roles, social behavior, or educational objectives must be understood on two levels: subject and theme. And, in many cases, the underlying theme came back to ground zero: Civilization now existed, for better or for worse, under the shadow of the mushroom cloud, and everyone must learn to live with this new reality.

Educators were so concerned about the social and psychological impact of the atomic bomb that they sought to combat apathy by encouraging participation in a multitude of school athletics, clubs, and organizations. Students themselves joined in school activities and peer-bonding as a means of feeling secure and gaining self-identity. Chapter 1 examines these various activities within the context of their relationship to the Atomic Age and Cold War. Chapter 2 continues the discussion of adolescents' exposure to atomic narratives by entering high school classrooms, corridors, and auditoriums. Here, students read about, watched, discussed, and interacted with an array of fictional and factual, written and visual, atomic narratives. This chapter provides specific examples of what postwar youth encountered.

Chapter 3 traces the evolution of schoolwide themes of international brotherhood in the years immediately following the bombings of Hiroshima and Nagasaki, to themes of self-reliance and survival in the early 1950s. It also discusses the emphasis placed on safeguarding democracy, opposing communism, and preparing for civil defense—from the perspective of atomic narrative and social experience. Chapter 4 returns

to the classroom, this time providing an analysis of one of the more important supplemental texts from this era, *Senior Scholastic* magazine. As with
other narratives, the changing themes in the magazine's factual and fictional
atomic narratives mirrored societal changes taking place as the Cold War
deepened. The magazine used its factual reports and fictional stories to
inform students, as well as to influence their attitudes and behavior.

Chapter 5 travels to the movies, where the science-fiction genre
exploded in the early 1950s with atomic mutants and sinister enemies, and
where mainstream and so-called "teenpics" reflected such atomic themes
as loss of identity, alienation, anxiety, and fatalism. Chapter 6 leaves the
movie theater and returns home, where radio, television, magazines,
comics, and books provided myriad atomic narratives for young minds.
In an attempt to ascertain the attitudes of this generation, Chapter 7 provides a sampling of poems, essays, editorials, letters, and stories written
by male and female adolescents, white and African American, from large
cities and small towns, from the eastern seaboard to the West Coast.
Although these narratives reflect a diversity of thought, they clearly
demonstrate a universal awareness of the atomic bomb's virulent potential and concerns about its impact on the individual, American society, and
civilization itself. This is followed by a discussion of the fusion of the postwar youth culture, connecting the tenets of this generation with those of
the generation coming of age in the new frontier of the 1960s.

This book draws on the writings of adolescents from around the country, although high school newspapers and yearbooks from Kansas City,
Missouri, are cited extensively thanks to the Special Collections in the
Kansas City, Mo., Public Library, which provided access to every school
newspaper and yearbook published between 1945 and 1955. Kansas City,
however, is cited here as a city representative of most urban areas during
this era. In addition, letters, articles, and poetry have been gleaned from
the pages of *Senior Scholastic* magazine, read by thousands of high school
students throughout the country and thus representing a cross-section of
attitudes, opinions, and themes expressed by youth from cities, suburbs,
small towns, and rural America.

A conscious decision has been made not to explore other, and equally
significant, contributing factors in the socialization of youth (e.g., expansion of corporate America; technical, scientific, and medical developments;
urban to suburban migration; racial confrontations; working-class and
middle-class dichotomies; ethnicity, racial, and family issues; etc.). The
steady increase in the number of adolescents attending and completing
high school also is recognized as a factor contributing to the emergence of
an adolescent culture. Notwithstanding these exclusions, it is historically

clear that the atmosphere between 1945 and 1955 was highly pressurized. Americans struggled to understand the new Atomic Age with its many repercussions, as they simultaneously readjusted to peacetime and prosperity in a heated Cold War.

Adolescents are, for my purposes here, the protagonists playing out the roles assigned to them, and searching for self-identity as they are constantly reminded of the threat lurking in the background of their daily lives. For those moving through adolescence during this decade, moreover, exposure to atomic narratives and the wider social narrative of the atom resulted in a reality bursting with conflicting images: at times full of promise; at other times seemingly on the brink of oblivion.

Introduction: Postwar Adolescents and the Atomic Bomb

There are no longer problems of the spirit. There is only the question: When will I be blown up?
— William Faulkner, acceptance speech for
Nobel Prize for Literature, Stockholm, 1950[1]

In June 1962, a group of college students and young activists gathered in Port Huron, Michigan, to adopt what one called a "manifesto of hope." This manifesto, known as the Port Huron Statement, has become part of the historical archive of a decade noted for civil rights demonstrations and urban riots, the counterculture and psychedelic drugs, political assassinations and the Great Society, student protests and the Vietnam War.

Upon closer examination, however, the Port Huron Statement takes on added significance. Not only does it reflect the attitudes of American youth during the 1960s, but it also stands as a finely crafted expression of an earlier generation growing up during the dawning of the Atomic Age, in a world constantly threatened by the potentialities of nuclear Armageddon. In fact, the Port Huron Statement is both a precursor to the concerns and conflicts of the new decade and the concluding chapter of an earlier encounter with an anxious society reeling from atomic explosions and desperately searching for stability and security.

Led by Tom Hayden, a 23-year-old college student, and Alan Haber, the 26-year-old president of Students for a Democratic Society (SDS), the young students who gathered in Michigan that summer of 1962 were concerned about their future based upon the realities of their past. Wrote Hayden:

We are people of this generation, bred in at least modest comfort, housed
now in universities, looking uncomfortably to the world we inherit... . The
enclosing fact of the Cold War symbolized by the presence of the Bomb,
brought awareness that we ourselves, and our friends, and millions of
abstract "others" we know more directly because of our common peril, might
die at any time.[2]

Hayden addressed a "half-century of accelerating destruction [that]
flattened out the individual's ability to make moral distinctions." Anxiety, despair, and hopelessness were rampant, according to Hayden. People suffered from apathy and loneliness. They felt isolated. Society, he said,
had been forced to project public silence as it worried privately. Americans, particularly the young, had lost a sense of identity in an increasingly
technocratic world. This, in turn, had given rise to the vacuity of an entire
society. Beneath the calm was "the pervading feeling that there simply are
no alternatives, that our times have witnessed the exhaustion not only of
Utopias, but of any new departures as well."

Americans were feeling the emptiness of life. Only an "invisible
framework seems to hold back chaos for them now," Hayden lamented.
He criticized depersonalization, while endorsing belief in the "unrealized
potential for self-cultivation, self-direction, self-understanding, and creativity." Personal freedom needed to be recaptured before all was lost. He
emphasized independence, spontaneity, and "an intuitive awareness of
possibilities, an active sense of curiosity, an ability and willingness to
learn."

Hayden and his perspicacious colleagues understood the dire threat
both to the country and to civilization itself presented by the atomic bomb.
The only hope for survival was a commitment to human interdependence — international brotherhood. Hayden acknowledged the dichotomous nature of the atom, as both a new source of peaceful energy and the
harbinger of mass destruction. Yet it was more likely, he believed, that the
world would ultimately "unleash destruction greater than that incurred in
all wars of human history." On this last point, Hayden acknowledged a
quiet sense of desperation, almost fatalism, about the future, unless something was done immediately to change the country's direction.

The Sixties Generation — born between 1942 and 1954, inspired by the
New Frontier and the Great Society, confronted by the Vietnam War, and
concerned about segregation, sexual mores, social constraints, and nuclear
conflict —changed American attitudes, morals, and foreign policy. It was
not the first to come of age in a world threatened by world destruction,
though. Nor was it the first to confront its place in history. The themes
that underscored youthful protests during the Turbulent Decade were a

continuation of those themes accessible *to* youth, directed *toward* youth, and expressed *by* youth between 1945 and the late 1950s.

An earlier generation, coming of age in the aftermath of Hiroshima and Nagasaki, first espoused concerns over world peace and democratic values, and articulated the pivotal theme of postwar youth: a commitment to security in a world precariously balanced on the brink of destruction. More than twenty years before the Summer of Love in 1967, this earlier generation created the framework for a mass youth culture. Born between 1928 and 1942, this generation has carried many banners (Depression babies, Silent Generation, Shook-up Generation, Luckiest Generation, Beat Generation), but it is best described as the "Atomic Generation." No generation before or since has been as informed about the actualities and repercussions of the atomic bomb and the inherent dangers associated with its constant threat.

The Atomic Generation may be best understood as a cohort: the aggregate of individuals (within some population definition) who experience the same event within the same time interval. Writing in this area, sociologist Norman Ryder, in his often-cited 1965 essay, "The Cohort As a Concept in the Study of Social Change," contended that social transformations modify people of different ages in different ways; and, equally important, that youth is the primary locus of social change. Ryder maintained that although everyone alive at the same time is considered a contemporary, they respond and contribute to historical occurrences in different ways, that is, unless they are coevals. "In particular," he wrote, "the potential for change is concentrated in the cohorts of young adults who are old enough to participate directly in the movements impelled by change, but not old enough to have become committed to an occupation, a residence, a family of procreation, or a way of life." In addition, Ryder argued, the concept of change itself expedites youths' development of other orientations than those of their parents and their social environment.[3]

Ryder proposed further that cohort differentiation is not based solely on birth; it may be the result of "traumatic episodes like war and revolution [that] become the foci of crystallization of the mentality of a cohort." Technological change, for instance, may make the past irrelevant to the adolescent who is preparing for an adult role in an uncertain, even frightening, future society. The years immediately following the conclusion of the Second World War, which witnessed the unleashing of the Atomic Age with its many perceived and real dangers, created a cohort unified by birth, as well as by its movement through adolescence in age-segregated high schools.

Karl Mannheim's landmark 1928 article, "The Problem of the Generations," also dealt with the concept of cohort differentiation, which produces "fresh contact" with the historical world, and results in a "stratification of experience." Bernice Neugarten and Nancy Datan later expanded on Mannheim's argument by formulating the notions of life time (an individual's chronological age), social time (the system of age grading or age expectations), and historical time. Their position that historical events are filtered through life time and social time, so that an event (e.g., the exploding of the atomic bomb) affects an adult much differently than an adolescent, corresponds to Glen Elder's position on the three major features of the life course: timing, the events of an individual's life; interaction, individual life-course transition in changing historical situations; and integration, the cumulative impact of earlier life-course transitions with later ones.[4]

The fact that the world had experienced the destructive power of an actual atomic bomb, and had entered an era of intensified themes about living in an Atomic Age, is a useful historical reference point in understanding the impact of the bomb on individuals at different stages in the life course. Jeff Smith, in his study of nuclear weapons and western culture, *Unthinking the Unthinkable*, argues that it is impossible to address history in terms of pre-1945 and post-1945 as if these were totally different worlds. Obviously, the influence of the Depression and the war itself contributed to the worldview of this generation; and the mores, attitudes, lifestyles, and social ecologies of this generation continued from war to peacetime.[5] Nonetheless, for the Atomic Generation, the internalization of atomic narratives (often containing contradictory points of view) and the interaction with atomic-related activities, undoubtedly contributed to the formation of its social reality and self-identity in an ambivalent society.

Robert Thom, a student at Midwood High School in Brooklyn, New York, not only defined this generation; he also captured the dichotomies later expressed in the Port Huron Statement in his poem, "I Am a Child of the Age of the Atom," published in *Senior Scholastic* magazine in 1947. The poem expresses a fear that the atom is "nailing Christ to a second cross." It also acknowledges the power of an emotionless, controlling, authoritarian society. But this is balanced by a spiritual belief, a hope, that perhaps the world will not explode into chaos. Thom wrote:

> I am a child of the Age of the Atom
> And I must make my roots in this age.
> But I am afraid
> And I would go back into my mother's
>   womb where it is quiet and dark.
>
> I am afraid of the buildings for they are too tall,
> And I am afraid of the streets, for they are too long,
> And I am afraid of the noise of the cities, for it is deafening

But most of all I fear the atom, for it is nailing
Christ to a second cross.

I am a child of the Age of the Atom.
I shall be taught to See,
And I shall be taught to Speak,
And I shall be taught to Think.

I shall be taught a Science of Chaos,
And I shall be taught a Language of Chaos,
And I shall be taught an Art Form of Chaos,
For I have been begotten by Chaos and I am a Son of Chaos.

I shall be taught to Agree and to Disagree,
And I shall be taught to Participate and to Direct;
In brief, I shall be taught how to Live
And eventually I shall be taught how to Die.

All these things I fear,
But I am a child of the Age of the Atom.
I shall learn everything that may be learned and I shall
    be denied nothing.

But I shall learn nothing and I shall be denied everything.
I shall lead a life that is predicted,
My emotions shall be explained to me and I shall control them,
My talents shall be revealed to me and I shall develop them,
I shall be told I am free and I shall always be commanded.

All these things I fear,
But I am a child of the Age of the Atom.
Yet I shall turn to God of my own accord,
Although I am a child of the Age of the Atom.[6]

Thom was part of the first wave of the Atomic Generation — or the
initial *Blast*— born between 1928 and 1931. These youth were old enough
to fully comprehend the Second World War and actively participate in
schoolwide and community-wide projects as adolescents. The economic
hardships, insecurities, and social tribulations of the Great Depression,
followed by a mobilized homefront and newsreel images of a war-ravaged
world, framed their formative years. Many experienced absent fathers,
family dislocation, and personal tragedy during their childhood and early
adolescence. Their perspective of the atomic bomb was first and foremost
as the weapon that brought an abrupt end to a devastating war. After all,
they had been conditioned to massive bombings and death for nearly five
years— through newspapers, comics, movies, newsreels, and radio broadcasts.

Immediately following the war, "One World or None" became a major
theme in their lives, with emphasis on cooperation, brotherhood, and the

hopes of the United Nations. By the late 1940s, though, as they entered young adulthood and accepted the mast as America's Silent Generation, the world had entered what New York financier and statesmen Bernard Baruch first labeled a "cold war" against the Soviet Union, which had drawn an Iron Curtain across eastern Europe. Between 1946 and 1950, the United States threw its economic power against the expanding communist empire through the Marshall Plan and the Berlin airlift. Yet in 1949, as the initial *Blast* graduated from high school, the Soviet Union exploded its own atomic bomb. Now, the weapon that had won the war had been transmuted into a fearful weapon of mass destruction that might lead to another, perhaps apocalyptic, third world war.[7]

The *Heat*, or core, of the Atomic Generation was born between 1932 and 1937. They graduated from high school between 1950 and 1955. And during their adolescence, they experienced the Korean conflict; the development of the hydrogen bomb (1,000 times more powerful than the bomb used at Hiroshima); and the escalation of the Cold War, McCarthyism, and the introduction of civil defense as part of their daily lives. Amplifying these events, of course, was the simultaneous explosive expansion of television, a new medium that unleashed an unprecedented era of immediacy and social conformity. In 1950, *Senior Scholastic* magazine, read by hundreds of thousands of students each week in classrooms across the country, reflected that this generation had a date with destiny:

> You were born some time between 1932 and 1937. One of the first things you remember outside the four walls of your home was the Japanese bombers roaring down on Pearl Harbor. Five years ago ... you heard about the giant mushroom blast of smoke and flame that blossomed over a town called Hiroshima. And then — peace broke out![8]

This core group would become the vanguard for rock 'n' roll; be mesmerized by the ever-encroaching television medium; encounter atomic thrills in science-fiction movies; emulate and mourn James Dean; go steady and marry early; and, ultimately, complete the cultural barrier between a well-defined adolescent, or "teen," culture and adult society.

The last wave (the *Fallout*), born between 1938 and 1942, came of age as the 1950s blended into a new decade. By their adolescence, hopes of "One World" and international brotherhood had been replaced with the themes of individual preservation and survival. This last installment of the Atomic Generation would be the last youth to remember childhood before the atomic bomb. They entered adolescence in mid-decade as society slowly embraced the new teen culture. And they approached adulthood listening to the country's youngest president encourage them with the same rhetoric heard throughout their childhood: to accept their social responsibility to safeguard democracy. Many would enter college or the workforce as the 1960s exploded into racial, gender, and generational fragments.

The connection between the Atomic Generation and the Sixties Generation — both captives if not casualties of their social environment — is illustrated by pointing out that Tom Hayden (b. 1939) and Alan Haber (b. 1936) experienced their adolescence in the mid-1950s yet founded Students for a Democratic Society and played major roles during the turbulent Vietnam-era student protests and antiwar movement. Likewise, 29-year-old Bob Moses directed the 1964 Mississippi Summer Project, which established "freedom schools" and registered black voters; and Abbie Hoffman (b. 1936) led the Yippies in Chicago during the 1968 Democratic National Convention. Legendary music promoter and Korean War veteran Bill Graham (b. 1931) brought the psychedelic sounds of the counterculture to the mainstream; and Jim Morrison (b. 1940) of the Doors and Grace Slick (b. 1939) of the Jefferson Airplane reigned as the first king and queen, respectively, of the new *underground* music.

Ken Kesey (b. 1935) wrote *One Flew Over the Cuckoo's Nest*, about one man's fight against "the Combine," and led the Merry Pranksters, the original hippies immortalized in Tom Wolfe's *The Electric Kool-Aid Acid Test*; and writer Richard Brautigan (b. 1935), in such works as *The Abortion* and *Trout Fishing in America*, became identified with the new literary style that emerged from the countercultural mecca, San Francisco. Finally, Martin Luther King, Jr., (b. 1929) and Eldridge Cleaver (b. 1936) represented the extended hand and closed fist of the civil-rights movement.

These individuals and many others involved in or sympathetic to civil-rights protests, the counterculture, student activism, the anti-nuclear movement, the Peace Corps, the ongoing struggle against communism and for democracy, and other social causes during the early 1960s, were themselves influenced by their education and the atomic narratives that formed an integral part of their formative years.[9] The basic tenets of the postwar youth culture — a belief in the individual; a desire for creativity and expression; a commitment to world peace, brotherhood, democratic principles, and one's social responsibility; anxiety over communist aggression and the hydrogen bomb; a sense of separation from mainstream adult society; and, for many, an apathetic and even fatalistic attitude toward life — were thus transmitted from the generation coming of age with the atom to a younger generation coming of age during a new era of social unrest and conflict.

Jerome Rodnitzky has written about the evolution of the American protest song, "[S]uddenly in the late 1950s and early 1960s came the cataclysmic events that called folk guitarists to arms. Along with the student-led Southern civil-rights movement, came a variety of songs. Northern songwriters picked up the spirit and spun out a mass of polemics against racism, the arms race, and middle-class conformity."[10] Among these young folksingers were Bob Dylan (b. 1941), Phil Ochs (b. 1940), and Joan Baez (b. 1941). Dylan became the most influential voice of caution and concern. In his song, "The Times They Are A-Changin'," released in 1964, he warned mothers and fathers not to criticize the younger generation. A year earlier, two years before the Vietnam buildup by President Lyndon Johnson and a year after the Port Huron Statement, Dylan reflected Hayden's warnings about the next world war. In his song, "Blowin' in the Wind," Dylan expressed concern that it might take another world war before society learned its lesson and banned war forever.[11]

As the country moves beyond the Cold War and its threat of all-out nuclear conflict, toward a world of terrorists armed with nuclear capabilities, it is time to view America's youth following the Second World War from another perspective. In so doing, historians may recognize that it was not the Sixties Generation but an earlier generation, coming of age with the atom in the late 1940s and 1950s, that gave initial life and meaning to the postwar youth culture.

American society, trapped in an age of anxiety, sought to protect youth while simultaneously preparing them for a potential atomic war. Exposure to atomic narratives and atomic-related social activities in school, at home, and in the community only intensified the self-awareness of the Atomic Generation as the protectors of democracy and civilization, and encouraged youth to seek security and a sense of identity within the generational boundary separating them from adult society. And the more difficult it became to adjust to the educational, social, and psychological requisites of this society in an ever-intensifying Atomic Age, the more committed adolescents became to their own culture.[12]

1

Future Homemakers and Boy Cadets: School Activities for "Atom-Agers"

Science has brought forth this danger, but the real problem is in the minds and hearts of men.
— Albert Einstein, 1946[1]

Adolescents moving through high school corridors between the fall of 1945 and the late 1950s confronted myriad issues and concerns never before faced by Americans, young or old. Coming of age in an era of prosperity, following years of depression and world war, they were constantly reminded not only of the possibility of an atomic war but of the end of civilization and Earth itself. Told to take advantage of educational pursuits, America's postwar youth were chastised for not accepting their responsibilities, being apathetic, threatening the country's security through juvenile delinquency, and, by the mid–'50s, challenging acceptable social mores and behavior with rock 'n' roll.

Most postwar youth maintained an outward faith in the future, suppressing any fears of atomic apocalypse and emerging to fulfill their roles in the "organization," the "nuclear family," and the American dream. Many also held bifurcated views, vacillating between hope for the future and fear there may not be one, as illustrated by high school student Robert Thom's 1947 poem, "I Am a Child of the Age of the Atom": "I am a child of the Age of the Atom/And I must make my roots in this age/But I am afraid...." These views would take time to crystallize, however.

On Tuesday, August 14, 1945, at 6:57 P.M. (Eastern War Time), when Americans finally heard the long-anticipated announcement that Japan had finally surrendered, no one had any thoughts of the future. The victory celebration had been a long time coming. As radio broadcasts and late-edition newspapers spread the word, the pent-up emotions of a war-weary nation exploded. America's children joined their parents in unbridled celebrations from the eastern seaboard to the West Coast, in major metropolitan centers and the outermost communities, on city streets and rural roads. The focus on this summer night was not on the opening of the Atomic Age. Rather, it was on the final victory in a war that witnessed more than 400,000 American deaths and estimates of 50 to 70 million deaths worldwide.

Teenagers took to the streets en masse, along with Americans of all ages, to throw confetti, shoot fireworks, honk horns, and unbutton tensions caused by four years of war. Young women and men reveled through the night and into the first morning of the postwar era. Others attended religious services with their families. More raucous Americans burned effigies of the Japanese, piled into overcrowded streetcars, and blocked traffic as they spilled their cars onto busy intersections. Happy civilians and military personnel embraced, kissing wildly and passionately — strangers before, strangers after.[2]

When high schools reopened that fall — the first time in peacetime for this generation — girls looked "neat" in their black chesterfield coats and ballerina slippers, while boys were "really a zoot" in tee shirts, jeans, "drapes," and club jackets. On the radio and on jukeboxes, white youth listened to the swing music of Benny Goodman and Harry James and danced to the crooning sounds of Frank Sinatra and Hazel Scott, while black youths enjoyed the harder swing and jazz rhythms of Duke Ellington, Fats Waller, and Lionel Hampton.

Returning students enrolled in Cooperative Occupation Education (COE), which gave them credit for working while still in school. Boys turned their attention toward completing their training in the Junior Reserve Officers' Training Corps (JROTC) program. Girls joined the Y-Teens and Junior Red Cross. Both signed up to support "teen town," school- or community-sponsored social events combining dancing with ping-pong, basketball, chess, checkers, and shuffle board. Schools that had abandoned cheerleaders, proms, and other social activities during the war announced their reintroduction. Indeed, students' immediate concerns appeared far removed from the war's battlefields and devastation. Yet behind the talk of dating, teen town, the upcoming football game, and the latest fashions, a more serious awareness existed among America's adolescents who were already conditioned to the realities of world war. After all, those entering high school had watched newsreels, read newspapers, and participated in school and family discussions about the struggle in

Europe since the late 1930s, long before America responded to Japan's attack on the naval base at Pearl Harbor in Hawaii.

Over the next few years, the Atomic Generation slowly coalesced behind a burgeoning high-school-based culture with distinct — and, to some, threatening — values and shared outlooks. But this emerging youth culture was not an accident. Although the use of schools to encourage moral values and social conformity had been well established by the early 1900s, it was nonetheless rearticulated to reflect the realities of the postwar era. Government spokespersons and educators throughout the late 1940s and early 1950s expressed strong views on the school's role in providing a positive moral and cultural environment for America's children. Clearly, one of the main objectives among educators was the encouragement of adolescents to accept their social responsibilities to be good citizens and, even more urgent, to safeguard democracy and civilization itself. These ideas were expressed in countless narratives appearing in magazines, books, and journals aimed at America's school administrators and teachers. The impact of these narratives, moreover, can be seen in school activities, student organizations, and the many community-wide programs and projects directed at the younger generation and which formed adolescents' social narrative of the atom.

Educators, in an elemental sense, encouraged youth to attend high school as a means of preparing for a challenging and precarious future. As historian William Graebner has pointed out, postwar educators transformed the school into a laboratory for the social engineering of youth.[3] William Reaves of the University of Chicago argued that schools must use all their resources — including extracurricular activities and assembly programs — to prepare students for the future. Reaves believed students learned from one another in informal associations on the school ground, in the school corridors, and even on their way to and from school. "The almost innumerable activities in which students engage outside the high school classrooms," he wrote, "provide further opportunities for education through participation in the pursuit of common interests and purposes." According to Reaves, even students who did not participate in school activities benefited indirectly because well-organized extracurricular activities contributed to a school environment "more conducive to the natural and normal development of youth."[4]

Gerald Van Pool, director of school activities for the National Association of Secondary-School Principals, suggested that students should feel school is a better place because they were there that day. "Everything a student does," he wrote in 1953, "ought somehow to contribute to his civic competency." That same year, Gordon Dean, former chairman of the

Atomic Energy Commission, commented that educators were the ones who could ensure that America's youth developed a healthy outlook toward the Atomic Age. Likewise, Lyman Graybeal, associate professor of education at New York University, was a strong proponent of a student activity program he called "democracy in action," aimed at discovering and developing individual talents, needs, and abilities. "To discover, liberate, develop, and perfect the intrinsic powers of every citizen of the school is the central purpose," he wrote, "and its furtherance of individual self-actualization is its greatest glory."[5]

Educators stressed, even demanded, student involvement as verification of an individual's commitment to democracy. Their most significant concern, though, was student apathy resulting from fear of unstoppable death and destruction. Bonaro Overstreet, writing in the February 1952 issue of *Journal of the National Education Association*, suggested that internalized fear and the atomic threat were allogamous: each contributing to the growth of the other. "The present balance between life-affirming and life-denying forces is too nervously precarious to be maintained," he wrote. "The eventual swing of that balance may generally depend upon what we come to understand about fear and what we do as a consequence." The author of *Understanding Fear in Ourselves and Others*, Overstreet felt legitimate fears contributed to the ability for human survival. People, he maintained, *should* fear authoritarian personalities, defeatism, the influence of so-called "hate-mongers," the growing sense of helplessness, human tendencies like obtuseness, and threats to free institutions—not the atomic bomb itself.[6]

Although fear among America's children and youth became an obsession for many educators, anxiety was an even greater concern among others. Laurence Sears, professor of American political theory at Mills College, addressed this issue in *Educational Freedom in an Age of Anxiety: The 1953 Annual Yearbook of the John Dewey Society*. In defense of progressive educators, he issued a sharp rebuttal to the tactics of McCarthyism and the growing fear of communist subversion within society, as well as within the educational community. These tactics had fostered an atmosphere of panic, according to Sears, in which people were willing to give up personal freedoms because the danger appeared too formidable to overcome. "War might conceivably result in the destruction of America by Russia," he wrote. "[But] the *threat of war* may result in the destruction of American democracy by ourselves."[7] Sears's central thesis was that because fear is focused (i.e., the enemy is known, and a means of attack or escape can be definite), it can be overcome through knowledge. Anxiety, on the other hand, was more diffuse and therefore more difficult to counter. He described anxiety as "a sense of bewilderment, of being lost, of having shelters destroyed, guards beaten down, of helplessness in the face of over-powering, if ill-defined, threats." Anxiety arose when danger not only seemed overwhelming but also unmanageable, with no surety that it could be controlled. "There are times when the expectation of danger, instead of precipitating a rational fear, calls forth an overwhelming panic," he wrote. "It is this very sense of helplessness, of being unable to find any appropriate action to meet the danger, that marks the transition from fear to anxiety."[8]

Other eras had surely experienced anxiety, Sears acknowledged. Yet none had encountered the struggle of the United States, virtually alone and without strong allies, against the Soviet Union, the explosive power of the atomic bomb, and the subversive nature of communism. Thus, the Atomic Age contributed to a more acute sense of anxiety, particularly among those susceptible to emotional immaturity.

H. Gordon Hullfish, editor of *Educational Freedom in an Age of Anxiety*, also warned that anxiety would be compounded if educators did not recognize that maturation was a slow process, and that young people were undeveloped, helpless, and dependent. The Ohio State University education professor reminded teachers of the necessity of remaining positive as they worked to reduce anxiety and prepare the new generation for an uncertain future. "[T]hough we dare not rule out the possibility that our world may blow up as we work to improve it," Hullfish wrote, "...we are entitled to have faith in the future."[9]

This faith was repeatedly placed in the context of group solidarity and identity — the basis of any culture. A special 1949 report on health education by *The High School Journal*, for example, called group dynamics an area of knowledge of first importance to every health educator, "for group thinking strengthens democracy." The report went on to read: "Knowledge of how a group is built and how it works, insights and understandings of the part each group member can play, and familiarity with the psychology of group behavior are indispensable to such success."[10]

Youth's commitment to group welfare — and to democracy itself — was the central theme of a *Life* magazine article published in December 1944. Titled simply "Teen-agers," the article said that teenage girls lived "in a world all their own — a lovely, gay, enthusiastic, funny and blissful society almost untouched by the war. It is a world of sweaters and skirts and bobby sox and loafers, of hair worn long, of eye-glass rims painted red with nail polish, of high-school boys not yet gone to war." A June 1945 article in *Life* proclaimed that teenage boys were most concerned about having to fight the Japanese. But "they have responded to this stern prospect by behaving exactly as they have always behaved, connected with the complete enjoyment of playing, eating and sleeping...."[11]

The lives of teenagers had become more institutionalized during the Second World War as high school attendance continued to increase. More important, teenage culture flourished as adult society concentrated its energies and concerns on the war effort. *Life*'s portrayal of "a welter of fads and taboos" dominating the lives of adolescent boys and girls, however, glossed over the serious side of the initial *Blast* of the Atomic Generation. More than a million teenage boys and girls actively participated in youth centers during the war, setting the stage for the teen towns that would become widespread in peacetime. Of more significance, teenagers sold War Stamps and conducted community collection drives. They joined Y-Teens, JROTC, and the Junior Red Cross. Students across the nation made Christmas packages for veterans and visited veterans hospitals. In short, during the war, America's adolescents immersed themselves in national and international affairs, even as they attempted to live a *normal* teenage existence of slumber parties, dates, boyfriends, and the latest fads and fashion.[12]

In the fall of 1945, *Senior Scholastic*, which was distributed to high schools across the country, offered students an opportunity to respond to *Life*'s portrait of the teenage world. Those responding represented committed young women sensitized to the war and traumatized by the recent atomic explosions. Mildred Baach of Blooming Prairie (Minnesota) High School summed up her feelings by commenting that "we teen-agers have learned about war through experiences. Our dreams, our plans, our hearts cannot help but be battle-scarred." Adelaide Brothers of South Orange (New Jersey) High School took exception to the notion that girls did not participate in the war effort. "These two articles in *Life* made me mad as hops!" she wrote. "What about the girls who became Junior Aides in hospitals? Was it a 'lark,' giving up two or three afternoons of an already-crowded week? What about those who joined Art Service units or knitted sweaters for the Red Cross? Or sold stamps or worked in canteens?" Phyllis Kane of Midwood High School in Brooklyn, New York, reflected the involvement of many of her classmates when she wrote:

> Do we appear silly and juvenile at our Red Cross meetings, Child Care centers, at our G.O. elections? Did we do too badly as hospital aides? Weren't we in there pitching with paper collections and War Stamp sales? Didn't we take jobs after school? Didn't the 4-H'ers can tons of fruits and vegetables? Didn't we dig Victory gardens? Didn't boys of 17 enlist in the Merchant Marine? Boys of 18 help fight on all the battle fronts? Why should the serious many be criticized because of the silly few?

Finally, in the view of Jean Rancourt, from Solon (Maine) High School, the magazine had failed to recognize that teenagers, even in small towns, thought a great deal about the deeper and more important things in life, including religion and social problems. "Perhaps we haven't solved any of them," she added, "but we're trying. Isn't that something?"[13]

These girls were part of a generation that had grown up with a world war only to face a world now on the brink of an even more frightening and potentially fatal war. Only a month before the new school year began, *Time* magazine announced "the age of atomic force," saying the atomic bomb had presented civilization "a brutal challenge" to save itself from destruction.[14] This viewpoint emerged in countless atomic narratives over the next decade, including high school newspapers, which no longer merely chronicled school activities but promoted educational objectives. As one educator wrote, "A newspaper can no longer be a mirror, a reflector of the school. It must be a participant in the promotion of the educational program. It must be able to affect the attitudes and improve the learning of all its readers."[15] These newspapers, therefore, form relevant historical repositories, revealing the concerns of educators as well as students. Shortly after the *Time* article, for instance, a high school newspaper in Kansas City, Missouri, commented:

> Few of us can remember clearly the problems which confronted a world at peace. Certainly none of us can remember when the world was challenged with such a glorious opportunity of rebuilding a world torn by war and strife into a world in which all nations would live together in peace and harmony.... Perhaps the newly developed atomic bomb affected the sudden conclusion of the war more than any single factor. It has also brought us the realization that we are living in the age of science. If this is to be the age of atomic power, and if civilization hopes to survive, it is imperative that an enduring world government be established. The necessity of hard study while we are in high school is undiminished. It is our most valuable contribution to peace.[16]

Another school newspaper wrote, "When in the science class, remember the atomic bomb and all the other scientific strides which our country has made during this war — and remember that to keep peace, we must be scientifically 'tops.'"[17]

Within the first few weeks of returning to school, 500 girls at a senior high school in Kansas City signed up to sell forget-me-not flowers made by veterans, sponsored by the War Veterans Association. Combat veterans spoke before students and told of their experiences in Japanese concentration camps. A new veterans program opened at the city's technical high school, which joined other high schools in planning memorials for alumni who had died in the war. War films were shown in school auditoriums and classes, and groups like the Y-Teens and Junior Red Cross continued their efforts to provide food and other goods for veterans and war-torn Europe.[18] Even as students made the transition from war to peace, they were reminded of the continuing struggle for human survival. The social narrative of the atom was rapidly taking shape.

Students participated in national radio hookups addressing the issue of whether the United States should keep the atomic bomb's makeup a secret. In fact, a poll taken at one high school, as part of the nationwide poll sponsored by *Senior Scholastic,* found that 58 percent of students opposed sharing the atomic secret with other nations. Students listened as teachers warned that unless the Soviet Union cooperated in a world government, it would be "the end." A student wrote at Thanksgiving that the best way to honor this tradition was "by seeing that peace reigns, and that atom blasts do not rend the world." An editorial, in response to a national

Images of the mushroom cloud and the textural themes of the atomic bomb became incorporated in high school yearbooks. In this 1947 yearbook, the attitude is nonchalant, even humorous. The photograph of a girl in science class has the caption: "An atomic bomb?— maybe."

poll that showed most Americans believed a third world war inevitable, told students that "very little hope for all mankind in this atomic age" existed without a strong United Nations organization.[19]

Images of the mushroom cloud and the textual themes of the atomic bomb also became incorporated in high school yearbooks. But what is most interesting is the seeming acceptance of, even nonchalance about, the bomb's factuality. The 1947 yearbook at Kansas City's Southwest High School featured the photograph of a girl in science class, with the caption, "An atomic bomb?—maybe." Another yearbook featured an illustration of an atomic explosion to chronicle the events occurring during the senior class's high school years. Next to the drawing it read, "The control and production of atomic energy took the public limelight in the fall of 1947. As its control was turned over to an international agency, the halls ... rocked from the terrific impact of the returning tide of students."

A Kansas City high school made "Fusion" the theme of its 1951 yearbook, using the atomic lexicon to describe the school experience: "motivation .. faculty; mass .. student body; matter .. honors, events; motion .. activities." In Los Alamos, New Mexico, home of the atomic bomb, the 1952 graduating class dedicated their yearbook to the work on atomic energy, with photographs of the Los Alamos Scientific Laboratory interspersed with student pictures. In 1954, the school featured an atomic explosion on the cover. Inside, the director of Scientific Laboratory wrote, "[T]he mushroom cloud of an atomic explosion is a familiar shape drawn in colored crayons by the smallest schoolchild. Textbooks have been rewritten to include the principles of nuclear physics and atomic fission. Students everywhere are preparing to apply these principles to their work in the future."[20]

For students in Los Alamos and across the country, the atomic bomb posed a serious threat to the future and required a serious and immediate response. In December 1945, the sons and daughters of atomic scientists formed the Youth Council on the Atomic Crisis in Oak Ridge, Tennessee, site of a major atomic research installation. This came just four months after the bombings of Hiroshima and Nagasaki. The council, dedicated to the peaceful use of atomic energy, began as an idea following a student discussion of Norman Cousins's *Modern Man Is Obsolete*, which foretold of civilization's fateful date with apocalypse unless the world formed one government. The council finally took shape after a physicist, speaking at a school assembly, commented to students, "There is no defense against the atomic bomb. If another war comes along, one out of every three persons in this auditorium will die from atomic blasts."[21]

The reality of the Atomic Age had penetrated the insular environment

$\mathcal{I}t's \quad \mathcal{A}bout \quad \mathcal{T}ime$

That we recorded some facts for posterity. ....

1948

In September 1946, the headlines gave day by day accounts of the war criminal trials in Nuremberg, Germany. As the world awaited the results of this great event, so the members of the senior class of 1951 were awaiting a big day in their history; and after a late start due to a polio epidemic, it finally came. We were eighth graders at last! In spite of being the youngest group in Westport, we soon proved to be among the top Westport supporters and carried our bubbling school spirit with us to all games, mixers, and other activities.

The control and production of atomic energy took the public limelight in the fall of 1947. As its control was turned over to an international agency, the halls of Westport rocked from the terrific impact of the returning tide of students. Joining the literary societies and departmental clubs ranked high on our list of freshmen achievements that year, and Bud Kramer was elected a second time to the office of president, which he was to hold for two more years.

Presidential campaign speeches and many union strikes due to the rising cost of living were prominent in United States affairs as we, as sophomores, greeted the clock in the front hall and looked forward to a great year. Many of our boys started on the road to an all-star position in football or basketball, and some of the girls displayed their musical talents by joining the choir or glee club.

So near and yet so far might well have been said in 1949 in regard to world peace. But it would have applied equally as well to the fact that we were now juniors with only two years to go! A small senior class was no match for such a large group of juniors and we were soon found to be close rivals in running school affairs. Another first-place basketball team gave a proper finishing touch to our fourth year in Westport and after an unusually long summer due to the shortened term, we felt rested enough to continue our education.

In 1950 the world was in an ever increasing turmoil as the cold war had become the Korean battlefront, but one thing stood out clearly in our minds as we entered these friendly halls again. We were SENIORS at last! Dave Clark took over the presidency, and we were on our way. That long and eagerly awaited year had finally arrived. Among the highlights of the first term were that never-to-be-forgotten football assembly in which the coach's dreams of a championship team were publicly analyzed, and the musical play, "Meet Me in St. Louis," The second term had a thrilling beginning as Westport's Tigers played their way to an Interscholastic Basketball League Championship. As we came closer and closer to our graduation goal, we grew sadder and sadder at the thought of having to leave Westport and all the good times we had had there, but the thought of the coming Senior Day raised our morale considerably. As the last strains of "Pomp and Circumstance" faded away at the Distinguished Service Award Assembly, the Senior Class of 1951 said a fond farewell to Westport, the "school above all others."

1947

1950   1949   1946

Kansas City's Westport High School featured an illustration of an atomic explosion to chronicle the events occurring during the senior class's high school years. Next to the drawing it read, "The control and production of atomic energy took the public limelight in the fall of 1947. As its control was turned over to an international agency, the halls ... rocked from the terrific impact of the returning tide of students."

of these youth. Sally Cartwright, in an article on the council published in *Progressive Education*, wrote, "Oak Ridge students know that no more terrible destruction can be imagined than that caused by atomic blasts. Another war is unthinkable in the face of the complete devastation shown by the two dead cities of Japan…. The issue is clear: We shall have peace or extinction!" According to Richard Glasgow, the sixteen-year-old Youth

This yearbook's theme is "Fusion," using the atomic lexicon to describe the school experience: "motivation .. faculty; mass .. student body; matter .. honors, events; motion .. activities."

Council president, "We may be children, but if atomic war should come, we'd be just as dead as the other people." Added Richard Sawyer, whose father worked on the Manhattan Project, "The atomic bomb may mean the death of my family and friends if something isn't done about world control of atomic energy."[22]

The Youth Council promoted discussions about atomic energy in school, public meetings, and the media, as well as among family groups. It encouraged letter writing to influential persons within the scientific and political communities to urge them to prevent the destructive use of atomic energy. The council also endorsed a proposition that atomic energy should only be used for peaceful applications. Committees were formed on technical aspects of atomic energy, national legislation, the United Nations, international friction, bomb damage, and world government. The council assisted the school librarian to create an atomic energy bookshelf. The council even worked with teachers to develop atomic units throughout the school curriculum, including social studies, literature, speech, physics, and chemistry.

By August 1946, Youth Council members from Oak Ridge High School had traveled to ten states, participated in numerous radio broadcasts, and written more than 1,000 letters in support of peaceful applications of atomic energy. After school, council members met with teachers, parents, journalists, business people, ministers, and scientists in informal roundtable discussions. Newspapers coast to coast published a Christmas editorial written by Oak Ridge Youth Council members. The editorial, which also was quoted by radio commentators, read, in part: "We have never known a peaceful Christmas. While the atomic bomb threatens, we fear that there can be no peace for us nor for the world.... We are alarmed that this terrible menace has not been more generally recognized. We, the youth of America, must help the people see it, or we, with them, are lost." Council members spoke at schools in Philadelphia and New York City, where they also participated in the *New York Herald Tribune* forum on atomic energy. In a special edition of the Oak Ridge High School newspaper, distributed free to more than 12,000 schools, student editor Dee Chambliss wrote, "The wiping out of 40,000,000 autobiographies— of 40,000,000 futures— in a hour of atomic warfare is a 'probability' that must not happen, ever."[23]

Following the lead of the Oak Ridge Youth Council on the Atomic Crisis, schools around the country began to integrate atomic issues into their activities. Similar Youth Councils were formed in twenty-five states and included both school and citywide councils. Students at Suffern (New York) High School formed an Atomic Energy Club in the fall of 1945, and continued it well into the next decade. The club was open to all students interested in the Atomic Age: those who wanted to make cyclotrons, reactors, or atom smashers; art students; English and journalism students; and even technicians and stagehands, for assistance in conducting school programs.

Similar to other atomic youth councils and clubs, the one at Suffern High worked with teachers to incorporate atomic themes into classroom discussions. The term for this schoolwide, interdepartmental approach to atomic education was coined in 1946 by Aaron Goff, a junior high school teacher in Newark, New Jersey. He wrote that "atomics" had significance for every class and age group because it didn't need to be justified or rationalized, only given sympathetic treatment.[24] At Suffern High, introductory science classes conducted experiments in atomic energy, while the study of atomic energy became required in senior science classes. Social studies teachers discussed the implications of atomic energy, with student discussions focusing on such relevant topics as the desirability or futility of using atomic weapons for strategic and tactical purposes. In 1953, students sponsored an open house that featured tours of the science department. As other students, parents, and community visitors moved from table to table, club members summarized the atom's history. They discussed the atomic bomb and explained the principles of fission and fusion. Students then interpreted Einstein's formula for the equivalence of matter and energy. Also featured was a display of a model of a Brookhaven atomic reactor. Gerrit Swart, faculty advisor, commented, "We feel the atomic surface hasn't been scratched — that results will stagger even the wildest imagination. We believe that the language of science, although only too recently concerned with war and weapons, can be directed just as effectively toward the betterment of human understanding ... that atomic energy can be put to such peaceful uses as to make a utopia for all mankind."[25]

At Boys' Technical High School in Milwaukee, the Atomic Age became an environmental issue to the Forestry Club, formed in the late 1940s. The club blended conservation into everyday life through botany, chemistry, biology, English, mathematics, music, and art. In this early version of the "back-to-the-earth" movement that emerged in the 1960s, the club promoted the idea that humankind had to take care of Earth in an era ripe with the potential of mass destruction. Its fifty members planted trees, tilled gardens, built bird sanctuaries, and distributed grain to animals during the winter. They helped the library obtain materials on the environment, and they toured lumber yards, tree nurseries, pulp and paper mills, and newspaper plants. In a 1950 article titled "Atom-Agers Look to the Future," published in *Progressive Education*, a veteran forester and club advisor wrote, "They sensed that the atom bomb threatens less damage than the efficiency that rids us of the forests nature gave us for free, and which we are still felling to plaster the country with Sunday unfunnies—exceeding even the buzz-saw and fire-bug antics of our ancestors."[26]

Educators formally introduced students to the new era in November 1946 by proclaiming "Education for the Atomic Age" as the theme of American Education Week, during which schools across the country provided numerous events for students, parents, and the community. Teachers formed committees to advertise school activities and to urge parents to attend open houses. They presented talks on atomic energy, emphasizing its benefits, such as decreased dependence for coal and other fuels, which in turn would lessen the need for conflict between nations. Students, making their own contribution to atomic education, conducted townhall meetings dealing with such questions as "What Are the Major Issues Which Serve As Obstacles to World Peace?" In addition, they presented talks to various civic, religious, and business groups.[27]

Kansas City, Missouri, reflected cities across the nation, where atomic issues became a substantive topic in and outside the classroom. Kansas City's *Central* (High School) *Luminary*, for example, addressed the atomic challenge to education in its November 1, 1946, issue. A student editorial maintained that education had to prepare youth for the Atomic Age by stressing social engineering and technical skills, and by emphasizing that cooperation and international harmony were essential to lasting peace. Education also had to make it clear to everyone that "our future security lies in a world community in which atomic power is controlled by moral law." In strikingly similar words, the cross-town school newspaper, *East Echo*, editorialized that "education must train the leadership needed to rebuild a world in which lasting peace will replace recurrent wars and to prepare youth for living in the atomic age."[28]

Homerooms (twenty-minute periods prior to the second hour of school) served the schools' social-engineering aims. They started with the playing of "The Star-Spangled Banner," then discussed the day's relevant issues, such as the atomic bomb and its implications. Some schools, in an attempt to utilize more fully the allotted time, divided homerooms into topical areas, including English, mathematics, science, American problems, and world history. One school newspaper wrote, "These democratic units, though small in size, are very important organizations in our school; for if they are managed successfully, they become the training ground for democracy."[29]

In the eyes of educators, school organizations formed the foundation for this training. Indeed, the first postwar decade became the era of student

TO THE PATRONS, STUDENTS, AND TEACHERS OF AMERICAN SCHOOLS

THE week beginning November 10 has been designated for the twenty-sixth observance of American Education Week. It should be the occasion for all citizens to visit their schools and to give serious thought to the theme selected for this year's observance, "Education for the Atomic Age."

Atomic energy can contribute immeasurably to man's welfare, or it can destroy civilization as we know it. Whether its powers shall be harnessed for good or for evil, the adult citizens of the United States will in large measure decide. It is the task of education to bring about a realiza-tion of the issues at stake and to develop the practices of human brotherhood that alone will enable us to achieve international cooperation and peaceful progress in the atomic age. —*Harry S. Truman*

EDUCATION FOR THE ATOMIC AGE is the general theme for American Education Week this year. This school-and-community-wide week throughout the Nation is sponsored by the National Education Association, the American Legion, the National Congress of Parents and Teachers, and the U. S. Office of Education.

The schedule of subjects for discussion follows. It is hoped by the sponsors that valuable results will come in every community from the 1946 American Education Week.

Practicing Brotherhood—Sunday, November 10.

Building World Security—Monday, November 11.

Facing New Tasks—Tuesday, November 12.

Developing Better Communities—Wednesday, November 13.

Strengthening Home Life—Thursday, November 14.

Investing in Education—Friday, November 15.

Promoting Health and Safety—Saturday, November 16.

Educators formally introduced students to the new era in November 1946 by proclaiming "Education for the Atomic Age" as the theme of American Education Week, during which schools across the country provided events for students, parents, and the community. Teachers formed committees to advertise school activities and to urge parents to attend open houses. They presented talks on atomic energy, emphasizing its potential benefits, such as decreased dependence for coal and other fuels, which in turn would lessen the need for conflict between nations.

clubs, societies, councils, and other organizations. These multifarious groups provided social outlets and, essential to educators, opportunities for students to pursue democratic ideals and social issues. But so-called secret societies (e.g., fraternities and sororities) were discouraged, even outlawed, by many schools because they threatened the schools' social-engineering functions and did not adhere to the democratic principles felt important in postwar American society, particularly the notion of brotherhood, equality, cooperation, and the belief in individual value.[30]

High schools, such as Forest Park High School in Baltimore, Maryland, formed United Nations Youth, affiliated with a statewide organization, to develop a spirit of cooperation and understanding among youth of all countries. Schools also formed Current Affairs Clubs, International Relations Clubs, Youthbuilders, Green and White Clubs, Pan-Am Leagues, Discussion Clubs, and Forum Clubs, all designed to encourage values of brotherhood, cooperation, and understanding, and to foster knowledge of the world in the Atomic Age. These clubs sponsored assemblies, gave talks to homerooms, created hall displays on a variety of subjects, and held informal discussions with other students. A national survey published in 1949 found that 78 percent of students had some organizational affiliation, such as a school sorority or fraternity, YMCA or YWCA, or other social group. The following year, another survey of more than a thousand high school students found that 26 percent belonged to a group or club, either in school or out of school, specifically devoted (at least in part) to the study of world affairs. Yet those conducting the survey believed the number was too low.[31]

The tenets of religious understanding were reinforced in Youth on the Beam Bible Clubs (YOBs). Members met each week in classrooms for Bible discussions and every Saturday night for "Singspirations." The Hi-Y (for boys) and Y-Teens (the renamed Girl Reserves), groups associated with the YMCA/YWCA, were devoted to civic projects such as providing relief to veterans confined to local hospitals. Students also continued the work begun during the war through such activities as War Stamp Councils, War Safety Clubs, Safety Service Clubs, Red Cross Councils, and Peace Clubs—organizations encouraging social responsibility and community involvement.[32]

Service societies brought these principles into the school. Each homeroom nominated a service society representative, an honor recognized as second only to the National Honor Society. This representative agreed to donate his or her time to improve the school in some way. Corridor Patrols, consisting of boys and girls, acted as official guides to school visitors and maintained order in the hallways. Proctors, called "Sentinels of the Halls," became integral to high schools. They cleaned hallways, inspected lockers, discouraged loitering, and supervised cafeterias. Girls served as Nurse Proctors, ready to assist any emergency no matter how large or small. Some schools formed Cafeteria Courtesy Committees (CCCs) to maintain order and decorum during the lunch hour. At Sumner High School in Kansas City, Kansas, an all-boy Committee on Beautification provided the upkeep and general appearance of the grass and shrubbery of the lawn and athletic field. All these activities reflected the aims of school administrators to teach democratic values and to foster involvement rather than apathy. For the students taking part in these activities, the democratic spirit was no doubt tempered by the opportunity to participate with friends in a socially acceptable group activity.[33]

Among the many other school-based organizations open to the Atomic Generation were teen-town committees, drama clubs, pep clubs, speech clubs, home economics clubs, radio clubs, art clubs, science clubs, book clubs, chess clubs, stamp clubs, traffic squads, auto clubs, photography clubs, engineers clubs, commercial or business clubs, printers clubs, zoology clubs, debate teams, craft clubs, and even charm clubs. Outside of school, as well, boys and girls formed fan clubs, informal "clubs," and even gangs— expressing their desires to belong to a group with similar interests and needs.[34]

Schools also sponsored chapters of national organizations, including the American Association of University Women, National Art Honor Society, Future Teachers of America, National Beta Club, National Honor Society, Future Farmers of America, and Future Homemakers of America. Although many of these school and national organizations crossed gender lines, race was another issue. Black students were forced to participate in segregated associations such as New Farmers of America and New Homemakers of America, which had 33,000 members compared to more than 250,000 members of Future Homemakers of America open to white students.[35]

In addition to clubs and organizations, athletics also became a key part of schools' democratic programs. And, once again, the position of educators on sports became part of the social narrative of the atom. School officials saw sports— by focusing on more positive and physically vigorous pursuits for girls and boys— as essential as other activities in developing good citizens, teaching democratic values, and, perhaps most important, allaying anxieties and fears emanating from the Atomic Age.[36]

Charles McCloy, editor of a book titled *The Organization and Administration of Physical Education*, published in 1958, endorsed the necessity of building group values based on cooperation and brotherhood. Such values, he felt, were critical to the survival of democracy as well as the survival of the country against atomic attack. "In team competitions," McCloy wrote, "the only measure of a man is what he does as a member of the team — his race, creed, wealth, and class are all forgotten. No better training for citizenship in a democracy is available anywhere in the school system." Team sports helped develop loyalty, leadership, followership, sportsmanship, respect for the rights of others, and other qualities deemed essential in a democratic society — all themes consistent with atomic education in the classroom.[37]

The relevance of athletics did not stop with the social and physical benefits. Athletics, according to McCloy, also lessened anxiety, decreased juvenile delinquency, and kept minds off "sex matters." McCloy expressed critical concern about youth controlling their emotions, a theme often contained in atomic narratives. War and the unleashing of the atom had resulted from an inability to control one's emotions. Moreover, athletics were particularly important in this quest. "Man's behavior," he wrote, "has sprung from emotions and instinct for so many thousands of years that we cannot expect our conduct today to be based largely upon intelligence. What is needed in our schools, as much as anything else, is provision for the education of the emotions."[38]

McCloy argued that emotional stability was achieved only through practice of controlling and modifying the feelings released. Any curriculum of physical education, he maintained, should include activities valuable in "arousing and offering an outlet for emotional expression," particularly contact sports like football, basketball, soccer, and wrestling. Ironically, by the mid–1950s, the notion of controlling another's emotions and the more dreaded fears of losing control and one's self-identity had become prevalent themes in fictional narratives, such as Jack Finney's *Invasion of the Body Snatchers* and J. D. Salinger's *Catcher in the Rye*; in nonfiction works, such as David Riesman's sociological study, *The Lonely Crowd*; and in movies ranging from *Invaders from Mars* to *Rebel Without a Cause*.

McCloy's overall endorsement for high school athletics contained distinct objectives based on gender. Sports competitions benefited both boys and girls by emphasizing group solidarity and teamwork. Boys, however, gained self-confidence and leadership abilities through sports. Girls, on the other hand, learned the importance of sportsmanship, loyalty, and cooperation. That these traits, he wrote, "have been underdeveloped in the girl and are not foreign to her nature is shown by the big improvement in these qualities since the girl has had the chance to engage in big-muscle play activities, particularly play competitions."

Unfortunately, McCloy said, girls faced major handicaps in athletics. Not only did they exhibit less endurance and upper-body strength than boys, they had smaller hearts. A girl's menstrual period only exacerbated the problem.[39] But despite these so-called "handicaps," girls were given an opportunity to develop democratic principles through such intramural sports as basketball, ice skating, bowling, horseback riding, swimming, shuffleboard, ping-pong, aerial darts, archery, volleyball, square dancing, modern dancing, tennis, field hockey, and softball. Unlike boys' athletic competitions, girls' "playdays," held two or three times during the year, were not intended to inspire a competitive spirit. Instead, in the words of one school newspaper, they were conducted "to promote a spirit of friendship."[40]

Elaine Tyler May is among recent historians who have addressed the issue of gender during the 1950s, concluding that the uncertainties and anxieties of the Atomic Age led to a renewed emphasis on the family and traditional gender roles. In her study of the family during this era, *Homeward Bound*, she writes, "The modern family would, presumably, tame fears of atomic holocaust, and tame women as well." The emphasis on family and women's role within it, however, must be balanced with the impact on male roles resulting from atomic insecurities. In fact, girls *and* boys were instructed very carefully about their specific roles or obligations. And many accepted them. The Atomic Generation, in fact, was the most marrying generation on record: 96.4 percent of females and 94.1 percent of males would marry.[41]

A survey among girls at one high school, for example, found that most planned to become homemakers after graduation. The high school experience became, in many ways, a training ground for domesticity and mothering. In family-living and home-economics courses, nursing and first-aid activities, and organizations such as Future Homemakers of America and the Junior Red Cross, girls received the message that their purpose in life was to serve as wife, mother, and homemaker — in short, to nurture, to provide emotional support, and to repopulate the world. According to Marion Nowak, who examined female education in the 1950s, marriage and family "seemed to be a defense measure against the stress of the rest of the world."[42]

The family provided a safe refuge for males, too, as William Whyte revealed in his 1956 book, *The Organization Man*. Young men sought the safety of the corporate environment as a defensive measure against the insecurities of the times. This was a "generation of bureaucrats," Whyte wrote, who sought security within "the organization." Preparing for this adult role, however, proved difficult for many. For example, social psychologist

Kenneth Keniston, in his study of college youth in the late 1950s, found that boys rejected the male role, overidentified with their mothers, and consequently experienced a high degree of alienation from society and confusion about their social roles.[43]

In the end, though, it is clear that both boys and girls wanted security. Yet an interesting note to this orientation toward security is the fact that despite the high number of young marriages, the marital rate among adolescents remained virtually unchanged in the 1950s. In 1950, 98.9 percent of those between the ages of 15 and 17 were single; among 18- and 19-year-olds, the percentage was 93.4. Ten years later, 98.8 percent of adolescents aged 15 to 17 were single. And for those 18 and 19, the percentage of those single had dropped slightly to 91.1. So although it was true, for instance, that females were marrying earlier (with the average age at marriage decreasing from 20.5 in 1947 to 20.1 by 1956), this did not directly affect the adolescent culture. Although girls may have prepared for marriage and boys may have wanted to marry, the vast majority completed their high-school–based cultural experience.[44]

Several educators, Lynn White, Jr., being among the most celebrated, actively encouraged female youth to accept their traditional roles, but they did so within the context of the Atomic Age. The overriding message of White's 1950 book, *Educating Our Daughters*, reflected the view that society must protect the family and prepare for an uncertain future. Despite the obvious emphasis on women's domestic functions, his critique of postwar education was more of a response to the spread of insecurity rather than the often-cited attack on female educational and occupational aspirations.[45] White, president of Mills College, stressed that life adjustment was the objective of education. Although this *did* mean preparing girls for "the whole process of adult living," it also meant that boys should be taught to be good "weekend" fathers and husbands, and that both girls and boys should take courses in child development. Girls must be exposed to liberal arts education, not just domestic skills, however. White believed that managing a house and raising children were only part of a woman's responsibilities, which also included enriching the family's and the community's intellectual and emotional lives. Education must become family-oriented, and both men and women should put the family ahead of personal careers and goals.

According to White, though, distinct differences separated males and females. "The pattern of a man's existence," he wrote, "is fairly simple. He is born; he is educated partly to be a person and partly to earn a living; he earns a living, gets a wife; begets children and works until he dies." Women, on the other hand, are far more complex, White argued. Women are mentally and emotionally hardier than men. Life presents many more challenges: career, family, or both. Therefore, girls must be educated and trained to deal with their unique roles. Girls must be prepared to handle their lives in their twenties, when they would be raising children and maintaining a family. At the same time, they must learn how to deal with the crisis of their forties, when they would reenter the workforce after their children had grown. White, above all else, believed women would survive the next atomic war and, for this reason, schools "must educate for catastrophe." Women, not men, would be able to rebuild society if they nurtured their domestic responsibilities.[46]

Home-economics classes, in fact, instilled the importance of a stable and secure home life during these anxious times. Between 1946 and 1950, as the first *Blast* of the Atomic Generation completed its adolescence, the number of girls in home economics increased more than 60 percent, reaching 1.43 million, even though overall high school enrollments remained unchanged during this same period. Mary Laxson and Berenice Mallory, experts in home-economics (or "homemaking") education, captured the importance of this training in a 1950 article in *School Life.* "Helping girls develop the skills involved in managing household tasks and finances is only part of the job of homemaking education," they wrote. "Success in the job of homemaking can be judged only by such intangible outcomes as the quality of family life, the happiness, health, and sense of security of family members, or *the ability of the family to adjust to emergency demands or unexpected catastrophe* [emphasis added]."[47]

Perhaps this growing sense that nothing could prevent the unexpected catastrophe was one reason for the inexplicable decline in interest for home economics in the early 1950s. Despite a 30 percent increase in government expenditures for this form of education, home-economics enrollments increased just one-tenth of 1 percent between 1950 and 1955, even as high school enrollments were expanding by some 14 percent during the same period. This trend corresponds to the entrance of the second wave, or *Heat*, of the Atomic Generation, which would experience a modified social narrative of the atom. By the early 1950s, the Soviet Union had exploded a nuclear bomb, the communists controlled China, schools conducted civil-defense drills, war raged in Korea, and Senator Joseph McCarthy of Wisconsin railed against communist infiltrators and traitors.[48]

Throughout this period, nonetheless, the Future (and segregated New) Homemakers of America remained a vital organization in high schools. The club's motto was "Toward New Horizons ... learning to be better today in order that our lives and those of our families may be better tomorrow."

Girls helped persons in need and, in general, promoted an appreciation of the "joys and satisfactions of homemaking." Family-living classes, consisting solely or largely of girls, were designed to prepare students for their future lives. Kansas City's Central High School dedicated its 1950 yearbook to the theme "Central's Happy House" because "the home is the foundation of every life." A 1952 yearbook called the purpose of the Future Homemakers of America "to promote a growing appreciation of the joy and satisfaction in homemaking, to encourage democracy in home and community life, and to work for the good home and family life for all." In 1957, the government officially established the essence of home economics, publishing a booklet titled *Civil Defense Practices and References for Homemaking Classes* that gave directions for furnishing and decorating a bomb shelter and for stocking it with provisions.[49]

While girls prepared for their home duty, boys prepared to defend the country through the Junior Reserve Officers Training Corps (JROTC), a three- or four-year school requirement that encompassed training in drill, physical development, tactics, first aid, map reading, weapons, and military leadership. In addition, the Navy offered a similar NROTC program and gave exams for the Naval Aviation College Program. Although girls could serve as cadets, they usually assumed the role of helpmate, often serving as secretaries for sergeants. But they seemed to have enjoyed the experience nonetheless. One female cadet was quoted as saying, "We love every minute of it — not to mention the boys!"[50]

The JROTC program varied slightly from school to school, but generally it included some thirty-five hours of drill, ten hours of physical education, five hours of recreation, and the remaining time in military training. Third-year cadets took a voluntary nine-hour officers' training course before school. Throughout the late 1940s and early 1950s, military recruiters made routine visits to high schools, encouraging boys to enlist immediately after graduation. Schools held special assemblies featuring guest military lecturers, veterans, government representatives, and members of the American Legion. In addition, representatives from the Navy, Marines, Army, and Air Force, as well as war veterans, met with boys and their parents at school and citywide functions about choosing the branch of the service that most appealed to them. Educational magazines, like *Senior Scholastic*, published recruitment ads, offering special courses in atomic weapons. Cadets held school dances and annual military balls, complete with ROTC queens and attendants. Social studies classes discussed military training and the duties and responsibilities of youth in the Atomic Age.

With the introduction of civil-defense drills in the early 1950s, cadets served as messengers and air-raid wardens. During an actual attack, they were to evacuate the injured and guard the various installations throughout the school, such as water valves and electrical switches. Boy cadets attended summer camps to receive additional training in military tactics and weaponry. They also sponsored special hygiene and first-aid events, designed to demonstrate their ability to respond in any emergency. Cadets formed Memorial Clubs, providing firing squads at military funerals. Many boys also joined the Junior Rifle Corps, a branch of the National Rifle Association, to receive additional experience with weapons.

Even the Boy Scouts were not immune to military indoctrination. In 1949, the Scouts launched a three-year crusade called "Strengthen the Arm of Liberty," which saw a 33 percent increase in membership by the end of 1951. The crusade continued the Boy Scout tradition of promoting conservation and sponsoring collection drives for domestic and foreign relief efforts. But it also involved survival training and cooperation in local civil-defense efforts.

In short, military training was an integral part of the high school and community experience. Moreover, the draft law in 1948 required 18-year-olds to register and allowed for induction of those 19 years of age for a twenty-one month tour of duty. Thus, many of these boy cadets were thrust into the front lines of the Atomic Age. And, beginning in June 1950, they became immersed in "the coldest war"— Korea.[51]

Whether a boy cadet or future homemaker, America's youth encountered the social narrative of the atom firsthand through various clubs, organizations, and athletics. But the social narrative went beyond the school environment. Students had ample opportunities to learn about their world — and their roles within it — through community events, townhall meetings, and traveling exhibits. The Freedom Train, an ambitious project in which a train filled with 133 historical documents, including the Bill of Rights, the Constitution, and Lincoln's Gettysburg Address, traveled to 322 cities between September 1947 and January 1949. According to the American Heritage Foundation, the organization that planned and directed the exhibit, approximately 50 million people — or one in every three Americans— participated in Freedom Train program activities. The purpose, one researcher has written, was to articulate a national identity following the war and to rekindle an awareness of citizens' duties and responsibilities in the Atomic Age, a purpose congruent with that of educators for America's youth. Along the train's route, cities sponsored Rededication celebrations and Youth Days to reinforce the exhibit's primary aim: to strengthen democratic principles and national identity. High schools sponsored fund-raising drives to help buy grain for Europe, with the grain transported on the Freedom Train. In Council Bluffs, Iowa, students contributing at least ten cents received a "Wheat Tag" in recognition of doing their democratic duty. In addition, students signed Freedom Pledges, going on record in support of democracy and in opposition to communism.[52]

During the summer of 1948, thousands of people, including 30,000 children, attended the month-long "Man and the Atom" and Atomic Energy Book Exhibit set up as part of New York City's Golden Jubilee Exposition. Sponsored by the Atomic Energy Commission, Westinghouse Corp., General Electric, and the New York Committee on Atomic Information, the exhibit featured a wide array of presentations on the peacetime applications of the atom as well as its more destructive uses. The display featured the essential radiation detector. Other items included a giant model of an atomic nucleus and a chain reaction based on mousetraps. General Electric also distributed thousands of copies of *Dagwood Splits the Atom*, a comic book aimed at school children that explained the principles of atomic energy. The book exhibit, sponsored by the American Book Publishers Council, featured twenty-eight titles recommended for all Americans to read. Among the titles were Norman Cousins's *Modern Man Is Obsolete*, John Hersey's *Hiroshima*, Bernard Brodie's *The Absolute Weapon*, and Daniel Lang's *Early Tales of the Atomic Age*, all narratives found in school classrooms during the dawning of the atomic era.[53]

Although the exhibit included information about the atomic bomb, the main emphasis focused on the positive aspects of the atom. A survey conducted of those attending the exhibit, in fact, found that people's fear and insecurity had been reduced, and feelings of hope had increased. With this positive response, the sponsors decided to have the exhibit tour the country, allowing millions of Americans to become better informed about the atomic bomb itself and the many positive aspects of atomic energy. Three years later, another traveling exhibit, sponsored by the National University Extension Association, the Atomic Energy Commission, and the Oak Ridge Institute of Nuclear Studies, allowed parents and their children an opportunity to learn about the peacetime role of the atom in industry, agriculture, and medicine.[54] Many cities also held Atomic Energy Weeks, bringing information about the atomic bomb and the benefits of atomic energy to young and old alike.[55]

Training in citizenship and democracy included All-City High School Days, where students elected representatives to serve as local government for one day each year. During a typical school year, students attended assemblies on loyalty, democracy, brotherhood, citizenship, the Red Cross, the Atomic Age, civil defense, Pan-American relations, and military service. In 1947, the same year that Jackie Robinson became the first African

American to play Major League baseball and President Truman's Committee on Civil Rights issued its landmark report, "To Secure These Rights," condemning segregation, female students and graduates of the University of Southern California traveled the country, presenting assemblies on racial harmony. Students throughout Kansas City attended a performance by The One World Ensemble, an interracial, intercultural, interfaith vocal group. Four years later, many high schools sponsored another program, "In Our Hands," as a means of presenting "the true picture of democracy" to America's youth. Central High School in Binghampton, New York, conducted a "Peace — How to Keep It" assembly in 1950 to recognize youth's role "in the monumental task of securing and retaining world peace." A speech assembly at Kansas City's East High School featured a drama titled "The Bomb That Fell on America," which dealt with the Hiroshima explosion and its effect on the rest of the world.[56]

In 1952, students around the country attended the "Alert America" civil-defense exhibition. Three convoys of ten, 32-foot trailers carried portable exhibits on the possible impact of an atomic attack. Over a two-year period, more than 600,000 people in fifty-six cities visited the exhibit. Among the displays was a model of a city destroyed by an atomic bomb, with a spokesperson speaking on "This Could Be Your City." A dental laboratory truck, ambulance, and blood center truck also were shown, as well as infantry weapons. Posters accompanying the exhibit stressed the importance of civil-defense preparation. One declared, "TRAINED, ALERT CIVILIANS will cut our casualties in half." Another said, "IF WE ARE PREPARED, WE CAN COME BACK FIGHTING."[57]

America's youth also heard about the atomic bomb on the radio and used the radio to express their views on the Atomic Age, especially after March 22, 1951, when the Federal Communications Commission reserved 209 channels for educational broadcasting. Students throughout the country had opportunities to broadcast comments over Radio Free Europe on the meaning of democracy and living in America. The National Scholastic Radio Guild, sponsored by Scholastic Inc., provided scripts for student productions on local or school stations. One script, titled "The Youth Crusade for Freedom," concerned what youth could do for the people behind the Iron Curtain.[58]

Radio and (by the early 1950s) television stations offered students an opportunity to discuss a variety of topics, such as the atomic bomb and its implications in their lives and the world. In 1954, a Kansas City television station broadcast a program three days a week that, according to one school newspaper, called "public attention to the leadership, good citizenship, and outstanding ability shown by students." Ottawa Hills High

School in Grand Rapids, Michigan, sponsored Youth Forum Broadcasts. These thirty-minute broadcasts were held each week from a different high school. Two boys and two girls first gave a three-minute speech, then joined in a roundtable discussion of a specific topic, such as "Can we utilize the atomic bomb for peacetime uses?" At Suffern (New York) High School, students broadcast a one-hour radio play, "The Peaceful Atom," over station WLNA in Peekskill, New York. Students involved in radio clubs or radio workshop classes participated in over-the-air programs and broadcasts on school networks. The Radio Guild of Proctor High School in Utica, New York, broadcast school-of-the-air programs to elementary classes. Students in Stamford, Connecticut, participated in radio station WSTC's weekly fifteen-minute broadcast, *Report to Parents*, on topics ranging from civil defense to career choices. Students in Binghampton, New York, used a radio program to promote the goals of world cooperation, while schools in Philadelphia cooperated with station WPTZ to present a weekly program in 1951 called *Self Help in Civil Defense*, a short-lived series that provided practical knowledge and skills in first aid, home nursing, and safety measures in case of an atomic attack.[59]

Beginning in 1953, the emergency network, CONELRAD, routinely interrupted broadcasts with dire warnings of atomic attack, serving to remind students and their parents about the importance of civil defense. Announcements advised the public to turn their AM radios to 640 or 1240 for official information. Cities across the country initiated air-raid sirens, testing them at regular intervals, often at least once a month. After school and on weekends, students volunteered for the Ground Observer Corps and Civil Air Patrol (CAP). Boys and girls gathered at local airports and took classroom instruction on the identification of aircraft silhouettes, tracking flight paths, and implementing emergency procedures in case of enemy attack. Girls served as CAP officers and participated equally in all activities. They also worked side-by-side in control towers to watch the skies for the unexpected — the unexpected devastation far more deadly than possibly imagined.[60]

In case Americans did not fully comprehend the need for continual preparedness in the Atomic Age, the federal government introduced Operation Alert in 1954. Operation Alert, taking the social narrative of the atom to a new level of intensity, consisted of a three-day hypothetical attack on Washington and fifty-four other cities designed to keep people keenly aware of the atomic threat. As Russian bombers supposedly approached the United States, Americans were instructed to seek shelter immediately. The press then fused reality with fiction by announcing that 8.2 million Americans had been killed and 6.6 million injured. The following year,

125 hypothetical H-bombs and A-bombs fell on the United States, hitting seventy-five cities, military bases, and atomic installations. The government continued Operation Alert through the 1950s as a reminder to all Americans about the constant need to be prepared and on the alert for an unexpected, catastrophic atomic attack.[61]

A few months before an Operation Alert in 1955, students in Kansas City attended a play titled "45 Minutes—or Eternity," written by the civil-defense chairman of the Jackson County Medical Society and performed by the wives of doctors. The play, presented in school assemblies, dealt with a hydrogen bomb attack on the city. The first scene focused on women discussing the improbability of an atomic attack as they shopped in a fashionable district of the city, with a civil-defense volunteer warning them to be prepared. Scene two opened in one of the women's homes. Just as she again says that it's ridiculous to believe an attack could occur, a siren goes off. All the women panic, except for the volunteer. Because of her calmness in the face of this unspeakable emergency, she is able to help the women gather the necessary supplies and safely escape from the city. A school newspaper reported, "As the play ended, the people were praying, their heads bowed, some on bended knee. As they heard in the background the singing of 'The Lord Is My Shepherd,' new hope and renewed faith were evident in their hearts."[62]

The students in attendance had heard the message of new hope and renewed faith many times before. School-sponsored activities, such as this play, as well as the diversity of community and national events relating to the promise or the threat of the atom must be understood as chapters within a social narrative written by educators, the government, and adult society in general. Furthermore, in their attempts at social engineering within the school, educators purposefully endorsed group activities as a means of demonstrating the proper values and requisite behavior for a brave new world. Thus, educators contributed toward the solidification of the high school culture. At the time, adolescents themselves participated in these various activities as a way of contributing to the school, improving self-esteem, and, undoubtedly for many, merely associating with friends and having fun. Whether it was cleaning a rifle, competing in school athletics, or belonging to a club or organization, the unifying theme was how to live — indeed, how to survive — in the Atomic Age. This would be even more evident in the classroom.

2

Mouse Traps and Chain
Reactions: Atomic
Education in the Classroom

> Q: *Where do we stand, Mr. Arbuthnot?*
> A: *At the threshold of a new era.*
> Q: *Will civilization survive?*
> A: *Harness.*
> Q: *Harness, Mr. Arbuthnot?*
> A: *Harness and unleash. You had better learn to use those two*
> *words, my boy, if you expect to talk about the atom.*[1]

David Lilienthal, chairman of the Atomic Energy Commission, delivered clear instructions to the class of 1948 on a warm June evening. Speaking at the Gettysburg, Pa., High School commencement exercises, Lilienthal encouraged graduating students not to succumb to the unwarranted alarm being expressed about the atomic bomb. Rather, Lilienthal urged, they needed to remain positive and accept the challenges awaiting them in the Atomic Age. "Some people (usually, though not always, older people) find in new discoveries—and atomic energy in particular—a cause for the deepest despair," he told the students and their parents. "It is not uncommon, as you well know, to hear predictions that the end of civilization is near at hand.... But I doubt, somehow, that you young people will take much stock in these predictions of dire and utter calamity.... This is surely no time to despair and lose hope, just because we are acquiring more knowledge than we yet know how to apply for human benefits." Lilienthal attempted to inspire the young people in the audience by emphasizing that through knowledge, love, and faith, "the Atomic Age, the age in which you shall live, can become an age of mercy, of joy, and of hope, one of the blessed periods of all human history."[2]

This same message radiated out to students across the country, as educators strove to uphold their obligation of preparing America's youth for an uncertain and dangerously precarious future. Teachers and school administrators, moving swiftly to incorporate atomic issues into school curricula, were aided by the federal government, which advocated the need for this generation not merely to protect democracy but also to protect civilization. The message delivered by Lilienthal would be rearticulated often during the next few years. In Kansas City, Kansas, for example, the principal at an inner-city high school wrote of his concerns about these youth — some of whom had seemingly abdicated their responsibility to safeguard the world — in the 1949 yearbook:

> Now, you have the responsibility of taking account of a new world — that which will be created by atomic power. So far, you give the impression that you are taking atomic energy for granted, that it is just one new discovery which will lead to a few new inventions, but it will be in YOUR lifetime that entirely new adjustments will have to be made, if you are to survive. There has been nothing so far in history that can be compared with the changes that will come shortly due to (1) rapid communication, (2) rapid transportation, (3) atomic bombs and atomic energy. Will your generation prepare for these? If so, CONGRATULATIONS. If not, God help you.[3]

John Perkins of Boston University reflected the opinion of many educators when he said that although scientists had won the war, social scientists must win the peace. The harnessing of man's actions, according to Perkins, was social scientists' atomic bomb, their Manhattan Project. "Upon their success now rests the fate of all mankind," he wrote in the fall of 1945.[4] As the country braced for an uncertain peace, teachers clearly understood the importance of providing a fundamental understanding of atomic energy in both social *and* general science curricula.

The June 1946 issue of *School and Society*, published by the Society for the Advancement of Education, presented educators with a six-point program relative to the atomic bomb and potential peacetime applications of atomic energy. The program, issued by the Society for the Psychological Study of Social Issues, a division of the American Psychological Association, said the dangers of the atomic bomb and the possibility of another war should be made clear to everyone. Teachers should stress that no military defense could guard against "the horrors" of the atomic bomb. In addition, they needed to support international control of atomic energy. The program advanced the principle of international brotherhood, while emphasizing the potential benefits of atomic energy. Finally, to achieve these goals, teachers needed to endorse a moratorium on the further manufacturing of atomic bombs.[5]

President Harry Truman further defined education's role in the new Atomic Age in 1946. When Fordham University invited the president to deliver the address commemorating the granting of its charter, his message was unequivocal: Schools must teach the younger generation to be tolerant of others regardless of religion, race, or national origin. "Until citizens of America and citizens of other nations of the world learn this 'science of relationships,'" he said, "the atomic bomb will remain a frightful weapon which threatens to destroy us all." The potentiality of atomic destruction, however, would only result from ignorance — the hallmark of tyranny and dictatorship.

The president told his audience that when a citizenry is denied access to knowledge, to education, it eventually turns toward dictatorship. Nations that ignore the necessity of international cooperation, likewise, create an unstable world situation. Thus, America's essential task was educating for democracy in order to protect the future. The only palpable defense against the atomic bomb, according to Truman, was tolerance, understanding, intelligence, and thoughtfulness. "When we have learned these things," he stressed, "we shall be able to prove that Hiroshima was not the end of civilization but the beginning of a new and better world." Truman then issued a challenge for teachers and a mandate for the Atomic Generation. Youth must come to school prepared to learn the meaning of democracy, underscored the president, because the fate of the world depended upon them. "I know that education will meet that challenge," Truman concluded. "If our civilization is to survive, it *must* meet it."[6]

Pupils in New York City, from kindergarten through junior high school, were given an opportunity to explore the new world order beginning that same fall. The atomics-based curriculum, called "A Better World," sought to promote world organization and international cooperation by incorporating these themes in social studies, music, art, health education, English, and foreign languages. The ten-point program reflected similar objectives for the Atomic Generation expressed in numerous educational narratives of the time, both relating to classroom assignments and school activities. These included developing respect for the individual and understanding the importance of cooperation and working together. Students were to acquire a sense of family devotion and responsibility. It was important not only to be a loyal American but also to accept the role of world citizenship, learning that nations as well as individuals need one another. Accepting the equality of different races, religions, and nationalities was paramount, as was realizing the importance of economic and social security for all people. Moreover, teachers were to encourage students to practice responsible freedom, display the American spirit of justice, and honor the rights of others. "For the first time," wrote Benjamin Fine, education editor for *The New York Times*, "the teachers will emphasize not only the place of the child in his own community and his country, but his place in the world. In this way, it is hoped, world citizenship will not be a foreign concept to the children in the nation's largest school plant."[7]

In 1949, Dorothy McClure and Philip Johnson of the Office of Education articulated the government's position on atomics in the journal, *School Life*. In their view, teachers and schools should prepare students with a multifaceted curricula, beginning with a comprehensive unit on atomic energy that presented the basic scientific facts, discussed problems related to domestic and international controls, and made "clear both the destructive capacity and the hopeful potential of atomic energy."[8] This unit was to be taught in no less than three weeks' time and be supplemented elsewhere in the curricula. This meant incorporating atomic issues into English, mathematics, art, industrial arts, health, science, and other courses—atomics at its finest. Teachers also were encouraged to assist one another across disciplines (e.g., science teachers speaking to social studies classes, art students assisting science classes, etc.).

In the science program, McClure and Johnson proposed that comprehensive units be introduced in general science, biology, chemistry, and physics. General science students were to consider such issues as the definition of atomic energy, the necessary raw materials for its development, and controlling atomic energy once it is released. Biology students should examine the impact of atomic energy on living things, including the harmful effects of radioactivity. Chemistry and physics courses were to examine the structure of atoms and the chemical changes that occur during nuclear reaction. Even beyond these more concentrated units, McClure and Johnson recommended that atomic issues be included in other classroom discussions. General science classes, for instance, could integrate atomic topics into units on energy, power, transportation, health, astronomy, and control of diseases. Units on nutrition, the nature of matter, chemical changes, inventions, electronics, industrial processes, and laboratory techniques also could be used to educate students about the atom. Unquestionably, the government promoted the total immersion of this generation into the postwar realities of life in a new Atomic Age.

It didn't stop with the hard sciences. Social, political, and economic implications of the atom were equally important, and McClure and Johnson encouraged schools to provide similar comprehensive units for social science classes, as well. For example, a unit in American history could examine world events since World War I, the development of the atomic bomb, the actions of the United Nations, and the current state of international controls of atomic energy. Civics students might consider whether the United States could control and use atomic energy for the best welfare of all, or examine the potential applications of atomic energy in industry, conservation, medicine, power production, and agriculture. In addition to these comprehensive units, the authors recommended that world history classes discuss the atom in relation to the Industrial Revolution, modern warfare, postwar problems, and foreign policy. Geography students might examine the various regions containing the raw materials for atomic reactors and the proximity of the Soviet Union to the United States and its allies.

Where comprehensive units were not appropriate, McClure and Johnson argued, so-called atomic "pegs" could be used without violating the course or curriculum objectives and still broaden students' understanding of atomic energy. In English classes, the plethora of books, pamphlets, and magazine articles on atomic energy made the subject excellent for research projects and oral reports. Mathematics teachers could use atomic energy materials for the study of exponents, geometric progressions, conversion units, space models, and problem solving. Art students could arrange displays, murals, and bulletin boards on atomic energy. Industrial arts classes could make models of atomic piles, demonstrate a chain reaction, and assist in school displays. Health classes could study the effects of radioactive poisoning along with the use of radioisotopes in medical research and treatment.

The importance of educating the new generation mandated this all-out effort, according to McClure and Johnson. This all-inclusive approach was critical because time was of the essence. Under normal circumstances, they wrote, new scientific and social developments moved into the school curricula by a slow, casual, unsystematic process. Eventually, the basic concepts of atomic energy use would pervade the entire curricula as the country moved deeper into the Atomic Age. "But do we have the time?" they questioned. "Perhaps a half century would be required for this casual approach to achieve an adequate atomic energy education. It is doubtful that the resulting compartmentalized instruction would be effective."[9]

Teachers found many opportunities to prepare themselves for this challenge. The University of California; the Institute of Nuclear Studies at Oak Ridge, Tennessee; and the Brookhaven National Laboratory on Long Island, New York, offered summer courses. The Atomic Energy Commission (AEC) assisted in the development and operations of dozens of teacher workshops, seminars, and teacher institutes on atomic energy and its implications for education. In New York City, the AEC helped sponsor a thirteen-week, two-hour-a-day course for 300 selected biology, chemistry, and physics teachers in the handling and use of radioisotopes. Similar programs were conducted in Springfield, Massachusetts; Baltimore; Glen Ridge, New Jersey; Minneapolis; Chicago; and Reno, Nevada, among many other cities. Nebraska's department of education issued a special teachers' guide, titled *Facing the Facts of Atomic Energy*, to spearhead a statewide program on atomic energy. Teacher workshops were held at the University of Idaho, Oregon State College, Ohio State University, Morgan State College, and many other institutions of higher education. States across the country offered similar assistance to teachers, many of whom expressed a need to maintain pace with their students on the scientific, social, and political implications of the atom.[10]

In Chicago, more than 700 teachers attended a seven-month Atomic Energy Institute for Teachers, sponsored by the Chicago school district, Argonne National Laboratory, AEC, and the Museum of Science and Industry. Sessions, held each Saturday from October 15, 1949, to April 15, 1950, were technical for science teachers and more superficial for general-education teachers. Presentations covered such topics as radiation detection and measurement, the biological and medical aspects of atomic energy, and the physics of atomic energy. The history and organization of the government's atomic energy project were discussed as well as the atomic energy business in the United States.

Teachers were encouraged to attend this in-depth training program in order to prepare America's youth for their destiny to safeguard the world, a point emphasized by Dr. Harvard Hull of the Argonne National Laboratory. "I believe you have a unique opportunity," he told the educators, "to guide your students and others so they will be prepared to live the Atomic Age to the fullest and make all of our best hopes come true." For the final session, some 400 Chicago-area high school students listened to presentations on the deadly effects of atomic radiation, viewed films on atomic themes, and attended an atomic energy exhibit.[11]

Through these various programs, teachers learned what to discuss and how to present the material. Among the more effective materials in this regard were educational films. *Senior Scholastic* and the annual *Educational Film Guide* listed films available for free or a nominal fee. Literally hundreds of films made their way into American classrooms during the early years of the Atomic Age — used by teachers both as informational resources and as propagandizing tools about the benefits of atomic energy and the destructive nature of the atomic bomb. These films, often presenting dichotomous views of the atom, formed one of the more significant atomic narratives for the Atomic Generation.

Westinghouse's *Dawn's Early Light*, a 33-minute film released in 1955, is an excellent example of this type of film. It concerns a high school senior who reads a frightening article about the atom's destructive power. His father, a scientist, attempts to reassure his son by explaining the many benefits of atomic energy. Together, they begin working on a model of an atomic reactor. Throughout the film, the father traces the development of atomic power from the first atomic pile to the nuclear-powered submarine *Nautilus* and the atom's future in generating electricity. The message is simple: If you understand the nature of the atom, there is nothing to fear.[12]

The Atomic Energy Commission cooperated with various companies, including McGraw-Hill, General Electric, MGM, The Encyclopedia Britannica, and Handel Film Corp., to make films for classroom use. These films were intended to allay anxieties by explaining the nature of the atom — in war *and* peace — using an objective, scientific manner. One of the most ambitious projects was undertaken by Handel, which in 1954 and 1955 produced the *Magic of the Atom Series*, consisting of some twenty films, each 12½ minutes long. Titles included *Atomic Furnaces*, explaining the principle of atomic reactors and featuring footage of the installations at Brookhaven, Oak Ridge, and Los Alamos; *Atomic Cities*, emphasizing the safety measures necessary to protect atomic workers and their families from radioactivity; *Atomic Detective*, describing the various types of radiation counters; *Atomic Biology for Medicine*, explaining various research experiments in bio-medicine using atomic energy as a tool; *Atomic Age Farmer*, showing applications of atomic energy in the mutation of corn and animal studies; and *Atomic Zoo*, exploring the effects of atomic radiation on sheep and fish. Other films in the series looked at atomic applications in health, industry, and the weather. The overall goal was to educate youth about the potential good emanating from atomic energy.[13]

In 1949, Coronet made *Nature of Energy*, a 10-minute film showing the relationship of atomic energy to other forms of energy. Young America released *How We Get Our Power*, a survey of various sources of power, including wind, water, fuel, and the atom, with illustrations of water wheels, electric generators, and the atomic bomb. McGraw-Hill's *Report on the Atom* (1950) looked at non-military uses of atomic energy. Three years later, Encyclopedia Britannica produced two films: *Atom Smashers*, which explained the importance of cyclotrons and described the workings of atom smashers, and *The Atom and Biological Science*, a 12-minute film on the biological effects of high-energy radiations on plants and animal cells. In 1954, it released *The Atom and Agriculture*, a film that discussed how radioactivity might benefit farmers.

The numerous films on more positive aspects of atomic energy were balanced by an equal array of ones projecting strong visual images and accompanying narratives about the bomb. *Atomic Power*, produced by MGM in 1946, was one of the earliest in this educational film genre. This 19-minute film traced the beginnings of atomic power from 1905, when Einstein theorized that matter could be converted, to the bombings of Hiroshima and Nagasaki. *One World — Or None*, also released in 1946, emphasized that no country could maintain the secret to the atomic bomb. It also compared the atomic bomb's impact on Hiroshima with other major cities around the world, and argued that no defense existed against atomic attack.

Hiroshima and Nagasaki were the focal points in *A Tale of Two Cities*, a 1946 U.S. Army documentary on the effects of the first atomic bombings. The atomic tests in the Pacific, conducted the same year, were the subject of *Atomic Bomb Test — Bikini Island*, produced by the U.S. Navy, and of *A.A.F. Special Delivery*, a U.S. Air Force film that combined footage of the Japanese bombings with those at Bikini. A number of films were released over the next decade on the atomic bombing of Japan and the atomic tests conducted in the Pacific and the desert southwest of the United States: *The Atom Strikes* (1948), *Operation Crossroads* (1949), *Operation Sandstone* (1951), *Target Nevada* (1953), and *H Bomb* (1953), to name a few. The effects of radioactivity were the central themes in *Bikini — Radiological Laboratory* (1951); *Effects of Atomic Bomb Explosions* (1952); *Medical Aspects of Nuclear Radiation* (1952); and *Fundamentals of Radioactivity* and *Properties of Radiation*, part of the U.S. Army's 1952 series on radioisotopes.

MGM's 1946 commercial release, *The Beginning or the End*, a fictional story about the morality of dropping the atomic bomb, became the basis of two educational films: *Beginning or the End* (1947) and *First Atomic Pile* (1947). The first of these documentaries used excerpts from the original film dealing with the development of the atomic bomb and the destruction of Hiroshima, and included comments by Albert Einstein. The second concentrated on the theories of nuclear fission and the moral questions surrounding the use of the atomic bomb.[14] Another film about the moral justification of using atomic weapons was The Film Forum Foundation's *Atom Bomb — Right or Wrong?* (1948), which questioned the atomic bombings of Hiroshima and Nagasaki as a means to end the war.

Teachers had a clearly defined role: to interpret these films and other visual or written atomic narratives in terms that students understood — and in terms that minimized (or downplayed) any fear or anxiety about the atom's destructiveness. As historian Lisle Rose has argued, the Cold War had slowly engulfed the country by the late 1940s, with the Berlin crisis, communist coup in Czechoslovakia, fall of China to the communists, the Alger Hiss spy case, and the testing of an atomic bomb by the Soviet Union. By the end of 1950, America's mood had "plummeted dramatically," according to Rose.[15] This only intensified the challenge confronting the educational community. According to three respected educators, R. Will Burnett, Ryland Crary, and Hubert Evans, teachers needed to help students analyze and evaluate the diverse issues surrounding the impact of atomic energy on the nation and the world, which they admitted was a task not necessarily easy to accomplish.

Writing in a 1949 article titled "The Minds of Men," the authors said that teachers had to realize students might express fear, apathy, or fatalism. "The Atomic Age can become a Frankenstein monster of public apathy," they wrote, "and ineptitude become widespread and persistent." For students' part, the authors pointed out, they must accept their own social responsibility "that leaves small margin for error." Students not only were expected to understand *why* the atomic bomb was used but whether it *should* have been used. The authors told teachers they had to emphasize, and students had to be able to understand, the issues related to controlling atomic energy, both domestically and internationally. Even if the intricacies of the atom were not fully understood, students needed to know its implications in war and peace. One result of this approach was the intensely felt self-awareness of this generation about the world's tenuous state.[16]

In 1948, Crary, Evans, and Glenn Haas applied these tenets in a handbook published in cooperation with the Atomic Energy Commission and the National Association of Secondary-School Principals (a department of the National Education Association). The 96-page handbook, titled *Operation Atomic Vision (OAV)*, was mailed free in the fall of 1948 to every high school in the country and instantly became an integral tool in the education of America's youth.

The authors stressed that democratic survival depended upon "an informed, active public vision and enlightened leadership." According to Crary, Evans, and Haas, *OAV*'s major purpose was to provide schools with up-to-date information for their students. The handbook would help schools raise the level of understanding and concern about atomic energy. In addition, the authors hoped that students would be encouraged to help

Opposite: In 1948, the Atomic Energy Commission and the National Association of Secondary-School Principals (a department of the National Education Association) published *Operation Atomic Vision*, a 96-page handbook mailed free to every high school in the country.

Operation Atomic Vision

New Teaching-Learning Unit
for High-School Student Use

*****Operation Atomic Vision,** a teaching-learning unit for use of secondary-school students, is now off the press.

***This 96-page unit has been prepared by the National Association of Secondary-School Principals under the direction of Dr. Will French, Chairman of the National Association of Secondary-School Principals' Committee on Curriculum Planning and Development to encourage high schools throughout the nation to incorporate a unit on the peacetime use of atomic energy into the curriculum so that the youth of the country, and through them the adults, will understand the enormous peacetime potentialities of the split atom.

*****Operation Atomic Vision,** a project in community education on atomic energy for senior high schools, was prepared by Hubert M. Evans and Ryland W. Crary of Teachers College, Columbia University, and by C. Glen Hass of the Denver, Colorado, Public Schools.

***Every high-school principal of the nation has been sent **one complimentary copy** of **Operation Atomic Vision.** Additional copies may be purchased direct at 60 cents each with discounts for quantities.

National Association of Secondary-School Principals
1201 Sixteenth Street, N. W.
Washington 6, D. C.

—Examine **Operation Atomic Vision.**
—You will want to be a part of this nation-wide discussion project.
—**ORDER YOUR COPIES TODAY.**

those in the community understand atomic energy, thus building confidence in the democratic process. Through such activities, public lethargy and apathy toward atomic issues could be overcome. Underlying these objectives, though, was the most essential goal of simply replacing the scare approach to atomic education with an optimistic one.[17]

Writing in the *Journal of the National Education Association*, the authors told teachers, "Let us face realistically one absolute fact now: *There is no hope for the future in the A-bomb or anything connected with it* despite its apparent usefulness at the moment."[18] Because of this, schools had to assume their share of the responsibility in meeting the challenge of protecting the democratic way of life, even life itself. If successful, they wrote, *OAV* would make youth feel more optimistic about themselves and their country because they would be better informed. When students opened their handbooks, they read statements like the following:

> Atomic energy! What do you think of when you hear these words ... war, destruction, the atomic bomb? This is not strange for, after all, the press and radio and prominent people have emphasized the great hazard of war and the A-bomb.... You may even wish to bury your head in the sand and resign yourself to fate. But there is a much brighter, a much more constructive, and a much more thrilling side of the atomic energy picture. If we look long enough and hard enough at this side of the picture, we might be able to see a world free from war, strife, poverty, and sickness; a world of hope and of great possibilities for human welfare.... Why not keep the bright side of the atomic picture in the center of your attention?[19]

The handbook discussed such topics as the Atomic Energy Act of 1946 and the work of the AEC. It even reviewed the current international situation. But the bomb overshadowed the entire text. Wrote the authors, "We dare not leave out a frank facing with young people of the terrible atomic hazards that might destroy the world."[20]

OAV's purpose, in part, was to dissuade students from succumbing to internalized, irrational fear. In another article published in *Teachers College Record*, the authors argued that students would be able to control their fears about impending disaster by obtaining knowledge about atomic issues. "Fear can induce irrational adjustments," they wrote. "[I]t can result in a refusal to confront facts; it can impel toward escape in reckless hedonism. But knowledge of fearful things is not necessarily compounded of unreasoned terror. There are awful facts of total war — the atomic bomb is one of them." The atomic bomb dropped over Hiroshima had killed more than did the entire blitz over England, they pointed out — a fact that students must never be allowed to forget. "There is still no defense," they continued, "and atomic bombs have not diminished in potential fury since Nagasaki."[21]

The handbook encouraged teachers to offer these "awful facts" but not to dwell on the atomic bomb's horror, which would only contribute to fear. Rather, teachers should minimize emotional rhetoric and instead present a reasonable, balanced view of the atom: its promise and its *possible* peril. To overcome growing lethargy and apathy evident among the younger generation, *OAV* urged students to promote interest in atomic energy by forming discussion groups, writing letters to their newspapers, sponsoring lecture series, and forming atomic energy councils.

Within a few months of its publication, *OAV* had become an important adjunct to teachers' reference materials on the Atomic Age. At James Monroe High School in New York City, teachers incorporated *OAV*'s tenets into a schoolwide atomics program. In December 1948, the school's *Bulletin of World Affairs*, published biweekly for the faculty, devoted an entire issue to the "Operation Atomic Vision" theme as part of a comprehensive two-week unit on atomic energy. The issue dealt specifically with social and scientific problems associated with the production, utilization, and effective international control of atomic energy.

In an effort to involve the entire student body in a discussion of atomic issues and concerns, extra copies of the *Bulletin* were distributed to all homerooms and used to persuade students to confront the complexities of living in an Atomic Age. Part of the program also required teachers to prepare more in-depth units on atomic energy. Although homerooms stimulated general discussions, social studies and science teachers used the *Bulletin* as a formal text for in-depth analysis and study. In addition, they promoted an atomic energy exhibit and showed films like the March of Time's *Atomic Power*. Schools developed units for English classes as well, with students reading and discussing David Bradley's *No Place to Hide* and Norman Cousins's *Modern Man Is Obsolete*, among other books, which contributed to classroom exchanges about the ramifications of the atomic bomb on American society and the world.[22]

Not only was the immutable fact that no defense existed against the atomic bomb integral to the unit, the *Bulletin* also pointed out that once an attack occurred, it would be impossible to decontaminate areas against persistent radioactivity. Perhaps even more direful, students' readings suggested that other nations would soon be capable of developing their own bombs. Furthermore, unless international controls of atomic energy were in place, such a nation might unleash a surprise attack with devastating consequences, even threatening the survival of civilization. The *Bulletin*'s special report went on to discuss current U.S.-U.S.S.R. relations, the work of the United Nations, and the Atomic Energy Act of 1946. It also featured a point-by-point comparison of the American Baruch Plan and the Soviet Plan for controlling atomic energy. Biological and chemical aspects of atomic energy were covered. In addition, the *Bulletin* offered a suggested reading list and questions for classroom discussions. One question asked students to analyze Bernard Baruch's often-cited 1946 statement before the United Nations Atomic Energy Commission, in which he stated, "We are here to make a choice between the quick and the dead.... Behind the black portent of the New Atomic Age lies a hope which, seized upon with faith, can work our salvation. If we fail, then we have damned every man to be the slave of fear. Let us not deceive ourselves; we must elect World Peace — or World Destruction." Again, students were given the choice between life and death — a choice they were told they had to make.[23]

In the years immediately following the mushroom cloud's initial ascent, the government outlined the atomic bomb's consequences, educators implemented a plan to deal with the bomb's impact on youth, and students received heavy doses of atomics to help them cope with living in the Atomic Age. Science students demonstrated chain reactions with mousetraps and built working models of atomic reactors, cyclotrons, scintillation counters, and Van de Graff generators. At Mount Baker High School in Deming, Washington, students built a model showing the idea of a plutonium production plant. Other students, like those at Anacostia High School in Washington, D.C., even set off miniature A-bomb explosions. Social studies and history students discussed the development of the atomic bomb and its economic, political, and social implications. Art classes constructed clay models of the bomb, painted murals, and decorated hallways and classrooms with charts, illustrations, and collages with atomic themes. Sewing classes made bandages in case of atomic attack. English students covered atomic issues in school newspapers and on corridor bulletin boards, while speech students gave presentations on the Atomic Age in classrooms, assemblies, and even before community organizations. At a senior high school in Missouri, science, language arts, and social studies teachers, with student assistance, conducted an all-school atomics program that subsequently led to a school-community study of the United Nations and the possibilities of world government as a way of securing world peace.[24]

Opposite: At Mount Baker High School in Deming, Washington, students built a model showing the idea of a plutonium production plant. At Anacostia High School in Washington, D.C., however, students set off a miniature A-bomb. Photographs reprinted with permission of the AP/Wide World Photos.

A NEW BRITISH DOMINION?

A second British dominion may be formed in the Western Hemisphere.

Britain's scattered possessions in the Caribbean area may in time be united into a "British Caribbean Federation," which would enjoy the same amount of independence as Canada.

(See major article in this week's issue on Hispaniola for background on another part of the Caribbean.)

The proposed Federation would consist of British Honduras in Central America; the islands of Jamaica, Trinidad, and the Barbados; and the Windward and Leeward Islands. Nearly 3,000,000 people inhabit these colonies.

Two other British colonies in the general Caribbean area—Bermuda and the Bahama Islands—are not included in the plan. Nor is it certain whether British Guiana in South America would join the Federation.

A "blueprint" of the Federation was recently drafted at a meeting of political leaders from the British Caribbean colonies. The following governmental set-up was suggested:

1. A single Caribbean Governor-General, appointed by the Crown.

2. A two-house parliament, with 23 senators appointed by the Governor-General and 50 representatives elected by the people.

3. A prime minister, chosen by the house.

4. A cabinet selected by the prime minister.

Like all the other dominions in the British Commonwealth of Nations, the Caribbean Federation would enjoy complete independence in its conduct of foreign and domestic affairs.

The advantages in having these small

Understanding the NEWS

colonies united into a Federation are many. It would bring about a common currency in the area. At present each of the colonies issues its own money. Some of the colonies base their currency on American dollars and others on the British pound.

A Federation would stimulate greater trade among these colonies through the elimination of existing tariffs. Generally, it would lead to more efficient public services, a more stable economy, and possibly a higher standard of living.

All that is needed now to bring the Federation into existence is approval by the various local legislatures in these colonies.

It is known that Britain is in favor of the Federation but she cannot force the plan upon the colonies.

Perhaps the chief obstacle to an early realization of the plan is inter-colony jealousy. Squabbles may develop over such issues as the selection of a capital for the Federation, the fixing of the number of representatives in parliament from each colony, and the powers of the federal government. The islands are composed of Indians, Negroes, mulattoes, and whites—many of whom have conflicting interests and backgrounds.

The principal exports of these colonies are sugar, bauxite, lumber, molasses, rum, coffee, and oil.

UNDERWATER FOR 21 DAYS.

A U. S. submarine traveled 5200 miles under water before coming up for air.

Leaving Hong Kong, China, on March 15 and arriving at Hawaii's Pearl Harbor on April 5, the U. S. submarine *Pickerel* made a new U. S. Navy record. It stayed submerged for the entire distance of 5,200 nautical miles (that's about 6,000 land miles).

The *Pickerel* is a snorkel-equipped sub. The snorkel was a Dutch idea, developed by the German navy during World War II. It uses a sort of "breathing tube" from the submerged ship to the ocean surface. Through the tube the sub takes in fresh air and gets rid of fumes and gases. The snorkel sub is propelled by diesel engines.

Before the invention of the snorkel, undersea ships were driven by electric engines using batteries. The ships had

Wide World

Madame Ambassador "at work": Mrs. Eugenie Anderson, U. S. Ambassador to Denmark, gets acquainted with the Danish mode of travel, with son, Hans. Mrs. Anderson, our only woman ambassador, is a favorite with the Danes.

to come to the surface to re-charge their batteries with the aid of diesel engines.

The crew on the *Pickerel's* voyage consisted of 67 enlisted men and eight officers. When asked what the men did for 21 days, the captain said "we took 30 movies along. We saw them all. Our main 'athletics' were card games. We didn't feel like eating much."

PROGRESS REPORT.

The 81st Congress completed action on bills to aid displaced persons. U. S. Indians, and house-hunters. All three bills are assured of speedy approval by President Truman when they reach his desk.

1. **Displaced persons.** Last year the House approved a bill to ease restrictions in the Displaced Persons Act of 1948 (*see Feb. 22 issue*). After a long debate the Senate followed suit earlier this month with its own bill, slightly different in form. Debate in favor of the Senate measure was spearheaded by a bipartisan group of 18 Democrats and Republicans.

A conference committee was expected to iron out the differences between the House and Senate versions. Both bills provide that the limit of DPs entering the U. S. be raised from 205,000 to about 340,000. The bills eliminate existing provisions which require 30 per cent of the DPs to be farm

Wide World

To get a more graphic understanding of atomic energy, Anacostia H. S. students in Washington, D. C., set off a miniature A-bomb explosion under science teachers' direction. No super-secrets were revealed; sulphur and zinc were used in the mushroom-like blast.

Whether comprehensive atomic units lasting from one week to two months, or atomic issues integrated into English, history, geography, physical science, and art classes, stark thematic similarities were evident. Atomic discussions usually began with a baneful warning about the apocalyptic dangers of uncontrolled, unleashed atomic bombs, against which there was no defense and no protection from the effects of the blast, the heat, or the radioactive poisoning. From the depths of fear and trepidation, students would then be led methodically toward the light of atomic promise: the peacetime applications of atomic energy in medicine, industry, and agriculture. Ultimately, educators issued a call to arms, encouraging their students to accept the challenge of saving civilization from an adult society that had taken the world to the brink of oblivion. David Lilienthal's message that "this is surely no time to despair and lose hope" was repeated in junior and senior high schools from Maine to California.

The curriculum offered at the University of Chicago's Laboratory School provides a glimpse into the classroom approach used by teachers in the months and years following the bombings of Hiroshima and Nagasaki. As with many students, eighth- and ninth-graders at the Laboratory School began studying the atomic bomb in the fall of 1945, relying exclusively on newspaper and periodical articles because of the paucity of textbook materials. Units continued to be offered to freshmen students each year, incorporating social and scientific information about atomic energy, although in subsequent years they were moved to the end of the ninth-grade year rather than the beginning.

Writing in a 1954 issue of *The School Review*, two teachers at the Laboratory School described a typical atomic energy unit in which students attending summer school studied the atom during two, 45-minute morning periods. Instructors introduced the unit by demonstrating several scientific principles and showing students how to use them in solving a problem. During the first phase of the unit, students also read biographical sketches of Albert Einstein and other scientists involved in the discovery of atomic energy. The objectives, according to the teachers, were threefold: to stimulate interest, to increase the reading rate, and to prepare students for the more difficult reading ahead.[25]

Once students had a basic appreciation of the history and science of the atom, they were exposed to its awesome power in films of atomic explosions: *Operation Crossroads*, on the Bikini test; *Operation Greenhouse*, which described the atomic explosions on Eniwetok; and *Target Nevada*, on the 1952 desert tests. Following the movies, teachers amplified the destructive nature of the atom even further by explaining the immediate impact of the blast and heat on living creatures and inanimate objects, as well as the harmful effects of radioactivity emanating from the blast and the fact that radioactivity could contaminate other substances.

Within a few days, students confronted the frightening realities of their world. "On the basis of the principles which they had learned," the teachers wrote, "the students reasoned that some materials near the blast were vaporized; that the air was violently expanded; that the high pressure produced a strong wind; that, because cooler air holds less water vapor than hot air, the cloud which appeared was formed by the expanding column of air above the explosion."[26] In short, students learned the origins of the mushroom cloud and achieved an appreciation of the atomic bomb's overwhelming power to vaporize life itself. The only hope was to protect oneself as best as possible. Thus, the ability to survive atomic warfare was critical to the unit, as exemplified by the movie *Atomic Alert*, which outlined the protective measures that could be taken, and by the booklet *ABC's of Radiation*, which served as a reading exercise and instructional bible for survival.

Students then prepared their own exhibits and visited the University of Chicago's betatron and synchrocyclotron. Positive movies followed the devastating ones: *Making Atomic Energy a Blessing* introduced students to the constructive uses of atomic energy; *Unlocking the Atom* tracked the discoveries that finally led to a successful chain reaction. Students completed the unit by reading about the splitting of the atom, followed by an objective test on what they had read. During this same period, students also did laboratory work, interacted with scientific exhibits, and participated in lecture demonstrations. Overall, the teachers concluded, the unit had been very successful. The students were interested in their work, and the tests and evaluations indicated they had learned more about atomic energy — its promise and, particularly, its peril.[27]

The perilous aspects of the atom became even more pronounced as America soon found itself confronting a war in Korea, a war against communism, and a war of survival against atomic attack. Beginning in the late 1940s, Americans felt the impact of the House Un-American Activities Committee, Representative Richard Nixon, Senator Joe McCarthy, and others who assailed the communist infiltrators destroying the country. At school, the Atomic Generation attended Loyalty Day assemblies and discussed the threat of communism. School newspapers continued to publish articles on alumni killed or wounded in Korea. And commentaries extolled youth's responsibility to safeguard the future. A school editorial warned, for example, "We are fighting to keep the youth of America free. So that when they become adults they may have a better world in which to live." As the Atomic Age hardened into a Cold War, the social narrative of the atom escalated into anti-communist rhetoric. Yet at the core of the often-heated diatribes against the nation's foes was atomic fear.[28]

A Gallup Poll taken in September 1947 found that 58 percent of those responding felt war was inevitable within ten years, and 75 percent felt war would occur within twenty-five years. Within a year, however, two-thirds of Americans felt World War III would occur in ten years. In another Gallup survey conducted in June 1950, 73 percent of those responding felt U.S. cities would suffer atomic bombings in another war.[29] The government's answer to this rising social anxiety was to encourage teachers to use radio, magazines, newspapers, books and booklets, and other outside materials to illustrate the importance of democracy, civil liberties, human relations, and world citizenship. The "Zeal for American Democracy" program, initiated by the Office of Education in 1948, reflected the growing emphasis placed on the teaching of loyalty, civic duty, creative spirit, respect, and the constant search for truth. Equally important, this program was designed to offset the growing fear, apathy, and pessimism among America's younger generation.[30]

As part of Zeal for American Democracy, Charles Peters, a visiting professor of education at the University of Miami, compiled a book documenting what he termed an experiment in "democratic, action-centered (DAC) education" conducted by some 1,000 high school students.[31] The DAC method, used by history, social studies, civics, sociology, and psychology teachers, stressed democratic participation, with teachers as part of the group and students as the leaders. Some 8,700 books were sent free of charge to teachers across the country to encourage the adoption of the DAC method.

Peters reported great success in incorporating junior and senior high school units that combined democratic tenets with present-day issues. A unit on war offered to a high school history class in Bedford, Pennsylvania, for instance, featured panel discussions on subjects such as the United Nations and its chances for success as a means of preventing an atomic war.[32] Teachers were not only encouraged to use the unit outlines contained in the book; they also were instructed to read portions of the book to students. An introductory narrative, as provided by Peters, read:

> Now that, by the skin of our teeth, we came out victorious from a war that threatened to destroy civilization, we have before us the possibility of great strides in our civilization and of rich and abundant living if we know how to manage our society so as to realize these possibilities. Or we have the possibility of strains and stresses and suffering, and even of another war that will wipe out our society, unless we can bring up from our young people citizens for the future who are competent to run a democracy that will be much more complicated and difficult than any we have had to operate in the past.[33]

In 1950, high schools became the focus of yet another educational experiment: the Citizenship Education Project, headed by Ron Davis of the Teachers College at Columbia University in New York City. Funded by the Carnegie Foundation, the project emphasized the learning of citizenship through so-called laboratory practices. It began initially in eight cities, located in New York, New Jersey, Pennsylvania, and Connecticut. By 1953, however, it had been adopted by more than 500 school systems in thirty-seven states and Hawaii. This included some 970 individual schools, 1,857 teachers, and approximately 55,000 students in junior and senior high schools.[34]

The laboratory approach was similar to Peters's concept of democratic participation. Students collected information firsthand, conducted mock trials to practice democratic principles in action, and visited actual courtrooms. Among the more important activities was encouraging readiness for a potential disaster — natural or manmade. Students made plans for using school facilities during a local disaster. They organized air-ground observer teams. They even ventured into the community to discuss the need for disaster preparedness. Disaster drills in schools were often organized and conducted by students enrolled in the Citizenship Education Project. These students formed civil-defense medical aide teams, planned emergency child-care centers, organized disaster rescue teams, and helped take civil-defense block census.

Students heard the same message throughout their daily class schedules: Save democracy from atomic attack *and* from communism. World topics were incorporated into citizenship and history classes. Students discussed the day's news at the beginning of each class; political and social topics were chosen for intensive study, with students required to prepare oral and written reports. The Problems in Democracy course offered at Quincy (Massachusetts) High School included the study of propaganda, economic security, minority rights, crime prevention, and family stability. Psychology courses emphasized good citizenship values. Hundreds of thousands of junior and senior high school students also saw films, such as Encyclopedia Films' *Democracy* and *Despotism*, to become sensitized to political realities. In 1950, the Eisenhower Foundation sponsored a citizenship program in all Kansas schools aimed especially at youth not attending college. The classroom, in essence, became a training ground for learning social responsibilities to be better citizens and to take any action necessary to protect the nation.[35]

Atomic education even found applications beyond those instilling the requisites for surviving in the Atomic Age. Atomics also benefited students with learning difficulties and inspired highly motivated students.

William Cullen Bryant High School in New York City, for instance, incorporated a unit on atomic energy into the school's XG, or experience, classes.[36] The average IQ in these classes was 80. Although this unit was offered in a ninth-grade class, students were reading at the sixth-grade level. According to their teacher, these students normally sustained interest in a problem for two weeks. For the atomic unit, however, they maintained involvement for two months, during which time teachers showed films and used magazines and other supplemental texts in an attempt to answer six specific questions, again beginning with the basics of atomic energy and the apocalyptic aspects of the bomb. The questions included the following: What is it [atomic energy]? How is the atomic bomb made? Where is it made? How dangerous is the bomb? How can we use atomic energy for the good of humankind? And how can we control it?[37]

To facilitate learning, the XG class formed an art committee, which built a clay model of an atomic bomb (with all parts labeled) and a miniature version of the Oak Ridge, Tennessee, atomic installation. A newspaper committee planned and wrote articles. A play committee and story committee provided special presentations and readings. And a scrapbook committee documented the class's activities. Students had the benefit of English teachers, who assisted in the writing of papers, and mathematics teachers, who helped to calculate the number of electrons, protons, and neutrons in various elements. Social studies teachers even offered background information on the current atomic energy situation in national and world affairs.

Because the hydrogen bomb became front-page news during the unit, the school made the chemistry lab available so students could prepare hydrogen and learn its properties. Following the study of chemistry, they discussed the military and moral implications of the H-bomb. This, in turn, led to a discussion of the control of the bomb and the workings of the United Nations by conducting a mock General Assembly meeting with each student representing a different country. Scientific principles were reinforced through class participation as well. An atomic model set was built using multi-colored rubber balls. Students were then shown how to build complex nuclei by using plastic tubing. Teachers further engaged students' interest by having them dramatize a chemical reaction by throwing the balls from one student to another, and then moving pupils around

Opposite: The classroom, in essence, became a training ground for learning social responsibilities to be better citizens and to take any action necessary to protect the nation. The 1951 Better Schools Campaign, for example, proclaimed that America's military and children were both a "line of defense."

the room to demonstrate the meaning of fission as well as the concept of motion and space within the atom.

At the other end of the spectrum, freshmen students at University High School in Chicago, with IQs ranging from 110 to 160, actively participated in a similar unit on atomic energy.[38] Titled "What It Means to Live in the World with Atomic Energy," the unit was presented in the common-learnings class, which met each day for two hours. Students read and discussed atomic issues in class. They also were given an opportunity to visit the library for additional research and to participate in science lab projects to obtain a better appreciation of the atom's physical properties. More impressive, though, was a visit from the principal of a laboratory school in Hiroshima, who along with his assistant answered questions about the atomic bomb's immediate impact and the lingering effects of radioactivity on the environment and local population. This unique opportunity allowed students to learn about the moral implications of atomic energy and not merely the science or history of the atom.

The class also constructed models of atoms, molecules, an atomic pile, a cyclotron, and a chain reaction. Students drew charts and diagrams illustrating the structure of both the atomic and hydrogen bombs, future plans for the layout of cities, and comparisons of conventional and atomic/hydrogen bombs. Maps were made plotting the distances and routes from Moscow to strategically important U.S. cities. The unit concluded with students visiting the University of Illinois to see a betatron, a device that accelerates electrons to create beams of high-energy X rays.

Students at University High gained benefits beyond the central topic of atomic energy. Upon completion of the unit, the teacher reported that students were excited about learning more about the atom in magazine articles, and they were anxious to tell their classmates what they had read the night before. It was a pleasure, she said, "when they groan with disappointment and amazement when the bell rings. When a student calls you during summer vacation to ask you excitedly if you have seen the article that just came out. Teaching the exciting and timely story of atomic energy and its implications can do these things. I've experienced it."[39]

Alarming, though, was her report that students came away from the unit believing war was imminent. Students felt the United Nations lacked an ability to deal with the atomic crisis, and the Soviet Union continued to loom over the country both in its immensity and power. The feeling of security, which had resulted from the country's sole possession of the atomic bomb, had been replaced with a fatalistic sense of insecurity and increasing obsession with civil defense and the decentralization of cities.

Student statements were telling: "Why don't we go ahead and drop the bomb on Russia now while we have a chance and get it over with?" And, "why don't we just forget about atomic energy? The destruction it causes isn't worth the peacetime uses."[40] In the end, students became acutely aware of the portentous nature of the atom and, more important, their role in deciding the fate of the world. One student commented: "I feel that it was very worthwhile studying atomic energy since it is so important and our generation will be the ones to decide how we're going to use it —for our betterment or our destruction."[41]

For the adolescents enrolled in this atomic unit, and for hundreds of thousands more across the country dealing with similar curricula, the atomic bomb became a daunting reality. Each day in class, adolescents coming of age in the early years of the postwar era were exposed to both the atom's inimical repercussions and to its potentially beneficial nature. Their textbooks reflected the fact that the world teetered precariously on the brink of instant termination unless the world achieved international cooperation and peace. This was confirmed by a study of high school textbooks published between 1945 and 1947, which found increased mention of atomic-energy issues, with concentration on the atomic bomb and international control.[42] A 1948 review of Magruder's *National Governments and International Relations* textbook said the content "rightly feels that we are in a midway era between military madness and world federation."[43] The term *military madness* may be somewhat hyperbolic; nonetheless, postwar youth encountered maddening instructions in their schools. What began as a call to protect civilization soon escalated into a call to arms against communism and, ultimately, a call to action in the name of civil defense.

3

Communism, Democracy, and Civil Defense: High School Days and Drills

*Today there is nothing in the papers except communism and war,
and that ... has a great bearing on the young mind. We have got
a terrific problem.*

— Irvin Beltrame, Balboa High School,
San Francisco, 1949[1]

Immediately after the Second World War, students embraced international brotherhood and world government as two of the best guarantees for preventing a third world war of atomic proportions. A high school editorial in 1945, for example, pointed out that few students could remember a world at peace or when another generation was given such an opportunity to rebuild a wartorn world into one "in which all nations would live together in peace and harmony." The unleashing of the atomic bomb had verified that the world had entered the age of science. And "if this is to be the age of atomic power, and if civilization hopes to survive, it is imperative that an enduring world government be established."[2]

As the postwar evolved into the Cold War, however, the challenge facing America's youth to maintain world peace and protect national sovereignty became more precarious with the Soviet Union's emergence as an atomic adversary in 1949. The social narrative of the atom, which had focused initially on the dangers of any form of totalitarianism, now crystalized more forcefully as a direct attack against communism. Then, as the country entered the 1950s, with both China's and the Soviet Union's increasingly antagonistic roles and burgeoning military prowess, civil defense and survival became the benchmarks for narratives in school as well as in the everyday lives of the Atomic Generation.

Kansas City's East High School exemplified this emphasis on world government "...or else" in its 1946 yearbook. The theme, "Horizons Unlimited," reminded graduating seniors that "the Class of '46 came to East in a world of bloodshed, chaos, and war; emerged, with their learning, into a world preparing for peace." The Dedication read:

> The birth of the atomic age has been heralded in all circles as a vital factor in determining world events. Certainly atomic power is a potent force as a weapon of war. Science must strive to render it an equally powerful implement of peace. Our high school years have been tremendously influenced by war. Having witnessed the chaos wrought by a world gone mad, we fervently hope that we may aid in establishing an enduring world organization. It is to this hope that we dedicate the 1946 *Eastonian*.[3]

Another school newspaper marked the opening of the Atomic Age by writing, "Nations, great and powerful, were fused together to constitute the most colossal destructive force the world had ever seen. Now the fighting is over.... Just as peoples banded together to win the war, we must now unite in our efforts to win the peace." A crosstown high school newspaper reminded students that they had to live in the world created by their parents. But they would have to "hope and pray that they will try to make a world of peace and growth, not a world of war and corruption." A school reporter likened youth to "soldiers on the home front" whose collective duty and privilege were to "hereby resolve to perform each task efficiently and willingly in order to help in every way possible to establish a lasting peace." Other high schools dedicated yearbooks to the "One World" theme and youth's opportunity to promote international goodwill, tolerance, and understanding. "The fate of humanity is in the hands of the youth of today," the inscription in one such yearbook read, "who have learned in school to practice tolerance, observe the Golden Rule and to live together as good neighbors in One World."[4]

During these early postwar years, many Americans endorsed some variation of One World or world government. This translated into support for a strong international body, such as the United Nations. A 1946 Gallup Poll found that 54 percent of Americans wanted the United Nations to have the power to control the armed forces of all nations, including the United States. By that same year, fourteen states had adopted the Constitution for the Federation of the World, advocated by Robert Humber, to symbolize their belief in the concept of One World or None. "A world in chains to armament and conscription, or a world made free?" wrote Tracy Mygatt of the Campaign for World Government. The choice, according to Mygatt, was life or death: a world doomed to self destruction by the "fiery breath of the split atom," or a world that recognized "man's morning vision of his destiny as an authentic potentiality." He urged teachers to do their part in eliminating the concept of national sovereignty, "that breeder of wars which Mankind, in this atomic age, can never again afford if he is to survive."[5] William Fisher, a history teacher at Fieldston School in New York City, wrote further that students "must learn that the intensely nationalistic boundaries of custom and government which keep men apart must be erased if mankind is to survive." Additionally, he said, they must learn that "it is hypocritical to preach about democracy unless it is a growing, living thing."[6]

If students were to accept this doctrine, then teachers had to demonstrate a commitment to world cooperation through their own actions. And they did. State education associations formed World Citizenship Committees to promote international education as well as the role of teachers in the Atomic Age. At a district conference held under the auspices of the Colorado Education Association's World Citizenship Committee, teachers and invited students discussed such issues as how atomic energy could be diverted from human destruction to human service. In August 1946, representatives from teachers associations in twenty-eight nations met in Endicott, New York, to establish the World Organization of the Teaching Profession. At the first official conference, held a year later in Glasgow, Scotland, delegates pledged to support worldwide cooperation among teachers, to promote world peace and to aid in various activities of the United Nations. The United Nations itself supported this international perspective by offering a summer school for teachers and students devoted to the study of the organization's various efforts in the international arena.[7]

As the Soviet Union assumed its adversarial role, safeguarding democracy became closely linked to international peace; and, ultimately, this peace resided in the success of the United Nations as an effective international organization.[8] Each year, schools conducted a United Nations Day (or expanded United Nations Week) featuring classroom discussions and special assemblies, guest lectures, and films in classrooms, auditoriums, and hallways. Radio broadcasts by President Truman, addressing world and international affairs, were heard in school auditoriums. Schools across the country, like Herman Ridder Junior High School in New York City, sponsored one-day programs in which they opened their doors to students from different ethnic, racial, and socioeconomic backgrounds as a gesture of goodwill and brotherhood. Throughout the late 1940s, school classrooms and newspapers continued to emphasize the need for a strong world organization, even world democracy, to ensure the peace, even as students became more pessimistic about the possibility of another war.[9]

Fear of a third world war accentuated much of the rhetoric in the late 1940s—both as it related to the need for international cooperation and the need for One World government. As the *Heat* of the Atomic Generation entered adolescence, Atomic Age rhetoric became increasingly focused on fear of an increasingly aggressive and atomic-armed enemy. One civil-defense official warned that fear could "produce a chain reaction more deeply destructive than any explosive known," citing an increase of 1,447 percent in the use of the word *panic* by the media between 1947 and 1952.[10]

By the second anniversary of V-E Day, a school editor, prompted, perhaps, by recent atomic bomb tests in the Pacific, wrote, "[B]ack of everything that has gone on is the fear of the Atomic Bomb, of what its terrific power can do and what it might do when developed more."[11] This fear, the editor said, had prompted some countries into a more desperate effort to maintain the peace by using "unscrupulous means to obtain the secret to this power or some stronger power." A 1948 editorial appearing in an urban, African American high school newspaper commented:

> Although we live in 'peace,' we do not know when some enemy will drop a series of atomic bombs on us and start a Third World War.... The United Nations is the latest attempt by man to have world peace, but no one can reach an agreement. If this state of things lasts between countries, the U.N. will fail and war will be inevitable.... The younger people of the world play an important part in shaping the world of tomorrow. Will this world be war torn or will we enjoy peace?[12]

For the Atomic Generation — urban and rural, male and female, white and black — the central theme in the social narrative of the atom was articulated clearly in the classrooms, hallways, auditoriums, and school newspapers: Safeguard democracy and ensure the world peace ... or face certain death.

That same year, students were given another opportunity to demonstrate their allegiance to democracy through the Voice of Democracy contest. The National Association of Broadcasters, Radio Manufacturers of America (later renamed Radio and Television Manufacturers Association), and U.S. Junior Chamber of Commerce sponsored the contest, which was promoted in local communities by radio stations and All-City Student Councils. Students submitted a five-minute broadcast script titled "I Speak for Democracy," with the winners permitted to read the entry on the radio. "During these unsettled times," proclaimed a school editorial, "each one of us, young and old, should be more conscious of the democracy we take so much for granted." Twenty thousand students participated the first year; by 1951, more than one and a half million students representing some 30,000 high schools participated annually.[13]

The views expressed by students reflected a strong belief in the country and democracy, and the need to fight apathy and indifference while maintaining democratic principles of brotherhood, cooperation, understanding, fairness, and peace. Additionally, some of these student-written atomic narratives, such as the one submitted by Howard Hartzell of Chautaugua (N.Y.) Central High School in 1948, framed democratic principles within the context of "the expansion of the forces which seek to destroy the peace of mankind." Hartzell's comments contain the same concerns expressed by Tom Hayden and his cohorts fourteen years later:

> Blows need be struck against class hatred, economic disunity, the fear and bias of one race, one religion, for another. Blows need be struck against political corruption, the refusal of the potent citizenry to wield its full power as the ruling electorate, and against the suppression of legitimate minorities. Indeed, blows need strike down that sense of false security which has led so many Americans to believe their system safe and indestructible, that it has no responsibility to the rest of the world, that it can ignore the cries for help from fellow nations across the seas, or that it can ignore the expansion of the forces which seek to destroy the peace of mankind. And who shall strike these blows? We, the people of the United States, shall strike them — strengthened by faith in ourselves, by a rediscovery of our highest heritages, by the basic philosophies of our religions, and by our potency as free and enlightened individuals.[14]

The Universal Declaration of Human Rights, approved by the General Assembly of the United Nations in 1948, also contained these same themes. The declaration endorsed personal and political freedom, and opposition to brutality and oppression. More significant, it supported the inherent dignity and equality of all people regardless of race, color, gender, language, political or other opinion, social origin, nationality, property, birth, or other status. "Fear, want, and insecurity are the breeding ground of communism," wrote Education Commissioner Earl McGrath. "Democracy's greatest hope — and in the end, democracy's only real hope — lies in putting into practice the Universal Declaration of Human Rights."

Educators must teach youth to have respect for these principles, McGrath said, in order to ensure universal peace and prosperity. He argued further that teachers should take loyalty oaths to disarm their critics. He wanted communism taught in the schools so that young people would fully understand the nature of the country's adversary. Youth must not only understand democracy; they must maintain a keen interest in democracy on a local, national, and international level. The most urgent responsibility of schools, according to McGrath, was the cultivation of "proper attitudes of citizenship in a democratic society, attitudes which help the student define the role government plays in the good society, and the role the citizen plays in good government."[15]

James Bryant Conant of Harvard University was among the more vocal educators leading the battle against the rising tide of communism in the late 1940s. He argued that this struggle would not be won by weapons of mass destruction but by adhering to the democratic ideal of equal opportunity for everyone, especially children. The country's ability to survive the Soviet Union's challenge, according to Conant, depended upon a "vigorous demonstration" of democratic beliefs and freedom. Dual loyalty to America and to democratic societies elsewhere in the world was "the essential condition for the freedom of this nation and the continuance of Western civilization."[16]

In the end, as with most commentaries during this era, the critical issue was how to overcome the fatalistic attitude that another world war was inevitable. Wrote Conant: "In some quarters nothing but pessimism is in fashion. Atomic bombs and other new methods of warfare, we are told, will soon be upon us in a global war. No one can say this is impossible. Perhaps the fated task of those of us now alive in this country is to develop still further our civilization for the benefit of the survivors of World War III in other lands."[17] Democracy would prevail — that is, atomic war would be averted — if everyone worked together, Conant believed. Educators and America's youth held fate in their hands.

The 1948 theme of American Education Week was "Safeguarding Our America." In just three years, educators had moved from educating youth about the atom and stressing One World as the best way to save civilization, to accenting democratic principles while attacking communism as the primary foe of peace. And school newspapers heeded the call. One high school newspaper warned students to wake up to the communist menace, proclaiming that 80,000 communists in the United States, all taking orders from Moscow, were at work in every union, school, church, and business. An editorial also informed students that they would "have to decide in the future years to come whether or not communism will rule the world." Student reporters wrote, "We, the youth of America, must accept the challenge set before us and determine for ourselves whether or not communism will rule the universe."[18]

After 1949, with the fall of China to Mao, the Soviet Union's successful testing of an atomic bomb, and the outbreak of hostilities in Korea, it became even more difficult to separate the issue of ensuring world survival from that of opposing communism. Schools across the country soon began conducting Democracy vs. Communism Week, highlighted by assemblies with guest speakers and films. Teachers incorporated *Senior*

Scholastic and other materials into lesson plans centered around educating students about the "Red Menace." Many cities held week-long "Democracy Beats Communism" programs, during which high school students were elected to city offices for a day and taught classes on democracy. In 1951, thousands of students joined the "Crusade for Freedom," donating money to fight communism and adding their names to "the Commies' black-list." *The Northeast* (High School) *Courier* in Kansas City, Missouri, wrote, "Russia won't lick us, but we will lick ourselves by failing as citizens. Do you want to live in a 'Master State'? Well, it's up to you, youth of today, because you will be the men and women of tomorrow."[19]

"United for Freedom," the 1951 theme for American Education Week, stressed the escalating need for social solidarity against communists. A high school editorial in honor of Education Week said, "We have no fear of the government, for in America, the government is run by the people." Students read on that "unless America can show the rest of the world that democracy is the only hope for freedom, our chance for peace is small." Yet another paper cautioned students to "always be on your guard for any activity that has the making of communism." As Christmas approached, students were asked to remember the fighting men in Korea and to say a prayer for their safe return.[20] A student editorial commemorating the attack on Pearl Harbor asked students to remember a decade of war, and to remind themselves of their special role in preventing another war:

> We, in America, are the most privileged people in the world. We have more rights and liberties than have ever been known to any other country. These privileges we enjoy are taken for granted by most Americans— perhaps because they have never been in a situation where they have had to fight for them. Now, more than ever, we must stick together. Stop where you are right now! Think it over! Are you a true American, fighting in your own individual way to prevent a similar occurrence on the December 7th in the future?[21]

For students at Northampton (Pennsylvania) High School, the reminder about their role in protecting democracy was delivered in the fall of 1953 during the annual installation of the student council. As the new president gave his acceptance speech, the doors suddenly burst open. A man clad in an army sergeant's uniform, and safeguarded by a police officer, rushed down the aisle toward the stage. "At one o'clock today, the United States government as such no longer exists," the sergeant proclaimed. "It has been taken over by the Nationalists Party. Upon the signal from our headquarters in Washington, our party members will assume complete control of the entire country." Stunned students listened as the sergeant continued, "Anyone offering resistance will be immediately removed to a correction camp."

Murmurs spread through the crowd. Surely this was all a joke. The sergeant yelled, "Silence!" The officers stationed around the auditorium grabbed their weapons. During the next hour, the sergeant told the students that they were now controlled by the state and, after the assembly, they were to go home and listen to their radios. Boys over the age of fourteen were to report back to the school at five o'clock with a few belongings and be prepared to leave immediately for military bases around the country. Anyone not reporting would be shot when captured. Girls over the age of fourteen were to return to the school at 6:30 a.m. At that time, they would leave for government service — destinations to be determined. When a teacher in the audience objected, he was arrested and dragged from the auditorium, leaving students startled and even more confused. They sat white-faced with fear, some holding back tears.

Then, just as suddenly as when the doors had burst open, the teacher who had been subdued reappeared. All was fine, he announced. What had taken place was an example of what *might* happen if they, the students, did not fulfill their social responsibilities to serve their country and protect the American way of life. The students, who had been unsuspecting participants in yet another atomic narrative, heard the message: Democracy and communism were on a collision course, with democracy's future threatened by a formidable and precariously dangerous atomic foe that must be defeated.[22]

This demonstration — or social narrative — of democracy's future in an age of ominous uncertainty underscored the importance for students to comprehend democratic principles and to be able to contrast them to those of communism. This required active participation in and awareness of the current world situation. Stanley Dimond, education professor at the University of Michigan, typified this viewpoint by suggesting that all youth achieve an intellectual understanding of democracy and strong emotional loyalty. Students had to practice democratic procedures, wrote Dimond in *National Parent-Teacher* magazine. Moreover, they had to study controversial subjects, be able to solve problems, and participate in out-of-class activities and public affairs.[23]

The threat of communism and the threat of atomic annihilation had become, in an elemental sense, one and the same. High schools held assemblies dealing with communism and the Soviet Union's potential atomic capabilities. In 1948, at Kansas City's Manual High School, for example, students watched the film, *A Tale of Two Cities*, showing the devastation at Hiroshima and Nagasaki, and listened to scientific explanations of the atom. Presentations, however, stressed the need for international cooperation in atomic research in order to ensure world peace. Without it, said student Rollie Baldwin, "our civilization is apt to be destroyed." Another student then spoke on "Requisites of Atomic Control," which pointed out that the Soviet Union was the only nation dissenting to such international controls because it was "desperately trying to find out the secret of the atom, herself." Shortly thereafter, the school newspaper asked simply, "Do you seriously feel that you will be able to take your place in the world — this great world of ours that might, at any minute, be plunged into an inferno?" After a city-wide meeting with a Navy admiral, another school reporter wrote, "Just think of what it would mean to us to live under a Communist regime instead of in a Democracy. We, as the youth of today, will have to decide in the future years to come, whether or not Communism will rule the world."[24]

These threats coalesced on June 24, 1950, when the communist-led North Koreans crossed the 38th parallel and attacked South Korea. Although schools continued activities in support of veterans throughout the late 1940s, most school newspapers had suspended columns on alumni in the service and updates on war-related issues by the end of the decade. But the personalization of war was again in student news. Newspapers reported teachers and former students who were called-up, wounded, or killed in action. Military recruiters increased their efforts to enlist boys after graduation. Students set up exhibits on the Korean conflict and signed so-called "freedom scrolls," pledging their support of individual freedoms. "Government Of, By, and For the People" became the 1950 theme of American Education Week (a reflection of the country's current obsession), as the government and educators emphasized the necessity of defending democracy against all foes. The generation coming of age as a new decade began learned quickly that their world differed even from the world encountered by their older siblings just a few years earlier.[25]

With the escalation of real war, not merely an anticipated one, concerns about the growing fears and anxieties among children and teenagers became more pronounced. These concerns were reflected in textbooks, which increasingly became more pessimistic about the future and more alarmist about the communist challenge to democracy. *The Story of American Democracy* provides an excellent example of this change. The 1950 edition portrayed the United States as a leader in the struggle for democracy and the United Nations as essential for maintaining world peace. In addition, it stressed the importance of international control of atomic energy. By its 1955 edition, the book contained myriad anxieties about the future. The United States was now locked in a struggle with the Soviet Union. The text warned youth to guard against "false news," "dangerous propaganda," and "subversion anxieties." They also were instructed to demonstrate their responsibilities (i.e., loyalty) to democracy by serving in the military, serving on juries, and paying taxes.[26]

The fear of communism became the overriding passion of history textbooks in the 1950s as prospects for a peaceful future became more dim. According to historian JoAnne Brown, "If panic was the present danger, fear was the future threat." She suggests, however, fear and panic were minimized by the use of such euphemistic terms as crisis, tension, emergency, and disaster, as well as phrases like "any emergency which may occur" and "threat to our way of living," in place of the most frightening, yet more accurate, descriptors such as war, death, bombings, attack, atomic warfare, and atom bomb.[27] Yet the tone of the atomic narratives found in classroom texts, collateral materials, films, and even oral discussions nonetheless contained fearful messages of possible atomic doom.

In 1953, a representative of the Ford Foundation asked simply how anyone could live without fear, citing the Soviet Union's atomic arsenal, better delivery systems for atomic weapons, and inadequate defense systems. "How in particular can one live without fear in the second half of the Twentieth Century?" he asked. "Plainly, we are facing greater dangers and are having made upon us greater demands than any other generation." Ryland Crary, co-author of the high school handbook on atomic energy, *Operation Atomic Vision,* and chief of the Federal Civil Defense Administration's School Branch, called upon educators to counteract fear by instilling emotional stability in their students. Moreover, they should assist them in coping with any intimidation by teaching defensive skills. "The hazards of the changed world have become known to America," he wrote in 1953. "These hazards are simply the conditions of life in the twentieth century. They will be adequately met through education neither by hysteria nor by avoidance."[28]

Crary recognized that young people had to be concerned not only with defending democracy but also with dying in their own homes. As society prepared for the potentiality of an atomic offensive, the Atomic Generation became the principal players in the country's next act in the social narrative of the atom: the civil-defense drama. Before long, America's children and youth scurried down tiled corridors and along underground passageways. Bodies merged and voices murmured in crowded boiler rooms as boys and girls huddled together in mock drills that took less than three minutes to conduct but promised the continuation of life.

Following passage of the Federal Civil Defense Act in 1950, President Truman moved quickly to name Millard Caldwell to head the Federal Civil

Defense Administration (FCDA), created on January 12, 1951. The FCDA, which consolidated the functions of the wartime Office of Civil Defense and the postwar National Safety Resources Board, oversaw the defense of the nation against atomic attack. America's youth, who represented the future, became its major focus, with schools quickly enlisted in the civil-defense effort. The FCDA issued the information to state and local governments, which quickly produced their own booklets.

Although students had been indoctrinated in the values of cooperation and teamwork under the guise of brotherhood and international relations, they now received instruction in the new Atomic Age formula for survival: cooperation, teamwork, and self-reliance — the same message reflected in countless *Senior Scholastic* narratives (see Chapter 4). Urban Fleege, director of the FCDA's Educational Institutions Division, suggested that teachers aid students in becoming emotionally stable, cooperative, mutually responsible, and helpful. To survive an atomic war, he said, people had to cooperate with others. They had to be team players. They had to follow instructions. And they had to be able to take control of the situation: to stand strong and to stand alone. According to Fleege, self-reliance and cooperation were everyone's responsibilities. Civil defense, in other words, meant personal survival.[29]

To ensure survival in a surprise atomic attack, James Ridgway, writing in the *American School Board Journal*, said school services should be expanded to include housing, feeding, medical care, recreation, and liaison with the community. "This is a huge order," he wrote, "but World War III, if it should come, will be a fight to the finish; and in view of the size of the major powers that may be involved, it may last a long time." Education Commissioner Earl McGrath announced that the Office of Education and American Red Cross would cooperate in an effort to train some 20 million people in first-aid.[30]

Schools across the country immediately introduced massive identification programs. Early proposals to tattoo children, mark clothing, and distribute ID cards were rejected because severe burns would make identification impossible. Fingerprinting, likewise, was abandoned because gathering and filing thousands of fingerprints of the dead would be a slow and tedious job. The FCDA ultimately recommended heat- and corrosion-resistant metal "dog tags" as the most practical and indestructible form of identification. Millions of children — including two and a half million in New York City alone — eventually received dog tags (for boys) and identification necklaces (for girls), even though the government still encouraged parents to use indelible ink to write their children's names in their underwear, or to sew their names into clothing. The FCDA also instructed schools to institute emergency drills, especially in so-called target cities such as New York City, Los Angeles, Detroit, Milwaukee, San Francisco, and Philadelphia. These drills, however, soon spread throughout a nation at risk.[31]

To overcome potential panic among students, John Sternig, assistant school superintendent in Glencoe, Illinois, urged teachers to outline specific disaster situations and discuss the psychological aspects of such emergencies. Students also were to be encouraged to develop the qualities of self-reliance and group self-sufficiency, and the ability to help others. "The greatest danger in any catastrophe," he wrote, "always has been panic." Echoing the words of other educators and government officials, Sternig reiterated that panic resulted when uncontrolled emotions led to uncontrolled behavior. If the individual is able to understand the facts, he argued, then — and only then — would rational behavior become possible, which would then lead to behavior appropriate to the facts. But this was difficult to achieve, Sternig warned, and "almost impossible in times of catastrophe unless we are well trained." Dealing with atomic facts, not fiction, was heralded throughout the educational community. The Geneseo (New York) State Teachers College even developed an intensive civil-defense program for public schools. The training course, designed to be adapted to the needs of any school, provided background information on postwar developments and the current national emergency, including potential atomic warfare.[32]

The bottom line in the Geneseo program, and others like it, was atomic survival. Teachers could learn about civil defense themselves, but the real test came in translating its importance to their students. Teachers were not without resources, however. Numerous books, articles, and government publications were available for classroom use. One of the most widely used publications used to teach civil defense was *Survival Under Atomic Attack*, published by the Office of Civil Defense in 1950. The federal government, in cooperation with school districts across the country, distributed this booklet to more than 20 million students from elementary to high schools.[33] State, county, and local civil-defense agencies also reprinted the booklet for general distribution.

The opening page of *Survival Under Atomic Attack* read:

You
Can
SURVIVE
You can live through an atom bomb raid and you won't have to have a Geiger counter, protective clothing, or special training in order to do it.

REPRINT OF THE

OFFICIAL BEAVER COUNTY CIVIL DEFENSE
Court House
BEAVER, PA.

U.S. GOVERNMENT

BOOKLET

The secrets of survival are:

KNOW THE BOMB'S TRUE DANGERS.
KNOW THE STEPS YOU CAN TAKE TO ESCAPE THEM.

Yet the life-threatening aspects of the atomic bomb were made clear, even as the booklet attempted to minimize them. "Should you happen to be one of the unlucky people right under the bomb," it read, "there is practically no hope of living through it," although chances for survival increased to 50-50 from one-half to one mile away from ground zero. The booklet pointed out that 70 percent of Nagasaki residents and slightly more than half of those in Hiroshima who were a mile from the blast survived to tell of their experiences. It compared radioactivity, which should be less feared than the blast and heat, to a sunburn. A sunburn might hurt but was not necessarily harmful unless it covered your entire body, in which case it could make you very sick, or sometimes even cause death. "In the same way," it read, "the harm that can come to you from radioactivity will depend on the power of the rays and particles that strike you, upon the length of time you are exposed to them, and on how much of your body is exposed."

Surviving an atomic attack (assuming, of course, a person was not located at ground zero) came down to following six survival secrets, which should be memorized: 1) try to get shielded, 2) drop flat on ground or floor, 3) bury your face in your arms, 4) don't rush outside right after a bombing, 5) don't take chances with food or water in open containers, and 6) don't start rumors. The booklet ended by reinforcing its real message that survival depended upon avoiding panic:

> [A]lways remember that blast and heat are the two greatest dangers you face. The things you do to protect yourself from these dangers usually will go a long way toward providing protection from the explosive radioactivity loosed by atomic explosion…. If you follow the pointers in this little booklet, you stand a far better than an even chance of surviving the bomb's blast, heat, and radioactivity…. But if you lose your head and blindly attempt to run from the dangers, you may touch off a panic that will cost your life and put tremendous obstacles in the way of your Civil Defense Corps.

Opposite: One of the most widely used publications used to teach civil defense was *Survival Under Atomic Attack*, published by the Office of Civil Defense in 1950. The federal government, in cooperation with school districts across the country, distributed the booklet to more than 20 million students from elementary to high schools. State, county, and local civil-defense agencies also reprinted the booklet for general distrbution.

MEMORIZE THESE SIX IMPORTANT POINTS

1

**Your First Warning . . .
May Be a Brilliant Flash of Light**

TRY TO GET SHIELDED . . .

The next few seconds might save your life—if you are inside get down in a basement, or under a desk or table. Should you unexpectedly be caught out-of-doors—get alongside a wall or doorway of a building—or drop in any handy ditch or gutter.

2

DROP FLAT ON GROUND OR FLOOR . . .

You have a few seconds before the swift blast hits you, lie flat—to keep from being tossed about—and to lessen the chances of being struck by falling and flying objects.

3

BURY YOUR FACE IN YOUR ARMS . . .

When you drop flat—hide your face in the crook of one arm—place free hand over back of neck—to protect your face from flash burns—and to keep flying objects from crushing you.

**Keep Calm and Cool . . .
Protect Your Family and Property**

DON'T RUSH OUTSIDE RIGHT AFTER A BOMBING . . .

After an air burst—wait a few minutes—put out minor blazes. After ground bursts wait at least one hour—to give lingering radiation some chance to die down.

DON'T TAKE CHANCES WITH FOOD AND WATER —IN OPEN CONTAINERS . . .

To prevent radioactive poisoning or disease—select your food and water with care. When there is reason to believe they may be contaminated—stick to canned, covered and bottled things.

PLAN AHEAD FOR HOUSEHOLD SAFETY . . .

Don't let trash pile up, keep waste paper in covered containers. Know which is the safest part of your cellar —learn how to turn off your furnace and what to do about utilities. Always have on hand—a good flashlight, a radio, first-aid equipment, and a supply of canned goods.

4

5

6

YOUR SAFETY DEPENDS ON YOU

6 Survival Secrets for Atomic Attack was another publication that was widely distributed to the public.

Another key narrative used by teachers and parents alike was *How to Survive an Atomic Bomb*, written by Richard Gerstell, a consultant to the Civil Defense Office of the National Security Resources Board (predecessor to the FCDA). Promoted as a complete, easy-to-read guide for every home, office, and factory, this book presented facts, not "scare-talk," although the message was congruent with the one found in *Survival Under Atomic Attack*: "Ignorance makes fear. Fear makes panic. Panic can be an enemy's best weapon."

Gerstell warned that initiating

a single wild rumor could start a panic that might result in the loss of one's life. Everything came down to keeping calm. "Don't give in to panic," he wrote. "Don't forget that atomic rays and radioactivity are not some mysterious magic against which we're all helpless. You are *not* bound to die at the least touch of it."[34] He even took extra measures to minimize the impact of radiation, suggesting that although "atomic rays" near the blast could be lethal, they were completely harmless just a mile and a half away. More important, radiation exposure would not lead to cancer, Gerstell argued, because no "ray-caused" cancer was discovered in studies conducted among Hiroshima and Nagasaki survivors. He also pointed out that of the 42,000 servicemen and scientists participating in the atomic test in the Bikini Atoll, all of whom had been exposed repeatedly to some radiation, and even got "bomb ashes" in their hair, not one came down with radiation poisoning.[35] (Only recently has the government acknowledged the lethal effects of these tests on the participants, many of whom developed cancer, leukemia, and other diseases.)

Still, Gerstell believed that the eventuality of atomic attack was very real; it was not some science-fiction plot. All Americans had to know what to do because the entire country was a possible target. "Don't think that because you live in a village of five hundred people or because the nearest town is ten miles away that you shouldn't know what to do," he wrote. "You still must know the facts of this book." He urged parents to conduct home drills and to instruct their children on the absolute necessity of taking cover immediately and, above all else, remaining calm. "You must stay down," Gerstell wrote. "You don't know when it's coming. You probably won't hear the enemy planes. An atomic bomb goes off in a split-second. In much less time than it takes to blink. So stay down until you know the danger is over."[36]

One of Gerstell's main concerns was what to do if an atomic attack occurred during school hours. He urged parents to insist that teachers and school administrators have a plan for safeguarding their children. But there was no need for such urgings. Following the lead of the FCDA, schools throughout the country quickly implemented three types of civil-defense drills. The "duck and cover" drill was used to demonstrate proper procedure when an enemy attacked without warning. Advance-warning drills, or "shelter drills," allowed students an opportunity to proceed to the shelter. Dispersal drills meant students had enough time to get home before the bomb struck.

In 1952, the FCDA published *Civil Defense in Schools*, which described the various drills and outlined schools' responsibilities during an emergency. The training of students to react properly was paramount. The booklet read in part:

A BANTAM BOOK
Every Book Complete

845

If there's ATOMIC WARFARE
this book may save y<u>our</u> life!

COMPLETE
EASY-TO-READ
GUIDE FOR
EVERY HOME, OFFICE
and FACTORY

How to Survive an Atomic Bomb

RICHARD GERSTELL

CONSULTANT, *Civil Defense Office*

Training should continue by means of frequent drills. It may be well to announce the first few drills in advance. Younger children especially should be prepared to prevent emotional upset. When routine satisfactory procedures have been established, drills should come at irregular intervals and without warning. These drills will uncover weaknesses in planning, coordination, and communication.[37]

By the end of 1952, most high schools had some form of civil-defense education program. States also issued special publications to assist local school districts in establishing proper procedures.

A policy statement issued by the New York City Board of Education said bluntly that the child "should be trained in self-reliance, imbued with faith in his ability to survive, no matter what the danger." In other words, the emphasis on international cooperation and brotherhood, heard by adolescents in the early postwar years, had been replaced by an emphasis on strength and self-reliance. Millions of copies of *You and the Atomic Bomb*, distributed by the New York State Civil Defense Commission, provided the public with information about the atomic bomb and how to survive its effects. The introduction of the hydrogen bomb, however, with a thousand times more power than the Hiroshima bomb, prompted even more extreme civil-defense measures. In 1955, for example, a city-wide atomic drill in Mobile, Alabama, evacuated 37,000 children some seventy-five minutes from the city, beyond what officials called "the danger zone."[38]

During so-called "cover" drills, a teacher shouted, "Drop!" Children immediately assumed a kneeling position, hands clasped behind their necks, and their faces covered as much as possible. New York City distinguished between "take cover" drills, with no warning of attack, and "shelter area" drills, when there was at least an eight-minute warning. In Detroit, more than three hundred schools conducted monthly schoolwide drills in addition to more frequent individual school drills. For the city's drills, schools received air-raid warnings through a telephone relay system, supplemented by announcements on the school system's own FM radio station. A yellow message meant an air raid was possible and children should be brought in from outdoors. A red message signalled an imminent raid, sending children to their assigned refuge area.

Opposite: Another narrative used by teachers and parents alike was *How to Survive an Atomic Bomb*, written by Richard Gerstell, a consultant to the Civil Defense Office of the National Security Resources Board (predecessor to the FCDA). Although promoted as an easy-to-read guide with facts, not "scaretalk," its message was the same as *Survival Under Atomic Attack*: "Ignorance makes fear. Fear makes panic. Panic can be an enemy's best weapon."

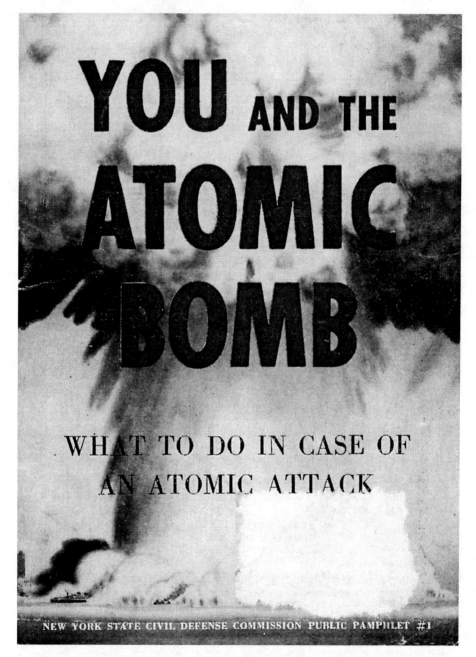

Millions of copies of *You and the Atomic Bomb*, distributed by the New York State Civil Defense Commission, provided the public with information about the atomic bomb and how to survive its effects.

Columbus, Ohio, first introduced individual homeroom drills, then school drills, held at least once a month. L.W. Huber, principal of the Indianola Junior High School in Columbus and chairman of the school system's civil-defense committee, told delegates at the 1952 convention of the National Association of Secondary-School Principals, "We have before us ... a long-range and continuous problem of educating all pupils as they come along in our schools. We must teach the facts of the atomic era: We must point out the true dangers of the atomic bomb and must teach pupils how to escape its dangers."[39]

Kansas City, Missouri, schools were representative of schools elsewhere in preparing the Atomic Generation for the next phase of their atomic education. In December 1950, Master Sergeant Walter Halverson told Southwest High School students that if they understood the principles of the atomic bomb, there would be no panic in the school's first air-raid drill, planned for February. At a special assembly, he discussed the three phases of an atomic bomb attack: the flash, which causes fires; the blast, which breaks windows and topples buildings; and the radioactivity. If the school received a thirty-minute warning of an actual attack, students would be sent home. With a ten-minute warning, they would go to the designated safety area within the school. Students would learn more about the bomb, he said, through a series of school bulletins and films, including *A Tale of Two Cities*, about Hiroshoma and Nagasaki, and *Operation Crossroads*, about the Bikini atomic tests. A student editorial in January stressed that "air-raid drills are for a real purpose, not for amusement and enjoyment. When we realize the seriousness of this matter we will have self-discipline."[40]

Kansas City students also heard Dr. Carroll Hungate, chief medical officer at a nearby naval base, explain the nature of atomic energy and precautions to take against atomic attack. Part of his program featured the film, *One World or None*, which compared the destructive force of early weapons to that of the atomic bomb. This was followed by another film, *Pattern for Survival*, providing the specific steps to take against atomic attack. A student reporter commenting on the showing of these films wrote, "Gasps in the audience demonstrated the reaction to the pictured results of an explosion. Tension was at a level seldom seen in a school assembly." Hungate then reiterated the survival secrets: Students should drop flat on the ground, shield themselves, stay inside, not use water or food in open containers, and not start rumors.

During another assembly program, students heard from the regional civil-defense director, who explained the "appalling conditions" resulting from an atomic bomb attack. All were being prepared for the introduction

VOTE FOR
DICK SMITH

SOUTHWEST TRAIL

SEE THE
REVELS

Vol. XXVI — Southwest High School, Kansas City, Missouri, February 21, 1951 — No. 11

Student Talent Show To Be Seen March 1 and 2

Put the best talent in the school in a pot, season with tiptop directors, and out comes the 1951 edition of the Redskin Revels.

The Revels will be presented on Thursday and Friday nights, March 1 and 2, in the auditorium. The price of tickets is 50 cents. Miss Pauline Wolfe is faculty director and Jack Glenn and Janet Eckert are student directors.

This year's show is composed of nine scenes, all built around the central theme of a "Winter Vacation." The scenes are spots well known to winter vacation travelers.

Scene one is entitled "Before School" and features Sue Bletkey, Patty Ferris, Nancy Hoglund, Shirley Riley, Mary Lu White, Eleanor Snyder, Betty Perkins, and Diane Mookin.

Scene two, "The Station" stars the dancing feet of Saul Ellis and Bob Hackler as well as the clever antics of Bill Gilmore.

Scene three called "The Radio Show," has a flute duet by Betty Davis and Gail Loomis, a scene by Ron Kuntson and his puppets, a vocal rendition by the Whatnot Quartet, and two piano numbers by Trudy Gibson and Eleanor Herbet.

Scene four takes place in Florida and has Nancy Wells and "The Thing."

Scene six, "Sun Valley," uses the talent of Patty Taylor, Miss Davidson's vocal group, Dickie Vrooman, and Margaret Donnelly.

Scene seven takes place at one of the well-known winter festivals. Sandy Haas, Pete Rush, and Marilyn Schwarts are featured in this scene.

Speaking parts are held by Max Bergman, Bruce Bellamy, Mary Weddendorf, Marvin Rich, Bev Robbins, and Sue Schmiederer.

Several of the various departments at school are doing their bit toward moulding the Revels. The Spanish department is doing some work on the fiesta scene, Miss Pusateri is helping with the chorus lines, and Mr. Nivens is directing the choir.

Betty Davis Chosen Southwest Candidate For R. O. T. C. Queen

Southwest's candidate for this year's R.O.T.C. Regimental Queen is Betty Davis. This active senior girl was chosen by the cadets from five candidates from this school. Cadets from all over the city will participate in this gala affair to be held in the main arena of the Municipal Auditorium February 23.

Four attendants were chosen for the Southwest Queen. They are: Gayle Rimann, Nancy Jones, Ruth Remley, and Joyce White.

The first thing on the program will be the Grand March in which all the cadets and their dates will participate. It is to be a program dance and dancing will start immediately after the Grand March.

The music will be furnished by a military band from Fort Leavenworth. This band is reported to be the best in the Fifth Army Area. The bandstand will be decorated with the National Colors and the Regimental Colors on the front and the eight school flags on the back.

The highlight of the evening, which is the crowning of the queen, will come at intermission. The battalion queens will be crowned before the Regimental Queen.

Each battalion queen will be presented a locket with "ROTC Queen 1951" inscribed on it. There will be a Banquet of Roses in honor of the Regimental Queen.

Radio and TV Jobs To Be Discussed

"Careers in Radio and Television," will be discussed in a meeting at Junior College, 39th and McGee, at 3 p.m. on February 27, Tuesday.

This will be the fourth annual "Jobs in Radio and Television" conference sponsored by the Radio Council of Greater Kansas City.

The meeting is open to students of high schools, junior and senior grades, and all college students, both public and private. There is no admission charge.

Coming Events Planned For Rest of the Year

Looking ahead into coming events for the rest of the year, we see that the Senior Play will be presented on the evenings of April 20 and 21. A busy schedule is planned for May with the Literary Contest scheduled for the 4th. Following that the National Honor Society will hold its annual induction May 11, and the Spring Concert is planned for May 18. Installation of N.A.H.S. and Quill and Scroll members will be held May 23.

The last day for the seniors is June 1 and commencement will follow June 6. For the others, June 8 will be the closing date of school.

Looking Ahead

Feb. 21—Hestia Meeting
Feb. 22—George Washington's Birthday—No School
Feb. 23—R.O.T.C. Ball
Feb. 27—Student Council Meeting
  Chess Club
Feb. 28—N.A.H.S. Meetings
Mar. 1—City Hall Election
  Engineers Meeting
  Y-Teens
Mar. 1-2—Redskin Revels
Mar. 5-9—Jr. Red Cross Drive
Mar. 7—Hestia Meeting
Mar. 8—Trail out

Students Are Orderly In First Air Raid Drill

The scene above is typical of those that were witnessed by the students during the first air raid drill practice. In the foreground are the students of Miss Davidson's music class. —Photo by Jim Carter.

The comments were very favorable as students returned to class after the first air raid drill Wednesday, February 7. Mr. W. Lawrence Cannon and M/Sgt. Walter L. Halverson expressed themselves as being very well satisfied with the practice drill.

Mr. Frank Gunther, Office of Civil Defense, and Mr. J. Glen Travis, Supervisor of Public Information Service from the Board of Education, visited Southwest principally to watch the practice. They were impressed with the good behavior and co-operation of the students. To them, it was remarkable for the first time.

Wardens on Duty

The air raid wardens were on duty at their individual posts immediately after the alarm was sounded. They reported that everything was quiet and the students orderly. However some straggling was noticed and the students are cautioned to stay closer together.

Placed at the most critical spots, the air raid wardens have a tremendous job. Their main duties will be to prevent panic and to enforce safety rules. The boys chosen to shoulder this responsibility are: Roger Heiskell, Dee Williams, Fritz Heath, Mark Stein, John Handley, Cooper Allen, Duke Duncan, Dudley Gilmore, John Rudolph, Harold Michaels, Jerry Shaw, Tom McKee, Jack Henslip, Ed Enfield, Richard Oglesby, and John Collet.

R.O.T.C. Trained for Emergency

The members of the R.O.T.C. have also been instructed to aid in the air raid drills. They report quickly to the drill hall after the signal has been given and assume their duties as messengers. In case of a real air raid their services will be important, as they will be equipped to meet all emergencies. It will be their joke to evacuate the injured, in addition to guarding the various installations throughout the school, such as water valves and electrical switches.

First Aid Instruction Given

First aid is to be taught so that

the students in general will be more able to handle dangerous situations in case of an emergency. The course is for eighteen hours, given to the upperclassmen in physical education and human science classes, and to the eighth graders in physical education health classes. The instructors are Mr. Lou House, Miss Jane Joyce, Miss Marie Pusateri, and Mr. George C. Ewing.

Definite plans have not, as yet, been worked out as to how and where medical treatment will be administered in time of disaster. It is thought that students will receive aid in teams. The way it stands now, girls will be cared for in the shower room and the girls' gymnasium and boys will be taken to the R.O.T.C. drill hall. The school nurse, Miss Elma A. Dreyer, will be on duty where needed. Equipment will be necessary to outfit these first aid stations.

Other Precautions in Case of War

If the situation grows very critical more precautions will be taken. The windows will be barricaded just as England had to do in the previous war. During an air raid all utilities will have to be shut off. Four people, probably two custodians and two students, will be assigned to each so that as soon as the alarm is sounded, at least one will reach his specific assignment.

It has also been suggested that the basement of the school be used for an air raid shelter. There is adequate space and it is suitably built. However, there is only one small exit, and before it could be put into use, other exits would have to be built.

Red Cross Elects New Officers

The remaining Junior Red Cross officers for the second semester were elected at the first meeting of the council, February 6, 1951. Jerry Jurden and Elaine Smith, president and vice-president, respectively, were elected by the entire student body in the election before the first semester ended.

Dee Williams, senior, was elected secretary. Among Dee's activities are Student Council representative and alternate, first and second team letters in football, and member of National Art Honor Society.

Petres Doty, junior, was elected treasurer. Her activities include, news editor of the Trail, Student Council representative, Red Cross representative two semesters, 8th grade class representative to the Sachem, honor roll two semesters, and member of Thalian.

Don Olson, senior, is the newly elected parliamentarian for the council. His activities include: Student Council alternate, Red Cross representative and alternate, honor roll four semesters, and member of Zend Avesta.

Ann Welch, junior, will keep order in meetings, as the new sergeant-at-arms. Listed among her activities are Student Council representative

The new Red Cross officers shown above are: top row, left to right, Dee Williams, Jerry Jurden, Don Olson; front row, Elaine Smith, Ann Welch, and Petres Doty. —Photo by Jim Carter.

three semesters, Red Cross representative two semesters, vice-president of the Glee Club, and a squad leader in gym.

The various classes elected representatives to All-City Red Cross. They are: senior, Elaine Smith and Jerry Jurden; junior, John Powell and Paula Oviatt; sophomore, Barbara Eckstein and Mary Inwood; freshman, Kathy Williams; and 8th grade, Sandra Bottis.

Tooters Club To Sponsor Benefit Card Party

A benefit canasta and bridge party, sponsored by the Tooters Club will be held tonight at the Country Club Methodist Church. Profits will be used for purchasing risers for the band and orchestra.

Several table prizes and a door prize will be given.

Dick Smith Speaks to Schools In Campaign for Student Mayor

For the second time in the history of Southwest the school is represented in the election for mayor of Student Government Day. Dick Smith, a senior, is the number one candidate, and is running against John Sablo of Central, and Stan Levine of Paseo. The date of the election has been set for March 1.

As a candidate for mayor, Dick has presented his campaign speeches to all of the Interscholastic League high schools except the ones

from which his opponents come. He has also gone to the three junior high schools and the two Negro high schools—Lincoln and R. T. Coles.

Dick has already made several radio broadcasts and plans to appear on T. V. in the near future.

Dick's campaign managers have been hard at work boosting him for Mayor. Small handbills with his picture on them have been given out, while the Pep Club has honored him at basketball games.

Following a drill at Southwest High School in Kansas City, Missouri, the school newspaper reported that observers from the Office of Civil Defense was satisfied, but unfortunately "some straggling was noticed and the students are cautioned to stay closer together."

of atomic survival drills. Boys were enlisted as junior air-raid wardens. ROTC members were messengers and assigned the task of guarding water valves and electrical switches. Girls made bandages in their sewing classes. Boys and girls enrolled in public-speaking classes prepared talks on how to protect oneself from an atomic attack. Schools published shelter locations. One school newspaper commented: "'Keep calm. Do as you are instructed. This is an air raid.' What will you do when you hear this kind of a message? An air raid is very serious, whether it is practice or the real thing, and should be considered as such."[41]

Students in Kansas City conducted their first drills between January 12 and February 7, 1951. High school students were notified by a person at the public library, who first announced an air raid and then gave the appropriate color code: green, twenty minutes to get to shelters; blue, less time; red, very little time. Once notified, the high school telephoned several elementary schools in the area and repeated the warning. Students were alerted by three, one-minute periods of the continuous ringing of bells.

Prior to the drill, members of the Southeast High School newswriting class were taken on a visit to the air-raid shelter. A reporter, describing the experience, began, "This is the story of a door that may save your life. I want to tell you about this door." The article went on to describe how the class walked in a column of twos through the first-floor halls, down the middle stairs, to the ground floor, and into a tunnel, where a small door was located. "I had never really noticed [the door] before," the reporter wrote, "but now the chalked lettering Air-Raid Shelter No. 1 on it, made it stand out." The door opened into a forced-air room under the auditorium. The article continued:

> There were pipes in the middle of the room. We had to stoop under some of them in order to get to the other side of the room. Rectangular chalked spaces had been marked off all over [the] floor of the room. Each one had a number. Finally we came to a spot marked No. 2, this was our space. A space in which we might spend many hours. It was hot. We crowded into the space, got down on one knee and covered our faces as well as possible. Although it was just a practice, it brought out the seriousness of world affairs closer to us all.... As we walked out of the door each of us took a better look at it. This door that meant little to us before, might turn out to be a trusted friend.[42]

Following another drill, it was reported that observers from the Office of Civil Defense were satisfied, but unfortunately "some straggling was noticed and the students are cautioned to stay closer together." To overcome any lack of concentration or seriousness among students, educators

PAGE TWO   THE WESTPORT CRIER   FEBRUARY 23, 1951

Leaders In Our Community

By Bruce Power

Westporters who attended the first Tiger Den last October quickly became aware of a tall, dynamic man with a welcoming smile and a friendly word for everyone—a man whose winning personality and untiring efforts have helped to make our Tiger Den such a huge success, Dr. E. N. Vegiard.

As Chairman of the Tiger Den Committee, Dr. Vegiard holds numerous open discussions with representatives of the Student Council and the P.-T. A. to iron out Tiger Den problems and co-ordinates financial and entertainment operations so that on the night of the Tiger Den everything runs smoothly. As a result of his efforts, a great number of parents have become interested in the Den and its future.

Even though Dr. Vegiard devotes a great deal of time to school activities and his profession of being an orthodontist, he finds time to take an active part in the Alpha Lions Club, the Calvary Baptist Church (as Assistant Superintendent of the Sunday school), Boy Scouts (as committeeman for Troop 10), American Legion, Disabled American Veterans of which he is Past Commander, Veterans of Foreign Wars of which he is Past Surgeon of the 4th District, Sojourners Association, Ararat

Shrine, Missouri Peace Officers Association, and the Sheriff's Flying Air Squadron of which he is a deputy sheriff. Dr. Vegiard is also a member of the Missouri State Dental Association and takes an active part in the Kansas City Dental Society.

During the Second World War, Dr. Vegiard served in the First Cavalry Division three and a half years, acting as Division Dental Surgeon under General Swift. After being wounded while serving in the Southwest Pacific and spending six months in the hospital, Dr. Vegiard was discharged from the Army as a Major. The thing which gave him the greatest pleasure during his war experiences was helping the Chaplain's Corps with their music on the beaches of the blue Pacific at Oahu in the Hawaii Islands when the churches overflowed and the boys had to hold their services on the beaches.

Dr. Vegiard's gracious and charming wife is a regular helper at the Tiger Dens while his daughter, Peggy (a junior), and his son, Bobby (an eighth-grader) are also regular Den-goers. Another daughter, Evelyn, who was recently married, also attended Westport.

Whether known as "Doc" or "Major" to his many friends, to all Westporters he will always be looked upon as one of their "best friends" and a true leader in our community.

The Red Cross belongs to everyone, including YOU, and without your help it cannot function. It belongs to the people who want to help, and those who need help.

The goal for the 1951 Red Cross Campaign is $85,000,000, a boost of $18,000,000 over last year's goal. This 27% increase is due to the enormous load placed on the Red Cross by the expanding military forces and the civilian defense program.

The new duties and responsibilities of the Red Cross, assigned by the Government, include procuring blood for military and civil defense use, and training 20,000,000 people in first aid.

The month long drive, which begins March 1, deserves your help and support. Your contribution to the Red Cross in 1951 will help support the many services it renders at home and abroad.

Air Raid Instructions

"Keep calm. Do as you are instructed. This is an air raid." What will you do when you hear this kind of a message?

An air raid is very serious, whether it is practice or the real thing, and should be considered as such. When an air raid occurs at school, go with your class to the place assigned. The shelter spots are listed below.

Boys' Dressing Room	Room 1
Engine Room	Rooms 2, 4, 5, 119, 120
Remain in Rooms	Rooms 6 and 7
Boys' West Shower Room	Room 9
East Entrance of Engine Room	Room 104
Auditorium Under Balcony	Rooms 107 and 116
Auditorium Dressing Room	Auditorium Stage
Column Near Office Door	Rooms 106 and 110
Column Near Health Center	Rooms 114 and 115
Boys' Gym	Rooms 118, 216, 217, 218, 219, 220, 312, 313, 314, and 317
Cafeteria	Rooms 204, 205, 206, 207, 208, 210, 211, 212, 213, 214, 215, 303
By R. O. T. C.	Room 304
By Kitchen	Room 305
By S. E. Entrance to Boys' Gym	Room 306
West End of Second Floor Corridor	Rooms 307, 309, 310, and 311
By Metalwork	Room 315
By Woodwork	Room 316
Entrance to Boiler Room	Room 318

THE WESTPORT CRIER

Published bi-weekly during the school year by the newswriting class of Westport High School, Kansas City, Mo. Entered as Second-class matter April 4, 1928, at the postoffice at Kansas City, Mo., under the Act of March 8, 1879.

Address: The Westport Crier, 315 East Thirty-ninth street, Kansas City, 2, Mo.

Co-editors: Shirley Krenkel and Bruce Power; Managing Editor, Barbara Ross; Assistant Editor, Addie Dennis; News Editor, Shirley Lance; Page 2 Editor, Joan Yent; Feature Editor, Jo Ann Lewis; Sports Editor, Stan Gibson; Assistant Sports Editor, Ted Dixon; Art Editor, Carolyn Smith; Circulation Manager, Cynthia Carswell; Advertising Manager, Suzanne Carter; Photographers Jim Haynes, Jerry Shapiro, Cecil Foley; Reporters, Jerry Balls, Roberta Robinson, Barbara Wright, Dick Temple, Mildred Russell, and Joyce Miller. Faculty Adviser, Virginia Welch; School Treasurer, Lorena Card.

continually stressed the importance of these drills, even incorporating the dire reality of surprise attack into otherwise benign activities. For example, two weeks after a school's first civil-defense drill, the film *You Can Beat the A-Bomb* was shown at a school assembly at the conclusion of the drama class's presentation of "Our Miss Brooks."[43]

In March, the Red Cross conducted first-aid training in all Kansas City high school physical education and human sciences classes. The next month, a school newspaper announced that almost 100 students had been trained and could serve during an atomic attack. Furthermore, it said the school would have three or four volunteer ambulances on duty during an attack, with radio operators available if an atomic boom destroyed telephone lines. A school invited crosstown students to present Herman Hagedorn's poetic drama, "The Bomb That Fell on America," in a schoolwide assembly. The school's paper reported that "students listened attentively to Hagedorn's emotion-packed story of America's misuse of atomic power and the fear inspired by the bomb dropped on Hiroshima."[44]

When a high school conducted an air-raid drill in early 1953, the newspaper proudly reported that the school was "very fortunate in having three approved air-raid shelters." Students were informed that instructions would be posted in each room telling them what to do and where to go in an atomic attack. The article continued:

> If the action must be taken at school without warning, drop to the floor against the wall where the windows are located to prevent contact with any shattering glass. Bury your face in your arms. If the alert is given with warning, follow the directions given and go to the assigned shelter quickly.... In seeking protection in a building from an atomic explosion, make certain that you cannot see windows or openings in doors. This will assure you that the direct waves (the dangerous waves) cannot strike you. In case of urgent necessity, many of the outside and inside doors will be boarded up to give protection from possible direct waves.

The newspaper concluded by saying that these instructions were not intended to arouse alarm; they were "merely the routine assignments that must be carried out."[45]

In addition to frequent atomic drills, the nation's schools quickly adapted the concept of atomics education to include civil-defense issues.

Opposite: In preparation for civil-defense drills, a school newspaper printed a list of shelter locations within the school and commented: "'Keep calm. Do as you are instructed. This is an air raid.' What will you do when you hear this kind of message? An air raid is very serious, whether it is practice or the real thing, and should be considered as such."

ist # TOWER

Kansas City, Mo.   March 2, 1951

The newswriting class poses in the air raid shelter beneath the auditorium. Most of the students here have the correct position which is on one knee, with one hand protecting the back of the neck and the other arm covering the face.

Uniforms and Create Festive

Gerry Heuermann Southe Batallion Cadets Honored

The annual R.O.T.C. Regiment Municipal Auditorium was a colo uniformed cadets and their dates. the ball proceeded in military fash Fort Leavenworth "Commandants Band.

Clean-Up Campaign To Brighten Castle

Attention all school-spirited Knights and Ladies! Have you noticed the paper and rubbish cluttered about in the halls and the cafeteria? If so, you will be interested to know that plans aare under way for an all-out effort to improve the general appearance of our school. This clean-up campaign will start next week.

Let's make this clean up job not merely a campaign to be extended over a short period of time. Let's make it a habit!

Musicians At Work

Girls Glee, Choir, Band, And Orchestra All Perform

The Southeast music department has a rather full schedule of engagements.

The Girls Glee Club, composed of 84 girls, is singing March 6 and 7 at 8:30 in "The Children's Crusade." The program will be presented in the Music Hall. Our Glee Club was chosen along with the Southwest Girls Glee, to sing with the K. C. Philharmonic Orchestra under the direction of Hans Schweiger.

Since before Christmas, the group has been hard at work on "The Children's Crusade" a musical legend in four parts. The story is of the band of children who perish while on a crusade to Palestine.

The a cappella choir is also very busy. They sang Sunday evening, February 17, at the Broadway Baptist church and are singing again Sunday morning, March 4, for the Business Men's Bible Class. They are doing work in preparation for a radio broadcast, March 31. Some of their numbers include: "Rock'a My Soul," "Send Forth Thy Spirit," "Bells of St. Michels Tower," "Music a Link with God," and "To Thee We Sing."

Colorful Circus Week Comes to Kansas City; First Show, March 6

Hamid-Morton, the world's largest 3-ring indoor Police Circus is brought to Kansas City by the Police Benefit Association. The circus, which will present forty-two new 1951 features, will start March 6 in the Municipal Auditorium.

Clever animal acts help the circus moving in a fast and merry mood. Helen's chimpanzees will offer an engaging blend of careful training and purely unpredictable monkey business. Fearless Dick Clemens and Alert Anna will enter the arena and put the vitamin-charged savage jungle brutes through their intricate paces.

Dr. Cooper's beautiful, waltzing and rearing horses provoke gasps of admiration when presented. The antics of five baby elephants will be the hit of the show for many youngsters.

The tickets will sell at the same prices as last year, which are $1.22, $1.60, and $2.00 including tax. As a special service to groups, seats may be obtained in a block for any desired performance by contacting either Chief Johnson, Captain Keilerstrass, or arranging their reservation with the box office in the Municipal Audi-

News Students View Shelter

Southeast Prepares Atomic Bomb Shelter; Small Door a Hazard

This is the story of a door that may save your life. I want to tell you about this door.

During the past few weeks every school in Kansas City has been drilling for atom-bomb air-raids. The Tower Staff made their initial visit to the air-raid shelter one day last week. We followed our air-raid leader in a column of twos through the first floor halls, down the middle stairs, to the ground floor and into the tunnel. We made a couple of turns down the tunnel and there it was, the door.

I had really never noticed it before, but now the chalked lettering Air-Raid Shelter No. 1 on it, made it stand out. The door was very small. We had to hurry through it. When a great many students are trying to get through it, there will be a need for haste to keep the passageway from being blocked.

(left margin fragments:))ened olors :ross, ntro- e ra- oks." y the lirec- ht of was pring the rooks Seth him. get her star .each- mmer s has Hoff, .onnie 'eggy Joyce vorse, and had libra- only atitled was there for in : the iation. ind in et of efense t and

Jack Johnson, former FCDA assistant administrator, told the Florida Education Association in 1953, "Because of the potential danger of attack, the schools in target areas must make certain adjustments quickly." Shelter areas should be designated, he said, and schools should implement programs for self-protective drills. It was paramount that schools inform parents about plans for children under emergency conditions. Most important, schools had to provide specialized training for students because of the real and imminent danger of atomic attack. Teachers needed to prepare training materials for students and the community and to serve as advisors to civil-defense directors. Moreover, according to Johnson, the entire educational community had to focus on the problems of the Atomic Age. Rather than be an adjunct to school, civil defense needed to become an integral part of current educational programs. Johnson described this as functional civil defense, or "protective citizenship." Biology must provide information on biological warfare. Psychology should discuss the problems of panic during an attack. Home economics should even emphasize skills to handle emergency mass care.[46]

D. B. Roblee, an FCDA school relations officer, concurred with Johnson, writing that protective citizenship should emphasize an intensified sense of social interdependence and group solidarity. It also should broaden understanding of interpersonal responsibilities. Knowledge of the world situation should be improved. Finally, Roblee said protective citizenship must stress the "widespread mastery of the skills which enable mankind to meet adequately the dangers and tensions of emergency situations." The State of Connecticut's booklet, *A Guide to Teaching Civil Defense in Our Schools*, summarized the role of education in terms already well established, and once again exemplified the inextricable tie between democracy and the atom:

> Our way of life, including democracy, a good standard of living, and important cherished human values can be preserved. Education can and must be geared to perform its inherent role in winning the battle for democratic ideologies as well as world understanding and international cooperation. This may be a long battle and we must be prepared for any emergency including the possibility of another war.[47]

Opposite: Prior to a drill, members of a newswriting class were taken on a visit to the air-raid shelter. A reporter described how the class walked in a column of twos through the first-floor halls, down the middle stairs, to the ground floor, and into a tunnel, where a small door was located. The reporter wrote: "I had never really noticed [the door] before, but now, the chalked lettering Air-Raid Shelter No. 1 on it, made it stand out.... This door that meant little to us before, might turn out to be a trusted friend.

Save Your
Papers

SOUTHWEST TRAIL

Remember
May 12th
The Prom

'ol. XXVI   Southwest High School, Kansas City, Missouri, April 5, 1951   No. 14

$1,300 Paper Drive Goal; 75 Pounds per Student

April 18 or 19 is the date now set for the paper sale to raise unds for the restoration of the stage facilities which have been in 1se since the school was built some 26 years ago.

The Student Council Research Committee, which is planning he paper sale, is headed by Charles Goldenberg, and Miss Shipey is the faculty advisor. This committee has set a goal for each .tudent at 75 pounds per student. This will give a total of $1,300 and will bring the stage total to almost $2,000 of the $2,500 that is needed 'or the complete restoration of the stage.

The paper should be tied or in cardboard boxes because the school will not receive as high a price from the paper house if it is loose.

As a reward, some of the teachers are offering not to give their classes finals if the classes have an average of 100 pounds per pupil in the class.

Each homeroom will have a weighing station where the students of that room will bring their paper to be weighed before the truck takes it away. The Student Council will man the stations and it is hoped that the paper will begin coming early as the Council representatives will be on hand at 7 o'clock or shortly after.

The weather will have to be the deciding factor in whether or not the paper sale is held the 18th or the 19th. Students should be sure to watch their homeroom bulletin for the exact date of the sale. The sponsors point out that a great deal of outside collecting is not necessary in order to gather the 75 pounds for each student, because if each person gives all the papers and magazines that come to his house between now and the date of sale he will have easily accumulated the necessary amount.

While 75 pounds is the minimum, the Student Council hopes the students will keep in mind the fact that there is no maximum. Even if the students are unable to bring their quota, they are urged to bring whatever they can.

R. O. T. C. Circus To Feature Scottish Band

The R.O.T.C. Circus, to be held April 6, in the Municipal Auditorium it is one of the highlights of the year. The cadets from Southwest are busy practicing the Queen Anne's Manual which is a manual of fancy drills.

Every city battalion plus some visiting battalions will participate in this gala affair. The main attraction is the all-girls Scottish uniforms valued at over $25,000.

There will also be an expert crack squad from the Shattuck Military Academy of Fairbault, Minnesota. This squad, which has been on a tour of the Midwest, started in Kansas City and ends here with the Circus. They have taken part in several events and have never lost. They wear army costumes dating back to the War of 1812 and the Revolutionary War.

The Kemper Battalion will be here with its famous band. The R.O.T.C. units from La Fayette High School in St. Joseph and Joplin High School will participate. Also the William Chrisman High School Battalion from Independence will be here.

General admission tickets may be purchased from any cadet for 50 cents and box seats may be purchased for $1.00. The Circus will consist of many interesting and educational events and will be something worth while to see.

Miss Jackson's Class Reaches Red Cross Goal

Another homeroom, Miss Jackson's 316, not mentioned in the last issue of the Trail, reached its quota in the Red Cross drive.

Looking Ahead

Senior Play Will Feature Satire, Comedy

"Riddle Me Riches," a comedy in three acts, directed by Miss Grace Brees, will be the title of the senior play to be presented at Southwest on April 20 and 21.

The original story was written by Anne Ferring Weatherly. It involves a typical American family in the confusion of winning a 20,000 dollar quiz program prize.

The play will be under the supervision of the seniors and the different committees will be composed of those seniors who tried out for this event. The various committees will include Pat Holdren, Gitta Kaperl, "Duke" Duncan, Carolyn Blagg, Pat Ferris, Mark Stein, Mary Wallace, Caroline Ennis, Gloria Ramquist, Nancy Hougeland, Connie Lounsberry, Betty Davis, Janet Pfefer, Ann Straulman, Frank Leltz, Nancy Bodwell, Ken Peltzie, John Sands, Bennie Marks, and Ralph Schmidt.

This year, the play will feature entirely new scenery along with new furniture.

The cast has prepared for plenty of rehearsing. It includes Mary Weddendorf, Maryolive Manly, Jack Glenn, Janet Eckert, Virginia Orthwein, Phil Cline, John Sands, Susie Schrader, Bruce Bellamy, Bev Robbins, Dick Neff, Joan Hunt, Max Bergman, Ralph Schmidt, and Dave Davis.

Practice of First Aid Is in Full Swing

Sue Ragsdale (left) and Carolyn Carrier (right) are displaying their skill at bandaging, which is being taught in the First Aid classes. (Photo by Jim Norman).

As the students of the first aid classes sit in their assigned seats in the auditorium they learn to apply the definition of first aid to all types of illnesses. The definition is simply "the immediate and temporary care given to a victim of an accident or sudden illness until the services of a physician can be obtained."

So far the students have learned how to give immediate care to anyone who needs some attention given to a broken bone. They know how to make the proper kind of splint and bandage, which will hold the bone in place until a physician can set the bone for correct healing.

They have been taught the do's and dont's on serious illnesses and accidents, and also what to do in the cases that are not so serious. Learning how to bandage and what type of bandage to use on the different parts of the body is one of the most interesting parts of first aid. All the fundamentals of bandaging make it interesting—for example, the use of the square knot, which is a required type.

How to care for burns, wounds, and types of bleeding also is part of first aid.

Constantly the beginning first aiders are being reminded of these things that a good first aider should know and practice whenever he encounters any illness or accident. Even if in the home, at work, or on the street he should be able to render temporary, efficient first aid to the victim; keep the patient calm and himself calm; notify a doctor and give him an intelligent report of the case.

Many other things are also required of a first aider, but the above play the main part.

Plans for Junior-Senior Prom Announced at Senior Meeting

At a meeting of the senior class on March 29, the plans for the Junior-Senior Prom were announced. It is the wish of the Senior Business Committee that the Prom will be a grand success this year.

Full Schedule Arranged For City Hall Day

Students elected to the City Hall for Student Government Day, April 5, will have a busy schedule beginning at 7:30 a.m.

At 7:30 they will assemble in the Little Theatre to see City Manager Cookingham introduce all-city councilmen who are present, and hear Mayor Kemp talk on "Your City Government."

Following Mayor Kemp's talk, one boy and one girl from each high school, working as a team, will participate in the "Know Your City Government" contest. Ten dollars will be awarded the team with the best score.

Equipment from the various city departments such as police, fire, street, etc., will be displayed in the arena of the municipal auditorium, where there will also be an exhibition in which the Police Department and the Fire Department will demonstrate their equipment and tactics.

The Prom will be held on May 12 from 9 to 12 o'clock at the Little Theater. Music will be provided by Larry Boyle's Orchestra.

The tickets, two dollars per couple, will go on sale April 23 and will be sold until May 11.

The rules for the Prom as decided by the Senior Business Committee are as follows: Any junior or senior, boy or girl, who is a student at Southwest may buy a ticket and attend. No sophomore or freshman may attend. Juniors and seniors may bring outside dates if the dates are at least a junior in high school. Upon the purchase of a ticket, the purchaser must give his name and the name of his date and the school if he is an outsider. The ticket holder's name and date must be written on the ticket. The dance is to be formal.

Stags will be permitted to attend for the same price of admission as a couple. "Stag" will be marked on the ticket when it is bought, and if the stag obtains a date afterwards he must notify the committee before the dance. These rules will be enforced by the Senior Business Committee.

Decorations for the Prom are being worked on by a junior-senior committee.

Spotlighters Entertain Students

The first step toward new props for the stage started when the Spotlighters presented three one-act plays for the students during sixth and seventh hours Tuesday, March 20. The profit was over $400.

"No Banners Flying," the first play presented, starred Valle Loomis, Mary Weddendorf, Janet Pfeffer, Pat Holdren, and Carolyn Blagg. This play was a serious drama based on the theme of an organization of peace being more important than a preparation of war.

Charles Bishop, Ann Straulmann, Richard Neff, Janet Eckert, Joan Hunt, Phil Cline, Betty Carr, Frank Leitz, Kenneth Peltzie, John Campbell, and Kay Walton were the actors in a comedy "The Third Act." The story was a tale of some of the troubles and comic situations that arise behind the scenes of a stage production.

Good manners plus a pleasing personality are the makings of popularity, was the theme of the comedy "Princess Charming," the last of the plays by the Spotlighters. This comedy had the cast of Susie Schrae-

On stage for "The Third Act." This scene was one from the plays given by the Spotlighters for money toward new stage props. The players shown are Jack Glenn, Kenneth Peltzie, Janet Eckert, Betty Carr, Ann Straulmann, and Frank Leitz. (Photo by Jim Norman).

der, Maryolive Manly, Jack Glenn, Bruce Bellamy, Dave Brock, Susie Liebermann, Gitta Kaperl, John Sands, and "Grey" Orthwein. This last play showed vividly the comedy of the social life of the college campus.

Between the plays there were musical numbers. The "What-Four," a boys' quartet with Harold Michael,

Bob Kamberg, Fred Roehr, and Bob Hatfield, sang "Swing Low, Sweet Chariot" and "Chattanooga Shoe Shine Boy." Bob Pearce played two selections on his saxophone.

"Duke" Duncan was master of ceremonies and introduced each musical number. Marcus Fuhrer representing the Spotlighters, introduced the names of the plays and players.

In March 1951, the Red Cross conducted first-aid training in all Kansas City, Mo., high school physical education and human sciences classes. The next month, a school newspaper announced that almost 100 students had been trained and could serve during an atomic attack. Furthermore, it said the school would have three or four volunteer ambulances on duty during an attack, with radio operators available if an atomic boom destroyed telephone lines.

In 1951, Mary Meade, principal of Washington Irving High School in New York City, told a national conference of school principals that science courses should include the essentials of the atomic bomb and ways to defend against it. Safety, nutrition, and health education classes, she said, should include units on an atomic bomb attack. Students also should be encouraged to work with the Civil Air Patrol to spot incoming enemy aircraft. Meade and other educators felt strongly that schools should integrate civil defense into classroom narratives on the Atomic Age. Schools, in turn, recognized their obligation to prepare the younger generation for the unexpected catastrophe. Teachers urged students to demonstrate leadership skills through small group activities. Schools introduced "messenger" exercises, allowing students to learn techniques for informing others quickly and correctly. School trips reinforced the importance of following instructions outside of the school environment, while camp outings and similar activities taught self-reliance techniques. Schools sincerely believed that these activities worked to protect lives. By the early 1950s, civil defense not only had become written into the social narrative; it also had formed a vital aspect of adolescents' social experience.[48]

The Parent-Teachers Association, in its own contribution to civil defense, moved to create a positive mental health program to ease atomic anxieties by urging parents and teachers not to react unnecessarily to newspaper headlines and news broadcasts. Instead, they were to maintain a calm and assured demeanor. Speakers at the 1951 annual convention in Miami Beach told delegates to prepare students and themselves to "deal bravely" with the possibility of atomic attacks and to teach the younger generation to "come to terms with the actual world they live in now" so that they might achieve real peace in the world.[49]

The Virginia State Department of Education booklet, *A Guide to Organizing the School for Civil Defense*, summarized the need for civil defense within the scope of the larger narrative of "education for democracy." It was imperative, it read, "that each school continually explore the meaning of the principle: 'We must love democracy enough to practice it and practice it enough to love it.'" Only by making this principle more meaningful in every classroom would students confront the issues "in such a way that they do not become frustrated or develop a feeling of 'What's the use? Who cares?'" This same approach — merging civil defense with democratic principles — was heralded by William Shunck, superintendent of the Waterford Township Schools in Pontiac, Michigan. Shuck urged teachers not to focus solely on specific drills for specific emergencies, but to stress "the daily practice of group and individual discipline in the classroom, in the corridors, and on the stairways."[50]

Classrooms soon became civil-defense theaters as well, with students watching an array of movies on what to do in case of atomic attack. *And A Voice Shall Be Heard*, a 1951 General Electric Film, showed an imaginary attack on the city of Syracuse, New York, and the importance of civil defense. In *Survival Under Atomic Attack*, sponsored by the FCDA and based on the government publication of the same name, radio and television journalist Edward R. Murrow explained the dangers of the atomic bomb and the effects of radiation. Among the films aimed primarily at younger children were *Atomic Alert* (1951), produced by Encyclopedia Britannica, which illustrated the basic methods that children could use to best protect themselves and their friends from the effects of an atomic bomb; and *Duck and Cover*, the 1952 animated classic starring Bert the Turtle, who demonstrated the steps to be taken in the event of an enemy attack. Bert was more than a cartoon character; he was the mascot for civil defense. As such, he also became widely known to adolescents.

Several movies addressed the central concern of understanding civil-defense procedures. McGraw-Hill's *Disaster Control* (1951) provided a blueprint for organizing such an effort. Castle Film's 1952 release, *Our Cities Must Fight*, explained the importance of maintaining a well-organized civil-defense effort. The following year, the Health Education Service addressed the reasons behind civil defense in the first place. *The Injured Can't Wait*, for use with the Civil Defense Medical Aids program, was a sixteen-minute film that traced the movement of injured citizens to various medical installations.

Canada's National Film Board (CNFB) and the British Information Service (BIS) produced several films available to American educators. *Debris Clearance* (BIS, 1953) focused on cleaning up after a bombing. *Atomic Bomb — Its Effects and How to Meet Them* (BIS, 1953) provided a step-by-step account of what would happen if an atomic bomb were detonated one thousand feet above a major metropolitan city, and the civil-defense problems that would result. *Homeless Ones*, another CNFB release in 1954, detailed how an atomic attack on the center of a major city would cause death and destruction, and how civil-defense workers needed to be prepared to act immediately. These films joined many others in the arsenal of visual narratives that helped prepare the *Heat* of the Atomic Generation for what appeared to many as an inevitability: atomic attack.[51] Children were taught it was not normal to fear the bomb and to consider civil defense as a ritual not to be questioned. Rather than eliminate or at least minimize fear, however, films such as *Our Cities Must Fight* and *Survival Under Atomic Attack* projected what might be called atomic fatalism. One movie merely advised that the best defense against the atomic bomb was to be somewhere else when it bursts. Of course, this was not very reassuring.

Civil defense had become part of the educational routine by the early 1950s. Schools published periodic articles on what to do in case of atomic attack — at school, at home, or on the street. One high school newspaper wrote in 1952, "In case of sneak attack, if you are in a car, drop to the floor, or in a building lie under a table, bed, etc. If you are on the street and have a few seconds, get into a building; otherwise, get close to the curb, but by all means lie flat wherever you are.... The main thing is to keep your head all the time, no matter what happens."[52] High schools introduced Civil Defense Clubs, which became responsible for teaching first aid, addressing homerooms on the importance of civil defense, and assisting during air-raid drills. Students at one high school formed seven teams, each composed of one boy and one girl, who spoke on topics such as "Survival Under Atomic Attack" and related subjects.[53] A school newspaper, editorializing in 1955 in support of the school's Civil Defense Club, amplified the importance of civil defense with this portent of an atomic attack:

> The steady drone of bombers breaks the silence of the cold winter night. Closer they come to their target. The sky is lighted by the flashes of anti-aircraft fire searching out the enemy. The bursting shells blanket the sky, but still they press on. The interceptors attack the enemy viciously. Many of the enemy are destroyed, but finally they are over their target. From the bellies of the bombers fall the missiles of death and destruction. A huge eery ball of flame engulfs the city while a great mushroom of smoke hangs overhead. This was once a city of tall buildings testifying of the ingenuity of man, but now there is nothing but ruin. Here was once a city of culture and education ... a city where thousands of people worked, loved, and played. Now there is nothing but death. This has not really happened, but it could.[54]

Even the Girl Scouts joined in the civil-defense effort by forming monitor teams for detecting radioactivity, providing first aid, and working in the evacuation and shelter program during civil-defense practice.[55]

By the early 1950s, the Atomic Generation realized that losing the battle against communism would result in a war in which civilization itself would ultimately become the fatality. As the new decade progressed, civil defense became more integrated into the ever-changing social narrative of the atom. Students soon learned the familiar sounds of atomic alarms and teachers' methodical instructions to duck and cover. The shift from international brotherhood to survival of the fittest became more pronounced as the Cold War escalated.

Teachers, called upon to educate and to protect America's children,

CIVIL DEFENSE

Paseo inaugurated a Civil Defense program
this school year as its part in the program of
general national preparedness. Seven student
teams, composed of a boy and girl each, spoke
to homerooms on "Survival Under Atomic Attack"
and other related subjects.

Under the leadership of Mr. Chubb various
members of the faculty, including Sgt. Strayhall,
Sgt. Turner, Mr. Lindley, Mr. Stephens, Mr.
Wehrle, Mr. Lindwall, and Mr. Morrissette, prepared and administered the plans for the drills
and the student instructional program.

High schools around the country introduced Civil Defense Clubs, which became
responsible for teaching first aid, addressing homerooms on the importance of
civil defense, and assisting during air-raid drills. Students at Paseo High School
in Kansas City, Mo., formed seven teams, each composed of one boy and one
girl, who spoke on topics such as "Survival Under Atomic Attack" and related
subjects.

utilized all necessary means to assist them in their mission. One of the most popular tools used by teachers was, in fact, aimed specifically at America's youth. *Senior Scholastic*, published each week and read by thousands of high school students across the country, integrated fact and fiction in an effort to educate, to influence, and to entertain. *Senior Scholastic*'s editorial progression from promoting international brotherhood to opposing communism to encouraging strength and self-reliance occurred concurrently with the shift in America's school programs from protecting civilization to saving oneself from all-out atomic war.

4

Brotherhood, Self-Reliance, and Survival: *Senior Scholastic* in Text and Images

> *In our culture, children necessarily are exposed to many fear pro-*
> *voking and destructive influences. These are a part of reality.*
> — Dr. S. Harcourt Peppard, 1948[1]

S enior Scholastic, read each week by thousands of teachers and their students, provided a wide range of atomic narratives between 1945 and 1955 — from portents of impending atomic annihilation to unlimited potentialities of atomic applications in science and medicine. Bulk subscriptions were as low as three cents a copy for students. Teachers also received a special edition with guidelines on how to use the magazine in the classroom, as well as suggestions for class projects, discussion questions, and additional references for further study.[2] Among *Senior Scholastic*'s objectives, as stated in its Editorial Platform, were promotion of the democratic way of life and the "cooperation and understanding among all peoples for the peace of the world." According to John W. Studebaker, former U.S. Commissioner of Education and chairman of the editorial board for Scholastic Magazines after 1948, teachers were to read this platform to their classes, then use the magazine to encourage discussion in classrooms and in students' homes. "The competent and worthy teacher," Studebaker wrote, "will inculcate zeal for American democracy." Moreover, he said, teachers should "accept the challenge and be grateful for the big privilege of helping young people to become sincere and intelligent participants in the great adventure of preserving our freedom and making democracy work."[3]

To achieve its objectives, *Senior Scholastic* published news and editorials on national and international events. Regular departments dealt with teenage concerns and lifestyles. Letters to the editor and a department devoted to student writings allowed interaction with readers. Crossword puzzles on select topics were included, too, including one submitted by a high school teacher on the Atomic Age. A fictional discussion (or forum) on a topic of particular relevance appeared each week. The magazine presented these forums as conversations between diverse individuals—typically a scientist, housewife, journalist, politician, and student—representing all sides of a question, such as whether or not the United States should share the secret of the atomic bomb with its allies. This approach provided both teachers and students with an opportunity to discuss issues more objectively. But upon closer examination, these fictional discussions often appeared slanted toward the incontrovertible eventuality of atomic war—and with it the end of civilization.

Many of the magazine's atomic narratives, including these forums, were accompanied by cartoons reprinted from metropolitan newspapers and national magazines. These illustrations, selected purposefully and intended to be discussed, reflected the prevailing attitude toward the atomic bomb by the magazine's editors and, in a larger sense, by the mass media of the day. The cartoons, therefore, form a repository of visual narratives that can be read according to what E. H. Gombrich calls the code, the caption, and the context.[4] In the case of *Senior Scholastic*, the caption and the context (or placement of the cartoon within an atomic narrative) amplified the code (atomic power or atomic bomb). Edmund Burke Feldman, in his study of art as image and idea, also has written that the visual arts, like other arts, can operate as "language of praise and celebration, anger and protest, satire and ridicule." Even more significant, says Feldman, is the fact that art, like the written word, influences the attitudes of people in groups, affecting the way they think or feel and, ultimately, the way they act.[5]

Many cartoons accentuated the duality of the atomic bomb as friend and foe. The May 13, 1953, issue accompanied one such cartoon with a short True/False quiz that instructed students to base their answers on the cartoonist's viewpoint. The quiz read:

_____ 1. There is only one way of looking at the atomic bomb.

_____ 2. Uncle Sam would rather start a war with the atomic bomb than use it to prevent a war.

_____ 3. Our Government is deeply concerned about the possible use of the atomic bomb.

_____ 4. It is possible that the atomic bomb can be used to prevent wars from breaking out.

Brookhaven

(Continued from page 8)

The exciting highlight of our tour was a visit to the "hot lab." Here radio-isotopes are handled just after they come from production in the atomic pile. For these "hot" experiments, there are three "cells," sealed behind 11-ton steel doors and backed up by three-foot-thick concrete walls. A "hot" experiment can be sealed off inside one of these cells and operated from a distance by controls outside the doors, while scientists observe the experiment through periscopes.

As we left the hot lab, we stepped on an instrument resembling a weighing machine (although we didn't need a penny to operate it!). And instead of telling us our "wate and fate" the machine recorded radioactivity on our hands and feet. This is an extra precaution to be certain that workers do not absorb too much radioactivity.

In addition to safeguards for workers themselves, Brookhaven maintains an alert Meteorology Department. Weather and wind experts conduct regular tests at the Laboratory site and for miles around, to measure gases emitted from the 320-foot stack which carries out the large quantities of air cooling the atomic pile. If wind conditions ever became such that the mildly radioactive gas did not move quickly and harmlessly to the upper atmosphere, the atomic pile would be instantly shut down.

Brookhaven, like most other atomic research centers, is not run by Uncle Sam or the U. S. Atomic Energy Commission. The Commission prefers private operation of these centers. Brookhaven operates on a contract issued by the AEC to Associated Universities, Inc. —an organization set up by nine leading eastern universities to provide this major atomic research center.

All policy matters and operational directions are in the hands of AUI, although the millions of dollars needed to run Brookhaven's complex facilities are provided by the Atomic Energy Commission. As one Brookhaven worker told us, "By combining the scientific skills of our universities with funds provided by the Government, we can do work which would otherwise be impossible, on the frontiers of atomic science."

Answers to last week's puzzle

THE ATOMIC PUZZLE

By Herbert C. H. Myers
Winchester Ave. High School, Monroe, North Carolina

(Starred words refer to atomic energy)

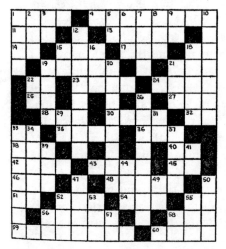

ACROSS

* 1. Atomic pile.
* 4. Proposed bomb, more powerful than A-bomb.
* 11. State in which uranium is found in nature.
* 13. Vacuum tube that serves as a rectifier.
14. 45 r.p.m. phonograph record.
15. Comes in a pod.
17. Edgar Allan _____, poet.
18. Alternating Current.
19. A likeness, semblance.
21. William Green's labor organization.
22. Battleship: The Big _____.
23. Penny.
24. Location.
25. Indefinite article.
27. Rural Electrification Administration (abbr.).
28. Winter sport equipment.
30. Cheer for.
32. Railroad (abbr.).
33. Exists.
35. Profound insensibility.
36. Finish.
* 38. Celestial body which depends on atomic fusion for its energy.
40. Nickname for Edward.
42. Aroma.
43. To hiss away a cat.
45. College degree.
46. To embroider.
48. Borders, rims.
51. Atop.
52. Part of a circle.
54. Lair of a wild beast.
55. Neuter pronoun.
56. Capital of South Korea.
58. Twice one.
* 59. Smallest unit of negative electric charge.
60. Loud noise.

DOWN

1. Cowboy, Tim _____.
2. European Recovery Plan (abbr.).
* 3. Atomic energy (abbr.).
5. Yard (abbr.).
6. To immerse.
7. Chamber.
8. Lyric poem.
9. General Electric (abbr.).
* 10. Energy released from the nucleus of an atom.
* 12. Atoms exploding other atoms, chain _____.
15. Afternoon.
16. To grow old.
18. Following.
* 19. Gas atoms.
20. Antonym for exit.
21. Atmosphere.
22. Mother.
* 26. Discoverer of X-rays.
29. Kilocycle (abbr.).
31. Ton (abbr.).
* 33. Atoms of same atomic number, but different weight.
34. Large area of tropical grassland in Africa.
37. Society gals.
39. "To be, or _____ to be."
41. District Attorney (abbr.).
44. To sum up.
47. A horse's gait.
49. Half an em (printer's measure).
* 50. Smallest particle of an element.
* 52. Atomic Energy Commission (abbr.).
53. Mongrel.
55. Famed battle of World War II: _____ Jima.
56. Compass direction.
57. Behold!
58. Toward.

STUDENTS are invited to submit crossword puzzles for publication in Scholastic Magazines. Each puzzle should be built around one subject, which may be drawn from History, Art, Science, or any field of knowledge. Maximum about 60 words, of which at least 10 must be related to the theme. For any puzzle published we will pay you $10.00. Entries must include puzzle, definitions and answers on separate sheets. Give name, address, school and grade. Address: Puzzle Editor, Senior Scholastic, 7 East 12th St., New York 3, N. Y. Answers in next week's issue.

Senior Scholastic featured crossword puzzles on select topics including this one on the Atomic Age submitted by a high school teacher in 1951. From *Senior Scholastic*, 1945–1955. Copyright © by Scholastic Inc. Reprinted by permission of Scholastic Inc.

18

3. a filibuster
4. an amendment

___c. *cloture*
1. cloak room for Senators
2. place where lobbyists meet
3. first step in introducing a bill
4. process of closing debate in order to bring a matter to a vote

___d. *fiscal year*
1. a year during which party in power loses office
2. a year of deficits
3. happy days
4. a 12-month period at the end of which accounts are reckoned

___e. *immunity*
1. contempt of Congress
2. inability to understand a law
3. privilege of Congressmen exempting them from prosecution for any statement made in Congress
4. freedom of the Supreme Court to set aside laws

___f. *nonpartisan*
1. a minority party
2. free from party domination
3. refusal to join majority party
4. Congressmen who ignore social functions

___g. *patronage*
1. the control of appointive jobs by a political party in power
2. the merit system of appointment to office
3. people who give generously to charitable causes
4. jobs under civil service

___h. *quorum*
1. a choral group assembled for functions in the Capital
2. number of members required to be present before business can be carried on
3. a majority
4. a minority

___i. *rider*
1. car pool organized to avoid traffic jams in large cities
2. measure asked by President
3. an illegal but effective parliamentary move
4. an unrelated controversial measure attached to a bill which the President cannot veto in part

___j. *seniority*
1. a custom of withholding approval on nominations if not approved by a Senator
2. respect owing to old age
3. custom that provides that the chairman of a Congressional committee shall be the person with the longest service
4. changing Congressional districts to keep experienced legislators in office

My score____

VIII. Pros and Cons

In each of the following groups a controversial question is raised. On the line to the left of each of the statements place a "Y" if it supports a *yes* answer to the question and an "N" if it supports a *no* answer. Each counts 1. Total, 10.

A. *Should we have a women's rights amendment to the Constitution?*

___1. It is silly to take the time from more important things to press for such a change.
___2. American women have more freedoms than any other women in the world.

B. *Can business be too big?*

___3. The big corporations serve the public more efficiently.
___4. Workers become cogs in a wheel.

C. *Should Alaska be admitted as a state now?*

___5. Huge new industries are getting under way in Alaska.
___6. Alaska should not be released from Federal control at a time when it is in danger of attack.

D. *Should members of the House be elected for four-year terms?*

___7. Congressmen would have more time to learn their jobs.
___8. The close tie with the voters at home would be cut.

E. *Should the American Indians remain wards of the Federal Government?*

___9. Indians could make more progress without the blundering help of white men.
___10. Even now, whites without consciences trade cheap liquor for prized possessions.

My score____

IX. Understanding a Cartoon

Study the cartoon on this page. On the line to the left of each of the following statements, place a "T" if it is *true* or an "F" if it is *false*. Base your answers on the viewpoint of the cartoonist only. Each counts 1. Total, 5.

___1. There is only one way of looking at the atomic bomb.
___2. Uncle Sam would rather start a war with the atomic bomb than use it to prevent a war.
___3. Our Government is deeply concerned about the possible use of the atomic bomb.
___4. It is possible that the atomic bomb can be used to prevent wars from breaking out.
___5. The atomic bomb has not been perfected to the point where we could use it in time of war.

My score____

Shaw-McCutcheon in the *Spokesman-Review*

Many cartoons accentuated the duality of the atomic bomb as friend and foe. The May 13, 1953, issue accompanied one such cartoon with a short True/False quiz that instructed students to base their answers on the cartoonist's viewpoint. Cartoon reprinted courtesy of the *Spokeman-Review*. From *Senior Scholastic*, 1945-1955. Copyright © by Scholastic Inc. Reprinted by permission of Scholastic Inc.

___ 5. The atomic bomb has not been perfected to the point where we could use it in time of war.[6]

These textual and visional narratives were designed to inform students about both atomic warfare and peaceful applications of atomic energy. The magazine also featured short stories that reinforced the social themes found in nonfictional articles.[7] With few exceptions, each issue featured a short story reprinted from another magazine, an original story, or a classic American story. Immediately following the Second World War, these stories often contained positive themes of brotherhood and teamwork, which reflected the early emphasis on the need for international cooperation found in the magazine's nonfiction articles—and in various educational narratives as well as the social narrative within schools.

Senior Scholastic's atomic narratives began in the first issue of the 1945–46 school year. The magazine's editorial concerned the "exciting events" of August that saw an end to the war and the destruction of the Japanese empire. The United States, the editorial read, had assumed a new role: school teacher to a classroom of 73 million "hard-to-handle pupils—the entire Japanese nation." The magazine proclaimed General Douglas MacArthur the new principal of "the world's largest reformatory school," with Emperor Hirohito reduced to school monitor. "For years to come," the magazine said, "it will be the stern task of Schoolmaster Uncle Sam to re-educate — by books and rod, if necessary — a warlike people to the way of peace and democracy." Japan's defeat had taught everyone that aggression does not pay. Unfortunately, the war had ended with the power of the sun being harnessed in a potentially world-threatening force: the atomic bomb.[8]

In addition to articles on the rise and fall of the Japanese empire, the long road to reconversion, and the shift from war to peace, the issue also contained two reports on the new Atomic Age: "Atomic Revolution" and "It Is Later Than We Think! The Atomic Challenge." "Atomic Revolution" discussed the scientific principles of nuclear fusion and offered a brief atomic narrative that defined the historic magnitude of the bomb:

> The atomic bomb that devastated two Japanese cities is the most significant invention since primitive man found out how to make fire thousands of years ago. And this unleashing of atomic energy may change our way of life more drastically than any of the inventions since that time.

Students were told further that scientists did not see any immediate peacetime applications for atomic energy, such as a power source for cars or planes; however, the article did express the hope that within ten years

It is later than we think!

Atomic bomb challenges United Nations Organization

THE ATOMIC BOMBS that fell on Hiroshima and Nagasaki did more than devastate those cities and shorten the Pacific war. They made an international organization to preserve the peace even more necessary than it was when the 50 United Nations signed the Charter at San Francisco last June. (Poland will be admitted later to make 51.)

In the terrible destructiveness of atomic energy, the world heard this message:

The atomic bomb is bigger than the Big Five. Its power is greater than the combined armed forces of the United States, Russia, Great Britain, China and France. If we permit another war, it will destroy us all.

The unleashing of atomic energy completely reversed the thinking of many men. For instance, Dr. Robert M. Hutchins, president of the University of Chicago, has strongly opposed the idea of world government. He did not believe that there was any "conviction of the world community" strong enough to keep all nations united. The atomic bomb changed his mind.

How Can We Control It?

Right now the secret of that bomb belongs to the United States and Great Britain. But scientists tell us that other nations can invent their own atomic bomb within three to five years. Finding the means to control the atomic bomb is one of the greatest tasks facing the statesmen of the United Nations.

Atomic power is expected to revise sharply United Nations' plans for armed forces to keep the peace. It seems likely that the mere threat to drop a few atomic bombs on a would-be aggressor nation would persuade it to behave.

Around 120 planes, each carrying one atomic bomb, would equal the destructive power of all the bombs (2,453,595 tons) dropped by Allied bombers on Europe during World War II.

How the United Nations will fit the atomic bomb into their peace force cannot be foreseen, because the organization does not exist yet. The Charter that was signed by 50 nations at San Francisco is only a blueprint of the world's peace-keeping machinery. Before this machinery can be put into operation, the Charter must be approved by all of the Big Five and a majority of the other nations—called the Little Forty-five.

The U. S. Senate approved the Charter on July 28 and President Truman later signed it. France, China, Russia and Britain also approved it. Among the Little Forty-five, Nicaragua, El Salvador, Costa Rica and Turkey have approved the Charter.

Meanwhile, the Executive Committee of a Preparatory Commission is meeting in London to draw up a program for the first sessions of the United Nations Organization. It has one representative from 14 of the 50 nations.

Unfinished Business

While these men are setting in motion the machinery for future peace, a Council of the Foreign Ministers of the Big Five will work out treaties of peace to settle the score of World War II. This Council was established by President Truman, Premier Stalin and Prime Minister Churchill and his successor, Clement Attlee, at the Potsdam Conference last July. It will draw up peace settlements with Italy, Romania, Bulgaria, Hungary, Finland — and eventually with Germany and Japan.

Once treaties have been concluded with governments in these nations, they can apply for membership in the United Nations Organization. According to the Charter blueprint this is what would happen:

Suppose the Council of Foreign Ministers negotiated a treaty with Italy which was signed by the Allies. Italy could then ask to become one of the United Nations.

Her application would be studied by the eleven members of the Security Council. The Big Five, who are permanent members, plus at least two of the six temporary members (selected from the Assembly) must approve Italy's application. If but one of the Big Five votes "no," the application would be turned down right there.

If the application is approved, it would go to the General Assembly. Approval by two-thirds of the members of the Assembly would permit Italy to join the United Nations.

It is hoped that eventually all countries will be accepted by the United Nations. Then a truly international organization could cooperate in making certain that atomic bombs never again are used in war.

UNITED NATIONS PROBLEMS

SENIOR SCHOLASTIC

---

atomic energy would be used for industrial purposes. Yet any sense of optimism was undermined with a chart comparing the destructive power of ten tons of explosives (6.5 acres) with that of the atomic bomb (2,624 acres). *Senior Scholastic* made it dramatically evident that the atomic threat, not atomic energy, was the real concern.[9]

The second article, "It Is Later Than We Think! The Atomic Challenge," dealt with the lamentable exigency for a strong United Nations Organization (UNO), "or else." The bombings of Hiroshima and Nagasaki had destroyed two cities and shaken the world, it said. The atomic bomb was bigger than the military forces of the United States, Russia, Great Britain, China, and France. If the world permitted another war, "it will destroy us all." The only hope, according to the article, was to find a means of controlling the atomic bomb. That, it said, rested solely with nations working toward international cooperation and brotherhood through the United Nations.[10] Once again, these narratives, while presenting a coherent message about atomic energy and particularly the potential danger of the atomic bomb, offered a multiplicity of discourses within each text.

The same issue's Teacher Edition warned teachers not to speculate in class about the peaceful applications of atomic energy, such as atomic-powered cars and planes; rather, "the important and immediate problem is the relation of the bomb to world organization." An article suggested that an informal class forum explore the bomb and its significance. Teachers also were urged to remind students that Germany almost beat the United States in the development of the atomic bomb. Additionally, they were to ask students whether it was feasible to keep the bomb a secret from other countries. The class discussion, the magazine said, should close by pointing out that the United Nations was an absolute necessity to ensure the survival of civilization. *Senior Scholastic* again clarified the issue: "Atomic energy may eventually bring new and undreamed of luxuries; new industries will spring up, new subjects will be offered in colleges, new professions will be open to the young scientists of tomorrow. But none of this dream can come true if we allow another war to break out, for atomic war would destroy the world."[11] A few months later, in one of an ongoing series of narratives on atomic energy control, the magazine once more reminded teachers that the United States faced a problem more difficult than any nation, or groups of nations, had ever confronted before. "[W]e cannot hope that time alone will offer a solution," it said. "*Tomorrow will be too late.*"[12]

Concerns about a future war of atomic devastation and the need to achieve international cooperation were not confined to the issue's nonfiction narratives. Even Stephen Vincent Benét's short story, "William

6-T

The Capsule News

MORE HISTORY, YES, BUT HOW?

Advisers Split on Issue of Chronology vs. Topics

Should history be taught by chronology or topics? This and other questions came before a six-man committee advisory to New York's Board of Regents. Their recommendations:

1. Eighth grade American history should shift from topics to chronology; include post-Civil War events.

2. High school history instruction should be increased from two years to three years, equally divided between American and world history.

3. World history should not be "indiscriminately global"; should center on European civilization, its world expansion, influence on the New World.

Committee split over twelfth grade history; two for topical teaching, four for chronology. Professors Schlesinger and Carman urged the teaching of controversial issues as "crucial in preparing youth for intelligent participation in our democracy."

Drama in Washington

Drama marked the closing sessions of the White House Conference on Children and Youth. After long arguments conferees voted:

1. Federal aid to equalize educational service in tax-supported public schools; auxiliary services for separate legislation.

2. Unalterable opposition to the use of public schools directly or indirectly for religious educational purposes.

3. That racial segregation in education be abolished.

Two Dismissal Cases

N.E.A. announces action on two cases of unjust dismissal.

In Pasadena N.E.A. with the A.A.S.A. will investigate the resignation under board pressure of Supt. Willard E. Goslin.

At Twin Falls, Idaho, N.E.A. called firing of two physical education teachers without hearing of charges unjustified; urged new contracts to both men.

PHILADELPHIA: Teachers receive $200 increases Jan. 1.

Associated Press Wirephoto
Just in case! Portland, Ore., children huddle in basement in bomb drill.

1950's BIG TEN

Ten Major Education Events of 1950 selected by the Educational Press Assn.

1. U. S. educators' support of universal military service.

2. Supreme Court decisions against segregation in universities.

3. Rising enrollment in Catholic schools.

4. Creation of National Conference for Mobilization of Education for the emergency.

5. Kellogg Foundation votes $3,000,000 for school administrator in-service training.

6. National Science Foundation created by Congress.

7. Social Security extended to non-public school employees.

8. Launching $250,000,000 Ford Foundation.

9. Federal aid to war activity-swollen school districts.

10. White House Conference for Children and Youth.

SCHOOLS MARCH BACKWARD

One year ago March of Time put out a documentary film called *The Fight for Better Schools.* It pictured the successful fight for better schools in Arlington County, Va. In November Arlington citizens voted on two bond issues, one for new sewerage and one for schools. Sewerage won, schools lost.

Teacher Hailed TV's Newest Comedy Find

Brightest new star on TV's horizon is a former Samuel J. Tilden H. S., Brooklyn, teacher of Spanish—Sam Levenson. This fall CBS filled a 15-minute spot following Jack Benny with monologist Levenson. Benny's Hooper hit .40; Levenson .38.

Quipped Levenson: "Reminds me of the time I got 98 in algebra and all mama wanted to know was who got the other two points."

Comedian Levenson now has his own regular show on CBS-TV.

Another schoolman appears on ABC-TV. He is Stuart Irwin, high school principal and key character of "The Irwins."

HOW CRISIS WILL HIT SCHOOLS

Graduation of Boys at 18 Proposed in N. Y. State

How will the proclaimed national emergency affect the nation's schools? In many ways.

State of Readiness
President Truman pushed the throttle forward one notch—the next to last notch. It is still short of full mobilization. Education's first duty is to operate as near normal as possible. Keep calm.

Military Service
We already have compulsory military service for all able-bodied males 19 to 26. Much-argued Universal Military Training is a "dead duck." Instead we will likely have Universal Military Service for every youth at 18 who can walk and isn't a moron. The Conant Plan calls for two years service. No one excused. N.E.A. prefers "selective service" with new eligibility standards to enroll those not fit for combat for "limited service"; defer high school students doing satisfactory work until their 20th year.

Gen. Hershey and educator advisers would send brightest boys to college; put all others in training.

Congress will decide early in 1951. Draft has dropped college enrollments 7 per cent; next year enrollment may shrink as much as 50 per cent.

Acceleration
New York State's Board of Regents proposes that high schools speed up; graduate boys at 17. This would permit one year in college before military service. Other states may follow this lead. Accelerated programs will return to the campuses.

Teacher Deferments
Small chance. With World War II veterans still not callable, local boards find it hard to fill quotas.

Teacher Supply
Prospects very dark. Number of emergency certificate teachers dropped to 80,000; now trend is up again. Wage-price controls may slow departure of teachers to war work. Teachers (like all workers) must expect longer hours, heavier loads, less take-home pay after taxes. Boards must raise salaries to secure teachers.

Curriculum Changes
More time for health and physical education. Gymnasium and teacher shortage will hamper this demand. More speed-up training for war industries. Congress must vote money for war training. More emphasis on mathematics, science, and world problems—especially communism.

School Building
In 1950 U. S. spent $1,000,-000,000 on much-needed school buildings. Schools plan in 1951 to spend $1,500,000,000. An N.P.A. order regulation M-4 appeared to block construction of gymnasiums and athletic fields. But construction for instructional purposes (not exhibition) is O.K. School building has high priority.

Civil Defense
All Los Angeles teachers now take Red Cross first aid training. Other school systems will follow suit. "Bomb raid" drills will be standard practice. As civil defense plans expand, schools will become key centers. May be asked to train civilians for emergencies.

PR BRIGHTIES

Newton, Mass., issues its annual school report in mock *Reader's Digest* style. Teachers, administrators, parents, pupils contribute articles.

Jackson, Miss., citizens hear an earful of school news over the public address systems in the warm-up periods before sports contests.

Dearborn, Mich., recruits school news reporters to feed stories to local press and monthly school bulletins. Each reporter receives a copy of *How to Wiggle Your Nose for News.*

Senior Scholastic's Teacher Edition kept teachers informed about activities at schools around the country, including "duck and cover" drills. From *Senior Scholastic*, 1945–1955. Copyright © by Scholastic Inc. Reprinted by permission of Scholastic Inc. Photograph reprinted with permission of the AP-Wide World Photos.

Riley and the Fates," which appeared in the same issue that warned "it is later than we think," reflected the magazine's message that only by taking control of one's fate and adopting the tenets of brotherhood would world destruction be avoided.[13]

The story, set in the early 1900s, focuses on young William Riley, a budding reporter for the *Snapperville Gazette*. On a day short of news, his editor tells him to cover a picnic being held by a group called the Sons and Daughters of Destiny, described as being "outside of time." The picnic is guarded from curious sightseers, but William manages to get inside, where he hears numerous American accents and foreign languages. He becomes confused by what he sees, but a girl he meets tells him, "[Y]ou're not one man alone — you're part of a nation and a time. And that nation and that time are going to be altered by all sorts of things and people.... For Snapperville isn't just Snapperville, William Riley. It's part of the world." The two then watch a movie of a future packed with war, death, chaos, and destruction. William expresses concern about what he sees, and doubts whether anything can be done. The girl responds,

> There's fate and there's destiny — and there's man as well. And too many people make fate an excuse for failure. They're bright and they're tired and they see something bad might come, so they just lie down and let it walk over them. Or else they're all wrapped up in their little concerns and hates and they won't listen to anything till fate grabs them by the scruff of the neck. But you — stand up, William Riley! Because you were born a free man.... You'll hear people say that they can't bear to have children with times so unsettled — well, if they feel that way, let them — I don't want their children. I'm young and I'm free and I'm growing, and I want the bold and the merry and the enduring. I want the laughers and the thinkers, the strong-hearted and the daring.[14]

William returns to the newspaper and writes his article. The girl and the Sons and Daughters of Destiny deeply affect William. He becomes convinced that humans are not the victims of fate but can determine their destiny by asserting themselves and promoting understanding among the peoples of the world. The story concludes with William telling his editor, "Fate's fate, but a country's what you make it. And we're going to need the bold and the free."[15] Even within this fictional work, the magazine delivered a message to the Atomic Generation: Through commitment, dedication, and brotherhood, peace will prevail ... or else.

The participants in a November 1945 discussion on the control of the atomic bomb included a congressman, a general, a professor, a judge, and a married woman. The article opens with the same stark warning found in countless atomic narratives: "We stand at the crossroads with that bomb.

One highway leads to the destruction of our civilization — backwards to the Dark Ages. Another road leads to benefits for all humanity — new leisure, new comforts, new freedom from disease — [that] can be the by-product of atomic energy." The professor then proceeds to argue that it is ridiculous to keep the atomic bomb a secret because scientists around the world already know how to make it. The judge, likewise, calls for a law-making body "higher than the law of individual nations" to settle international disputes. The housewife, however, is given the last word. She says matter-of-factly: "[I]t is even more clear that humanity must at last live by the Golden Rule. Otherwise we will all be destroyed." The article was accompanied by illustrations showing the choice between world cooperation and atomic oblivion, the increasing weight of responsibility being placed on the United States, the size of the atomic threat, and "the hot potato" that the atomic bomb was rapidly becoming.[16]

Another fictional discussion, titled "Does the UNO Go Far Enough?," included a judge, newspaperman, senator, scientist, and veteran. The ability of a world government (i.e., the United Nations Organization, or UNO, as it was originally called) to succeed is deemed improbable by the senator. But the scientist provides the doomsday alternative: "If the animal man is to survive on the face of the earth, the creation of a world government with security on the basis of laws is not merely desirable but imperative." The veteran believes that there will always be wars; therefore, the only thing you can believe in is "the world's biggest stockpiles of atomic bombs." As with many such discussions, this one ends on an apocalyptic note, offered by the newspaperman:

> The simple fact is that mankind must fashion a plan for enduring peace — or face extinction. There is no other choice. I know. I have covered two world wars. Another world war would carry the world to final and complete destruction.... There is no time to lose. We owe it to ourselves. We owe it to our children. Nothing less than world government can assure peace.[17]

The same message was heard again in yet another discussion on domestic atomic policy, appearing in May 1947. This exchange, led by fictional high school students Margie and Bill, included a senator, reporter, industrialist, and an obligatory scientist. When Margie asks whether people will always fear the dangers of atomic energy, the reporter answers that the only way to get rid of that fear is when the United Nations has established effective international control of atomic energy. The discussion ends, as many did, with the reporter's portentous warning for the younger generation: "All of us have got to keep working at this war-born problem if we don't want to be blown to powder within a few years."[18]

During the first three years following the war, articles were dominated by the One World theme and the belief that the United States held the hope for world peace and control of the atomic bomb. During these same years, the school years 1945–46 to 1947–48, the vast majority of the short stories with favorable outcomes contained themes of brotherhood, cooperation, or teamwork. Of the stories with unfavorable outcomes, all contained themes of self-reliance or related themes of withdrawal from or aversion to teamwork or alliance with others (i.e., the breakdown of the group). Taking control of one's fate and promoting better understanding and cooperation among neighbors and nations of the world were dominant themes during the late 1940s. In contrast, situations where an individual withdrew from his or her social responsibilities or became isolated resulted in negative outcomes. Stories continually differentiated between isolation, individuality, and self-reliance, all leading toward despair or death; and teamwork, cooperation, and brotherhood, all leading toward hope. Even stories dealing with apparently lighthearted or superficial plots often contained the same underlying themes reflected in *Senior Scholastic*'s more overt atomic narratives, expanding the magazine's editorial mission to inform and influence the Atomic Generation. Therefore, these short stories serve as atomic narratives, too.[19]

This is evident in Dr. Louis Ridenour's play, "Pilot Lights of the Apocalypse," reprinted in 1946 from *Fortune* magazine. The one-act play takes place in the operations room of the Western Defense Command, located hundreds of feet below ground in the San Francisco Bay area "some years after all the industrialized nations have mastered the production and use of atomic power." Nations have positioned approximately 5,400 atomic bombs (2,000 from the U.S.) in the stratosphere and mined major cities around the world with atomic bombs.

As the play opens, an apparent atomic explosion has shaken the command center, prompting the officers in charge to consider when and if to retaliate. Because Denmark has the highest negative rating in the latest State Department digest (as it relates to the most-likely adversary), the colonel decides to destroy Copenhagen. The Danes immediately suspect the Swedes and pulverize Stockholm. This prompts the Swedes to extirpate London, Manchester, Edinburg, and other British cities. The British, in turn, commence an attack on the Soviet Union, which then attacks the United States. As bombs beginning hitting U.S. cities, and the colonel finally realizes that the world is being annihilated, it is discovered that the initial "blast" was not a bomb at all; it was an earthquake. But by then it is too late:

Brigadier: To all stations: URGE IMMEDIATE WORLDWIDE BROAD-
CAST THIS MESSAGE: DESTRUCTION COPENHAGEN 1910 HOURS
THIS DATE INITIATED BY THIS STATION THROUGH GRIEVOUS
ERROR. ATTACKS MADE SINCE BASED ON IDEA DESTRUCTION
COPENHAGEN WAS ACT OF WAR, WHICH IT WAS NOT REPEAT NOT.
URGE ATTACKS BE STOPPED UNTIL SITUATION CAN BE CLARIFIED.
THERE IS NO REPEAT NO WAR. END.
    Colonel Peabody (who has been watching board): The hell there isn't.
New York's gone red, and Chicago, and ... (The room rocks, the lights go
out. With a dull, powerful rumble, the roof caves in.)[20]

Senior Scholastic's fiction and nonfiction narratives continually
emphasized the challenge to protect civilization from self-destruction. In
"The Delegate from Everywhere," published in May 1946, failing to join
together in a world of brotherhood was foreseen as inviting another war.[21]
The short story opens in a military hospital with war veterans listening to
news of an international meeting of nations being called to establish world
peace. They decide to collect money and elect "the delegate from everywhere" to represent them: an amputee who lost both legs at Iwo Jima. On
his way to New York, the amputee meets Senator Ballard, who has been
invited to address the conference. At the conclusion of the senator's speech,
the senator invites the amputee to address the meeting. As the veteran's
words are being broadcast over the radio, the doors open to allow veterans — in wheelchairs, with canes and crutches, and crawling — to come
down the aisles along with women carrying babies. The amputee continues:

I bear a message ... forged in a fiery crucible. Only this. That all nations
have a right to self-determination, and to live in comity if they so desire.
Small nations retain their honor and must be allowed to preserve it. We ask
no guarantee of economic bliss for any nation or any man. Systems that are
not valid have no right to survive, but let there be no more trading in human
unhappiness. Back of all your little national flags, we stand as one army,
without medals or insignia or rank. Make this peace free of small thought
or we shall rewrite it with the violence you taught us. The trumpets are
crumpled, gentlemen, and the drumheads are smashed. Our eyes are open,
and watching....[22]

As the delegate from everywhere walks out of the conference, leading the
army of women and war wounded, the representatives from around the
world stand up in homage.
    This story perhaps best exemplifies the themes of One World, inter-
national cooperation, and brotherhood. The venue of an international
conference; the camaraderie among the delegates, veteran soldiers, and

mothers; and the strongly worded request that there be no more trading in human unhappiness, delivered the message of "peace ... or else" with clarion amplification.

Nonfiction articles augmented the same message. "Make no mistake about it," wrote the magazine's aviation editor Sam Burger after witnessing Operation Crossroads (the atomic tests at the Bikini Atoll conducted in the summer of 1946), "at sea as on land, the atomic bomb is murderous and destructive beyond your most awful imaginings." The only known defense against the atomic bomb, according to Burger, was the successful cooperation of all nations to maintain world peace. "[I]t is not merely military and naval science which stands at the crossroads," he wrote. "All mankind stands there today. You and I alike took part in Operation Crossroads. Which road will we take?" The Teacher Edition urged teachers to discourage students from lulling themselves in the "excitement of looking on the bomb as a fine new mechanical toy." The only hope, teachers were told, was international cooperation through the United Nations.

An article appearing two weeks later, titled "Atomic Power ... for Progress or Destruction," reviewed the Baruch Plan, which proposed international ownership and control over all nuclear resources. Bernard Baruch, a leading statesman and political advisor, presented his plan to the United Nations Atomic Energy Commission on June 14, 1946. His opening remarks captured the core reality of the post–Hiroshima world. "We are here to make a choice between the quick and the dead," he said. "That is our business. Behind the black portent of the new atomic age lies a hope which, seized upon with faith, can work our salvation. If we fail, then we have damned every man to be the slave of fear. Let us not deceive ourselves: We must elect World Peace or World Destruction." The editors of *Senior Scholastic* agreed, declaring that the world was living "in the shadow of a primeval force which, if uncontrolled, may blast us off the face of the globe." The same issue's Scholastic Citizenship Quiz offered a four-word challenge to everyone faced with the problem of the atomic bomb:

> LacKing the coUrage To accept tHe dangerS of the Atom bomb, and Providing for Adequate Controls on anY InterNational basis, caN well bring Destruction to our civilizaTion.

The answer (worth five points for each correct word) was *think, study, plan, act.*[23]

The immutability of atomic war resulting from fear, misunderstanding, and the failure to cooperate was a recurring theme in images as well as text, particularly the many cartoons reprinted by the magazine. Illustrations constantly reminded adolescents of the precarious state of

Which Way? ". . . If a danger exists, it is a danger shared by all—if a hope exists in the mind of one nation, that hope should be shared by all."

—President Dwight D. Eisenhower

Fitzpatrick in St. Louis Post-Dispatch

Can We Win Freedom from Fear?

ON April 25, 1945, representatives of 44 nations gathered at San Francisco to draft the Charter of the United Nations.

At San Francisco, the U. S. Secretary of State, Edward L. Stettinius, read the historic words from the Churchill-Roosevelt *Atlantic Charter* of 1941. These words had been included in the *Declaration by United Nations*, Jan. 1, 1942.

The *Declaration* spoke for all the nations in the Grand Alliance against the despotic warmakers of World War II. It pledged these nations to establish "a peace which will afford to all nations the means of dwelling in safety within their own boundaries, and which will afford assurance that *all the men in all*

the lands may live out their lives in *freedom from fear* . . ."

On the same day that the San Francisco meeting got under way, Secretary of War Henry L. Stimson handed an explosive memorandum to the President of the United States.

The Atomic Age Opens

Said Stimson to the President, "Within four months we shall in all probability have completed the most terrible weapon ever known in human history, one bomb of which could destroy a whole city." These words introduced the atomic age.

Stimson further said to the President in Washington, ". . . Modern civilization migh\` be completely destroyed . . .

To approach any world peace organization of any pattern now likely to be considered without an appreciation by the leaders of our country of the power of this new weapon would seem to be unrealistic. . . .

"The *control* of this weapon will undoubtedly be a matter of the greatest difficulty . . ." It would involve, said Stimson, "such thoroughgoing rights of inspection and internal controls as we have never heretofore contemplated. . . ."

Mr. Stimson went on to point out that the "question of sharing it with other nations and, if so shared, upon what terms—becomes a primary question of our foreign relations. . . ."

A month later, while the delegates at

the world. One, for example, showed the Soviet Union, United States, and Great Britain all marching toward World War III, with the U.S. equipped with an atomic gun. The Russian says, "I'll call a haltski if you do," and the American replies, "Do you really mean it?" Of course, the answer is never given. But the strong implication in these types of illustrations is that the only option for maintaining peace is cooperation. The combination of written and visual narratives served to strengthen the magazine's overriding message about this generation's mission to prevent another war.

Early hopes for world peace based on the activities of the United Nations waned by the late 1940s. The U.N.'s failure to develop a plan to control the bomb created new fears about atomic war with the Soviet Union. Baruch's remarks before the U.N. Atomic Energy Commission in 1946 were reprinted the following year to remind students again about the dangers emanating from the mushroom cloud.[24] Increasingly, Americans saw the threat of world destruction coming from the Soviet Union, which continually blocked any proposals for the international control of atomic energy. Saving the world became synonymous with safeguarding democracy.

To this end, the magazine introduced a 30-article series during the 1947–48 school year titled "All Out for Democracy," designed to compare life in a democracy with life in totalitarian countries. According to Rosa Kohler Eichelberger, director of the series, the intent was not to indoctrinate but to emphasize the tenets of democratic education: "the free search for new knowledge and the understandings of other peoples besides our own."[25] Despite articles on such topics as "Freedom to Speak Our Minds," "Freedom to Be Well Informed," and "Counting Heads, Not Cracking Them," the underlying theme remained that this generation must accept its mission to protect democracy and to save the world from atomic extinction — a portentous message stated with exactitude in the final installment of the series:

> On every horizon new frontiers beckon to the young people of America who are now in school or college. You are the problem solvers of the future. It is up to you to build that more perfect union — to root out the defects of our democracy — to show how people of all groups can live together in harmony. It is you who will organize the nations of the world to work together for a just and durable peace. It is you who will tame the energy of the atom for the welfare and not the destruction of mankind.[26]

The magazine continued the trend of balancing the promise of atomic energy and the peril of the atomic bomb. The April 12, 1946, issue emphasized the peaceful uses of atomic energy but included fictional narratives about atomic war and atomic energy gone awry. In an editorial, the AEC's David Lilienthal urged students to pursue careers in science and technical fields in order to develop atomic energy. Again, as others had done before, he issued the ultimate challenge to the Atomic Generation: save the world and democracy. Unless America's youth became better informed about this new science so they could control their own collective destiny, Lilienthal said, "then democracy in its very essentials will be gravely imperiled, not by the action of a foreign foe, but by default by those who benefit most from it."[27]

Another article addressing the use of atomic energy in agriculture, engineering, and medicine also warned that atomic energy was "both a killer and a healer, a destroyer and a builder," and it was up to mankind to determine "whether Atomic Energy is to become his servant or his doom."[28] In addition, the magazine reprinted Louis Ridenour's "Pilot Lights of the Apocalypse" (for a new high school class) and published Theodore Sturgeon's "The Purple Light," a science-fiction story about an atomic-powered spaceship. "Read All About It," a review section, suggested that students discuss "The Purple Light" as an example of peaceful applications of the atom, and contrast the story with the atom's destructive potential as illustrated by Ridenour.

The Teacher Edition advised teachers to ask students about future scientific uses for the atom. Students were to be encouraged to look at how atomic energy would change their home lives, and to discuss whether their children would be safe from serious disease because of atomic isotopes. Most important, teachers should again solicit students' opinions on whether the United States should share the secret of the atomic bomb — an incessant debate in the late 1940s. The Citizenship Quiz, designed to test students on the articles in that issue, included an L (likely) and N (not likely) section with such questions as "Atomic energy will be used for fertilizer to increase crop production 500 per cent" and "Radioactive atomic energy will be used in cities to clear the air of smoke and dirt."[29]

A 1948 series of articles by Philip Knowlton, editor of the educational division of The Macmillan Company, continued to address both the peaceful and destructive aspects of the atom. At one point, he acknowledged that no past generation had ever faced such a complex and challenging situation. "War, slavery, disease, want, and fear have again and again preyed upon the human race," Knowlton wrote. "But never before have threats to man's happiness seemed to hold him so powerless when he had prosperity almost within his grasp. Never before has mankind been so frustrated by fear and anxiety." He then outlined "Planks for a Personal Platform," much of which would later appear in various forms among narratives for and by the Atomic Generation. The platform said to respect one's own mind; not to define people with hackneyed words, like communist or radical; and to consider the quest for truth as the highest function. Knowlton asked that youth listen to all sides of a question. They should remember that people are more important than property. Building on the theme of group solidarity promoted throughout this period, youth were to remain loyal to the larger group while not being disloyal to smaller groups that comprise the larger ones. Yet youth were to remain loyal to all of humankind as well. Commenting on this last plank, Knowlton wrote, "We must abolish war before it abolishes us. We must learn that no nation or group of nations can continue indefinitely to enjoy a standard of living far higher than that of the rest of the world."[30]

In another article, titled "Civilization's Race with Death," Knowlton outlined the current proposals to avoid another war, including such ideas as increasing the authority of the United Nations, maintaining a balance of power, and educating for world unity. "The atom bomb," he wrote, "made realists of the quacks." It also made the Atomic Generation's place in history of paramount importance:

> For more than three years people have been talking and writing as though the end of the world were right around the corner. What a bore! As one of the carefree younger generation might put it,
> >I'd rather see the players bat 'em
> >Than tear my hair about the atom
> >And I'd prefer to go a-fishin'
> >When dopes bring up atomic fission.
> A patient doesn't enjoy being told he has cancer. Humanity, especially young humanity, doesn't like to be told it has a social or collective cancer that will destroy it if it is not cut out. But it has, and it will, unless we learn to control the cancer of atomic war. So out of the sand with that head![31]

Even when addressing the peaceful applications of the atom, Knowlton warned his youthful readers, "[W]hat is to prevent its unpleasant twin — that atomic energy may be employed destructively for war until mankind, like a baby playing with matches, perishes in agony?"[32]

The emphasis on being loyal to humanity rather than to any one nation reflected the ongoing One World movement that *Senior Scholastic* endorsed through its support of the United Nations. Editor-in-chief Kenneth Gould wrote, "As citizens of the nation today that holds the secret of life and death in the atomic age, high school students have their chance to represent America. They can help shape the future toward 'One World or None.'"[33] Throughout the late 1940s, illustrations also stressed the U.N.'s role in preventing an atomic war. The magazine's position was stated clearly in a special issue on world government in 1948:

> Has the world resigned itself to suicide? We doubt it. The majority of people everywhere are disgusted with war. If left to themselves, they would want no more of it. They could never be got to fight in cold blood. They have to be shut off from facts and filled with distorted ideas and hot emotions about other nations. This happens constantly in dictatorships. But even in a democracy, when a certain temperature is reached on the thermometer of war, people can go "haywire," and decide that force is the only answer. We cannot blind our eyes to the cold facts that make war possible. Yet we know that there must be better ways to settle international quarrels. In previous times there may have been some excuse for not finding them. Today, in the infancy of atomic weapons, we must either find them, or else — .[34]

The potential destruction of the world moved closer to reality when, in November 1949, the magazine announced that atomic scientists had moved the mythical time on the clock signalling the start of World War III from 8 minutes of 12 o'clock to 3 minutes of 12. "If the world is to be saved from suicide," it said, "the atomic bomb must be outlawed and outlawed quickly." The reason: Compromise seemed impossible because of the wide disagreement between the plans for atomic energy control proposed by the U.S. and Soviet Union. Returning to a familiar theme, *Senior Scholastic* went on to say that nuclear scientists know "it is later than we think." This followed President Truman's announcement that the Soviet Union had exploded its own atomic bomb. [35]

The magazine earlier had published a news item on U.S. Navy officials informing the U.S. House of Representatives Armed Services Committee that the B-36 bomber was outdated and unable to carry out an effective atomic-bombing mission. Even if the U.S. won the war with an "atomic blitz of annihilation," officials were quoted as saying, the country would lose because "of the destruction and hatred created by use of the terrible weapon." Another report about a nuclear reactor nearing completion in Idaho stated that it would be used "to produce not only the stuff that goes into atomic bombs, but for many useful peacetime purposes."[36]

The confusing nature of these transitional years is evident in an Institute of Student Opinion poll, conducted in 1950 by *Senior Scholastic*, which found that 49.4 percent of high school students opposed placing atomic energy materials and the atomic bomb under international control, while 40.6 percent still supported the notion. The U.N.'s inability to enact controls for atomic energy, combined with the Soviet Union's testing of an atomic bomb, had begun to shift the emphasis from One World (i.e.,

The World in the Atomic Age

● This map is an azimuthal equidistant projection of the northern portion of the earth's surface. This means that the map is centered on a single point—in this case the North Pole. From this "center of projection" a straight line drawn to any other point represents a Great Circle—the shortest distance between two points. Note the ten-degree lines of latitude which circle about the North Pole. There are approximately 690 miles between each ten-degree mark of latitude.

Notice that the map shows Russia and the Russian-controlled area of the world in black; North and Central America are in color. From Alaska and the base of Greenland are shown some sample air distances to important cities in Russia. And from two points in Russia are shown similar distances to important U. S. cities. In the event of an all-out war, these distances would take on new significance. They might measure the routes of Russian or U. S. atomic attack.

The magazine repeatedly published its warning titled, "The World in the Atomic Age," showing the possible routes of a Soviet attack against targeted U.S. cities. From *Senior Scholastic*, 1945–1955. Copyright © by Scholastic Inc. Reprinted by permission of Scholastic Inc.

brotherhood and international cooperation) to survival against the very real threat of an atomic war. The magazine repeatedly published its warning, titled "The World in the Atomic Age," showing the possible routes of a Soviet attack against targeted U.S. cities.[37]

During the 1949–50 school year, short stories began to reflect less confidence in the group to triumph over adversity. As the country moved through the transition from being the only nation to have the atomic bomb, to being a nation confronting the threat of communism and another world power with atomic capabilities, stories began to reflect changing values. Again, the magazine's shifting emphasis reflected similar changes occurring in textbooks and other educational narratives as well as school-based activities. During the two school years immediately preceding the Korean War (1948–49 and 1949–50), fewer than half the stories with favorable outcomes contained brotherhood as a central theme, while more than two-thirds of the stories with unfavorable outcomes contained this theme.

Combined with a certain regret about the failure of group action and an increasing emphasis on self-reliance, there now was more imagery of war and death. Among the stories reflecting this trend was "Caesar's Wife's Ear," which portrayed most dramatically the breakdown of brotherhood as a means to ensure peace and security. The story focuses on Seppel Bergener, a lion tamer born in Hungary who now runs his own show with his wife. During an incident where his lions become unruly and threaten to attack him while he is in the cage, his assistant, Bert, stands by, frozen, unable to help: "Seppel gave a whimpering cry like a frightened child. 'Will no one helpa me?' he cried. 'Will I be alone forever — no one to helpa — me?'" Later in the story, Caesar, the main attraction, becomes angry when a tiger tears off the ear of his mate, Mariposa. He unleashes his anger by killing another lion and turning on Seppel, who yells out in vain for help. Before Bert can shoot Caesar, Seppel is killed. Venus, another lion, crouches near the dead body: "She licked his wounds with low, caressing growls; nor would she let anyone approach him, until she knew that he was safely dead."[38]

The failure of one person to save another became more pronounced as the country braced for the coldest war: Korea. As Michael Armine, former publications editor of the Federation of American Scientists, wrote in August 1950, "The most important effects of the [atomic] bomb and the most difficult problems it has created are those in the minds of men. Above all, we are indebted to the bomb for having shown us anew what priests and philosophers have been trying to tell us throughout the span of recorded history: man's greatest problem is man."[39]

Senior Scholastic continually accentuated the threat of war even as it published articles on the advancements in radioisotopes, atomic power, and other peaceful uses of atomic energy. An otherwise balanced, informative article on the merits of building the hydrogen bomb opened with the following fictional scenario:

> FLASH (from the Denver Radar Communications Center): New York City's eight million people and many more in the metropolitan area are believed to have been blotted out tonight at 8:22 P.M. EST by a hostile superbomb which struck without warning. No communication has so far been established with any point between Trenton, New Jersey, Bridgeport, Conn., and Poughkeepsie, N.Y.
>
> Will twentieth century Americans— or citizens of any other nation — ever hear news of such shocking horror and doom? It is not impossible. It is, in fact, definitely possible.[40]

The only recourse to the distinct likelihood of atomic war was to be prepared for any threat at any time. *Senior Scholastic*, in its continuing series of mythical discussions, contributed to the civil-defense effort by explaining how national, state, and community defenses were being organized against atomic attack, although the real theme was the necessity of finding shelter. In a 1950 article, "If . . the Bomb Falls," Everett, a fictional high school student, exclaims, "In our science class we read that there is 'no defense' against an atomic bomb. Why do we bother to plan civilian defense, if this is true?" Mr. Banks, a local reporter, answers:

> When scientists say that, they mean that nothing has been devised yet, and probably never will be, to prevent an atomic bomb from doing a great deal of damage. Scientists mean that we have to 'live with' the A-bomb — and the hydrogen bomb, too. We have to assume that any enemy would be able to deliver one or more of these bombs to targets in our country....
>
> But does this mean that we should stand by helplessly? Certainly not. While I was in Britain I learned a great deal about this....
>
> Drawing on their wartime experience, the British have reduced it to this: A dependable warning signal of enemy approach, shelters to house people during attack, and an understanding by everyone that the only promising chance of survival lies in heading for shelter at the first note of warning.[41]

Survival became an increasingly important theme in short stories, too. By the early 1950s, with the diffusion of communism and the Soviet Union's explosion of an atomic bomb, the magazine's articles and short stories shifted toward more emphasis on self-reliance and self-preservation: the new requisites for survival in the Atomic Age. "Smoke Jumper," appearing in the first issue of the 1950–51 school year, is an example of this new emphasis. In this story, the breakdown of the group is offset by the protagonist relying on his own inner strength in order to survive and protect the group from disaster.

Logan, a 23-year veteran of the forest service, takes his crew into a fire zone. Despite their efforts, the fire rages out of control and finally blows up, forcing the crew into a mine shaft for safety. Adams, described as "a violin string that had been stretched too tight and ... about to break," accidentally cuts the foot of another crew member, who loses a great deal of blood. As the fire threatens the men, Adams, who concludes that the crew is going to succumb to the fire, disobeys Logan's orders and leaves the rest of the crew. Logan goes after him but to no avail. Adams is overcome by the fire and dies. Ultimately, Logan's self-reliance brings help to the others, who make it out safely. Thus, we find praise for individual perseverance and sadness for the symbolic death of the group.[42]

"Tzagan," another story combining themes of self-reliance and survival, is the name of a stallion that leads a herd of wild horses. In a fight with another stallion, Tzagan's shoulder is injured, and before the shoulder can heal, he is attacked by "black birds of prey" who come close to killing him. As the white stallion becomes weaker, he is forced to relinquish his role as leader of the wild horses to his nemesis, Wood Mouse. Saved from the black birds by a mountain eagle, Tzagan takes refuge in a cave, where he grows strong enough to take back his rightful place, as Wood Mouse returns to his place behind the leader. Tzagan fought against his attacker, struggled alone to regain his strength, and once again asserted his power. He survived through self-reliance.[43]

In "Conquest," appearing in the December 6, 1950, issue, Joe Dixon and Brad Vierling, his partner in a Shanghai export business, go hunting blue sheep and bear near the Chinese-Tibetan border. Joe Dixon has always been mediocre and fallen short in everything he has tried. This climb was to be different. When Brad is hurt and can no longer proceed, however, Joe is faced with a decision: to stay with Brad or continue alone up a dangerous cliff. Joe knows Brad made the climb possible, but it was "now a lone conquest." Struggling against all odds, he reaches the summit alone:

> Dixon unfastened his binocular case. It came to him, confusedly at first, and then clearly, that he was no longer afraid. Afraid of height, yes; he would never lose that. But somewhere on the mountain he had lost his fear of failure. A small victory, perhaps, but one that gave him a certain warm satisfaction. And what had he found? ... Nothing, he supposed. But he would leave this summit without bitterness because in one sense, Joe Dixon had found himself.[44]

When it came to dealing with life in the Atomic Age, readers of *Senior Scholastic* repeatedly found themselves left to choose between life and death, hope and fear. In the March 7, 1951, issue on atomic energy, students read about atomic-powered planes and submarines, the advancements being made in radioactive isotopes for medical applications, and the "atomic pioneers" working at the Brookhaven National Laboratory on Long Island, New York. Articles also dealt with the scientific principles of the atomic bomb and the history of the U.N.'s failed efforts to control atomic energy. In addition, the Soviets were cited as the culprits in this failure because of their insistence on owning their own raw materials used to create atomic energy, thus permitting "a would-be violator to make bombs without fear of detection."[45]

The Soviet's atomic threat, and the U.S. responses to it, rapidly gained dominance in the magazine's editorial content. An article cited thirty-five cities as prime targets. And although U.S. defenses would stop some enemy aircraft, it said, "even our most optimistic military leaders admit that some of the enemy bombers would reach their targets." One answer to this possibility (or inevitability) was the dispersal of manufacturing centers. Under this plan, the government would encourage new industrial areas to be located ten to twenty miles from densely populated or highly industrialized sections of a city, preferably closer to hilly areas to minimize the blast effects. New plants would be built away from military installations, and separated from each other. An architectural designer was quoted as saying, "The size and concentration of our kinds of cities put us in mortal danger; their traffic congestion further cuts down the chances for escape or safety." The new Matador guided missile, the magazine also reported, now was equipped with an atomic explosive and guided by radio controls to its target.[46]

In October 1951, students read about the Soviet Union's second atomic explosion. Further, they learned that the Soviet Union already had amassed between twenty and eighty atomic bombs, while the U.S. was spending $1 billion a year on atomic production. The magazine reported that each atomic bomb now cost approximately $250,000, the same amount as a tank, and lighter atomic weapons were being developed for battlefield use. Even more alarming was the news that bombs were now more than six times as powerful as the atomic bomb dropped on Hiroshima. The hydrogen bomb, now under development, would be a thousand times more deadly. Another in the long series of articles on the deadlock in the United Nations over international atomic control featured cartoons showing an impatient atomic bomb. The October 31, 1951, cover featured a soldier preparing for atomic maneuvers in the Nevada desert, reading a copy of *The Effects of Atomic Weapons.*[47] Responding to the cover, one student wrote:

The expression on the soldier's face leaves a question mark in my mind. Perhaps he is thinking of the future and how it will affect him. Perhaps the picture of his parents, his family, or a girl he is going to marry is in the background of his thoughts. He might be thinking of his buddies, his leaders, or the people as a whole. Whatever it is, this is one of the most significant illustrations *Senior Scholastic* has ever printed.[48]

Reports continued on the Navy's request for appropriations to build ten new 60,000-ton, atomic-powered supercarriers. It was reported that a new artillery weapon fired shells with atomic charges. By the fall of 1952, the magazine was talking about the multi-million-dollar industrial giant: atomic energy. "This year is the biggest 'boom' period for atomic energy since the days of World War II," it said. Only 20 percent of the money spent on atomic energy is allocated for projects with no possible peacetime applications. New jobs were being created by the generation of electricity, the development of radioisotopes, and atomic-powered aircraft and ships. This was the era of the "expanding atom," which would help cure diseases and be used for many peaceful chores.[49]

Despite these advancements and the escalating dangers associated with the atom, progress still continued on the hydrogen bomb. A news article about the 1952 Eniwetok tests of the new bomb reported that despite the government's secrecy, thousands of letters "told of a flash of light and heat which warmed the backs of men thirty miles away, of a flame two miles wide and five miles high, of an island which burned for hours and then disappeared." In February 1953, the magazine brought credibility to the mutant-insect science-fiction movie when it declared that scientists had reproduced the "life-giving force of the sun" in a weapon that "could wipe out this civilization and leave the globe a habitation only for insects."[50] The article continued:

> Scientists point out that H-bombs are not like artillery shells. They are weapons of total destruction. Furthermore, there would probably be no victors—only [the] vanquished—in an H-bomb war.... Scientists believe it would take only a very few bombs—no matter which side dropped them—before the whole world would be so poisoned that human beings would be made sterile and unable to reproduce their kind, or could produce only subhuman monsters.[51]

Students were hard pressed to distinguish the unreal from the real, fiction from fact, as they read that the blast, burns, and gamma-ray poisoning from a four-megaton H-bomb could kill every human being over a ten-square-mile area. The blast, they were informed, would flatten 140 square miles. Third-degree burns would be inflicted within a 300-square-mile area. Moreover, scientists felt a bomb could be built that could devastate 300 square miles from the blast and 1,200 square miles by fire. The Soviets would be able to build a hydrogen bomb within two to five years, too. President Truman was quoted as saying, "The war of the future would … destroy the very structure of a civilization that has been slowly and painfully built up through hundreds of generations." An accompanying cartoon featured a one-eyed atomic bomb applying for the "World's Follies." The line beneath it read, "The overriding problem of our time is the question of atomic warfare. On the answer we find to that question may hang the future of the human race."[52]

The magazine intensified its offensive during the 1953–54 school year by publishing a series of twenty-five articles titled "Freedom Answers Communism." Each week, students read about people falling under the communist spell, the evil nature of communist objectives, the importance of family, the role of religion in fighting communism, and individual responsibilities in a democracy. In a December article, "Atoms for Peace," the Soviet Union's emergence as an atomic power was discussed, but students were reassured that "the atomic arms race, to all intents and purposes, is over. It has ended in a draw." The next race was to be the race to use the atom in peaceful pursuits. But the Teacher Edition urged teachers to caution students that civilization would be destroyed if the peaceful development of atomic power were not achieved. Whether or not to continue keeping atomic secrets from the country's allies became the forum topic of the week.[53]

President Eisenhower's January 1954 call before the United Nations for an international atomic energy agency kept the issue before students. According to the magazine,

> As the new year dawned, new hope filled the hearts of men. A mighty vision has been set before a war-weary world — the vision of beating atomic swords into atomic ploughshares. A man of peace — though a soldier by profession — saw the silver lining behind the dark, mushroom-shaped cloud that has hung ominously over the world for the past seven years.[54]

In April, however, *Senior Scholastic* reported the successful testing of a hydrogen bomb. Any hopes for world peace were dashed by the announcement that the dawning of the Hydrogen Age would have a major impact on the country, including the ineffectiveness of air-raid shelters against a bomb whose blast could destroy fifty square miles and whose resulting fire could burn 800 square miles. An eyewitness to the explosion was quoted as saying the test was "so far beyond what was predicted that you might say it was out of control." An accompanying cartoon contrasted the more deadly H-bomb to a now quite puny atomic bomb. The radiation exposure to nearly 400 persons, including twenty-three Japanese fishermen, also was recounted. The end of the world was no longer science fiction. Secretary of State John Foster Dulles was quoted as saying that "physical scientists have now found the means which, if they are developed, can wipe life off the surface of this planet."[55]

An article in May on President Eisenhower's proposal for international control of atomic materials—and the Soviet's rejection of this plan—told students, "While we search for the answers, we can overcome fear by asserting our faith in the methods of freedom. We can act in the great tradition of the founding fathers of our Republic." Cartoons encompassing atomic themes reinforced the growing schism between the Soviet Union and United States, as well as the continuing saga of international atomic controls. The H-bomb had made the need to overcome fear even more urgent. Survival in an atomic war was a real concern among Americans. For educators, this concern translated into greater emphasis on democracy and atomic war in curricula, classroom discussions, and school activities. It was now impossible to dismiss the threat of communism and the destructive nature of the atomic/hydrogen bomb.[56]

With the hardening of the Cold War (during the school years 1950–51 to 1954–55), *Senior Scholastic*'s short stories intensified the emphasis on the breakdown of the group and the need to be self-reliant, with the protagonist often surviving alone against a hostile environment. The 1952 story, "Killer in the Pass," for example, concerns Nanka Tol, a Tibetan villager who goes out to find food for his starving people. Left with only one rifle and fifty rounds of ammunition by the Chinese, the village faces certain death unless Nanka succeeds. He soon finds the track of a snow wolf and follows it through the mountains. Suddenly, he is attacked by a wolf and its mate, but he struggles free and escapes. Bleeding, he is attacked by a vulture. "He was used to solitude, to the empty brooding desolation, but today it mocked him. No help would come." Nanka was alone against nature; only his ability to be strong, self-reliant, would mean survival for him and for his village. Nanka is able to kill the vulture and one of the wolves. From his hiding place, Nanka watches three other wolves devour the dead wolf, then takes his rifle, aims, and kills all of them. He returns to save his village from certain starvation. Again, we see the importance of self-reliance as a requisite for individual survival as well as survival of the group, in this case the village.[57]

"A Matter of Time" concerns friends who take an adventurous trip somewhere in the wilds each year. The group includes an archaeologist, an engineer, a lawyer, and the owner of a dude ranch (the protagonist).

The story opens with the group in the Sahara Desert, lost and without water. Desperate, they attack a man who is crossing the desert, take his horse and water, and leave him to die. As the group leaves, the ranch owner turns to see the man draw a pattern in the sand and curse at the four Americans. Upon returning to the States, the four go their respective ways until the next great adventure. A few weeks later, the ranch owner hears about the accidental death of the archaeologist and the discovery of a strange pattern in the snow near his body. Not long after, the lawyer is killed on the docks of an eastern city and, again, a pattern is found in the dirt around him. Not daunted by these strangely related occurrences, the two survivors move forward on their planned trip to a secluded lake 150 miles from human habitation. Hiking toward the lake, they become lost and soon run out of water. The engineer decides to go for help and is killed during a sand storm. The story ends with the lone survivor, seeing the man from the desert standing in the wind, realizing he is doomed:

> The sand is still filtering through the tent door even though I have it tightly laced. The pattern nears completion. I could scatter it but somehow I know that if I do it will reform elsewhere exactly as it was. It is becoming terribly difficult to breathe. The sand is clogging my nose and throat in spite of the handkerchiefs I have tied over my face. It's only a matter of time. I should estimate about 40 minutes. The sand is coming in faster now. He must be growing impatient. Through the crescendo of the storm an undulating chant comes faintly to my ears.[58]

The story, with its focus on the breakdown of the group, the demise of brotherhood, man's inability to control fate, and the inevitability of death and destruction, could not have been missed by the least circumspect Atomic Generation reader.

By mid-decade, Americans realized that survival against communism, atomic war, and technology itself rested on the ability to be strong in an increasingly hostile environment. Two stories from 1955 illustrate *Senior Scholastic*'s continued use of fictional narratives to emphasize the necessity of being self-reliant. Additionally, the magazine selected stories that projected the prevalent 1950s theme of an inability to control one's fate.

In "Death of an Eagle," a man wants to shoot an eagle, a theme representing the failure of humans to protect the world from danger. The "world rare and uncharted" has been taken away, and now the eagle must die "among stones, gravel, loose earth, prickly grass, and entwining weeds." Climbing a mountain, the man finally sees the great bird and shoots it. But before he can get close, the eagle struggles and eventually falls over the cliff beyond the man's sight:

His muscles were twitching and the nerves or muscle cords were drawing tight. And all this mechanism that was limp and free would soon be hard, rigid, and dead. Dead as a rock is dead. Dead as the ground is dead. Dead like the things that surround man. His property. His money. His jewels and all his great hollow treasures. Dead like man who walks the earth a corpse, with pomp and grievances; and with his overpowering passion for hatred and his greatest desire his longing to kill.[59]

The eagle, all that was great, had to die. Any sense of brotherhood had been destroyed by a mad passion for hatred and a desire to kill.

Mike Gardener, the protagonist in "Alone in Shark Waters," is planning to spear fish on the Maldive Islands. While traveling on a ship from Ceylon to the islands, however, the ship breaks up during a storm and Mike is thrown into the water with only his fins, mask, and spear gun. His only thought is to stay alive any way he can. He kills fish and drinks their juices while avoiding shark attacks. He is alone; only his strength, endurance, and self-reliance keep him alive. After many days in the water, fishermen accidentally snag him in their fishing net, but his personal struggle for survival has made him part of nature, and he suddenly fears the unknown force pulling him from the water:

> He knew it was a net and that there were men around him — and he was afraid. The lamp seemed to draw his eyes till the flame filled his mind, and in the darkness all around there was terror. He gasped for air, but none would come. He struggled, and the other fish around him struggled, and he twisted and kicked, knowing only that he must get back to the sea, that he must slither back somehow into the dark cavern of the water and dart away through the softness and the silence where he belonged. It was a sensation of the purest fear — uninhabited by logic or pride or anything human, undiluted and nightmarish — such as only a wild creature might feel when it falls a victim to man.[60]

Michael Gardener's solitary struggle against the forces of nature was a world away from William Riley's encounter with the Sons and Daughters of Destiny, who stressed cooperation among all people and the importance of not succumbing to fate. The belief that brotherhood could prevent war and, thus, protect the individual, prevalent in the 1940s, had been replaced by the belief that self-reliance, strength, and even luck were the requisites for self-preservation in a world beyond control. Although *Senior Scholastic* portrayed the atom as friend and foe, its underlying message remained drenched in the fear of atomic war. The magazine exemplified this dichotomy in 1955, in an article appropriately titled "The Split Atom: For Peace, For War":

> The atom is a sort of Dr. Jeckyll and Mr. Hyde. It can be a benefactor or it can be a killer. Which it shall be lies within the power and wisdom of man.

12

THE A-BOMB MAY SOMEDAY DESTROY US FROM WITHOUT—BUT THIS IS DESTROYING US NOW FROM WITHIN !

Ray Evans, Jr., in Columbus Sunday Dispatch

The Awful Truth—A 30% increase in juvenile delinquency from 1948 to 1953.

psychologists all agree, it is that many of the causes of delinquency can be traced to the home.

In Boston, Mr. and Mrs. Sheldon Glueck of the Harvard Law School made a study showing the relationship of the home to juvenile delinquency. They took 1,000 young people from the same neighborhoods—500 who were delinquents, 500 who were not. These are some of the things they found about the family life of the delinquents:

In three out of five of the homes, the parents and brothers and sisters of the delinquents were heavier drinkers than those in the homes of the non-delinquents. Furthermore, the parents of the delinquents were emotionally less balanced.

In three out of five of the delinquents' families, the husband and wife had no affection for each other. Twice as many delinquents came from broken homes, as from homes in which the parents lived together.

Four out of five of the delinquent youngsters felt their mothers did not care about what they did, or where they went. Three out of five believed their fathers actively disliked or hated them.

Seven out of ten of the families of the delinquents never did things together—there was no real family life.

There is wide agreement that one of the basic causes of juvenile delinquency is the feeling on the part of the child—especially the child of pre-high school age—that he is not loved and is not wanted, that his parents are not interested in him, in what he does, or who his friends are. This breeds a feeling of insecurity, which in turn creates a devil-may-care attitude. And eventually the boy or girl may go out on the town in

search of pleasure, adventure, or romance—usually shady.

But if delinquents are recruited from the ranks of rejected children, they are also drawn from excessively sheltered or petted children. These have their own kind of frustration. They are not allowed to do anything on their own. They are never trusted to use their own judgment. They are encouraged to dodge responsibility. When they set out in protest against their restricted life, they are not equipped to withstand temptation.

Churches and Schools

There are those who argue that the rise in delinquency can be attributed to a decline in religious teaching. Others argue that the schools are no longer "building character."

But many experts who have studied the problem think that this criticism is an unfair one. They point out that the churches can hardly give religious training if the parents do not go to church or send their children to church. (In the Boston study, for example, three out of five of the delinquents rarely, or never, went to church.)

It is also pointed out that the parents of delinquent children are the very ones who usually take no interest in the schools, in Parent-Teacher Association activities, or the school-sponsored youth organizations which would keep their children occupied and interested.

Crime Comics

In the past couple of years, there has also been much discussion of whether crime comics contribute to delinquency. Many learned, and some not-so-learned, articles have been written on the subject. Recently psychologists and educators testified on the influence of crime comics for two days before the Hendrickson committee in New York.

The authorities did not agree. Dr. Frederic Wertham, a psychiatrist who works with two of the largest mental hygiene clinics in New York City, was certain that crime comics very definitely contribute to juvenile delinquency.

Dr. Wertham insists that "the increase in juvenile delinquency has gone hand in hand with the distribution of comic books." Moreover, he says that it is "primarily a normal child" who is harmed by crime and horror comics. He argues that "morbid children" are least affected because they are wrapped up in "their own fantasies."

But Dr. Laurette Bender, an associate professor of psychiatry on the staff of the New York University-Bellevue Medical Center, does not agree with Dr. Wertham.

Furthermore, many psychologists believe that if crime comics do cause harm, the harm affects only the already disturbed or maladjusted youngsters.

The answer to this, in turn, is that it is precisely the maladjusted child who may be inclined to delinquency.

In any event, there is a growing feeling that the comic book industry must soon begin to police itself, or be policed. Some states and communities have already taken steps to remove crime and lurid comics from the newsstands.

The Moral Climate of Our Times

There are many who believe that the increase in delinquency is a reflection of the general moral decline that is said to have taken place—in family life and in public affairs—in the past fifteen years.

Many reasons are given for this decline. During World War II, family life was disrupted as men were drafted and mothers went to work. Thousands of families migrated from rural surroundings into the centers of war industry, where they were suddenly thrust into a life totally strange to them.

For various reasons, war always brings a relaxation of moral standards. There is a prevailing attitude of "let's blow the lid off tonight, for who knows what tomorrow will bring." World War II brought an increase in juvenile delinquency.

After the war there was an almost immediate decline in juvenile delinquency as family life and old patterns of living came back.

Then in 1949, as the cold war became more intense, delinquency began to rise sharply. It continued climbing as the Korean war brought back the draft. Young people again felt insecure, unsure of the future.

This has also been the age of the "fast buck" and the slick deal. Some to whom the people have entrusted the conduct of public affairs have betrayed their trust.

For over a year the Kefauver Crime Investigating Committee uncovered tie-ups in some cities between gangsters and politicians. One Congressman was sent to jail for taking bribes from a company working on Government contracts. Three Congressmen have been convicted of padding their office payrolls. A Senator is reported to have taken a $10,000 fee from a housing concern when he was a member of a committee dealing with housing and Government loans. There have been scandals in the Reconstruction Finance Corporation, the Internal Revenue Bureau, the Federal Housing Administration.

Against this background, many educators believe that juvenile delinquency will begin to decline only when parents fully assume the obligations of parenthood, when the family becomes once again a happy, closely-knit social unit, and when public life is guided by the old—and still true—copybook maxims of right and wrong.

Senior Scholastic fused growing concerns about juvenile delinquency with the threat of the atomic bomb. In its May 12, 1954, issue, the magazine warned readers that the atomic bomb might destroy the nation from without, but delinquency was "destroying us now from within!" Cartoon reprinted, with permission, from the *Columbus Dispatch*. From *Senior Scholastic*, 1945–1955. Copyright © by Scholastic Inc. Reprinted by permission of Scholastic Inc.

If we let the atom 'blow its top,' it means mass destruction. If we harness the atom, it means peace and prosperity. Thus the choice before mankind is atomic construction or atomic destruction.[61]

Nonetheless, the cloud remained. As the school year came to a close in 1955, the magazine reported that the North Atlantic Treaty Organization (NATO) had finally achieved the "atomic punch" to reach every "profitable" Soviet target. Within a few hours, it said, some 800 atomic blows could be leveled against Eastern Europe. Reprisals would kill Americans, but "if the Soviets choose war, their armies will be hit at the Iron Curtain — with an atomic barrage."[62]

Well into the late 1950s, *Senior Scholastic* repeatedly presented incongruous textual and visual narratives about the atom. Although it objectively reported on peaceful developments in atomic energy, and kept students informed about national and international political events, it constantly reminded students about the atomic threat. Also evident are the concomitant references to atomic war within editorials concerned with safeguarding democracy. The shift in short stories from positive themes of brotherhood to positive themes of self-reliance and overcoming the failure of the group (or society) became more pronounced. Moreover, nonfictional articles emphasized the inability of the group (or nation) to protect the individual in the battle for survival in a world seemingly on the brink of destruction. Reflecting the broader scope of social discourse, *Senior Scholastic* even fused growing concerns about juvenile delinquency with the threat of the atomic bomb. In 1954, as delinquency among youth became emblematic of the emerging adolescent culture, the magazine warned readers that the atomic bomb might destroy the nation from without, but delinquency was "destroying us now from within!"[63]

The following year, James Dean personified the alienated, confused delinquent as Jim Stark in *Rebel Without a Cause*. Clearly, as high school populations increased in the early 1950s, so too did the solidification of a widespread adolescent culture — a culture pulling back from the edge of adulthood. Coupled with other factors, particularly the massification of a society bent on protecting youth as it sought to capitalize upon them, the threat of war — perhaps the *real* war to end all wars — became all the impetus necessary to warrant a cultural barrier behind which to enjoy the moment. Even outside school walls, however, the Atomic Generation encountered the same themes found in their daily lessons and activities. From movies to television to magazines to comic books, youth's everyday social reality, in essence, became shaded by a mushroom cloud.

5

Growing Up "in a Circus Like This": Atomic Repercussions in the Movies

> *[J]oin us and live in peace or ... face obliteration.*
> — Klaatu, *The Day the Earth Stood Still*[1]

W hen Homer Parrish, Fred Derry, and Al Stephenson come home from the war in the 1946 film, *The Best Years of Our Lives*, they discover that not only has the country changed; they, too, have changed and now must battle feelings of dislocation, awkwardness, and anomie. The story of three GIs returning to Boone City reflected the inquietude of a postwar America readjusting to a peacetime economy while attempting to absorb millions of veterans back into civilian life. Yet despite the film's troubling undercurrent, moviegoers made it one of the biggest hits of the year. Winner of seven Academy Awards, including Best Actor, Best Supporting Actor, Best Director, and Best Picture, *The Best Years of Our Lives* reflected a country in transition, as well as an America restive about the atomic bomb.

Despite his wariness about seeing his family after such a long absence, Al finally gains the courage and is reunited with his wife, Milly; his grown-up daughter, Peggy; and his teenage son, Rob. His family is anxious to welcome him home but not to hear about his battlefield exploits. Rob, in fact, is more concerned about the future than about the war just won. After Al proudly gives his son a Japanese sword as a souvenir, Rob thanks him politely, then asks whether he was at Hiroshima. "Yeah," his dad replies. "Well, did you happen to notice any of the effects of radioactivity on the people who survived the blast?" his son inquires. "Should I have?" Al asks. At which point, Rob says with a fearful tone, "We've been having lectures in atomic energy at school, and Mr. McLaughlin, he's our physics teacher, he says we've reached the point where the whole human race has either got to find a way to live together or … uh…." "Or else," Al interjects. "That's right," Rob says, "or else."[2]

As the postwar unfolded, replete with victorious euphoria commingled with restless angst, the movie industry altered its tone to reflect an increasingly disquieted social milieu. Film noir, expressing the era's underlying pessimism, emerged as a forceful cinematic movement that vividly contrasted earlier Hollywood happy-ending films with psychologically disturbing movies dealing with violence or mayhem that eventually overtakes and destroys existential lives. Even mainstream fare, like the award-winning *Best Years of Our Lives* and the memorable *What A Wonderful Life*, alternated between optimism and despair, and contained dark themes of frustration, depression, and alienation — themes permeating society in the aftermath of Hiroshima and Nagasaki.[3]

Congruent with movies' more serious tone was the intensifying interest in social-problem themes. Nearly 30 percent of all Hollywood films in the late 1940s dealt with social problems, such as racial prejudice (*Pinky*, 1949), anti–Semitism (*Gentleman's Agreement*, Best Picture of 1947), and political corruption (*All the King's Men*, 1949). Although this percentage decreased in the early 1950s, as the industry sweated under the watchful eye of communist-hunters, movies continued to incorporate controversial themes. *On the Waterfront* (1954) revealed the seedy world of labor corruption; *The Man with the Golden Arm* (1955) brought the problem of drug addiction to the forefront of America's consciousness; and *The Asphalt Jungle* (1950), *The Wild One* (1954), *Blackboard Jungle* (1955), and *Rebel Without a Cause* (1955) focused on the social problem of juvenile delinquency while reflecting society's growing identification of a youth culture.

This emphasis on what film historian Andrew Dowdy has termed "psychic malignancies" and "ambulatory psychotics," however, coexisted with the likes of upbeat musicals like *Let's Dance* (1950), *An American in Paris* (1951), *Singin' in the Rain* (1952), and *Guys and Dolls* (1955). Movies, in essence, mirrored the schizophrenic nature of the era: blindly optimistic and repressively depressed at the same time. In this sense, movies as narrative structures conveyed the same conflicting messages found throughout postwar America.[4]

The industry's obsession with reaching an increasingly fragmented audience was aggravated further by the emergence of television as a competitive entertainment and information medium. Weekly movie attendance spiraled downward from approximately 90 million in 1946 to just 46 million in 1955, with more than 3,000 theaters closing between 1950 and 1953 alone. During this same period, the number of households with television sets exploded from approximately 8,000 to some 31 million.[5] With the steadily increasing number of Americans staying home, as television extended its reach in the early 1950s, filmmakers were forced to cultivate audiences left unsatisfied by tepid, black-and-white television programs. The result was the introduction of innovative technologies, such as 3D and CinemaScope, and the discovery of segmented markets, particularly teenagers with their unprecedented economic clout.

As the movie industry began catering to youthful audiences as a means to boost attendance, young people themselves discovered movies as an important outlet for social activities, privacy, and cultural bonding. Many postwar adolescents literally came of age in darkened indoor and drive-in theaters. Movies— as visual atomic narratives— must be understood not only for their content and themes but for the participant interaction in these cultural expressions— the broader social narrative of the atom. "We forget too easily," historian Lawrence Levine has written, "that going to a movie or listening to the radio are in and of themselves events and that we may have as much to learn from the process, the ritual, surrounding expressive culture as from the content of the culture itself."[6]

By 1950, studies already had uncovered the fact that movies were being patterned to the tastes of a younger audience. A New York study of the Motion Picture Research Bureau in the late 1940s found that the 10–24 age group attended 4.6 movies per month, more than twice the average of those over the age of 50. An Iowa survey also concluded that 31 percent of those between the ages of 15 and 20 attended more than five movies a month, compared to just 1.9 per month for persons 50 years of age and older.[7] In addition, the dramatic rise of drive-in movie theaters, with their privacy and group orientation, contributed to the growing teenage audience. Drive-ins represented 25 percent of movie attendance in the early 1950s, and 30 percent of the total movie audience (at indoor and drive-in theaters) were under the age of 17.[8]

Thomas Doherty, in his study of movies aimed at the youth market, has written that during this era, producers perfected the exploitation formula to boost attendance: controversial, bizarre, or timely subject matter amenable to wild promotion, a substandard budget, and a teenage audience. The final product of this exploitation, the "teenpic," became clearly delineated by the middle of the decade. A movie industry survey in 1956 found that among movie exhibitors and producers, a film's appeal to the 15–25 age group was considered as the most important necessity for the success of their businesses.[9]

The two most significant teenpic genres were the juvenile-delinquent film and the science-fiction movie: one unleashing the stark realities of coming of age in a disillusioned, alienated, violent society; the other presenting the stark realities of radiation, contamination, and destruction in a world burnt out, exhausted, obsolete. "Each Saturday night," remembers Dowdy, an adolescent in the 1950s, "we witnessed the latest hostile surprise created by an environment more capriciously malignant than anything [Senator Joseph] McCarthy promised in his most lunatic moment."[10] Although many of these fictional film narratives stretched the limits of one's imagination, they also reinforced the factuality of atomic dangers ever-present among moviegoers. Movies exploited the fear of impending death by promoting "the aesthetics of destruction." Heroes and heroines constantly struggled against the threat of dehumanization. They were purged of emotions and rendered without volition. They lost their identities. They often sought urban renewal while rejecting the amoral, apathetic state of contemporary society. Many strove for spiritual rebirth or sexual awakening. Others discovered themselves trapped in a world beyond their control or beyond their comprehension. Film historian Joyce A. Evans has suggested that by 1950, transmutation had become the dominant motif in nuclear films. She argues that "atomic technology was presented as transforming all it came into contact with — nuclear survivors, atomic spies, and alien invaders.[11]

For audiences watching these films, the line between fact and fiction often became blurred. In his book, *What Stories Are: Narrative Theory and Interpretation*, Thomas Leitch notes, for instance, that all films are fictional if it is assumed that the action taking place on the screen is occurring in the present, during the time of viewing a piece of film being projected at twenty-four photographic images per second. "If, on the other hand," he writes, "the audience's assumption is that these states of affairs actually did come to pass at some point in the past, then all films are in a fundamental sense nonfictional, since, with the exception of special effects..., everything the audience is seeing is a record of something that actually did happen."[12]

If the audience is less sophisticated, such as children or adolescents, the impact is much greater. Among these groups, the film will more likely be viewed as true, or containing elements of reality. David Freedberg, writing on response theory and art, argues that diverse classes or groups indeed respond differently. Images are encoded as to communicate specific meanings to specific groups or cultures. Children and adolescents respond independently from adult society to the same images found in various media.[13] Postwar movies began to focus on the uncertain identity and adjustment problems of youth. Innocent children, dependent upon their elders, were now viewed as the most vulnerable to tragedy, unable to control their fate. Survival required self-reliance. Yet children, not adults, were the ones best able to understand the challenges associated with surviving in a post-atomic world. Adults were often confused and mistrusting of themselves and their children.[14]

The impact of movies (or any narrative form), in other words, is not so much a question of whether the audience believes the story line; rather, it is whether the audience gleans themes consistent with those encountered elsewhere. If the dangers of atomic warfare appear in fictional form and correlate with perceived realities of atomic dangers, and if a consistent plausibility appears in a variety of narrative forms (e.g., books, magazines, movies, etc.), the narrative takes on a stronger aspect of truth. The differences between the film *Operation Crossroads*, a factual account of the Bikini Atoll atomic tests, and *The Day the Earth Stood Still*, a fictional movie about an alien creature threatening Earth with atomic destruction, are therefore minimal (even indistinguishable) within the sociolect of some groups, such as children, because both appear to have actually taken place.

Filmmakers, in fact, have always sought to attain a sense of reality by incorporating actual film footage from actual events, a device used convincingly during the Second World War. Following the war, Hollywood continued this practice by presenting science-fiction movies, as well as movies with atomic themes, in a docudrama fashion: incorporating actual stock footage of atomic testing; shooting in black and white; using voice-over narration; displaying tanks, jeeps, and other military equipment; and featuring virtually unknown actors. The use of a desert as the backdrop also associated the film's narrative with Los Alamos, New Mexico, home of the atomic bomb, and the setting of atomic tests in Nevada — tests covered by the media on a regular basis and shown on television beginning in the early 1950s. Moreover, the desert amplified real-life fears of radiation fallout in neighboring states, such as Arizona. The threat of a mysterious or sinister enemy, whether Earth-based or extraterrestrial, presented as a docudrama provided the cinematic approach used in atomic science-fiction and atomic-espionage movies over the next decade. This technique has been called the "March of Time" style, in reference to the weekly newsreel series that provided theater audiences with updates on national and world events from 1935 to 1951. Directors used this style to portray significant historical occurrences within the context of an otherwise fictional movie.[15]

Although the first movie to feature an atomic theme was *Shadow of Terror*, released in November 1945, MGM's *The Beginning or the End?* (1947) was the first to define the docudrama method of postwar science fiction by framing a fictional story within a factual context. Made in cooperation with the Federation of Atomic Scientists, the War Department, and the White House, the movie explains the scientific principles of atomic fusion and traces the development of the atomic bomb. While the movie presents atomic weaponry in a positive light, as the technology ending the war, President Truman's moral agony over using the bomb is documented. To add realism, the movie re-created the actual atomic explosions at the Alamogordo test site and Hiroshima.[16]

The fictional narrative involves Matt, a young scientist who questions the morality of the bomb. At one point, Matt tells a colonel, "Most scientists don't really want to make the bomb." To which the colonel responds, "Get it done before the Germans and Japs, then worry about the bomb." Later, as he is arming the *Enola Gay* for its mission over Hiroshima, Matt contracts a lethal dose of radiation, although he is still able to prevent a premature detonation just before he dies. The final scene shows his widow standing before the Lincoln Memorial, reading a posthumous letter from Matt. Matt's voice is heard as his face is superimposed in the background. In his letter, he shares his hope that atomic energy will be used for the betterment of society. He then acknowledges that he is uncertain about the military implications of the atomic bomb, yet he believes in his government and trusts its judgment. *Senior Scholastic* commented that the triteness of the love story detracted from "the serious and unique problem that the bomb presents." One high school student reiterated the factual significance of the film, writing, "This is a very exciting and educational film which everybody should see. It shows how scientists worked day and night on the atomic bomb." This student, and likely many others, clearly understood the verisimilitude of the atomic threat, even in a maudlin movie containing an otherwise superficial fictional narrative.[17]

Two of the classics in the alien-invasion mold appeared in 1951: *The Thing* (also called *The Thing from Another World*) and *The Day the Earth Stood Still*. The Thing crashes to Earth in a flying saucer and is quickly frozen in the Arctic. The alien being, a radioactive humanoid vegetable that subsists on animal blood, is discovered by a small group of U.S. airmen and scientists stationed near the North Pole. Once inside the group's station, the Thing thaws and comes to life, exhibiting enough mental and physical power to destroy the world. Following some harrowing moments, the scientists finally win the battle as the Thing stands on a high-voltage grid and is consumed by flames. The movie ends with Scotty, a newspaper reporter, sending the story over the base radio as he looks toward the audience and delivers a caustic message as a warning of enemy infiltration and of the danger inherent in an unstoppable power:

One of the world's greatest battles was fought and won today by the human race. Here on top of the world, a handful of American soldiers and civilians met the first invasion from another planet.... Now, before I bring you the details of the battle, I bring a warning to every one of you listening to the sound of my voice. Tell the world ... tell this to everyone wherever they are: watch the skies ... watch everywhere ... keep looking ... watch the skies![18]

This scare tactic, of course, is vintage sci-fi and horror: Watch the skies for more alien beings. At the same time, the movie's warning to watch the skies reflected the overriding message that Americans received concerning a possible atomic attack by the Soviet Union. As with other movies in this genre, the dual meaning—one overt and one hidden—is often repeated with dramatic effect on the captivated, often fearful, theater audience.

Integrating social commentary within a science-fiction narrative was used most effectively in *The Day the Earth Stood Still*, the story of an alien being that lands in Washington, D.C., to warn the world about its misuse of atomic energy. Klaatu (played by Michael Rennie) leaves an eight-foot robot to protect his craft while he finds a nearby rooming house, where he befriends a boy and his widowed mother. Eventually, Klaatu is able to meet with a scientist (whose character is based on Albert Einstein) and tell him that an interplanetary United Nations is prepared to blast the planet out of the universe if it continues its violent nature. The scientist calls together his colleagues from around the world to listen to the ominous warnings. Klaatu tells them that soon atomic power will be used in rockets, and that if violence on Earth is extended into space, it will be reduced to a burnt-out cinder.

The choice is simple: "Join us and live in peace. Or pursue your present course and face obliteration"—the identical message being delivered by the media and educators.

Fatally wounded by gunfire, Klaatu is rescued by the robot, returned to the craft, and brought back to life. The message is delivered and Klaatu returns to where he came. According to one reviewer, the movie went "far enough in revealing the profound alienation of man in our ridiculous civilization, and in mocking the so-called values of our moral and political system, for it to gain our sympathy." The most dramatic message to the Atomic Generation comes when Klaatu explains, "Don't play with the atomic bomb. You are irresponsible children whose powers exceed your wisdom. Grow up, or stop playing with fire."[19]

The belief that nothing could save the planet, even if humankind tried, was promulgated in the 1951 movie, *When Worlds Collide* (1951). A scientist learns that the planet Zyra will pass so close to Earth that the oceans will be pulled from their beds. A few days later, a star will collide with whatever remains of the world. The only hope is to build a spacecraft for a few chosen humans (the young who are capable of breeding), and to fly to Zyra and begin a new civilization. According to *Senior Scholastic*, the only credible thing about *When Worlds Collide* was that the end of the world was "such a dull business."[20]

Following the Soviet Union's successful testing of its own atomic bomb in 1949, the conviction of Alger Hiss on spy charges, and the escalation of "Red Scare" tactics by the House Un-American Activities Committee and Senator Joe McCarthy, movies shifted dramatically from fantasy to potentiality. Filmmakers, intent on capitalizing on the mounting atomic stalemate, quickly introduced "I-battled-a-Communist" movies. Hollywood released more than 50 anti-communist films between 1947 and 1954, including *I Married a Communist* (1949), *The Red Menace* (1949), *The Big Lift* (1950), *I Was a Communist for the FBI* (1951), *The Steel Fist* (1952), *Red Snow* (1952), and *Big Jim McLain* (1952). Film noir, with its emphasis on the darker, more sinister, side of life, also was adapted as the prevailing style for several atomic-espionage films, including *The Thief* (1952), *The Atomic City* (1952), *Tangier Incident* (1954), *World for Ransom* (1954), *Pickup on South Street* (1954), and *Kiss Me Deadly* (1954).

In *Kiss Me Deadly*, adapted from Mickey Spillane's novel, Mike Hammer, the film's protagonist, struggles against communist spies and government agents over atomic secrets that threaten the country. Although Hammer, a self-reliant individualist, at first refuses to cooperate with the FBI, he eventually sides with the agents and leads them to a box containing an unknown atomic substance. The film ends in true film noir style, however, as Hammer and everything within miles of ground zero are annihilated in an atomic explosion.[21]

These stories concentrated on espionage and intrigue as the protagonists sought to destroy communist villains. Yet always lurking beneath the surface was the fear that failure in these efforts would result in atomic warfare and instantaneous oblivion. As historian Spencer Weart has pointed out, even movies not containing specific references to atomic war or atomic energy still featured scenes associated with these themes: mass evacuation, collapsing cities, troops mobilizing, military officers issuing warnings, and scientists assisting in each move.[22] This is an important point. During the late 1940s and early 1950s—an era of fear and paranoia, or what historian William Graebner calls the "age of doubt"—the implied if not overt threat was the atomic bomb in the hands of the country's major adversary, the Soviet Union. Children, viewed as the most vulnerable to tragedy immediately following Hiroshima and Nagasaki, now became the most vulnerable to communist ideology. Science-fiction filmmakers picked up on this by merging atomic narratives with story lines dealing with the threat of communism.[23]

Red Planet Mars, released in 1952, became one of the first movies to fuse the communist threat with the fear of atomic war. Described by *Variety* as "a fantastic concoction delving into the realms of science, politics, religion, world affairs, and communism," the movie centers around an American scientist (played by Peter Graves) who has achieved radio contact with Martians. Purportedly, the Martians reveal that they have prolonged their life span to 300 years and use cosmic power for energy. Back on Earth, pandemonium breaks loose as people fear the Martians' secrets will change the world's economic structure. As chaos prevails, government officials hold a high-level conference to avoid catastrophe. Eventually, the scientist and his wife discover that a Nazi war criminal named Calder, working for Russian communists, is behind the plot to take over the world. The clumsy but purposeful ending has Calder revealing that he did not receive messages from Mars. The communists are overthrown by a new spiritual leader, and actual religious messages are received from Mars where God resides. In an act of desperation, Calder accidentally ignites a hydrogen explosion, killing himself along with Graves and his wife. The movie ends as the president tells the nation that the final message coming from Mars was "Ye have done well My good and faithful servants." At that moment, the final title crosses the screen: "The Beginning." For the audience, this ending implied, not so subtly, that by defeating communism, a new era of peace would prevail.[24]

Invasion U.S.A., also released in 1952, contained similar fears of enemy attack and social disintegration. The movie opens with a television report about the takeover of Alaska by an enemy air force (understood to be the Soviet Union's) and subsequent capture of the state of Washington after atomic bombs are dropped. Adding to the grim realism was actual film footage obtained from the armed services and the Atomic Energy Commission. The film concludes with the revelation that the attack was fictitious (a fictional story within a fictional story framed by factual information). The television broadcaster explains to the audience that the future grows out of the present and past behavior of people, and that these events could happen "if Americans don't rise above their lethargy."[25]

Mounting fears about a communist attack were overshadowed only by the equally frightening threat of psychological or emotional takeover resulting from society's lethargy. Thus, another, more alarming, genre appeared: the body-takeover movie. In the first of these, *Invaders from Mars* (1953), culprits from the Red Planet use ray guns to disintegrate anything or anyone in their paths. The story revolves around a 12-year-old boy—children and youth often were central characters in science-fiction movies—who awakens during a thunderstorm to witness a spacecraft landing over a nearby hill. He immediately tells his father (a scientist, of course) and mother, who both ignore him. Within a short time, the boy becomes aware that the aliens are implanting crystals in people's brains and taking over their bodies. When his parents and police fall under Martian control, the boy goes to a woman doctor and a local astronomer who believe the boy and call in the army to destroy the invaders and save the townspeople. The movie ends with the boy, upon waking from a dream, gazing out the window and *actually* seeing a flying saucer once again landing behind his house. Film historian John Brosnan has written, "The film was the realization of a childhood nightmare, a world where all the adults become frightening enemies, even one's own parents."[26]

Invasion of the Body Snatchers (1956) is the best example of a movie that confronts the fear and anxieties in '50s American culture associated with the loss of individuality (or identity) and the threat of communism. Called a "tense, offbeat piece of science fiction" by *Variety*, *Invasion of the Body Snatchers* was based on Jack Finney's serialized story that appeared earlier in *Collier's* magazine. The movie focuses on the invasion of mysterious space spores, or "blanks," in a small town. As these blanks grow, they take on the form of a particular human. When the person falls asleep, a blank takes over his or her body, emerging devoid of normal emotions and all but the impulse to survive. The protagonist, played by Kevin McCarthy, discovers the dangers of the pods and desperately fights against sleep to prevent becoming another blank. As the movie ends, McCarthy is standing in the highway, yelling madly at passing motorists that the pods are being delivered to other towns. But everyone laughs, thinking he is drunk. He then turns directly toward the audience and screams: "They're coming ... and you're next!"—a common device in the docudrama style of abruptly ending the fictional narrative with a direct warning to the audience. The movie contained an overt anti-communist tone, particularly in the taking over of the minds and bodies of ordinary Americans. Yet it also expressed the same themes found in atomic narratives, particularly widespread fear, apathy, and the belief that people do not control their fates.[27]

Although many science-fiction movies dealt openly with the growing threat of the Soviet Union, others framed the escalation of social uneasiness in more fantastic representations of atomic realities. The interplanetary mayhem movie, which raged on through 1953 and 1954, continued to incorporate a documentary-style approach with social commentary about the growing intolerance in American society, the perceived external and internal threat of communism, and the potential of atomic annihilation. The director of *Phantom from Space* (1953), for example, created a documentary style by opening the movie without titles. The first visual images are of radar screens tracking an unidentified object as it moves across the skies and lands near the beach in Santa Monica, California.

In *War of the Worlds* (1953), the adaptation of H.G. Wells' novel, nightmares come to life to create an exhibition that *Variety* called "sock [*sic*] entertainment of hackle-raising quality." The fictionalized account of a Martian attack achieves a sense of reality through special effects that create "an atmosphere of soul-chilling apprehension so effectively audiences ... take alarm at the dangers posed in the picture." Even atomic bombs can't stop the spider-like monsters from Mars that demolish cities and char landscapes with "heatwaves." As one ray goes off, turning three men guarding a Martian craft into human-shaped piles of ash, one young theater-goer "backing slowly up the aisle, hypnotized by what was on the screen, fell flat on his back."[28]

From *War of the Worlds* to *Killers from Space* (1954), the onslaught of death and destruction continued in darkened movie houses on Saturday afternoons. In this sci-fi docudrama, an American scientist (again played by Peter Graves) is killed in a plane crash during atomic bomb experiments at Soledad Flats, Nevada, and brought back to life by Astronians from the planet Astron Delta. As the story unfolds, Graves is made to turn over top-secret atomic information needed by the Astronians before they can destroy everyone on Earth and take over the planet. At one point, the aliens explain their intentions of unleashing mutated creatures against the human race:

> We are accumulating the energy released in each of your atomic explosions.... We have stored several billion electron volts as a result of your atomic tests.... After your next atomic test, these animals will multiply at a rate beyond imagination, [and] at the proper time we will unleash them.... They will spread to every continent and devour every living thing on Earth.

Just before the Astronians' objective is realized, however, Graves destroys the underground lab by shutting down the electricity-generating plant, which the aliens have been using to siphon off energy. This, in turn, causes the lab to explode in an atomic cloud.

What is important about this film, and so many others, is not the improbable plot but the consistent blending of factuality and fictional narrative. In *Killers from Space*, this realistic blending again is obtained through the use of stock newsreel footage documenting the military preparations leading up to an atomic bomb test. During the precredits, the title is superimposed over an aerial view of a mushroom cloud, with the letters on the screen expanding and exploding outward as the cloud rises. The audience is thereby encouraged to realize immediately that the atomic threat is real as well as fictional.[29]

In addition to these "alien-as-enemy" movies, filmmakers incorporated the atom's destructive power into non-alien yet equally harrowing movies about the effects of atomic testing. During the 1950s, in fact, atomic tests became a regular event, even a tourist attraction, in New Mexico and Nevada. So when prehistoric beasts awakened or mutated by atomic explosions raged across the screens, it appeared to be merely the obvious result of America's explosive arms build-up. Moviegoers in the '50s witnessed the destructive power of giant ants, a giant spider, mutated wasps, giant grasshoppers, and a giant praying mantis—all the result of transmutation.

In *The Beast from 20,000 Fathoms* (1953), for example, an experimental atomic blast in the Arctic unfreezes a dinosaur-like creature. Rising out of the sea, the creature attacks New York City but is forced back into the ocean when it is wounded by an army bazooka. Angry, the beast returns to Coney Island, wreaking havoc and mayhem before it is destroyed by a harpoon containing a radioactive isotope. Beasts aroused from the ocean depths were also featured in *Godzilla* (1954), *Monster from the Ocean Floor* (1954), and *The Phantom from 10,000 Leagues* (1956). In *It Came from Beneath the Sea* (1955), an atomic submarine encounters a giant squid forced from its natural home far below the surface by H-bomb explosions. Following the lead of numerous other movies, this film sought a realistic tone by using documentary footage of actual naval personnel and the ocean.

Them!, one of the best of the beastly science-fiction flicks, became Warner Brothers' highest grossing film of 1954. Mutant ants, caused by radiation from the 1945 detonation of an atomic blast in the New Mexico desert, have grown to twelve feet in length and threaten the world with their radioactive deadliness. Actor James Whitmore, playing a sergeant in the state police, is assisted by two entomologists, an FBI agent, and Air Force personnel who seek to destroy the nest of mutated ants with flame throwers and gas. But two queens escape before they can complete their task. One nests on a ship, destroys its crew, and in return is destroyed when the Navy sinks the ship. The other, which has located in a Los Angeles storm drain, is destroyed in what *Variety* called "a real chiller-diller finale." Again, audiences had watched atomic testing on television and read about it in magazines. This movie, building on the popular awareness of the atomic bomb's power, thus reinforced for many the stark possibility of the atom's destructiveness through an unlikely yet plausible narrative.[30]

Not all movies blasted audiences with unrelenting thrills—from beyond the galaxy or within Earth. A more somber approach was typified by what Jeff Smith, author of *Unthinking the Unthinkable*, calls "postholocaust, cinema-of-victims" movies, which dealt with the strength of the human spirit to survive an atomic war and begin anew.[31] Postholocaust movies included *Five* (1951), *Unknown World* (1951), *When Worlds Collide* (1951), *Captive Women* (1952), *World Without End* (1955), and *The Day the World Ended* (1956).

Five, one of the first films to envision a world following a nuclear holocaust, was produced and directed by Arch Oboler and based on his radio drama, "The Word." It is the story of five survivors of an atomic war who find themselves together in a mountain-top lodge: Michael, a young Dartmouth graduate; Roseanne, a hysterical pregnant young woman; an African American bank attendant; an elderly cashier; and a sportsman-fascist explorer. The group forms a microcosm of society, replete with jealousy, rivalry, and violence. Its racial undertones also amplify the need for brotherhood and understanding among all peoples in order to survive. The elderly cashier dies soon after the movie opens; the sportsman murders the bank attendant, then dies himself from radioactive poisoning. *Five* reflects a pessimistic attitude toward the current state of society. Michael says at one point, "We're in a dead world ... and I'm glad it's dead.... Cheap honky-tonk of a world." In the end, Michael and Roseanne return to the city to confirm her husband's death. The final scene, with empty buildings and corpse-occupied cars, forms a distinctly realistic tone to the narrative. The message presents the audience with the same two choices contained in countless narratives: work together and survive, or continue on the current destructive path and be destroyed. As the movie closes, Oboler takes the optimistic path, presenting the pair as the new Adam and Eve, "hurled back from a technological age to work the soil."[32]

Many science-fiction exploits took place in the form of serials: continuous sagas pitting good against evil shown in movie theaters and, later, on television. Among these were *Superman* (1948), *King of the Rocket Men* (1949), *Atom Man vs. Superman* (1950), *Radar Patrol vs. Sky King* (1950), *Captain Video* (1951), *Flying Disc Man from Mars* (1951), *Radar Men from the Moon* (1952), *Zombies of the Stratosphere* (1952), and *Canadian Mounties vs. Atomic Invaders* (1953). Even with low budgets and farfetched scenarios, these serials often presented alien villains in ways that imitated real-life radiation-proof suits and military weaponry, such as the bazooka-like instrument used by the flying disc man from Mars.

Commando Cody, Sky Marshal of the Universe (1953) featured twelve chapters, including "Atomic Peril," "Cosmic Vengeance," "Robot Monster of Mars," and "Hydrogen Hurricane." In 1955, the atomic theme even traveled to darkest Africa in *Jungle Moon Men*. This Johnny Weissmuller adventure finds the hero joining up with a female journalist to save a white man from the queen of the Pgymy tribe known as Moon Men. The high priestess is afraid to leave her temple for fear that Ra, the Sun God, will destroy her as he did people in ancient times. The movie ends with her emerging into the open and "crumbling to dust when Ra beams his rays upon her." Even Mickey Rooney contributed to the era by starring in *The Atomic Kid* (1954). Rooney is a prospector who finds himself at ground zero while eating a peanut-butter sandwich in an old shack, only to appear unscathed but radioactive. These serials and lighthearted movies attracted a younger audience consisting of the *Fallout* from the Atomic Generation, those entering adolescence in the middle 1950s. But they, too, were being conditioned to the far-reaching effects of the atomic bomb.[33]

Many cinematic atomic narratives were not science fiction at all. *Atomic Power*, for example, released in 1946 as part of the *March of Time* series, and made under the scrutiny of the federal government, tells the factual story about the making of the atomic bomb. In addition to using actual footage of Hiroshima and Nagasaki, the film features the acting debuts of several real-life scientists involved in atomic research, including J. Robert Oppenheimer, David Lilienthal, and Albert Einstein. What makes the movie particularly interesting as an atomic narrative is the incorporation of fictional re-creations of events, decisions, and conversations. In the scene of the first Trinity test, only the footage of the explosion and fireball was authentic. The closeup of scientists James Conant and Vannevar Bush, seen moments later stretched out on the New Mexico sands several miles from ground zero, was shot in a Boston garage.[34]

General-interest movies also incorporated references to the atomic bomb, often setting the fictional stories within a factual (even documentary) context. *Destination Moon* (1950), described as a "highly technical space travel subject," concerned a flight to the moon by four American scientists. When they prepare to return, however, the scientists sadly learn that the spaceship is too heavy to break away from the moon's gravitational pull. Through their ingenuity, however, the intrepid explorers are eventually able to return home. Although the movie incorporated many scientific principles, *Senior Scholastic* commented wryly that "those movie-goers who are up on their atomic physics will enjoy catching the few technical boners." The Atomic Generation had learned its lessons well.[35]

Above and Beyond (1952), a semidocumentary starring Robert Taylor as Colonel Paul Tibbets, told the story behind the bombing of Hiroshima and promoted continued work on the atomic bomb; and *Run for the Hills* (1953) starred Sonny Tufts as a man wanting to use his life savings to convert a cave into a bomb shelter. Paramount's 1952 release, *The Atomic City*, concerned the FBI's successful efforts to foil a communist plot to kidnap the son of an American nuclear physicist, played by Gene Barry. The price for his return was the formula for manufacturing atomic bombs. Historian A. Constandina Titus has commented about the movie, "Directed by Jerry Hopper, who had previously worked only on army training films, it was done in psuedodocumentary fashion, in black and white, and bore great resemblance to the official reels being distributed by the government during the same period."[36]

Hell and High Water (1954), with Richard Widmark as soldier-of-fortune Adam Jones, captured a documentary tone by purporting to solve the mystery of an atomic bomb explosion actually occurring in 1953 north of Japan in the Arctic Circle. The narrative concerns a group of international scientists who become disillusioned with the government's inability to cope with the escalating nuclear threat. They hire Jones to command a submarine sent into the North Pacific to search for a suspected arsenal of atomic weapons. Jones discovers that communists plan to drop an atomic bomb on North Korea, which they will blame on the United States. But the plane carrying the bomb is shot down, setting off the mysterious atomic explosion. The fictionalization of an actual occurrence enhanced the dramatic realism of the movie's subject: the fear of atomic attack.[37]

Other movies, although not dealing overtly with the bomb, reflected the psychic numbing, search for identity, and meaninglessness of life congruent with postwar atomic anxieties. Film noir, particularly, epitomized the "psychologizing" movie where people's desires are able to be fulfilled in a world of abundance. But these desires are usually revealed to be full of evil possibilities and ultimately lead to despair or death. The main characters are, in the words of historian Lary May, "antiheroes often psychically tormented." Among the movies amplifying what Susan Sontag has called "aesthetics of destruction" were *The Postman Always Rings Twice* (1946), *White Heat* (1949), *Body and Soul* (1950), *D.O.A.* (1950), *Panic in the Streets* (1950), *In a Lonely Place* (1950), *Sunset Boulevard* (1950), and *Angel Face* (1952). These movies accentuated the nightmarish, fatalistic fears of many Americans—an attitude summarized by John Garfield in *Body and Soul*. When Garfield is threatened by gangsters, he defiantly tells them that he isn't afraid because "Everybody dies!" Although Freud had written his works years before, and had first become popular in the 1920s for liberating the libido, it was not until the post–Hiroshima era, when everybody huddled together under the mushroom cloud, that society embraced his tenets about the existence of subconscious desires and the underlying fear of death within each person.[38]

These tenets were personified in several juvenile-delinquent films. In *Gun Crazy* (1950), a young juvenile brought before a judge captures the essence of atomic fatalism when he says coldly, "Shooting's what I'm good at. It's what I want to do when I grow up.... It makes me feel good inside." A teacher in *Knock On Any Door* (1949), the story of teenage gangs, offers his solution to a classroom disturbance by declaring, "Drop an atom bomb on the whole slum." And Marlon Brando's Johnny in *The Wild One* (1954) became the spokesperson, in the view of one film critic, for those "beaten before they even had a chance to get started, by the ever-present insane possibility of a push-button war that could wipe all life off the face of the planet in a matter of minutes." When Johnny is asked what he is rebelling against, he replies, "Whadda ya got?"[39]

The seminal representation of teenage alienation and restlessness, however, was James Dean's portrayal of Jim Stark in *Rebel Without a Cause*: the story of a teenager torn between violence and apathy; searching for love from parents with whom he is unable to relate, in a society that has abandoned him and in a world beyond his control. As film historian Peter Biskind has written, Jim and his cohorts were "street-corner existentialists, filled with angst."[40] Dean, who died a few days after the film premiered in New York City, exemplified the emotional undercurrent of youth in the early 1950s. In the movie, Jim yells at his father, "I don't know what to do anymore except maybe die.... How can a guy grow up in a circus like this?"

Later, during a day trip to a planetarium, students stare blankly at the stars as an astronomy lecture concludes suddenly with the universe exploding into chaos, trapping them for one brief moment in total darkness as a vacuous voice conveys that

> the heavens are still and cold once more. In all the immensity of our universe and the galaxies beyond, the earth will not be missed. To the infinite reaches of space, the problems of man seem trivial and naive indeed. And man, existing alone, seems himself an episode of little consequence.

That same night, when Jim confronts his rival, Buzz, about why they must "chickie race" (in which the two drive stolen cars over a cliff, with the loser being the first one to jump), Buzz emulates Brando's Johnny when he responds stoically, "What else is there to do?" And when Buzz's shirt becomes caught inside the car and he is unable to jump out before plunging to his death on the rocks below, teens, who had just played the role of delinquent antagonists, disperse in panic, promising not to tell anyone what has taken place. Commenting on this scene, film historian Douglas Brode has suggested that the chickie race "symbolically depicts [adolescents'] chaotic but headlong rush toward an oblivion which, in a frightening way, is highly attractive to these impressionable young people trapped in a world without meaning."[41]

In a symbolic way, the fictional Jim Stark racing toward the cliff's edge and the real James Dean speeding along a deserted highway were one and the same, both rushing toward the edge of a world on the brink of finality. Said one fan after his death on September 30, 1955, "When James Dean was killed in that horrible accident, it seemed like a big, black curtain had been drawn in my life." Sam Astrachan, in a 1957 article titled "New Lost Generation," wrote of James Dean, "[I]n each of the Dean roles, the distinguishing elements are the absence of his knowing who he is, and what is right and wrong. Dean is always mixed up and it is this that has made him so susceptible to teenage adulation. His habits and his attitudes, exaggerated reflections of those of many youths, are seen all over the country." The identification of teenagers with the fictional persona and the real James Dean in many ways reflected the growing impact of media on postwar adolescents.[42]

Beyond the strict definition of film noir and the delinquent motif, other movies incorporated atomic-age themes or explicit atomic-bomb references. *High Noon* (1952) with Gary Cooper is hauntingly similar to *Invasion of the Body Snatchers*: A reluctant hero is put in the position of protecting a town that is unwilling—and unable—to protect itself from sinister forces. Fear and paranoia also run rampant in *Bad Day at Black Rock* (1955), in which the townspeople turn on Spencer Tracy, who has come only to present a posthumous medal to the father of a Japanese-American soldier killed during the war. And the classic *Shane* (1953) again finds the individualist as antihero fighting to protect a family and a society unwilling to protect itself.[43]

The Korean War reinforced the atomic threat, so it is not surprising that references to the atomic bomb or its bleak implications appeared in war movies as well. Samuel Goldwyn's 1951 movie, *I Want You*, concerns the owner of a pawn shop who sends his son off to Korea with instructions to kill a lot of communists, at which point his son explodes, "Why not drop the bomb if that's what the old men want?" Paul Douglas, as an NCO transferred to Berlin in the movie, *The Big Lift* (1950), says to another soldier upon his arrival, "This is where they should have dropped the A-bomb." Many of these films also reflected the growing sense of social anxiety. *The Steel Helmet* (1951) shows soldiers arguing among themselves, lacking any sense of purpose. When one dies, the central emotion is apathy, not patriotism. "Leave him be," the sergeant yells as a G.I. is shot. "A dead man is a dead man, and nobody cares." When Robert Mitchum orders a column of civilians liquidated by shelling in *One Minute to Zero* (1952), "even a slow-witted child, his teeth glued together with Milk Duds, was bound to remember the scene." All these films reflected the darker side of American culture in the 1950s: the underlying sense of uneasiness in the Atomic Age.[44]

What comes through in these films are the consistent themes of mass destruction; loss of identity or dehumanization; growing indifference and intolerance; fear of the unknown; sense of fatalism in an uncontrollable world; and the struggle for survival. The decade following Hiroshima was an era of anxiety and paranoia. Social anxiety resulted from the ever-present atomic threat and the belief that a third world war would bring an end to civilization itself. Social paranoia resulted from the equally potent fear of communist subversion, particularly in the early 1950s. As a result, even the most farcical or preposterous alien-invasion movie, replete with ray guns and other outrageous weapons, contained elements of truth concerning the potential of atomic warfare. At the same time, doomsday themes were balanced by equally strong messages about protecting democracy and Earth, and about the belief that the self-sufficient, inner-directed individual will survive to start again.

Mirra Kaminsky and H. Bruce Franklin have argued that science-fiction movies extolled society's fear of life and fear of the future, not the fear of death. "Often the fear of the future is more abstract," Kaminsky has written, "and represents our cultural feeling that we are destroying ourselves, losing control to the point where machines will take over and the scientist or superior intellect will turn us into slaves."[45] There is commonality, however, between film genres from this period. Science-fiction films dealt with anxiety about atomic weapons specifically or the implied threat of atomic warfare. Mainstream films often mirrored the sublimated anxieties, apathy, and indifference associated with postwar society. Historian Chester Eisinger's description of the mood during the 1940s as "one of fear, terror, uncertainty, and violence, mingled with sad satisfaction and a sense of relief at victory" can be applied to many of the movies discussed above. His comment addresses the disturbing, confusing, and contradictory messages presented to adolescents concerning their world, their futures, and their own sense of self.[46]

Film historian Patrick Lucanio also has suggested that fears of the Atomic Age manifested into a collective xenophobia, or fear of anyone and anything different. "To compensate for this imbalance," he argues, "the movies unpretentiously and overtly gave the public a manifestation of these fears."[47] As the 1950s matured and the Cold War intensified, cinematic atomic narratives made it clear that only the military or military scientists were capable of saving humanity from self-destruction.[48] Yet movies were not alone in the creation of this fear or the presentation of the atom as something to behold as well as something to beware. As the Atomic Generation came of age, it encountered an array of media—from books to television—blasting away at nearly equal decibel levels about the power and the promise of the atom.

6

Paper Bombs and Atomic Airwaves: The World of Print, Radio, and Television

...I'm sort of glad they've got the atomic bomb invented. If there's ever another war, I'm going to sit right the hell on top of it. I'll volunteer for it, I swear to God I will.
— Holden Caulfield, *The Catcher in the Rye*

If Jim Stark personified recalcitrant, misunderstood youth in the movies, then Holden Caulfied represented them in literature. J.D. Salinger's protagonist in his 1951 novel, *The Catcher in the Rye*, rejected "phonies" who fell victim to conformity. He felt alienated from his parents. His rebelliousness matched that of his cinematic cohort, capturing the trepidation among many postwar youth coming of age in an affluent yet suppressive society. But Holden, like Jim, also must be understood within the context of the Atomic Age. Both view adult society as a circus. Parents are vacuous bodies—"blanks"—unable to relate to the needs and the problems of their children. Jim "chickie races" because there is nothing else to do. Holden wants to save the children before they fall over the cliff, becoming victims of an unsafe world. Both characters approach life from an existential perspective: There is nothing to plan for because the future is too remote, too dangerous. Both attempt to salvage their identities. Both reject mainstream values—values seen as manipulative and authoritarian. Jim runs away with his new friends to an abandoned mansion; Holden wants to run away with his friend to the woods, away from people and problems and pain.

These themes suffused popular media in the late 1940s and 1950s, reflecting the criticism leveled against an increasingly technological, materialistic, bureaucratic, intolerant society. These are the themes of atomic narratives, too. From overt references to the atomic bomb to the Atomic Age as metaphor or subtext, Americans encountered the impact of the atom not only in movies but in popular literature, radio, television, comics, and magazines. Print and broadcast media, moreover, contributed toward the verisimilitude of the atomic threat by reinforcing the themes encountered in multifarious narratives, particularly those aimed at children and adolescents. In this sense, these mediums mirrored the same messages heard elsewhere and defined the social landscape — the social narrative — of American society. For the Atomic Generation, in particular, the intellectual and social interaction with these mediums constituted an influential dimension of its coming-of-age experience.

A 1949 study of teenage leisure-time activities found that 93 percent of adolescents listened to the radio on a regular basis, with no significant differences in listening habits based on economic or social group. One-third of teenagers had radios in their bedrooms, and more than half listened to the radio more than two hours a day. Nearly 34 million households had radios in 1946 — a number that would increase to nearly 46 million by 1955, even with the emergence of television. The introduction of the transistor and teen-oriented music programs contributed toward this growth. And radio's targeting of youth contributed toward the solidification of a modal adolescent culture that crossed socioeconomic barriers.[1]

Television, however, was the medium that greatly accelerated the massification of society and the emergence of a mass youth culture. Ten million households owned television sets in 1951. Four years later, this number had increased dramatically to more than 30 million. Yet as early as 1950, a survey of city youth had found that nearly two-thirds of high school students already had a television set in the home and watched fifteen hours of television each week. Unquestionably, urban, middle-class youth were able to embrace the new medium before rural and working-class youth.[2]

As television penetrated American homes and radio turned toward a younger audience, comics were becoming a national obsession. A 1948 survey conducted by the Institute of Student Opinion found that more than 73 percent of high school students read comic books at least on occasion. A study in Dayton, Ohio, conducted two years later, concluded that 54 percent of all comic-book readers were over the age of twenty, and 48 percent of all comic-book readers were female. Forty percent of those surveyed had read more than eight comic books in the past four months. On average, people read fifteen comics each month. Another study found that youth read twelve comic books each week. In one town of 4,000, more than

28,000 comic books were being sold each month — seven per month for each man, woman, and child. Among science-fiction readers, 95 percent were adolescent males. By 1954, at the pinnacle of comic-book mania, 150 million copies of more than 650 comic-book titles were being published *every month.*[3]

Comics were by no means the only reading material for the Atomic Generation, though. A 1951 survey of magazine reading habits, conducted at Long Island City (N.Y.) High School, revealed that over a six-month period, girls read an astounding thirty-seven different magazines, including romance, fashion, screen, and homemaking titles. Boys read thirty-one different titles on sports, adventure, mechanics, and hobbies. In addition, two-thirds of all students read comic strips or comic books. The number of juvenile book titles— another indication of society's focus on adolescents as a cultural group — increased by more than 50 percent between 1950 and 1955, compared to an 18 percent increase among all book titles. These titles reflected the trend in adult books toward naturalism, or the belief that people cannot overcome the power of nature. One contemporary observer wrote, "The naturalistic trends in adult literature engulf many [adolescents] before they have outgrown imitative behaviors."[4]

Among the magazines that engulfed youth with postwar naturalism were *Time, Newsweek, Collier's, Life, Saturday Review, The New Yorker,* and *The New Republic.* All these magazines (which were often used in classroom discussions) quickly reformulated the journalistic style adopted during the Second World War. This style combined factual presentations with the qualities of fiction: emotionality, plot, characterization, dialogue, conflict, cause-and-effect relationships, and, above all, colorful descriptors.

Mark Gayn, reporting for *Collier's* in June 1945, exemplified this style in an eyewitness account of the fire bombings of four Japanese cities that colorized and dramatized the horrors of mass destruction — in essence, desensitizing readers to what would follow in August. More than 3 million Japanese were killed, injured, or left homeless as a result of the attacks, Gayn reported. Rendering a vivid picture of the incoming American bombers, he wrote, "In a long, thin file they roared over Tokyo. They flew low, and out of their open bellies spilled bombs of jellied gasoline. When they hit, they burst, spewing out bellowing, all-consuming fire. The flames leaped across fire lanes, swallowed factories, destroyed skyscrapers." Gayn's report, however, was consistent with numerous others issued about the war in Europe and the Pacific. All Americans, young and old, had come to expect such graphic descriptions, which were considered part of the horrors of war.[5]

Time magazine expanded this horror when it reported just one week after the bombing of Hiroshima that "the atomic bomb was something more than an instrument to shape 1945's history. It represented a brutal challenge to the world to keep the peace." No longer was the issue winning the war. Accentuating the same warnings found in science-fiction stories, the magazine proclaimed that the atomic bomb "might wipe out with a few strokes any nation's power to resist an enemy." The next week, *Time* again wrote that this new age was "a new room, rich with hope, terrible with strange dangers." The door that slammed behind humankind at Hiroshima had locked, an event that completely overshadowed the winning of the war. Americans' fate would "forever [be] shaped between the hands of reason and spirit, now in collaboration, again in conflict." The only way to survive was to create an "indissoluble partnership" between the two. An accompanying illustration raised the question to be asked of all Americans in the next few years: "Life or death?" Appropriately, the choice was given to humanity, represented by a baby: a new generation. Sir James Chadwick, chief British advisor on the atomic bomb, was quoted in the same issue as saying any nation with raw materials could build an atomic bomb within five years, without U.S. assistance. The fire bombings that seemed so distant were quickly replaced by a more devastating threat at home.[6]

Life echoed the same wonderment on the one hand and trepidation on the other, cautioning its readers that they should fear the nature of man, not the atomic bomb. "No limits are set to our Promethean ingenuity, provided we remember that we are not Jove," it said. "We are not ants either; we can abolish warfare, and mitigate man's inhumanity to man. But all this will take some doing. And we are in a strange new land." An August 20 article, "The War Ends," included a Japanese account of the explosion: "A lightning-like flash covered the sky. All around I found dead and wounded ... bloated, burned with a huge blister.... All green vegetation ... perished." The same article featured a photograph of the Hiroshima blast with the caption, "Atom bomb no. 1 obliterated it," and an accompanying photo of Nagasaki with the caption, "Atom bomb no. 2 disemboweled it." "The atomic bomb," the magazine said, "had blown three fifths of Hiroshima off the face of the earth." *Life*'s Hanson Baldwin set the tone for later science fiction by proclaiming that "man has unleashed a Frankenstein monster."[7]

It would be Norman Cousins, in an article titled "Modern Man Is Obsolete," who would set the tone for subsequent atomic narratives in fact and fiction. "Whatever elation there is in the world today because of final victory in the war is severely tempered by fear," he wrote in the *Saturday*

Review of Literature's August 18, 1945, issue. He called it a primitive fear, "the fear of the unknown, the fear of forces man can neither channel nor comprehend." This fear was not new. In its classical form, according to Cousins, it was the fear of irrational death. But it had become magnified instantly, overnight, by the bombing of Hiroshima. This fear had "burst out of the subconscious and into the conscious," he wrote, "filling the mind with primordial apprehensions. It is thus that man stumbles fitfully into a new age of atomic energy for which he is as ill equipped to accept its potential blessings as he is to counteract or control its present danger." Cousins's article, later published in book form, became one of the most widely used narratives in American classrooms over the next decade.[8]

Three months after Cousins articulated the dangers of the new Atomic Age, *Life* melded a factual story about a report issued by General Henry Arnold, commanding officer of the Army Air Force, with a science-fiction plot remarkably similar to the movie, *Invasion U.S.A.* Titled simply "The 36-Hour War," the article described — in pictures and text — a hypothetical all-out atomic war in which more than 10 million Americans are killed instantly when atomic bombs hit thirteen key U.S. centers, ranging from New York City and Washington, D.C., to the Boulder Dam and San Francisco. Although, according to the story, the enemy has built rocket-launching sites in Africa to avoid detection, "the enemy's purpose is not to destroy industry, which is an objective only in long old-fashioned wars like the last one, but to paralyze the U.S. by destroying its people." With massive offensive weapons and a superior defense system, however, the United States is able to launch a counterattack. Despite the ability of enemy troops to invade the country and begin an assault using "light rockets of great destructive power," the United States ultimately triumphs. Victory comes despite losing 40 million people and having all cities with more than 50,000 population leveled.[9]

Magazines published ongoing narratives about the atomic bomb and related atomic stories throughout the late 1940s and 1950s. One of the most consequential of these many narratives appeared in the August 31, 1946, issue of *The New Yorker*. Written by journalist John Hersey and simply titled "Hiroshima," the article was a personal account of the first atomic bombing. Based on fact, it used such fictional devices as dramatic tension, dialogue, flashbacks, plot, characterization, and emotional involvement. The story focused on the lives of six survivors and was written as an unfolding story with the protagonists caught in a complex plot of survival. Hersey continually crossed the line between reporting and storytelling, using his characters as subtexts to his larger atomic narrative of destruction, death, and despair.

The article had a sudden and substantial impact, as readers were literally devastated by what they read. The National Committee on Atomic Information, the Army, and the Atomic Energy Commission immediately wanted copies to impress upon Americans the awesome power of this new weapon. The magazine gave permission for newspapers to reprint the article, as long as profits were given to the Red Cross and the article was not abridged. The American Broadcasting Co. (ABC) and many of its affiliates read the entire text, commercial free, in four special half-hour broadcasts. It also was published in book form later that year, was named a Book-of-the-Month Club selection, and became a best-seller. Scholastic, Inc., made the book a Teen-Age Book Club selection, available for just twenty-five cents. Teachers quickly placed *Hiroshima* on their recommended reading lists for students, incorporating it into their atomics curricula.[10]

One World or None, released in early 1946, had jolted complacent Americans who had already forgotten the bomb. The report by scientists, generals, and social pundits had discussed the atomic bomb's implications and previewed World War III. But *Hiroshima* changed Americans' concept of the atomic bomb from stark visual images of the mushroom cloud and factual, often clinical, government reports of the atom's potential, to an emotional, very personal narrative as readers followed the harrowing lives of the six survivors and the thousands of victims in the devastated Japanese city.

The contrast can be seen in an article published by *Life* in September 1945. The magazine described Hiroshima as a "flat, silent plain, a still-stinking junkpile" with dead trees standing like skeletons. Those near the blast had died suddenly; for others who only received small burns, the end was more painful. They lost their appetite, their hair fell out, their gums bled, they developed temperatures of 104 degrees, vomited, and died. The total dead at Hiroshima was listed as 125,000.[11]

Hersey brought this story into much tighter focus. In one passage, he describes two girls rescued from a river. The younger one had huge flash burns on her body and began to shiver. "Father Kleinsorge borrowed a blanket from someone nearby and wrapped her up, but she shook more and more, and said again, 'I am so cold,' and then she suddenly stopped shivering and was dead." The coldness and finality of death were overwhelming. More striking, however, was the inability of the survivors—anyone—to control their own lives and those around them. Another passage not only captures this feeling but also describes a scene that later will give credence to such science-fiction horror movies as *War of the Worlds* and *Invasion of the Body Snatchers*. It concerns the same German priest, Father Kleinsorge, who comes across a group of soldiers in the woods. One asks him if he has anything to drink. As Kleinsorge approaches, he realizes their faces are burned and eyesockets hollow, their eyes having melted from the heat. Hersey describes the scene:

> (They must have had their faces upturned when the bomb went off; perhaps they were anti-aircraft personnel.) Their mouths were mere swollen, pus-covered wounds, which they could not bear to stretch enough to admit the spout of the teapot. So Father Kleinsorge got a large piece of grass and drew out the stem so as to make a straw, and gave them all water to drink that way. One of them said, "I can't see anything." Father Kleinsorge answered, as cheerfully as he could, "There's a doctor at the entrance to the park. He's busy now, but he'll come soon and fix your eyes, I hope."[12]

Hersey's narrative shook Americans out of their apathy and resurrected the sense of awe and anxiety they had felt immediately after the bomb exploded in 1945. It also encouraged readers to empathize with the victims of Hiroshima and introduced them to the horrors of radiation sickness. Two years later, the Scholastic Book Service published David Bradley's book, *No Place to Hide*, and promoted it to teachers and high school students. This firsthand account of Operations Crossroads, the 1946 atomic test on Bikini Island, echoed Hersey's warnings. Bradley, a member of the Radiological Safety Section, wrote, "The devastating influence of the Bomb and its unborn relatives may affect the land and its wealth — and therefore its people — for centuries through the persistence of radioactivity."[13]

As more knowledge about radiation became known, particularly after the publishing of *Hiroshima* and *No Place to Hide*, writers increasingly focused on this deadly effect from the atomic bomb. Dexter Master's 1955 novel, *The Accident*, placed the dangers of radiation within the context of the overriding concerns about atomic energy itself. Masters became a noted advocate of One World when, in 1946, he and Katherine Way edited *One World or None*. As a member of the MIT Radiation Laboratory, he also was personally knowledgeable about the effects of radiation, which he used effectively in his novel.

Master's protagonist is a young physicist, Louis Saxel, who works at the Los Alamos atomic bomb laboratory. One evening, he becomes exposed to deadly radiation in an experiment gone awry but saves six other scientists in the process. The story unfolds around Saxel, who lies near death in a hospital room. Masters provides a brief history of the government's atomic research project, as well as Saxel's involvement in it. But the novel's central concern is Saxel, who ultimately suffers a slow and painful death as his girl, Betsy, looks on:

He saw also, although he did not comprehend at once what it was, one of his own hands—splotchy in red and white, a great blister between two fingers, dripping water. It was lifted somewhat above the bedclothes as though it were not to be touched by what was there. It hung against the yellow glow on the blind, and as he looked at it he pushed back involuntarily against the bars of the bed. He tried to speak to Betsy, but, although he could feel his lips moving, there were no words. Staring at his hand, retching dryly now, he lay half doubled up at the top of the bed, as though he had been pushed there.[14]

The works of writers like Cousins, Hersey, and Masters, combined with an array of accounts of the atom, contributed to society's eventual acquiescence to the atomic bomb's presence and to its attempt to sublimate atomic fears beneath the doctrines of containment and domestication. More than 300 atomic-related articles were published in 1946 alone; and, although the number fell over the next two years, it increased to nearly 200 in 1949 after the Soviet Union's testing of an atomic bomb. By 1950, society seemingly had recovered an unsteady balance between hope and despair, but it was a balance that remained precarious well into the next decade as narratives continually presented the atom as a massive force of destruction and as humankind's promise for future abundance. In 1953 and 1954, after the introduction of the hydrogen bomb, some 360 magazine articles appeared on the subject. The discourses within these narratives offered as much confusion as solace. At the same time that print media amplified both justified and unwarranted fears and anxieties, they simultaneously stressed the need to control them — implying indirectly that by controlling individual emotions, the atom could be controlled and, consequently, peace could be maintained.[15]

Even when articles contained the promise of atomic energy, the dangers of the bomb remained. Senator Styles Bridges of New Hampshire, in a 1954 *Collier's* article on the hydrogen test on Eniwetok, described the vaporization of dirt, trees, rock, and metal machinery by the hydrogen bomb, adding, "Those who saw the test wondered what more scientists must do to convince mankind that an era has ended … and that a civilization will end unless men reconcile their differences peacefully." The senator's words, framed as they are within a magazine article about the very real and serious dangers of the hydrogen bomb, were not unique; they merely reflected the same message contained in countless atomic narratives. Many general-interest magazines, like *Life* and *Collier's*, published science-fiction stories as well as factual articles about the atom. The twice-monthly *Collier's*, for example, published the science fiction of such noted writers as Philip Wylie, Ray Bradbury, and Jack Finney.[16]

For more serious science-fiction readers, magazines like *Beyond Fiction, Amazing Stories, Astounding Science-Fiction, Fantastic Adventures, Marvel Science Fiction, Thrilling Wonder Stories, Galaxy Science Fiction, Orbit Science Fiction*, and *Weird Tales* provided truly astounding atomic narratives.[17] In his study of nuclear fiction, Paul Brians concluded that immediately following Hiroshima, science-fiction writers expressed the same exhilaration that the war was over and the sense of anticipation about the new Atomic Age as most Americans. By 1946, though, the same themes found in later cinematic atomic narratives—enemy attack, mass destruction, survival, radiation, dehumanization, battles against atomic mutants, world peace, individualism vs. conformity—began to dominate science-fiction stories and books.

In Rog Phillips's "Atom War," published in 1946, the enemy is identified as Xsylvania, which is attacked by Australia and other U.S. allies. In the end, the development of inexpensive defensive "sterio rays" ends the threat of future wars only after millions of Americans are killed in a massive atomic assault. Ray Bradbury's "The Million-Year Panic," also published in 1946, concerned the demise of civilization through the eyes of survivors who escaped to Mars. In Edward Grendon's "The Figure" (1947), the survivors of an atomic war are humanoid beetles, while grotesquely mutated descendants inherit Earth in "Tomorrow's Children" (1947), by Poul Anderson and F.N. Waldrop, and Theodore Sturgeon's 1946 story, "Memorial."[18]

Total world destruction consumed many readers' nightmares. Louis N. Ridenour's "Pilot Lights of the Apocalypse" (1946), later republished in *Senior Scholastic*, envisions civilization coming to an end when an underground nuclear-weapons center wrongfully identifies an earthquake in San Francisco as an atomic attack. Rog Phillips's 1947 story, "So Shall Ye Reap," pictures most of humanity perishing during an all-out atomic attack, with only a select group able to reach safety in underground shelters. On the surface remain mutants who subsist by eating giant cockroaches and die at fifteen years of age. Within fifty years, it is learned, the contamination will end all life. Will Jenkins's *The Murder of the U.S.A.* (1946) finds the U.S. attacked by hundreds of nuclear missiles from an unidentified enemy. "The Blast," by Stuart Cloete, serialized in *Collier's*, is the fictionalized autobiography of a survivor of an atomic sneak attack thought to be launched by Russians but actually initiated by Nazi refugees living in Latin America. Most people who survive the initial blast subsequently die from radiation, although the survivor lives on as a lonely hunter.[19]

By 1947, the enemy within science-fiction stories changed from Nazis or unknown powers to the Soviet Union. In one of the earlier battles with

For more serious science-fiction readers, magazines like *Beyond Fiction*, *Amazing Stories*, *Astounding Science-Fiction*, *Fantastic Adventures*, *Marvel Science Fiction*, *Thrilling Wonder Stories*, *Galaxy Science Fiction*, *Orbit Science Fiction*, and *Weird Tales* provided truly astounding atomic narratives.

the communist menace, *World Aflame: The Russian-American War of 1950* (1947) by Leonard Engel and Emanuel A. Piller, 35 million Americans die in a nuclear-biological fight to the finish. Philip Wylie's *The Smuggled Atom Bomb* (1948) involves a sinister plot to carry atomic bombs into the country and detonate them in strategic locations, rather than conduct an attack by air that could be thwarted. Robert Heinlein's "Project Nightmare" (1953) finds the Soviet Union threatening to trigger atomic mines in thirty-eight American cities unless the country becomes a "People's Republic." When the U.S. refuses, the Soviets detonate the mines; paranormals are able to disarm all but one, which obliterates Cleveland. The country then launches its own atomic strike against the Soviet Union, putting an end to future threats.

Occasionally, however, the strike-retaliate scenario does not work, as in Robert Heinlein's "The Year of the Jackpot" (1952). This story finds the Soviet Union launching an all-out attack on the United States, followed by this nation throwing back all of its atomic arsenal. But the massive forces of destruction result in the sun exploding. The story, accentuating the most frightening outcome of atomic war, ends with the hero and heroine holding one another as the world ends: "He glanced down at the journal, still open beside him. 1739 A.D. and 2165. He did not need to add up the two figures and divide by two to reach the answer. Instead he clutched fiercely at her hand, knowing with an unexpected and overpowering burst of sorrow that 1952 was The End."[20]

Again, as reflected in the movies and other narratives, the atomic fatalism projected in one story was countered by spiritual rebirth in another. In Arthur C. Clarke's *Childhood's End* (1954), for example, Earth explodes "like a bombarded atom in a glorious imaginative fusion of spiritual illumination and nuclear explosion." Other postholocaust stories, emphasizing the ability to begin anew, included Leigh Brackett's *The Long Tomorrow* (1955), set in a post-atomic Mennonite community, and John Wyndham's *Re-Birth* (1955), which focuses on religious survivors who interpret the nuclear disaster as God's punishment. A concurrent theme to rebirth was the body-takeover: the persistent fear of losing your identity or becoming dehumanized. This was typified by Robert Heinlein's *The Puppet Masters* (1951), the story of giant slugs that attach themselves to people, turning them into mindless zombies, and Jack Finney's "The Body Snatchers," first appearing as a serialized story in *Collier's* and later in book and cinematic form as *Invasion of the Body Snatchers*.[21]

Comic books, which complemented science-fiction magazines, also contained a diverse range of atomic narratives. Dick Tracy began wearing an atom-powered, two-way wrist radio in 1946. In *The Battle of the Atoms*,

which appeared shortly after Hiroshima, Superman overcomes his nemesis Luthor's paralyzing atomic blast from a molecular impulsion beam that
melts steel, rocks, and trees. Captain Marvel joined the fray, too, battling
"the dread atomic way." By the early 1950s, Superman and Captain Marvel had been joined by such titles as *Strange Adventures* (1950), *Captain
Science* (1950), *Flying Saucers* (1950), *Strange Worlds* (1950), *Earthmen on
Venus* (1951), *Space Detective* (1951), *Space Busters* (1952), *Space Western*
(1952), and *John Carter of Mars* (1952).[22] *Panic,* published by Tiny Tot
Comics, caught the essence of the Atomic Generation on its May 1954
cover, which showed a boy exploding an atomic bomb in the middle of
his train set. Even Rex the Wonder Dog struggled against a 150-million-
year-old dinosaur unleashed by an atomic explosion, while fictional hero
Tom Swift battled the Kranjovians in *Tom Swift and His Atomic Earth
Blaster.* Comics also added a realistic Cold War slant to the bomb in titles
like *Atomic Attack* and *Atom-Age Combat.*

In December 1950, Marvel Comics introduced the first, but short-
lived, superhero of the new decade: *Marvel Boy.* Seventeen-year-old Bob
Grayson (aka, Marvel Boy) was raised on the planet Uranus by his father
but has returned to his real home, Earth. In his first adventure, Marvel
Boy discovers that evil aliens have kidnapped a scientist who has invented
an "anti-radioactivity ray" as protection against atomic weapons. Yet it is
soon learned that the scientist is actually the leader of the alien communists, and the antinuke ray is actually designed to weaken American
defenses. The final triumphant scene finds Marvel Boy dropping an atomic
bomb on the alien hideout in Arizona. Thus, Marvel Boy's ability to take
control of the situation and to wield absolute power in defeating the enemy
was merely another version of the increasing emphasis on self-reliance as
a requisite for survival in the Atomic Age.

The emphasis on self-reliance also is evident in another superhero,
the Human Torch. In a 1953 comic book, the Human Torch is awakened
from his burial spot in Yucca Flat, Nevada, by an atomic bomb test. Bursting once again into flames, he explodes out of his grave and exclaims,
"That terrific blast gave me a greater power than I had before! I couldn't
understand how or why ... not until I looked back as I blazed thru the sky
and saw a giant mushroom cloud rising from the post where I had been
buried!" In the first issue of *Captain Flash,* introduced in November 1954,
the hero fulfills Holden Caulfield's dream by straddling an atomic rocket
as it leaves an enemy launching pad. As he grabs hold, he exclaims, "I made
it! Now if I can only stop this baby before it hits Atom City!" All these
action superheroes conveyed mastery over the atomic bomb rather than
being victimized, even vaporized, by it. For those reading these stories, the

Panic, published by Tiny Tot Comics, caught the essence of the Atomic Generation on its May 1954 cover, which showed a boy exploding an atomic bomb in the middle of his train set. (Copyright © William M. Gaines, Agent, Inc., reprinted with permission.)

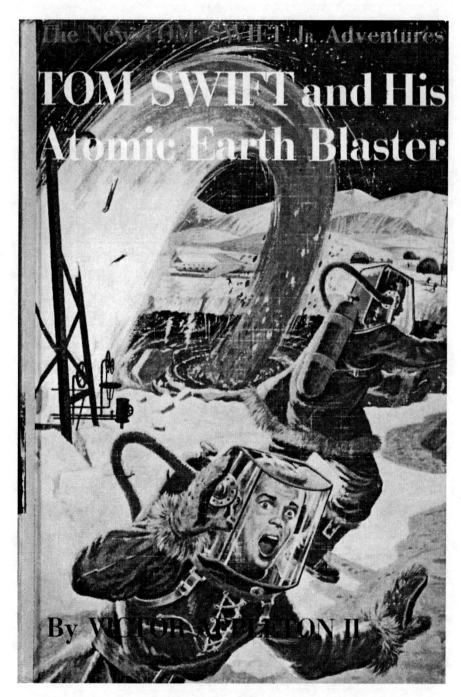

The New TOM SWIFT Jr. Adventures

TOM SWIFT and His Atomic Earth Blaster

By VICTOR APPLETON II

Young teens could keep informed about the atomic bomb by reading comic books or by following the adventures of Tom Swift, as the junior inventor battled the Kranjovians in *Tom Swift and His Atomic Earth Blaster*.

ability to overcome fear and survive against all odds was unquestionably a welcome respite from the more pessimistic atomic narratives they often encountered.[23]

Two works accentuating this pessimism were George Orwell's *Nineteen Eighty-Four* (1949) and Ray Bradbury's *Fahrenheit 451* (1953). Both delivered strong commentaries about contemporary society within post-atomic narratives. Orwell's story, set thirty years after an atomic war, describes a society controlled by Big Brother, who uses telescreens, the Thought Police, and the Two Minute Hate to indoctrinate and manipulate the masses. The protagonist, Winston, fights to retain his self-identity, individualism, and even his emotions. He writes in his diary: "To the future or to the past, to a time when thought is free, when men are different from one another and do not live alone — to a time when truth exists and what is done cannot be undone: From the age of uniformity, from the age of solitude, from the age of Big Brother, from the age of doublethink — greetings!" Winston is attracted to Julia, a younger woman, whose "body seemed to be pouring some of its youth and vigor into his." But Big Brother wins out in the end, destroying Julia and transforming Winston into another constructive member of society. Yet Orwell makes it clear that society's victory is the individual's defeat. As Winston gazes at Big Brother's telescreen image, "two gin-scented tears trickled down the sides of his nose. But it was all right, everything was all right, the struggle was finished. He had won the victory over himself. He loved Big Brother." The irony rendered by Orwell reinforced the belief that the individual had no hope in a world ravaged by atomic war and controlled by an authoritarian force. Also of note is the death of Julia, representing youthful beauty, innocence, and, above all, hope.[24]

Montag, Bradbury's protagonist, is a fireman charged not with extinguishing fires but with burning books in a post-atomic society in the twenty-first century. And, like Winston, he seeks to maintain his individuality and sense of identity by opposing the government's desire to destroy the written word. Montag also finds hope through a younger woman (seventeen-year-old Clarisse) who remains fiercely free of government control until she is killed. Two atomic wars have been won since 2022; now the government uses two-way television to monitor the populace, and burns books to keep them pacified. Montag refuses to succumb to social conformity, escaping to the country where he meets the last remaining free-thinkers: "human books" who have memorized the great works until such time that they can be reprinted. The story concludes with another atomic war, although unlike Orwell, Bradbury implies that in the midst of massive destruction, life will continue and society will be reborn.

As he ponders the future, Montag remembers something he once had read: "And on either side of the river [there was] a tree of life, which bore twelve manner of fruits, and yielded her fruit every month; And the leaves of the tree were for the healing of the nations."[25]

Bradbury envisioned a world scarred by atomic war. He, like Orwell, also portrayed a world where individuality was threatened by social control and authoritarian power, obvious allusions to the threat of communism. Although Bradbury offered a postholocaust ending, he reflected Orwell's overall negativity toward the massification of society. To both authors, media had become the primary means of monitoring the populace and placating it at the same time. These books are clearly atomic narratives because they contain themes of atomic destruction, loss of individuality, lack of control, fear of conformity, and alienation from society. From this perspective, both books contain similar themes found in film noir movies; teenpics such as *The Wild One* and *Rebel Without a Cause*; and countless science-fiction movies. More important, these themes are evident in popular literature, including *The Catcher in the Rye,* Sloan Wilson's *The Man in the Gray Flannel Suit*, and Saul Bellow's *Seize the Day*.

Many social issues or themes, including gender, corresponded with those projected in atomic narratives. Just as females were portrayed as curvacious helpmates, reproductive vessels, and nurturing homemakers in general-interest movies, popular literature, and television programs, so, too, were these characterizations found in science-fiction stories. This was particularly true in *1984* and *Fahrenheit 451*. Both books placed the hope for the future on female youth: Julia in *1984* and Clarisse in *Fahrenheit 451*. In Theodore Sturgeon's "Thunder and Roses" (1947), a female stops men from destroying the world. The story concerns a devastating sneak attack of atomic bombs designed for maximum radioactive poisoning. The attack wipes out the entire nation except for a few hundred people, who are dying off rapidly. A sergeant, faced with the decision to launch a retaliatory strike and destroy the world, is dissuaded from pulling the death switch by Starr Anthim, a female pop singer. Thus, as Albert Berger has suggested, we have the additional theme of woman, guardian of the home and hearth, overcoming "the rapacity of an unbridled masculine will [for] power and violence."[26]

Science-fiction magazines served as a stimulating genre for adolescents and adults alike. In many stories, women were exploited as shapely backdrops or objects of sexual gratification for men. Ward Moore's two stories, "Lot" (1953) and "Lot's Daughter" (1954), for example, dealt with a husband who flees an atomic inferno with his daughter, by whom he has a child. The daughter then commits suicide. Other writers portrayed women in delusional tones, particularly in the context of motherhood. Philip Wylie's book, *Tomorrow!* (1954), describes a gutted woman who attempts to stuff her fetus back inside her body, and another woman carrying the remains of her dead baby.[27] Judith Merril's "That Only a Mother," published in 1948, is about the pregnant wife of a nuclear scientist who works at Oak Ridge, site of the Manhattan Project. She is worried about the increasing number of mutants appearing after a low-level atomic war. After her daughter is born, though, she writes to her absent husband, explaining that their daughter is perfectly normal and not to worry. When he eventually returns home, he finds an exceptionally bright baby who has been born without a skeleton. The story ends with these words: "*She didn't know.* His hands, beyond control, ran up and down the soft-skinned baby body, the sinuous, limbless body. *Oh, God, dear God—* his head shook and his muscles contracted in a bitter spasm of hysteria. His fingers tightened on his child—*Oh, God, she didn't know....*" The mother's love created a self-delusion, not allowing the mother to see the *real* baby.

In *Shadow of the Hearth* (1950), Merril tells the more positive story of Gladys Mitchell, a happily married housewife who lives in a suburb of New York City. One day, she hears on the radio that Manhattan has been bombed and immediately begins to worry about the safety of Jon, her husband, and the potential of radiation affecting her children. Although atomic bombs have devastated America's cities, the novel ends with the belief that Gladys, Jon, and her family will be reunited. H. Bruce Franklin has commented, "[T]he situation gradually forces her to unleash repressed strengths, and her selfless nurturing, now coupled to an awakening consciousness, helps save her family."[28]

In 1954, Merril's story of atomic survival moved from the bookshelves to a mass audience when it was broadcast on the *TV Hour* under the title "Atomic Attack." At the same time that science-fiction editors began expressing their displeasure with so-called "atomic doom" stories, television quickly exploited the anxieties, fears, and even fascination with atomic narratives. But television's impact was even more pronounced than either print or movies because of its reach into the home and its socializing role, particularly among children and adolescents. In her book, *Make Room for TV: Television and the Family Ideal in Postwar America*, Lynn Spigel argues that despite concerns about its detrimental influence on children, television was heavily promoted to families with children. The emphasis on the family circle of television watching (i.e., televiewing), she points out, succeeded in encouraging families to gather together in the evening to watch the small screen. Further, television's creation of hyperrealism (or sense of "being there") made a more dramatic impact on younger family members, who usually watched along with their parents between 7:00 and 10:00 P.M., the prime-time hours of adult programming. By the early 1950s, studies found those teenagers with television sets in the home watched close to four hours a day and up to thirty hours a week, with more than half selecting their own programs. Teenagers even flexed their televiewing autonomy by selecting programs deemed inappropriate by their parents, such as science fiction and westerns.[29] Addressing the Conference on Reading in the Family in 1953, Robert Lewis Shayon, author of *Television and Our Children*, lamented that children watched television "hopping from a blow on the head to an embrace to a dance to a song to a sale to a corpse to a real war in a foreign land to a fantasy war in stellar space — all in a nervous, staccato, incessant rhythm of sense impression piled upon sense impression without human pact, relentlessly, mechanically, mesmerically."[30]

The dichotomous nature of television programming, described succinctly by Shayon, presented the same contradictory image of American society as found in movies, in print, and in the classroom. From the likes of Burns and Allen, Lucy, Ozzie and Harriett, and Milton Berle, to the fantasy exploits of Captain Video and Superman, to televised explosions of the atomic bomb and the explosive rhetoric of the McCarthy hearings, parents and their children received a barrage of incongruous and often violent messages about their world. Shayon and other social critics focused their concern less on the seemingly innocuous nature of variety shows and situation comedies than on the excessive violence being depicted on everything from children's Saturday morning cartoons to prime-time dramas. Even in these early years of the new medium, the trend toward violence for ratings was evident. A Chicago study conducted in 1953 documented some ninety-three murders occurring on television in one week. In addition, there were seventy-eight shootings, forty-four gunfights, thirty-three sluggings, nine kidnappings, plus knifings, whiplashings, poisonings, and even two bombings. The study concluded that the television industry and parents alike had to work together to minimize any effects from this content.[31]

The full impact of these effects must be understood within the context of the early 1950s. Conrad Phillip Kottak, in his book, *Prime-Time Society*, describes this era as Stage 1 in television viewing, in which the fascination with the technology results in devoted, almost obsessive, gazes "usually glued to the set."[32] Unquestionably, the hyperrealism of television, combined with its newness, led to an emotional involvement with the medium. The violence raging across the screen — as with the laughter and drama as well — thus became a representation, or extension, of reality.

George Gerbner, who has conducted numerous studies of television's impact on society, has called television the most pervasive medium in American culture, clearly dominating "the symbolic environment of modern life." As a narrative form, providing both visual and textual material, television promotes what he terms "mainstreaming," or the cultivation of a general concept of social reality encompassing beliefs, ideologies, social behavior, and world views. Additionally, television serves to amplify certain issues more salient to certain groups, which results in a more intense cultivation of the mainstreaming effect. In other words, the television world that tends to reflect the reality of particular groups becomes more closely associated with the actual world. Residents in the inner city, for instance, are more likely to associate with television's portrayal of urban violence; likewise, children and adolescents, who fear the dangers associated with adult society, including atomic war, are more likely, strictly from watching television, to have their fears and anxieties intensified. Television thus serves two functions: to solidify cultural bonding, and to create an identifiable representation of reality (i.e., a hyperreality).[33]

In 1951, NBC framed violence within the reality of the Atomic Age by stressing the importance of being prepared in case of attack in a seven-part series called *Survival*, which reached an estimated 12 million households. *Out of This World*, a mixture of science fiction and science lectures, and *Tales of Tomorrow*, a science-fiction anthology series, were introduced in 1952. In addition to *TV Hour*, other drama programs occasionally dealing with science-fiction themes were *Ford Theatre* (1954), *Front Row Theatre* (1955), and *Four Star Playhouse* (1955). *Inner Sanctum*, premiering in 1954, presented programs with such doomsday titles as "Face of Fear," "Tomorrow Never Comes," "Hour of Darkness," "Face of the Dead," "Pattern of Fear," and "The Fatal Hour." Additional family-oriented atomic-theme programs included "The Secret Weapon of 117," *Stage 7*; "Visit to a Small Planet," *TV Playhouse*; "Experiment Perilous," *Summer Theatre 54*; "U.F.O." and "It Might Happen Tomorrow," *Studio One*; "Flash of Darkness," *The Medic*; and "Ring Once for Death," *Studio 57*. *Science Fiction Theatre*, introduced in 1955, brought the atomic peril home each week in such titles as "The Negative Man," "The World Below," "Hour of Nightmare," and "Beyond."[34]

Americans also watched atomic developments on news and informational programs like *Meet the Press*, *The Big Issue*, and *The American Week*, while adolescents tuned in to *Junior Press Conference*, *Youth Takes A Stand*, *Johns Hopkins Science Review*, and *Youth Wants to Know*. In the spring of 1952, millions of Americans from coast to coast witnessed the first live broadcast of an atomic blast. Over the next few years, viewers would watch and listen to such noted journalists as Walter Cronkite, John Cameron Swayze, and Bob Considine as they described a hundred atmospheric atomic tests conducted in the Nevada Test Site between 1951 and 1958.[35]

Neither adults nor their children were being exposed to these radiating topics for the first time. Although this was the first television generation, radio still dominated homes well into the 1950s. And radio had begun grappling with the Atomic Age immediately upon news of Hiroshima. On the night of August 6, 1945, legendary radio broadcaster H.V. Kaltenborn set the stage for what was to later echo over America's airwaves: "For all we know, we have created a Frankenstein! We must assume that with the passage of only a little time, an improved form of the new weapon can be turned against us."[36] *The Human Adventure*, carried on the Mutual Broadcasting Network every Wednesday night, presented the first dramatization of the atomic bombing on August 9, 1945. *Bob Emery's Rainbow House*, broadcast Saturday mornings over the Mutual Broadcasting Network, devoted a program to the national high school debate question, "Do you believe that the United Nations Organization will prevent another world war during your lifetime?" CBS presented a special radio documentary, "The Sunny Side of the Atom," in June 1947 designed to change attitudes toward atomic energy from fear to optimism. A follow-up study indicated the program had been a success, despite such lines as, "When you get deeper and deeper into the secrets of life, you find them so fascinating you sometimes forget that the atom can kill you." Other programs included an eyewitness account of the Bikini atomic tests; a 20-part series titled "You and the Atom"; and an atomic bomb special called "The Fifth Horseman." The U.S. Air Force helped radio networks produce dramatizations of Soviet attacks that always managed to have some enemy bombers reach their American targets.

The Federal Radio Education Committee, within the U.S. Office of Education, recommended programs for high school students, including *American School of the Air*, *World Neighbors*, *Town Meeting of the Air*, *The Town Hall*, *The March of Science*, *Our Foreign Policy*, *Headline Edition*, and *University of Chicago Round Table*. *The Town Hall*, for example, presented a number of programs on the atomic bomb a month after the attack on Hiroshima, including "Who Should Control the Atomic Bomb?," "Does the Atomic Bomb Make World Government Essential Now?," and "Should We Share the Secret of the Atomic Bomb with Any Other Nation?" These programs were joined in the early 1950s by *Edward R. Murrow*, *Leading Question*, *Meet the Press*, and *American Forum of the Air*.[37]

When youth turned the radio dial to listen to the latest music, they often were exposed to atomic lyrics as well. In April 1946, "When the Atomic Bomb Fell," by Karl Davis and Harty Taylor, proclaimed that the bomb was "the answer to our fighting boys' prayers." On May 1, 1946, the Buchanan Brothers and Fred Kirby released individual versions of "Atomic Power," a song that quickly hit the *Billboard* charts and was covered by seven other artists in the next year. Other atomic songs exploding onto the airwaves in 1946 were "You're My Atom Bomb Baby," "There Is a Power Greater Than Atomic," "Old Man Atom," "Atom Buster," "Atomic Boogie," "Atomic Cocktail," "Atomic Did It," "Atom and Evil," and "When They Found the Atomic Power." The next few years saw such hits as "Jesus Hits Like An Atom Bomb" (1949), "When That Hell Bomb Falls" (1949), "When They Drop the Atomic Bomb" (1950), "Brush the Dust from the Old Bible" (1950), "Great Atomic Power" (1951), "Advice to Joe" (1951), and "Sh-Boom" (1954). Roy Acuff's "Advice to Joe" fused the fight against communism with the battle of atomic supremacy. The refrain, directed at Joseph Stalin, went "You will see the lightning flashing, hear atomic thunders roll/When Moscow lies in ashes, God have mercy on your soul."[38] When Bill Haley and His Comets first hit the pop charts in 1954 with "(We're Gonna) Rock Around the Clock"—perhaps the most played rock 'n' roll record of all time — teens listening to the flip side heard "Thirteen Women (And Only One Man in Town)." In this Atomic Age classic, a man dreams about being the only male left after an H-bomb attack, along with thirteen women.[39]

For the younger audience — those wearing their Lone Ranger Atomic Ring, compliments of Kix cereal — radio brought atomic narratives to life in such programs as *Captain Midnight, Superman, Space Patrol,* and *Tom Corbett, Space Cadet. Jack Armstrong, the All-American Boy* had searched for uranium in 1940 to take back to his high school science teachers, who were attempting to split the atom. Following the war, he faced more harrowing dangers. Soon after Vic Hardy is introduced as head of the Scientific Bureau of Investigation, Jack and his friends Betty and Billy Fairfield enlist and spend their final radio days protecting the country against mobsters with "superatomic knickknacks." The last broadcast in 1951 concludes with Vic warning that if a foreign power obtains the "cosmo-tomic energizer," America would become a pauper country; at which point Billy exclaims, "Golly! We *are* playing for big stakes!"[40]

As radio serials disappeared (only two were on the air in 1955), televised science-fiction sagas quickly replaced them. *Captain Video,* introduced in 1948, ran until 1956. *Space Patrol* (1950–1956) starred Ed Kemmer as Commander Buzz Corry. As grownups took care of the world's problems, the youngest members of the Atomic Generation were glued to the set, watching such terrifying sagas as "The Deadly Run Gun," "The Atom Bomb," "Danger: Radiation," "The Exploding Stars," "The Mutation Bomb," "The Deadly Radiation Chamber," and "The Plot in the Atomic Plant." Each week, *Tom Corbett, Space Cadet* (1950–1956) pulled back the black curtain on stories like "The Asteroid of Death," "Spaceship of Death," "Comet of Death," and "An Exercise for Death." *Flash Gordon* (1953) joined the fray in "The Breath of Death," "The Dancing Death," "The Red Planet of Death," and "The Race Against Time."

Jon Hall, as Dr. Thomas Reynolds in *Ramar of the Jungle* (1952), discovered an atomic poison gas that agents wanted to test on a tribal village in "Dark Venture." George Reeves brought *Superman* to life in 1953 and carried the battle through the 1957 television season. Cliff Robertson starred as *Rod Brown of the Rocket Rangers* (1953–1954), who waged a never-ending battle against invaders from Dimension X, the planet of ice, radioactive men, and the world of the doomed. *Rocky Jones, Space Ranger* (1954–1955) fought his way through "Menace from Outer Space," "Inferno in Space," and "The Cold Sun." *Captain Midnight*'s (1954–1958) first show was "Murder by Radiation." *The Atom Squad* (1953) featured a heroic trio who worked out of a camouflaged New York City headquarters and thwarted communist spies in such episodes as "The Bomb That Wouldn't Stand Still," "The Merchants of Death," and "The Five Steps to the Kremlin," in which the Atom Squad sneaks inside the Kremlin to find the only person who can disarm an atomic bomb. By the time *Commando Cody* joined the television wars in 1955 to once again fight the "Atomic Peril," this generation was already overexposed to a decade of cosmic rays.[41]

John Campbell, long-time science-fiction editor, has written, "Fiction is simply dreams written out; science fiction consists of the hopes and dreams and fears (for some dreams are nightmares) of a technically-based society."[42] The likelihood of an atomic war radiated through all mediums between 1945 and 1955: movies, television, magazines, comics, and books. Through their exposure to these mediums, adolescents were thus able to observe the threat of the atomic bomb and the social repercussions from this threat within apparently diverse, even highly farfetched, narratives.

From the believable to the ridiculous, this generation came of age with more than an ample supply of stimulants for their hopes and fears—and nightmares—as they prepared for an uncertain future in a brave new atomic world. The remaining and more important issue, however, is how America's postwar youth reacted to these stimulants: the myriad atomic narratives and the broader social narrative of the atom that framed their experiential reality.

7

"...to Escape the Fury of
the Blast": Young Voices
of a New Generation

Please God, let us all perish in the same catastrophe.
—Child's prayer, 1945[1]

The vast extent to which the atomic bomb imbued postwar popular culture is readily apparent. Ascertaining the significance of the atomic bomb's implications on America's youth, however, presents a more difficult challenge. As Lawrence Levine notes, historians all too frequently omit the participants' role in defining the popular culture, failing to recognize the process by which particular groups or individuals interpret and assign meanings to the myriad cultural expressions constituting their social reality. Documenting the narrative content and themes of movies, books, magazines, television, and radio may illuminate the cultural currents of any given era. Yet without acknowledging the participants' interaction with these narratives, much of history remains unstated, even inaccurate. "Audiences come to Popular Culture," Levine writes, "with a past, with ideas, with values, with expectations, with a sense of how things are and should be.... Thus both the performer and the audience have a role to play in determining the meaning and nature of the production and become collaborators with the creator."[2]

The audience — in this case, postwar adolescents— were not passive receptors of the popular culture; rather, they interacted with the culture around them, and translated social and political attitudes, beliefs, and policies (the social narrative of the atom) as well as atomic narratives to fit their values, needs, and expectations. From watching science-fiction movies and Saturday morning serials on television, to reading John

Hersey's *Hiroshima* and the latest *Marvel Boy* comic book, the Atomic Generation actively participated in giving atomic narratives specific relevance within their own perspective, both as diverse individuals and as part of an emerging subculture.

Levine argues further that it is dangerous to divide the world too neatly into reality and representations of reality because "the latter — the representations— when they become embodied in theater, tales, radio, movies, become forms of reality themselves." This does not imply that audiences confuse representation of reality with reality itself. Instead, according to Levine, the setting in which the representation occurs constitutes another reality that must be considered as well. This social reality provides the audience with an opportunity both to exhibit and to learn values, lessons, and behavior.[3]

The following student poems, essays, letters to the editor, newspaper articles, and other writings are offered as a qualitative sampling of the Atomic Generation. Editorials are included as well, even though it is recognized that among the objectives of school newspapers was the reinforcement of educational objectives. Nonetheless, these editorials were written by students, and thus provide insights into their attitudes. Taken together, these narratives reveal that while youths undoubtedly shared a strong, internalized sense of their historical placement, understanding clearly the intrinsic dangers of the Atomic Age, they also attempted, each in his or her own way, to grapple with the threats of war and possible world destruction.

Moreover, these narratives exemplify the contradictory themes projected throughout postwar culture. These adolescents, writing between 1945 and 1955, endorse democratic precepts. They promote values inculcated by an educational system and society bent on preparing them for their mission to ensure the future of democracy. And they endorse the need to defeat the inimical forces of totalitarianism in order to protect civilization from destroying itself. For many, hope for the future depends upon spiritual faith and international harmony; others convey a sense of fatalism. Some even articulate a quiet protest against a society considered nationalistic, indifferent to individual needs, and headed toward oblivion — all themes soon to become the slogans of a younger generation coming of age during the turbulent 1960s. Most important, these narratives verify an awareness of the atom as a confrontational force. In the words of Norman Ryder, the atomic bomb and its multifarious implications became the "foci of crystallization of the mentality" of those coming of age in the late 1940s and 1950s.[4]

For those entering high school at the conclusion of the Second World

War, the immediate challenge was learning how to adapt to a world at peace. "For the first time in four years," said an editorial in *The Southwest* (High School) *Trail* in Kansas City, Missouri, "the halls ... are filled with students who are going to and from their classes in an atmosphere far different from that which they have ever known before in their association with the secondary schools. This atmosphere is peace." The editorial continued:

> During this great and devastating war, Southwest students have learned much of the horrors of such a conflict and the hardships at home that go with them. Alumni have bled and died on the far-flung battle-fields of the world so that we could be free from those forces of evil which took root in Germany and Japan. At home we faced such perplexities as rationing, crowded transportation facilities, and clothing shortages. All in all, we became pretty tired of war and its complications.
>
> But — now that the war has ended, what shall be our attitude? Will we become frivolous and carefree, slackening in our lessons and duties? It's up to each one of us individually to see to it that this doesn't happen.
>
> When in the science class, remember the atomic bomb and all the other scientific strides which our country has made during this war — and remember that to keep peace, we must be scientifically "tops." When in a social studies class, learn well the history and mechanism of other countries as well as our own, for they do much to help you understand recent developments in the world.
>
> When in any class, no matter how large or small, we must strive for perfection — for this right of free education in a democracy was not easily won. Life blood was spilt for that privilege. We must not fail them, those who bled and died. It's up to us now.[5]

On the fourth anniversary of Pearl Harbor, the same newspaper reminded students that although peace had been achieved, a new power had been unleashed. In language repeated in untold atomic narratives, the editorial also framed the essential issue confronting all Americans as choosing between life or death:

> The elusive atom, sought after for centuries, has finally been isolated and smashed. In smashing the atom, we have discovered that inconceivable power is unleashed. This was demonstrated on a desert in New Mexico and taught the Japs the hard way over Nagasaki and Hiroshima.
>
> How can we be sure the world is ready for such unearthly power? Is our code of ethics sufficient to accept atomic energy? Even if the ethics of the United States should be upon a high enough level to receive the smashed atom, and turn its incomparable power towards the dove of peace, what of the remainder of the world? Give the power to Japan or Germany and there you have the base for World War III.

Do not answer these questions hastily. They contain the essence of future civilization. To ignore them is to challenge the continued existence of the earth. Who knows? The earth might disintegrate under the devastating effect of the infinite streams of neutrons emitted from atomic fusion.

There is but one statement sufficient to administer a warning about atomic power. It comes from the Bible, the book of the ages, and states simply: "I have set before ye good and evil, life and death. Choose ye good that ye may live."[6]

Although 1945 had brought an end to war, the year was "sad sometimes, and then joyous, but with an overall cast of gloom," according to another editorial. "We saw the establishment of the United Nations Organization," it continued, "the last hope for preservation in the progress of mankind. And we saw a new form of energy developed and brought into use in a deadly manner to produce the atomic bomb."[7] As 1946 began, students wrote that "we are now beginning a new year. This year ... is one of most hopeful anticipation, because in it will possibly be determined whether man is to dwell peacefully on the face of the earth and enjoy its growing benefits or if he is continuously to argue and war with his fellow man and ultimately either eliminate himself or be forced to burrow deep into the earth to escape war's ravagement."[8]

Following the war, adolescents confronted a world they were told might literally blow up at any moment. As a result, many considered maintaining the peace and safeguarding democracy as requisites to life itself. For seventeen-year-old Marcia Hildreth, a student at Deering High School in Portland, Maine, these were times of perilous challenge. The human race would either learn to get along peacefully or be forced to "escape the fury of the blast." Her poem, "A Plea for Democracy," appeared in the April 1, 1946, issue of *Senior Scholastic*:

> If choice of a disease were left to us,
> Who must in later time succumb to it,
> We would do well to choose the ills of man
> And shrink from those which man himself inflicts.
> Illness of the mind, the tender bud,
> Source of man's rise and cause too of his fall,
> Do rip the very roots of sanity,
> Resetting in their place a deadly plant,
> An all-consuming weed that bends and twists
> And snaps the mind at last by its swift growth.
>
> A mind-disease is fear, a torture rack,
> That stretches endless night and smothers sleep,
> That chains poor souls forever to its power

And whips that sensitivity which lifts
Man from the lower ranks of beasts and yet
Subordinates its victims to itself.

Fears of starvation, insecurity,
Toss men like flying foam from wave to wave,
Till to escape the fury of the blast
They grasp for safety at the nearest port.
What matter if that port contain the means
To dash to earth the sacred pyramid,
The record of man's slow and stumbling climb
From beast to intellectual freedom.
Twinkling with names like stars, it shines forth as
A Christmas tree set in a shabby world.
But they are blind: A ram calls, "Follow me
For I can give you life devoid of fear."
The others jump; but one remains behind,
Regards the pyramid, then turns and leaps.

The tall sun shines without impediment.
A small child near the ruins finds a page,
A yellow, trampled, old, forgotten page,
A line, "These are the times." These are the times.

Even as America returned to peace, the amplification of the potential risk of another war — a more horrific atomic war — made this generation realize rather quickly that it occupied a critical place in history. Its responsibility, as outlined in atomic narratives both inside and outside the classroom, was to safeguard America and save the world from atomic destruction. In 1962, Tom Hayden and his cohorts wrote in the Port Huron Statement, "Our work is guided by the sense that we may be the last generation in the experiment with living."[9] For those who had journeyed from childhood to young adulthood in the early 1950s, that catastrophic sense was born on August 6, 1945. A poem appearing in a 1946 yearbook captured the importance of America's youth:

O Youth, the world is in your hands;
A tragedy of war, it still
Remembers peace and understands
Life's formerly ecstatic thrill.
From you mankind derives its hope
For lasting bonds of harmony;
Yours is the future's horoscope,
And yours is opportunity.[10]

The opportunity to build a better future would be challenging, indeed, as the Atomic Age unfolded. America's youth encountered their adolescence in the midst of atomic fallout — real and perceived, factual and fictional. Kansas City student Dorothy Shearer addressed youth's choice in improving the world situation in 1946. "We face an era of revolution in human history," she wrote, "an era of momentous changes." Youth could either drag through the atomic crisis and surrender under its stress, according to Shearer, or create "something beneficial to all mankind."[11] School newspapers often emphasized the need for students to remain positive and active. Without their commitment to peace, their dedication to democracy, said one editorial, the world might not be there when they grow up:

> Look around you. These boys and girls you see now, today, are the men and women of tomorrow. Look at yourself. Do you seriously feel that you will be able to take your place in the world — this great world of ours that might, at any minute, be plunged into an inferno?
>
> Many of today's teen-agers don't realize just how much depends upon their stability and character. For most students, high school life is the last grip on childhood. From this carefree life they must meet the world, and the demands it puts upon them....
>
> Think ahead, prepare now for the future.... This is our country and will always be great if today's youth are prepared to be tomorrow's leaders. Set your goal high, and strive toward it. Keep the ideals of your countrymen before you, and remember who you are![12]

Joachim Ries's essay, "A Bicycle Without Wheels," was published in *Senior Scholastic* in 1947. In words more commonly associated with the 1960s protest movement, Ries espoused an almost desperate tone concerning the heavy responsibility of his generation. "We can do nothing about the past, little for the present," Ries wrote, "but we have in our grasp a powerful and promising future. What is this future? What is the future of any generation if not its youth?" Ries voiced his concern over an oppressive society that sought to repress youth. He continued:

> To tell a man that he must keep his tongue is to insist that he stifle his thoughts. To tell the youth of the world that they must be seen and not heard is to betray the lives of theirs [*sic*] and the coming generation. To tell Youth to be still and wait is to murder the initiative and industry of later age.
>
> In our elders' endeavors to preserve an almost-destroyed world, they overlook the very factor which will determine their success or failure. Youth. Man *must* take notice of the world's youth. For too many years, for too many centuries, fathers have played treason to their sons. We have fallen heir to the legacy of man's delight: the savagery of war. Why cannot we "children" make the world realize that we do not intend to betray *our* descendents!
>
> The greatest enemy of today is the ironic hand of war. Yes, man has been

most ingenious in his devising of war's machinery. But where are the inventions for peace? Man has toyed with alliances, signed treaties, and attended congresses; but he has never drawn together *and listened to* those who must fight in any future battles. A World Youth Congress, no longer just a theory, is commendable; but it functions like a bicycle without wheels when the adult population takes no heed of it.

Today's Youth does not wish to waive its responsibility. Time, of course, will not loosen his hold on us, and we in turn will step down in favor of tomorrow's young men and women. But let us live for peace while we can![13]

For Yoshio Kishi, a senior at the Bronx (New York) High School of Science, the future was one of science and world cooperation. When the words of Kishi are combined with those of Hildreth and Ries, the self-awareness of postwar youth as the Atomic Generation becomes more evident. Kishi, in an article titled "What It Means to Me to be Growing Up with Nuclear Energy," wrote this:

The importance of the atomic age is easily comprehensible, ushered in as it was, abruptly and importunately by the necessity for ending war. I realize, too, what this atomic age will mean to me as a member of a generation which will have to grow up and live with the delicate knowledge of both the atomic bomb and the more beneficial atomic sciences.

In my time, most probably, there will be extensive advances in pure sciences, advances perhaps more remarkable and astounding than those which led to the development of the bomb itself....

To me, personally, the atomic age will not mean so much in terms of discoveries in biology, medicine, chemistry, physics, and engineering as in terms of the actual implications of the atomic bomb and its influence upon our society....

Advances in science must be understood by everyone or these advances will only be statistics. People will not realize or understand what to do with these uncorrelated facts. When this occurs, ignorance will foment fear and fear will arouse mistrust. Mistrust, in turn, is an ideal cauldron in which to brew war.

Without education, life would be like having a book when one could not read. It is for us, then, to see that all learn how to read.

The atomic bomb and the atomic age have succeeded in making me more aware of the importance of world cooperation and the necessity to be informed. They have illuminated sharply the necessity for myself and for others to be aware of this need.[14]

Between 1945 and 1949, the need for world cooperation was expressed as "One World or None." In other words, either a strong world government or world organization would control the development of the atom, or else there would not be a world to worry about. Although the emphasis on world government was most pronounced in the years immediately following Hiroshima, the related themes of international cooperation and brotherhood continued even into the 1950s as youth found themselves pushed closer to the front lines of the Atomic Age. The fundamental change, however, was that the initial *Blast* of the Atomic Generation heard that international cooperation — through a one-world government or the United Nations — was critical to saving the world from simply blowing up. In contrast, the *Heat* (or second wave) of the generation, those entering high school after 1950, learned that containing communism was the key to international cooperation and, thus, world peace. While the generational *Fallout*, those coming of age in the late 1950s, felt the omnipotent, inescapable power of the atom within discourses of massive retaliation and individual preparedness.

"We have discovered that isolationism is not only dangerous, but really impossible," said a 1945 high school editorial. "There cannot be such a thing because every country on the globe is influenced profoundly by all the others. We are the heirs of generations that have gone, as we are directly or indirectly the parents of all that shall be." In addition to an emphasis on international brotherhood, the same editorial raised a more specific social issue that would emerge in the years to come: the importance of racial harmony. "The beautiful tapestry that we call the American civilization," it continued, "is the fusion of many races and peoples, many varied cultures and religions. Even our language is an example of the process of give and take in all human progress."[15]

Equally concerned about the need for racial harmony, a girl from Montana wrote to *Senior Scholastic* in 1948, "If you are going to talk about democracy, I think it would be best to stick close to home and talk about undemocratic conditions that exist in our own country, such as racial prejudice, and poor conditions of sharecroppers and tenant farmers."[16] In a similar tone, a 1951 high school editorial suggested that Americans recognize the equality of their fellow citizens before they condemn the actions of foreign countries:

> We live in a critical age today, and there is one thing and only one that can save us. We who live in a democratic country find it easy to condemn foreign countries for their cruelty to each other and for their warlike acts of aggression against us and other nations, but do we face our own failures in brotherhood or our acts that often appear threatening and domineering to others?
>
> If we examine our acts and attitudes honestly, we may gain a sense of humility that will make more convincing our expressed desire for peace and our often proclaimed ideal of the dignity of every man.[17]

During these early postwar years, the issue of race relations emerged as a powerful force in America, following the defeat of Nazi Germany and learning of the horrific prison camps and crematoriums. The government, under President Truman, quickly went on record challenging segregation in the armed forces, a practice that finally ended during the Korean War. By the late 1940s, civil rights gained momentum, culminating with the Supreme Court's 1955 decision to end school segregation. Looking at the voices of youth during this period reveals, at least among some, an acute awareness of the dangers of racial strife and, conversely, the absolute necessity to adopt the tenet of brotherhood. This was the theme of Joyce Dominie Sloane's poem, "Brothers," published in *Senior Scholastic* in 1948. The seventeen-year-old student at Marymount Academy in New York City wrote:

> The crowning glory of His handiwork are we,
> To be as brothers all.
> God saw the multicolored tapestry of being—
> This flesh and blood,
> Its hopes, fears, and ambitions—
> Woven as but one.
> On earth as in His heaven,
> God made no class or difference
> Except as raised a greater soul
> Above a lower,
> And this depends upon the man himself
> For each may have God's grace as he desires,
> And each may climb the stairway to perfection
> Where God will meet His children face to face.
>
> There no question will be asked of creed or color,
> But did we love our Brothers as ourselves.[18]

As Sloane's poem illustrates, early writings of the Atomic Generation reflected the same themes found in educational and mainstream narratives about the importance of brotherhood and cooperation as requisites for world survival. *The East* (High School) *Echo* in Kansas City commented in 1946, for example, that the "atomic bomb might help weld the nations closer together so that lasting peace could be a reality instead of a plan. It is certainly a necessity."[19] Immediately following the war, hope for world peace was placed heavily upon the United Nations, which was perceived as the best alternative to world government. According to another 1946 editorial,

> [T]he problem of the atomic bomb alone is tremendous. The impact of atomic power on civilization is not yet fully realized. The atomic bomb has

rendered war, as it has been previously known, obsolete. Mankind's one hope lies in the establishment of a truly democratic world government, not a foolish speculation as to the probable affects [*sic*] of an atomic war.... Now while we are in high school, is the time to prepare ourselves as future citizens of the United Nations.[20]

In her poem, "Transition," Martha Ann Nichols amplified the need to "create one world, alert and strong":

> A war now ends; the silence rings aloud
> Against the ears of men throughout the world.
> The mighty din of battle now will cease;
> Slowly emerges the new dawn of peace.
>
> Alas, the harsh cold light shows well, too well,
> The fields which lately were a raging hell,
> Where deadly missiles through fraught space were hurled
> By men gone mad, and acrid smoke in torrents swirled.
>
> From crumpled shells of precious human life—
> The bitter tragic fruit of fatal strife—
> This silence will ring out, loud and long,
> To halls of state where men of many nations throng,
> To expiate this cruel age-old wrong,
> To create one world, alert and strong![21]

Hampton Stevens, of Kansas City's Southwest High School, argued that the creation of the atomic bomb had increased the potential for mutual self-destruction. In his award-winning oration, "Humanity Versus Nationalism," reprinted in the school newspaper, he said:

> On August 6th, 1945, an ominous cloud mushroomed over Hiroshima and declared to the world that the atomic bomb had arrived. In such a manner the last gap was closed in the wall that can block human existence from its continuance. Emphatic though it may be, the atomic bomb merely forces to immediate trial a case in the supreme court of human relations— Humanity versus Nationalism.
>
> Nationalism may be compared with feudalism, for both are outmoded forms of government. But there is one conclusive difference; the forces entailed in the struggle between feudalism and national government affected few exclusive of a small radius of the struggle itself. The struggle between world government and nationalism is similar in principle, but millions now die to settle the same issues formerly decided by the deaths of hundreds. To put it bluntly, the human race cannot survive a struggle comparable to the one in which feudalism finally expired....
>
> As science shrinks the earth and simultaneously increases each nation's potentialities for mutual and self-destruction, Necessity, the mother of Invention, pleads with us to adopt obligations towards world citizenship.

There is no such thing as an inevitable war. *IF* war comes, it will be from failure of human wisdom.

This is the important issue of the hour![22]

The underlying theme in this narrative and many others was that if world cooperation succeeded, humankind might enter a world of plenty for all; if it failed, the result would be world war — world annihilation. The same message is found in the Port Huron Statement, which cautioned that although nuclear energy could easily power entire cities, "the dominant nationstates seem more likely to unleash destruction greater than that incurred in all wars of human history." This sense of urgency, of hopes blasted away at Hiroshima, challenged the Sixties Generation to shake off its apathy and make a commitment to save the world and recapture the true democratic spirit. As these writings demonstrate, though, these warnings were not new.

In 1946, sixteen-year-old William Melvin, of Milton (Massachusetts) High School, warned of being "flattened" by something no larger than a pea. Melvin called his poem "The Bitter Apple":

> We who have tasted little of the bitter fruit
> Of a hard green apple
> Picked before its ripened redness
> Dare to speak in terms
> Of tens of thousands of creatures.
> The misused orange
> That flattened Nagasaki and vaporized
> That which was not meant to be vaporized
> Is a question of national or international policy
> Whether we should or not,
> Talked over not by those
> Who planted the tree that grew the orange
> But by the little boys who stole
> The orange from its owner.
> Some of the planters who sowed the seed
> From which the tree sprang to life
> Wish the thought had not occurred to them.
> And those who plucked with grasping fingers
> That heated orange of fire and vaporization
> Wish now to hoard its acidity.
> This is a world of little things,
> Of a man cleaning his garage, washing his car,
> Of a boy calling his dog to supper,
> A bluejay stealing suet, scaring the smaller birds,
> A man coming home early from work,
> A girl praying for her dollie [*sic*] at bedtime,

A key turning in the lock of the front door,
The sound of a bus passing at midnight,
The tick of a clock in an empty house,
A boy coming home after losing a fight —
These are little things,
Cereal and two fried eggs,
Mixed with worry over the morning headlines.

They say the size of a pea will do it now,
But we can flatten them faster than they
Can flatten us because we're bigger.
There's a hundred and thirty million of us to kill.
People disappear and life flies away
With little protest.
And now the path divides;
We inheritors of the peace must choose our way.[23]

If society — and youth — did not choose the right path, everyone understood the repercussions. Robert Blackwell, an African American student at Lincoln High School in Kansas City, Missouri, captured this "…or else" attitude in a 1948 article titled, "What Will Tomorrow Bring?" The world was at peace today, he acknowledged, but the future was uncertain:

> Today we are living in peace, but what will tomorrow bring? Man is becoming smarter in the various sciences. Will he destroy himself or will he improve the condition in which he now lives? …
> The methods of war have been revolutionized by the invention of the atomic bomb. The question now is how to control it. The world of tomorrow will probably be based on whether the U.N. controls the atom bomb or not.…
> The fate of the world depends upon how men solve the problems today. We shall either have world destruction or world peace. What will tomorrow bring?[24]

The same year, Robert Alan Levine, a sophomore at Waldon High School in New York City, voiced his concerns about world peace and world survival. "At the moment," he wrote, "a terrible spectre faces the world — a third world war — a war with the latest weapons science has provided for the mass killing of peoples. It can and must be averted." He based his formula for survival on Franklin Delano Roosevelt's four freedoms: freedom of speech, freedom of religion, freedom from want, and freedom from fear. In a tone closely reflecting the Port Huron Statement, Levine emphasized the need for world cooperation through the United Nations and endorsed individual political freedom as well as self-determination. He argued that the United States should shoulder its responsibility to make the people of the world free from want through such economic aid programs as the Marshall Plan, and overcome want for education by supporting the United Nations Organization for Education, Science, and Culture (UNESCO). He also believed freedom from fear was the paramount issue, and that this could only be accomplished by universal disarmament. "The atomic bomb has to be outlawed," Levine argued. "Its production should be stopped promptly and stockpiles scrapped." He went on to suggest that all nations accept this policy, and that the Soviet Union stop her military buildup. "This is the stand of many high school students with whom I have discussed the issue," he concluded.[25]

The dichotomy between peace and war, survival and annihilation, haunted many Americans in the late 1940s as the country struggled to contain communism and, in a metaphorical sense, to contain its innermost fears. For postwar adolescents, struggling to form a self-identity and prepare for one's social role, these issues were amplified. Some, like Mary Root, a fourteen-year-old student from North Tonawanda, New York, expressed a more fatalistic view of the future in which the world "in ashes cold lies dead." Her poem, "The Lost Hope," appeared in *Senior Scholastic*'s May 5, 1947, issue:

> O wait until the burning sun comes to an end,
> O wait until the world in ashes cold lies dead.
> Then will the hopes of man forever dwell
> In the pit of lost things that remained unsaid.
> "No more war!" "At last the perfect world!"
> "Peace on earth, good will towards fellow men."
> So have the words come flying down the years,
> The last-drawn signs of things that "might have been."
>
> But still the wars are fought and won and lost,
> And still the battles played and lost and won.
> Peace comes a little while between the wars,
> And leaves us with the things we *might* have done.
>
> But wait and when the world has disappeared,
> And when the sun gives off its golden fleece,
> Then shall the last of man look up and cry,
> "Now shall we have the everlasting peace!"

Eleanor Gibson of Kansas City's Central High School challenged her fellow students to remember war so "the world may be a realm of peace and unity." Additionally, she stressed the responsibility of her generation to meet the unprecedented challenge of working for the preservation of life itself. And she warned about not meeting this challenge. Her poem, "It Waits for Peace," was published in the school paper:

It stands abandoned by the road,
    No hint it gives that it once showed
Such lessons in the ways of life
    As unity in time of strife.

One peek into the dark inside
    You would not know how then it tried
To kindle in young minds a spark
    To blaze through years of lasting dark.
'Tis nothing but an empty room
    Enshrouded in foreboding gloom;
The vacant desks are lined with dust,
    The heating stove decayed with rust.

A generation has gone by,
    The school's last days are drawing nigh.
It's stood erect through all the years,
    Its hopes diminish varied fears.

Will students who here strove to learn
    Regard world peace with like concern;
Or will they think of their own good,
    Remembering not the things they should?

Oh, Spark, here lit in minds so young,
    Rekindle now and spread among
Our leaders so that the world may be
    A realm of peace and unity.[26]

The same year, a student at crosstown Northeast High School voiced her plea that "freedom must not die" because if it did, atomic destruction would befall America and the world. Dolores Ross titled her article "Freedom":

> The atomic bomb has become a household word and other, even more terrible weapons lurk in the dim shadows of the future. We are told that the next war will not be a long one, that it will be a matter of minutes and whoever drops the most bombs will be the victor. Now that man has a successful device invented for his own destruction he must not allow himself to be so stupid as to blindly bring about that destruction by his hesitancy to improve his condition. He must learn to live at peace with his neighbors, to reveal war as a barbarous custom and to work harmoniously for the good of all.... Freedom must not die. It is our heritage and our privilege to preserve it that humanity may live, so that the children of tomorrow may profit by the wisdom of today.[27]

At the same time that adolescents adhered to the precepts of democracy as the last hope for world civilization, they revealed through their writings an unease with the government's policies based on massive retaliation and mutual destruction — policies seen by many to be bent on destroying the country's nemesis, the Soviet Union, and possibly being destroyed in the process.

Hope for a strong world organization to ensure the peace dissipated in the late 1940s, and for the most part disappeared after the Soviet Union successfully tested its own atomic, then hydrogen, bombs. Narratives aimed at America's youth emphasized the threat of communism, and high school editorials and student writings indicate the message was heard. According to *The Southeast* (High School) *Tower* in Kansas City, youth had to stop communism, or else:

> America's youth has the greatest challenge confronting it in the history of our Republic. It is a challenge that is so great that only by careful planning and preparation can America hope to survive.
>
> Facing the world today is the father of all tyrannies. This idea, Communism, is a deadly, Godless, senseless ideology created by men whose minds were too twisted to comprehend the greatness of a free humanity. It was created by those who were too weak to travel the democratic road....
>
> We as young Americans are in our stage of preparation. Let us now prepare! We are not too young to understand what faces the world. While we may be too young to fully understand all the problems of the world, we can certainly become aware of the general challenges and responsibilities.
>
> Let us educate ourselves to the extent of being able to convince the whole wide world that democracy does work. When we assume the roles of leadership in the community, state and nation, let's be ready to win the masses not in enslavement, over to our side.[28]

Although democracy ensured freedom, communism meant the loss of freedom. And the protection of personal freedom — in terms of self-expression, individuality, and self-identity — had formed a consistent theme in atomic narratives aimed at America's youth. A 1952 high school editorial, titled "Democracy," underscored this message by warning students to oppose any legislation that might control people or deprive them of their freedoms. "Always be on your guard for any activity that has the makings of communism," it said.[29] Concurrent with this theme was the growing belief that opposing communism at all costs might actually lead to war, and war meant death. For many students, therefore, comprehending the dangers associated with communism was balanced by understanding that efforts to work together in a spirit of international cooperation would benefit all nations, all peoples. As a result, by the early 1950s the One World approach became contextualized within the new realities of the Cold War. This viewpoint was expressed by Carrie Lee Bates, of Cherry Valley, New York, who wrote to *Senior Scholastic* in 1951 to express her opinion on the current world situation:

> I don't advocate communism. I don't advocate capitalism either. In some parts of the world one might work where the other wouldn't. But how can we ever hope to solve any world problems, in the U.N. or otherwise, if people don't realize that there are two sides to every question? Can't people realize that there is something wrong about every plan and more than one thing right about another way of doing things?
>
> There have been other great nations in other times who have tried to cope with much the same problems that the U.S. and U.S.S.R. are facing today. There have been other smaller nations trying to decide "which way is for us, which side will give us the most?" What a headache it must have been to decide with one power knocking at the front door and another at the back! And in all the confusion how simple it must have been to choose the wrong one. Then the powerful nations came to blows. City after city was wrecked and destroyed. Thousands of miles of productive land was laid to waste. The nations grew weaker and then another nation rose and grew to power. Somehow that cycle never seems to end.
>
> I don't know — I guess I really don't know what I'm talking about. Most people today don't. But I — and other boys and girls like me — will have to live tomorrow in the world that our elders are making today. And we don't want war, cold war or otherwise. We want "peace on earth and good will to men" whether we happen to agree on forms of government or not. Please God, can't two ideas, both with some right and some wrong, get along together in one world?[30]

Even by 1955, at the height of the Cold War, Katie Shattuck of University High School in Urbana, Illinois, maintained her faith in avoiding war through world cooperation. In a letter to *Senior Scholastic* she pleaded for continued support of the United Nations, which she felt was still the best hope of the free world:

> One of the principal aims of the U.N. is to attempt to solve world problems. It is the hope of the free world that we can settle our differences with Russia through negotiations and avoid war. Our chances of reaching any agreements with Russia would be very slight if the U.N. could no longer be used as an organization through which we could negotiate.
>
> As futile as our efforts may seem, the U.N. is the only world organization where countries of all different political beliefs can solve problems peacefully. If it was made up of nations which agreed with one another, much of its purposes would be lost.
>
> I think that Russia should remain a member. The Communist delegates should be encouraged to speak often and loudly enough that the whole world may hear their views. If the peoples of the world can see the Communists at work, I'm sure the U.S. will win their support.[31]

Susan Vanderlyn Kohler, of Villa Victoria Academy in Trenton, New Jersey, wrote to the magazine the same year, with the same message:

> We here in America are quick to condemn those people who are a threat to our democracy. Today it is the Communists, a few years ago it was the Nazis; both have borne the brunt of our hate.
>
> Hundreds of Communists throughout the world are willing to sacrifice everything, their lives, their families, everything, to further their cause. During World War II, thousands of Germans were not only willing but did just that.
>
> God has given all men a conscience, and it is seldom that a man would fight and die for something he knew to be wrong. It is therefore quite obvious that these men believe they are right. Bad ideas have been put into their heads by a few evil leaders, who, through the use of propaganda have been able to poison thousands of minds.
>
> During World War II, the Nazi youth were a very important part of the strength of the Reich. Today throughout the U.S.S.R. children are being trained in the Communist doctrine.
>
> Therefore, do not let us hate the Communists as we hated the Nazis. Our Government has prepared us for defense. So, being safe on that score, let us all take the hate that we feel in our hearts and turn it into millions of prayers that the darkness which overshadows so many minds in the world today may be lifted, and the light of truth come through.
>
> If we, the followers of democracy, pray for our brothers, the followers of Communism, we may be able to avert the impending danger of war and gain the peace we all so fervently desire.[32]

Many postwar youth attempted to become involved, raising their voices for the cause of democracy and world peace. For others, the response was to withdraw into the world of fatalistic iconoclasts or to become existential rebels. These were the uncommitted youth: the apathetic, alienated, defeated, fatalistic members of the Atomic Generation who adopted the persona of helpless victims to the whim of fate. These were the Jim Starks and other rebels without a cause racing toward oblivion because there was nothing else to do.[33] An expression of this dark underside was offered by Robert Kwit. The fifteen-year-old student at the Bronx (New York) High School of Science titled his poem, "I Am Going Away":

> I am going away soon
>   a long, long way,
> To a land of misty sea green shapeless forms,
>   in the faraway longaway.
>
> Today is yesterday and tomorrow is today in this land.
> Life is death and death is life.

There is no present in this land,
Memory does not exist here.
Once a thing is done, it passes into senseless oblivion.

Future is not known.
Vague desires float away on a milky mist of dreams before
    they are thought of here.
I am going away to join the shadows,
soon, soon, soon ...[34]

The increasing emphasis on postwar naturalism is evident in a poem by David Dignwell, a student at Solomon Juneau High School in Milwaukee, Wisconsin. In "Solar Things," which appeared in a 1947 issue of *Senior Scholastic*, Dignwell proclaims that the sun and stars will exist long after civilization has destroyed itself:

Stars and stars forever in eternity exist,
Moving and passing in an endless pattern
Beyond the power of Mars, the moons of Saturn,
Or any other closer sunlit orb
To match or to approach in solemn grandeur.
This first you see, and wonder as you stare
What monument erected can compare
With this broad shining highway of the air.
You saw and wondered — soon you see no more.
Yet still in calmness and in solitude
Those eyes will guide some mariner to shore,
And when his bark has sunk below the sea,
Their glow will thrill some native into song:
They will exist when all the world is gone.[35]

Sharon Southworth's poem, "Atomic Theory," also reflected the meaninglessness of humankind within the larger universe. Writing in 1947, the Ogden (Utah) High School student wrote:

Matter, like a handkerchief perhaps,
Is made of atoms; and it seems each one
Is a universe complete with planets and sun
A molecular system with orbits in the gaps
To buzz through. The galaxies of melting tin
We live among are built, or seem to be,
The same except the scale's too huge to see
The outlined shape of what it is we live in.
The earth, a mere electron, turns in space
Around the sun, atoms source of heat,
The nucleus. With rhythmic pulsing beat.

Each atom in the system whirls in place.
Space is curved and time will always bend;
There is no beginning; and there is no end.[36]

The same sentiment — nature will survive humankind — was expressed as well by Mary Ellen Berneski, a sixteen-year-old attending Latrobe (Pennsylvania) High School. Her poem, "Mood 4, Second Variation," appeared in the February 2, 1949, issue of *Senior Scholastic*:

Once there was a flower,
A delicate, transparent white flower
That was beauty itself.
It was born gently
And feared the breeze,
For it had not yet bloomed.
Each sight of the sun
Added to its loveliness,
Heightened its perfection,
Glorified its shy tint.
But suddenly the sky darkened,
And winds lashed and roared,
And rain beat the earth with foaming fists.
The little flower saw its terrible fate,
But would not submit
And cried aloud:
"Not yet, oh, not yet!
For I have not bloomed!"
So a miracle came to pass.
The storm ceased
And the sun appeared
To shine upon the flower,
And the flower was consumed with ecstasy
So that it burst into full bloom,
Bloom that was unspeakable
In its awful beauty.
And so it was for one breathless day.
Then the sun went away
And did not return.
And the flower began to fade.
And soon ghastly whiteness
Turned to brown,
Then to black,
As the once-beautiful petals
Began to fray and rot.
And the flower cried and rebelled,
But to no avail.

And slowly in tortuous pain
The flower died.
And in its last moments,
As it stood naked and ugly
Under the sunless sky,
It thought of the storm's swift knife
And wondered.

Other students fused the precarious state of civilization with the increasingly cold, emotionless, technological condition of American society. These are the youthful writings of those within the Atomic Generation "beat down" by the world around them, such as Carol Van Alstine of Schenectady, New York, who placed civilization on a train to nowhere. The St. Joseph's Academy student titled her poem "Heartbeat":

A locomotive
Pounding, steaming,
Puffing clouds of smoke
Into a blue-block void.
Clashing sounds—
The wheeze of engines, purr of wheels,
Dismal drone of a whistle,
The hollow moan of a ghostly being.
Squarish windows of light —
Dashes of daylight in the night —
Faces peering from their frames,
Seeing nothing.
A train is like the world,
A racing world
Of speed and energy,
Inhabited by multitudes
Caught in its throbbing pace
But ignorant of their destination.[37]

For seventeen-year-old Jay Gellens, attending the Bronx (High School) of Science, the appropriate image was crawling ants who could die at any moment. He wrote his poem, "Fall Thralldom," in 1946:

Early autumn morning:
Columbus Circle stirs in wakeful dreaming
And welcomes dullness
Clad in fetching hues
Across the gutters once to harbingers
Thrilled, in binding rhetoric.
There is the stubborn intent

Of small, black ants
Preparing for the insurmountable:
The thing that only death
Can bring in view.

Crawling on bellies newly filled
With morning's meal,
They pursue the grail in their
Ephemeral despair,
And wait for a higher being
Who, with the hand, a foot, a maze,
Shall end their earthly thrall.[38]

If the future held no promise, and the present held only meaningless existence, then the only recourse was to enjoy the moment, *carpe diem*. This was the attitude of Bruce McIntyre, a student at Church Farm School in Glen Loch, Pennsylvania, in his poem, "To Those That Shall Be Born":

Laugh and live, you new people,
Whether your inheritance be the stench
   of a rotting civilization,
Or the glory of its awakening;
Men's faces like grave thoughts
Or the cries of childbirth.
Laugh and live while you can —
Before the clouds shadow the sun of your existence,
And the bread of life is a stale, dry crust;
Before your life is the testimony of a gravestone;
Your world a burned book;
And your name wasted space in the telephone directory.[39]

Don Richardson, of Corpus Christi (Texas) High School, believed that civilization's curiosity and quest for power would eventually lead to atomic destruction. But he also incorporated the belief, as Ray Bradbury did in his book, *Fahrenheit 451,* that humankind would survive to begin again. *Senior Scholastic* published Richardson's science-fiction short story, "Cornerstone," in 1949:

The face of the stone was covered with a peculiar blackish crust. Large chunks of it slowly fell away as the Young Man scraped at it with his knife. Gradually part of an inscription appeared. It was not yet clear enough to read, for the crust seemed to have been fused into the stone. He paused a moment and glanced at the two large metal cases that lay beside him on the ground, apparently containing scientific instruments. One was long and narrow with an antenna reaching several feet into the air. The lid of the other was open, revealing a maze of wires and gauges. After a quick check of the delicate needles, he looked reflectively toward the crater.

It was difficult to tell how wide it was— perhaps two miles, perhaps twenty. The ground sloped unevenly away until it was lost in the deep twilight that filled the abyss.

The Young Man was unaffected by the somber landscape he saw. Such surroundings were nothing new to him; this was merely a routine survey. He turned toward the stone again. Finally he had exposed the whole surface. In large letters near the top was written "Hall of Science" and below it, the words "Erected by the Society for the Advancement of Scientific Research, April 29, 1937." He mused over it a while and would have dismissed the matter from his mind as merely another curiosity, but somehow he was tempted to run back along the dust-covered paths of his memory. He seemed to recall dimly something about the inscription. A paragraph in a textbook? Perhaps an old newspaper account? He ran his hand over the rough surface again. Then he remembered...

Years ago, many years before he was born, this block of granite had been a cornerstone in the laboratory of a great scientist. He had contributed many important discoveries to the world. And then, just as everyone thought that he was on the threshold of a great new discovery, he had lost his life in an explosion that destroyed all traces of his work. When the incident occurred, there had been much speculation as to what had happened. Then the episode was quickly forgotten. Yes, the Young Man remembered now.

But he did not know all, nor did any other living person ...

No one knew the feelings and thoughts of the scientist when after months of exhausting work he held the flask to the light. His task was completed. Here, in this flask, he held an explosive four times more powerful than gunpowder. A thrill shot through him. The lamp of science had been carried forward another step into the darkness. It would shed light and knowledge where only ignorance and fear had existed before. Four times more powerful than gunpowder! He mused over the possibilities. But as he thought, a cloud of doubt drifted through his mind. Would this discovery, primarily an instrument of war, *really* help mankind? With an explosive four times more powerful than gunpowder, what could be done? A shell could be made to travel four times farther. A bomb manufactured on this principle would kill four times as many men. War would be four times more horrible! He stood there a moment, dizzy from the impact of this last realization.

The hand that held the flask trembled now. Mankind must never know of this terrible monster. The formula must be destroyed. He would tell no one of his discovery. But could he completely seal the secret? With a quick, terrible decision he knew there was only one way. Before he could weaken he raised the flask containing the explosive above his head and hurled it with all his force against the stone floor of the laboratory. There was a deafening roar.

From the busy streets a crowd of curious and terrified onlookers soon gathered. Everyone was appalled at the effects of the blast. That evening the newspapers carried a large spread on how the explosion had "completely wrecked the laboratory and shattered windows for nearly ten blocks in every direction." For a short time it was a featured item, but in a few days the story wore itself out.

The Young Man still sat gazing at the stone. Yes, he remembered now. He puzzled over the matter while he gathered up his equipment and strapped the two metal cases on his back. He wondered about what had really happened. What new discovery died at birth? But enough of this—he had already wasted too much time.

He took a last quick look about him. Silhouetted against the crimson skyline were the blackened shells of a few buildings. Except for these, there was nothing within range of visibility but the charred, blackened earth, where a great city had been leveled by a single bomb.[40]

Sheila Crofut, of Chicago's Hyde Park High School, accentuated a similar naturalistic theme that the world would survive despite the efforts of humankind to destroy it. In her 1948 poem, "Seasons," she wrote about nature's continual process of renewal and the necessity to move with the rhythm of the seasons:

> Cold stars look down on warm earth,
> Stirring music to pipe the coming of spring.
> Giant rivers, imprisoned, burst their icy chains.
> All nature sings and spring reigns.
>
> Gaunt earth reclothes her nakedness,
> New hope is born to rise again.
> Children swing on vine trees.
> And shattered buildings look wistfully outward
> With blind gaping eyes.
> The planted seed of earth bursts forth,
> New harvests gathered and frontiers made
> While waiting icy winter's tap.
> The fisher boy sleeps beside his gently flowing stream
> Trusting the world and the fish in it.
>
> A leaf has fallen
> Scarlet color in a green world
> And now the trees stand shivering, waiting,
> For their first white blanket made of snow.
>
> A new world
> Lattice work among the silent trees.
> And earth is wrapped warm and tight in her covering of white.
> Some in happy lands smile at the shouts of children streaming
>   down a snowy hill;
> In other places curses rise for blue lips and scarlet blood
>   upon the untrodden white.

So in all places—
Man falls in step with Season,
Matching her cadenced rhythm
Lest he lose his place in Time.[41]

Fourteen-year-old Mary Cahn expressed the identical sentiment in her poem, "Nature and Man," published in *Senior Scholastic* in 1949. The student at William Cullen Bryant High School in Long Island, New York, placed the future of humankind, again, in nature's power:

What is nature — a tree, a lake, a flower?
No, it is merely an echo of man's feelings.
Or perhaps man's feelings are an echo of nature.
God created man on the sixth day — the last day.
  What had man to do?
  He looked and saw rich trees
    And felt strong.
  He looked at dainty flowers
    And felt beautiful.
  He looked at the lake
    And had the overwhelming desire
      to reflect, to glorify, to magnify.
  He gazed at the lake feeding the trees,
      the trees helping the flowers
    And learned that each must help.
  Nature surrounded him, and man was trying,
      desperately to weave himself into the pattern of it
  But God willed that it was not to be.
    For he gave man WICKEDNESS.
    This is a strange weird gift, for because of it
  Man no longer tries to weave himself into the tapestry
      of nature
  And nature is no longer a willing loom.
    But the few woven threads are still there.
No longer is man brother to the quiet lake, the pensive tree,
    or the glorious mountain.
For we are only foolish humans that stand apart
    Because we are unworthy to stand equal.
Nature will call us if we are worthy,
      but we must not answer.
    For we have been conquered and nature has lost.
We must retreat — sink back to our own creed
    That is apart because it is inferior.
    Perhaps some day if God wills it
    We will be honored to stand with and equal to

  The pensive tree, the quiet lake, and the glorious mountain.[42]

This belief in the inseparable bond between nature and humankind became the hallmark of the counterculture in the 1960s, expressed in terms of "back to the earth" and even "flower child." Moreover, the themes of brotherhood, peace, and love would form the foundation for the youth culture — "Make love, not war." But as the writings here suggest, the Atomic Generation expressed these same feelings twenty years before the Summer of Love in 1967 and The Beatles' refrain, "All you need is love." Coming of age during an era seemingly on the brink of oblivion, many postwar adolescents invested their hopes in a new world free of the violence and hatred that had resulted in the atomic explosions, and placed their future — and the future of the world — in jeopardy. The following poems contain a sense of spirituality, rural romanticism, rebirth, and environmental sensitivity often attributed to youth of a later era. Concomitant with these expressions of faith in the essentiality of civilization's basic goodness, however, is a quiet anxiety underlined by the impending atomic doom: Peace must be achieved, lest humankind perish. Shortly after Hiroshima, Dorothy Finnell, a student at Southeast High School in Kansas City, Missouri, wrote that peace is the goal of all creatures that inhabit the earth. Her poem, "Peace," was written four months after the bombing of Hiroshima:

> I am the goal of all creatures,
> Large or small, that inhabit the earth.
> I am what all men turn to
> When love is lost or failure has beset them
> And the world has turned against them.
> When above the blood and gore,
> The waste of human flesh, the useless horror
> That is war, I rise shining in the darkness,
> Free men hail me with joy in their hearts
> And prayers of thanks on their lips.[43]

A strong sense that the world can change, that civilization can be improved, that youth can make a difference, was articulated in 1951 by Christine Wicht of Hattiesburg (Mississippi) High School. Her poem was titled, appropriately, "The Power to Build":

> We have within our grasp the power
> To build — truth refined.
> Let us analyze our visionary schemes,
> Draw our blueprints;
> Then, when we begin,
> Build the things we dream of —

Plastic yachts, automatic factories—a modern world;
Harness the energy of an atom to
Use for the good of all mankind;
Discover the secret of solar energy to
Apply for the world's advantage;
Constitute synthetic materials that will outrank
Their precedents in strength and usefulness;
Develop in science ways of conquering man's
Ills and sufferings.
We alone may paint the most inspirational
Picture of all time.
Ours may be the finest piece of sculpture
The world will ever see—
Write a book, poem, or essay that will be
Worthy of the highest honors—
We must build for everyone—
Mechanically, scientifically, and aesthetically.
Let us build—not only for present delights—
To last a day, a year, a decade;
But let us build *eternal* things
For all posterity!
We do not know what lies ahead;
We dare not stop and wait.
The answer to this mystery lies beyond
Our advancements.
We must be builders *of today*
For tomorrow![44]

In 1955, in the aftermath of the Korean War and the Joseph McCarthy debacle, Kansas City's *Lincoln* (High School) *Callotype* continued the plea for sanity, and embraced "new hope and new faith" that the world would survive. The school newspaper, in an editorial titled "Easter Then and Now," acknowledged that American society was engulfed by the threat of war and the constant fear of atomic annihilation. This theme was reinforced by an accompanying illustration showing a cross emerging from an atomic-scarred earth. Like so many atomic narratives before it, the editorial commingled the themes of hope and despair, suggesting that civilization must reaffirm its faith:

1955—These are turbulent times indeed. An Atomic Age, men call it. We read of unrest in Formosa, where there is a possibility of a crisis. We see how, more and more, the Atomic Energy Commission plans for new uses for the atom. Most of them are of a destructive nature. A "whopper" of an atomic test in Yucca Flat—a blast in the 50-Kiloton A-bomb class, or the equivalent of 50,000 tons of TNT—is planned. Governments keep extend-

THE Lincoln Calliope

| VOLUME XXIX | LINCOLN HIGH SCHOOL   APRIL 7, 1955 | NUMBER 13 |

SHORTHAND STUDENTS RECEIVE HONOR

The following students in Mr. Wilson's third hour Shorthand II Class have earned awards from the Gregg Shorthand Company. (The awards are the Order of Gregg Artists (OGA) pins and certificates which are given for excellence in shorthand penmanship.

Those receiving OGA Pins and Senior Certificates are as follows: Beverly Avery, Bessie Daniels, Marceline Dixon, Barbara Henderson, Almeda Mills, Elizabeth Randolph, Jocelyn Reid, Sandra Wilson, Doris Woods, and Erma Canada.

Those who received Senior OGA Certificates are: Pauline Lyons, Audrey Williams, Marva King, and Ethel Smith.

Those who have received Junior OGA Certificates are as follows: Ollie Bishop, Rochelle Kearse, Marva King, Diane McTyer, Bessie Powell, Ethel Smith and Patricia Saunders.

The class has also entered the Gregg International Contest. The results of this contest will be announced this spring by the Gregg Company.

INTERSCHOLASTIC PRESS WORKSHOP

April 20-23 at Jeff City

According to Armistead S. Pride, Dean of the School of Journalism, Lincoln University, the 7th Annual Headliner Week Interscholastic Press Workshop will be held April 20-23. Students are expected to arrive on Tuesday evening, April 19, 1955.

Students attending may participate in any one division, or they may divide their time between any combination of classes. There will be three divisions: newspaper, yearbook, and photography. Students will receive instruction and practice in newswriting, headline writing, feature writing, editing, photography, yearbook planning and production, and column writing.

Several students from newswriting are expecting to attend.

FORMER LINCOLNITE ON DEAN'S HONOR ROLL

According to a local paper, Sarah Lena Hatcher, a former Lincolnite who is now a junior at the University of Kansas, was placed on the dean's honor roll.

LINCOLN WINS ON TEEN TUNE PARADE

Shirley Toomey and Basil North represented Lincoln on the Teen Tune Parade, Saturday, March 19, 1955. They competed in a contest against Summer High School. The contest consisted of naming the tune, orchestra, label and vocalist of hit tunes. Lincoln won the contest 10 to 2.

After the contest, students who won the dancing contest at the Coke Party danced on the show. Barbara Sayles and Allen McClellan represented Lincoln.

EASTER THEN AND NOW

There came a quake. The earth trembled and Jerusalem was indeed troubled. Jesus Christ lay buried in the sepulcher where great stones blocked the entrance way. Suddenly, from the heavens an angel in glistening white raiment came. The stones were rolled away. Jesus Christ had arisen from the dead.

1955—These are turbulent times indeed. An Atomic Age, men call it. We read of unrest in Formosa, where there is a possibility of a crisis. We see how, more and more, the Atomic Energy Commission plans for new uses for the atom. Most of them are of a destructive nature. A "whopper" of an atomic test in Yucca Flat—a blast in the 50-Kiloton A bomb class, or the equivalent of 50,000 tons of TNT—is planned. Governments keep extending their nuclear arsenals. Our United States adds atomic anti-aircraft weapons to the growing defense measures.

Sunday, millions of persons will do as persons have done for more than 1900 years—they will attend Easter church services to renew their act-old faith. Many ministers will attempt to define the meaning of this season and to enlarge its application to embrace the present troubled times.

Out of the chaos must come new hope and new faith. Perhaps for one day—Easter Sunday—the dazzling cross will emerge from a troubled earth as a sign. Put down your arms and believe—in humanity and rightness of eternal peace. And let the calm which spreads through your being live past the miracle of Easter morning. Let it last here forever!

FOODS CLASSES TO RECEIVE NEW ELECTRIC RANGES FROM GENERAL

The foods classes of Miss Dixon, Miss Martin, and Mrs. Hopkins are to receive two new General Electric ranges to replace the two received last year from the General Electric Company. These ranges will be used by over 600 students in the two foods classes. Both ranges are valued at slightly over $1,000.

HERRERA TO CHAIR SENIOR DAY ACTIVITIES

Paula Herrera has been chosen student chairman for Senior Day activities, announces Mrs. Glee J. Hopkins, senior class advisor.

She will choose a committee consisting of one member from each homeroom. The seniors are in the process of choosing the class motto and colors.

SPANISH PLAY

The annual Spanish Play will be presented next month in the Lincoln High School auditorium. The play, "Caribbean Holiday," will consist of a classroom scene, dances such as the mamba, samba, and tango, and pantomimes and skits.

There will be a fiesta scene, with the whole group celebrating, and a variety of songs.

The play is centered around a group of first-year Spanish students who are planning to take a trip to some SOUTH AMERICAN country. They arrive in Columbia in time for the "Carribean Holiday."

This play promises to be the best of the productions undertaken annually by the Spanish students.

FRENCH PLAY COMING UP

As in recent years, the annual French play will be presented this spring to the student body. In the past they have dramatized various fairy tales. Several of the plays have been written by students of the French classes.

Plans have not been completed for the production, but, according to Mrs. Pennington, our French teacher, it promises to be different.

LEATHER CRAFT CONTEST ON

Mr. Hardiman's leather craft classes are in a contest. A prize will be given to the person having the best leather project. The project will be judged on the basis of originality, skill, neatness and beauty. The contest will end close May 15. The student project that wins will be placed in the contest that Macy's is sponsoring.

EASTER ASSEMBLY

The annual Easter Assembly will be presented April 7 in the auditorium at 8:55 a. m. The choir will present the Seven Last Words of Christ, which has been done very brilliantly in the past years. The seven last words are as follows:

First Word: "Father Forgive Them for They Know Not What They Do."
Second Word: "Today Shalt Thou Be with Me in Paradise."
Third Word: "Woman Behold Thy Son—Son Behold Thy Mother."
Fourth Word: "My God, My God, Why Hast Thou Forsaken Me?"
Fifth Word: "I Thirst."
Sixth Word: "Into Thy Hands I Commend My Soul."
Seventh Word: "It Is Finished."

The soloists are as follows: Shirley Toomey, soprano; Guest soloists Mike Hinojosha, tenor, a student of Ver. Stanley Deacon from the Kansas City Conservatory and John Schelstrate, baritone.

LINCOLN HIGH SCHOOL ON APPROVED LIST

The North Central Association of Colleges and Secondary Schools has placed Lincoln High School again on the list of secondary schools approved for the coming year.

The action was taken at the annual business meeting of the Association in Chicago, March 21-25, 1955.

SENIORS GET MEASURED FOR CAPS AND GOWNS

According to Mrs. Hopkins chairman of the senior class, the measurement for caps and gowns should be well under way.

The 1955 graduating class will wear traditional caps and gowns. Tassels on the caps will be made of gold and blue threads. Graduates are given the opportunity to keep the tassel from the cap for an additional twenty-five-cent fee.

SOCIAL SECURITY BENEFICIARIES NOW NUMBER OVER 1 MILLION

According to information received from the central office by Hugh P. McTernan, Kansas City Manager of the Social Security Administration, the 7-million mark was reached in February, 1955 for the number of persons receiving current monthly benefits under social security.

Monthly benefits under old-age and survivors insurance (social security) were first paid in 1940. By February, 1945 there were one million beneficiaries. Approximately 5 years later, the number of beneficiaries getting monthly payments had increased to 3 million. The 5 million beneficiary milestone was reached in December, 1952.

The old-age and survivors insurance plan first went into effect in January, 1937, and had been in effect 18 years at the end of 1954. However, monthly benefits under the plan have only been paid since 1940.

In 1955, in the aftermath of the Korean War and the Joseph McCarthy debacle, school editors at Kansas City's Lincoln High School embraced "new hope and new faith" that the world would survive, with an illustration showing a cross emerging from an atomic-scarred Earth.

ing their nuclear arsenals. Our United States adds atomic anti-aircraft weapons to the growing defense measures....

Out of the chaos must come new hope and new faith. Perhaps for one day — Easter Sunday — the dazzling cross will emerge from a troubled earth as a sign.[45]

For the Atomic Generation, this was a message encountered often — contained in narratives aimed at them or exposed to them. Further, the dichtomous themes of life and death, war and peace, were expressed by them, as the poems and other writings contained here demonstrate. As Lawrence Levine suggests in his book, *The Unpredictable Past: Explorations in American Cultural History*, these narratives contributed toward this generation's social reality, which encompassed the classroom, school auditorium, movie theater, and living room.

Unlike their parents, America's postwar youth confronted the issues of the Atomic Age practically every day. In fact, they read about them, watched and listened to them, discussed them in class, and were tested about them. This is not to suggest that all adolescents experienced atomic narratives at the same intensity or reacted in the same manner. Quite the contrary. The heterogeneous nature of American society prevents monolithic responses to any cultural stimulus. This is illustrated by youths' own narratives. Yet, as Levine notes, it *is* possible to argue that "deeply internalized points of view" do exist, which these narratives confirm. Although the Atomic Generation did not respond in a unified voice, it *was* highly cognizant of the dangers associated with the atomic bomb; and, as integral participants in atomic discourses, members of this generation assigned their own particular significance and meaning to them.

8

The Fusion of Youth Culture

[D]emocracy must be viable because of its quality of life, not its quantity of rockets.
— Port Huron Statement, 1962

Between 1945 and 1955, American society clearly witnessed a growing separation of youth from adult society. At the same time, youths' values reflected the quiet desperation and fear that permeated their parents' lives, albeit beneath the surface. The Atomic Generation became committed to attaining security *now*: Why plan for the future when there might not be one? For the fictional Jim Stark and his rival Buzz in the movie *Rebel Without a Cause*, racing cars toward a precipitious cliff in a chickie race was at least something to do. And when the real James Dean died in 1955, it meant for many youth that you must live for the moment because there are no guarantees in life.

Commenting on the emergence of this fatalistic philosophy, which would become the hallmark of the next decade, sociologist Todd Gitlin writes: "James Dean's death inaugurated the idea that living fast is living right, and yet that there is something ineluctably poignant at stake when youth commits itself to go beyond the limits.... This sense of a fatal connection to young martyrs, of death as the final refutation of plenitude, ran strong through all the phases of Sixties culture."[1] Gitlin addresses an important connection between the Atomic Generation and the subsequent Sixties Generation. As he illustrates, the underlying themes imbedded in the discourses of the 1960s were not new; rather, they were contained in countless narratives and activities throughout his childhood and adolescence.

The struggle to cope with the new Atomic Age is well substantiated. A 1951 survey of 10,000 high school students in ten states found that 47 percent of the respondents were concerned about atomic warfare; 36 percent worried about atomic radiation. In a 1949 survey of Washington State high school students, 40 percent said no one (parents or teachers) could help them in making a vocational decision because of the rapid changes in society and the uncertainty of the future. Eight out of ten Maryland students, surveyed in 1952, had serious problems adjusting to normal living, with four times as many boys as girls declared maladjusted. A 1955 study of college-age students in ten nations, titled "Youth's Outlook on the Future," found that everyone surveyed expected "a great war," possibly within the next ten years.[2]

A twenty-year study of incoming college freshmen, conducted between 1948 and 1968, revealed a steady decline in youthful attitudes in support of cooperation and group activities. Over the course of the study, youth showed tendencies of withdrawal from others and disconnection from social responsibilities. James Carey, in his study of courtship patterns in popular songs, found that in the mid-'50s love was considered to be in the hands of fate: externally controlled; something that just happens.[3]

A 1957 report by the World Health Organization stated, "[T]he use of atomic energy as a weapon has aroused a deep sense of fear and, in some people, also a moral involvement and guilt." Irrational fear, the report said, was expressed more often than irrational hope. Another study of youth (who were between the ages of 4 and 8 in 1945) discovered that death was equated with annihilation. Life was considered unmanageable, beyond control. Respondents expressed pervasive doubts about the future of the world and anything personally longlasting. As a result, they had no belief or faith in the concept of individual achievement. A survey published the same year said that 73 percent of teenagers felt the most dangerous threat to democracy came from communists and communist-dominated groups. One-third of those responding felt they could not prevent another war.[4]

In high school, atomic issues influenced homework assignments and classroom discussions, clubs and organizations, assemblies and civil-defense drills, social activities and behavior. Both in school and outside of school, atomic narratives conveyed the realities of the Atomic Age, and the broader social narrative of the atom contributed to the shaping of youth's experience. The exposure to the diverse ramifications of the atom in an era of insecurity, moreover, resulted in an intensified commitment to emotional, physical, social, and psychological security.

Sociologist David Riesman, writing in 1950, first articulated this tendency by suggesting that people were becoming "other-directed," defining their identity within the solace of the group. Youth, he said, sought emotional security in social settings by mastering the peer group's taste preference and modes of expression. According to Riesman, the peer group becomes the measure of all things, but in the process the individual loses a sense of self. Thus, society becomes, in essence, a "lonely crowd."[5]

William Whyte, in his 1956 book, *The Organization Man*, also wrote about the growing urgency to be secure among the younger generation. In his observations of recent college graduates, Whyte concluded that they were "almost psychotic on the subject of depression" and selected big corporations primarily because they combined an opportunity to be of service to humankind while ensuring a sense of security — two important tenets of the Atomic Generation. "With the new emphasis on human relations," he wrote, "college-to-grave security, extracurricular benefits, and the like, the ideal of an organization so beneficent of its members has become more than a possibility; it is, in the eyes of some, the constant the individual must have to keep himself on keel in a world changing so fast."[6]

More recently, historian Elaine Tyler May has reconfirmed this orientation in the 1950s toward personal security in her study of women and the family, *Homeward Bound: American Families in the Cold War Era*. Clearly, she argues, the insecurities related to the Atomic Age, from McCarthyism to Cold War militarism, resulted in the social containment of women within the domestic sphere of home, marriage, and motherhood.[7]

Howard Becker, another sociologist writing in the 1950s, clarified adolescents' growing commitment to the peer group — their own subculture — by writing that people follow certain lines of activity for reasons quite extraneous to the activity itself. That is, they make "side bets." Becker maintained that what appears to be a commitment is actually the result of commitment objectives sometimes far removed from the observed activity or role. In order to feel secure within the youth culture, for instance, adolescents made commitments to the socially accepted norm of going steady or becoming active in a club, organization, or sport. An individual's commitment to a "side bet," according to Becker, minimizes the negative impact for violating generalized cultural expectations. At the same time, the same commitment allows the individual to conform more easily to accepted social behavior or social positions. Most commitments are made consciously and deliberately, while others are realized after the fact. In these "commitments by default," said Becker, the individual "becomes aware that he is committed only at some point of change and seems to have made the commitment without realizing it."[8]

Becker's concept of side bets provides a useful way of looking at adolescents coming of age with the atom. As a result of their high school experiences and exposure to atomic discourses, many adolescents made a series of side bets in an era of atomic uncertainty. They joined clubs and organizations, participated in school-based group activities, and even formed gangs or fan clubs, all of which provided the requisite side bets for feeling more secure. For others, perhaps more apathetic, fatalistic, or individualistic, the peer culture itself — through its music, fashion, separateness from mainstream adult society, etc. — provided the requisite security rather than organized group affiliations.

The emergence of a widespread youth culture itself can be understood as a meta-side bet for the Atomic Generation. This unifying, yet diverse, culture — both for the committed, group-oriented youth, and for the seemingly uncommitted youth — evolved from the need to feel more secure. Writing in 1955, educational psychologist Howard McCluskey posited that American culture was creating "a situation which tends toward the detachment of youth from the central stream of society. In this state of detachment and loosening controls, there is appearing in society the soil for surrounding youth with a subculture of its own."[9]

It is no wonder that contemporary psychiatrists, psychologists, and social commentators focused so much attention on adolescence as a social institution as well as a developmental life stage. After all, this was the period of the most vigorous construction of the postwar youth culture by the Atomic Generation. S.E. Eisenstadt, writing in 1962, suggested that developments in modern societies had "flattened" the image of the future and placed the importance on the present. For the adolescent, who is in a state of transition from childhood to adulthood, the lack of a distinct and promising future results in a growing sense of alienation and disassociation. Modern societies, Eisenstadt argued, had made it more difficult for youth to link "the development of personality and the personal temporal transition with cosmic and societal time, on the one hand, and with the clear role models derived from the adult world, on the other." This had resulted in an increasing sense of insecurity and a lack of a clear definition of personal identity. The adolescent, in an effort to find purpose and direction, turns away from parental guidance, according to Eisenstadt, because family values fail to provide an adequate basis for identity development. Youth groups become critical, he said, as the adolescent "seeks some framework for the development and crystallization of his identity, for the attainment of personal autonomy, and for his effective transition into the adult world."[10]

James Coleman, in his 1961 book, *The Adolescent Society*, called adolescence "a Coney Island mirror, which throws back a reflecting adult society in a distorted but recognizable image."[11] The adolescent society, as he called it, was distinct from the adult society and provided its own set of rewards for its members. He subsequently wrote that youth culture is characterized by inward-lookingness, psychic attachment to the peer group, search for personal autonomy, concern for the less fortunate, and an interest in change.[12] Enlarging upon Coleman's thesis, Bruno Bettleheim maintained that if adult society looms ahead as something to be avoided, adolescence declines as a transitional period and becomes instead a life stage separate from adult society with its own cultural norms and behavior. Similarly, Edgar Friedenberg, in *The Vanishing Adolescent* (1959), warned that adolescence as a developmental process was being undermined by mass society.[13]

These rather poignant views of modern adolescence capture the reality of a postwar youth culture that upheld many of the same social values and aspirations as adult society but altered them to reflect the uncertainties and trepidations related to growing up to face an increasingly technological, hostile, fragmented, and even opprobrious society. "[T]he group," sociologist Hans Sebald has written, "is not only a membership group but becomes a reference group." Among the reasons not to deviate from this group, Sebald posits, is a fear "of an inhospitable larger culture."[14] Similarly, social psychologist Kenneth Keniston, who has written extensively about youth, argues that youth culture is a reaction against parents who cannot adequately prepare youth for the future and a reliance upon peers who are more sensitive to the needs and demands of the present.[15] A subculture, he suggests, is a way for youth to cope with the stresses and strains created by rapid social change, without necessarily creating social or political upheaval. He describes "unprogrammatic alienation" as rebellion without a cause, or dissent without well-formulated justification or a program of objectives for improving society. "'Silent generations' and 'angry young men,'" Keniston has written, "share a common rejection of their culture: the first rejecting it through lack of response, the other through open opposition."[16]

Many adolescents in the era immediately following the Second World War found the search for an identity and the ability to make a commitment to a social role increasingly difficult, particularly as the Cold War escalated in the early 1950s. For many, in fact, the future no doubt seemed clouded by confusion and fear rather than promising a better tomorrow. "Our generation lives between Hell and Utopia," wrote David Woodbury, author of *Atoms for Peace*, in 1955. "For the very force that can destroy the human race can create wonders without end on earth. It is small wonder that men's minds today shuttle between fears of doom and dreams of unprecedented bounty."[17]

While educators encouraged emotional control, peer solidarity, and group involvement, adolescents committed themselves to emotional, psychological, and social security as a means to come to grips with their identities and roles within the Atomic Age. Their commitment to security, however, often resulted in role rigidity: adolescents clinging to each other and to more traditional gender roles as a means to feel secure, yet at the same time searching for some semblance of self-identity, or individualism, within their cultural boundaries. One girl expressed her concern over this conflict between individuality and group identity in 1951:

> The individual is almost dead today, but the young people are unaware of it. They think of themselves as individuals, but really they are not. They are parts of groups. They are unhappy outside of a group. When they are alone, they are bored with themselves. There is a tendency now to date together. They have to be with a crowd. These kids in my group think of themselves as individuals, but actually it is as if you took a tube of toothpaste and squeezed out a number of little distinct blobs on a piece of paper. Each blob would be distinct — separated in space — but each blob would be the same.[18]

Psychologist Robert Lindner commented in 1954 that this group orientation, which destroyed individuality, was a symptom of severe, collective mental illness. But it was a social illness being fostered upon America's youth. "Our adolescents are but one step forward from us upon the road to mass manhood," he wrote. "Into them we have bred our fears and insecurities."[19]

Harvard history professor Oscar Handlin commented in 1951 that America's youth were working toward "a riskless security and to attain it, were willing to sink into a dull conformity." That same year, *Time* magazine wrote that youth were "waiting for the hand of fate to fall on [their] shoulders, meanwhile working fairly hard and saying almost nothing." This was a Silent Generation, it said, that "does not issue manifestoes, make speeches or carry posters."[20]

Perhaps this generation was silent in 1951. Only a few years later, however, the voices were beginning to be heard. Otto Butz, a young professor at Princeton, solicited the views of members of the Class of 1957 (those graduating from high school in 1953 and composing the *Heat* of the Atomic Generation). Titled, appropriately, *The Unsilent Generation*, the book documented the thoughts of eleven seniors, selected as representative of a questionnaire completed by the graduating class. Although the students did not specifically express concerns over the atomic bomb, and often spoke of their individual aspirations and hopes for the future, they also expressed concerns about the increasing emphasis on conformity and regimentation,

the loss of identity and individualism, the constant threat of war, the growing sense of insecurity and loss of control over one's life, and the decline
of morality and spread of materialism — all themes associated with the
Atomic Age and with the emerging youth culture of the 1960s.

"My continuing problem," one senior responded, "is to find my identity, to find my place in a society which demands a total commitment that
I cannot give." Another student commented that his generation's com-
placency and self-satisfaction was a protective shield to hide its basic insecurity. "Threats of war, the draft, the loss of identity in a big corporation,
loss of a spiritual ideal, and the pleasures of an ever-evolving mechanical
civilization," he said, "all make the individual feel isolated and overawed
in daily life."[21]

Historians have made significant strides in revising their conception
of the nature of the 1950s, dispelling the myth that this decade was one of
sterility, consensus, conformity, and contentment. More important, they
have illuminated the origins of the social themes and events of the decade
that followed, pointing out that civil rights, student protests, and social
criticisms began, not in the 1960s but during the Eisenhower years. "The
fifties was not a placid and sterile decade — how could it have been," J.
Ronald Oakley has written, "when it experienced the continuing paranoiac
fear of being blown up by the Russians." This, after all, was the decade of
the Korean War and McCarthy hysteria, bus boycotts and riots over integration, the birth of the hydrogen bomb and the space age, the explosion
of suburbia and the baby boom, and the spread of television to 90 percent
of the nation's population.[22]

Gaile McGregor has called the 1950s "an age that gave birth to both
the ruptures and the icons that would 'make' the sixties." She argues further that although this decade was one of conformity, people conformed
because they were afraid and anxious.[23] In the estimation of Elaine Tyler
May, the quest for security in an era of atomic insecurity resulted in the
social containment of women within the home and within traditional gender roles emphasizing motherhood and domesticity. The family provided
a psychological fortress offering protection from a world on the brink of
chaos. "The modern family would, presumably, tame fears of atomic holocaust," she has written, "and tame women as well."[24] Although the ideology
of compromise reigned during the 1950s, adds James Gilbert, so too did
social ferment that questioned conformity and consensus. He, along with
such historians as Paul Carter, W.T. Lhamon, Jr., Joseph Goulden, Fred
Powledge, and Jeffrey Hart, have helped revise our view of this decade.[25]
"What society interpreted as vulgarity in music, delinquency in young
people, or mindless spontaneity during the 1950s," Gilbert has written,

"was transformed by a very complex process into counterculture, radicalism, and liberation in the 1960s."[26]

Norman Cousins wrote in 1945 that Americans could put on blinders, dismiss talk of the Atomic Age, and claim that the threat of the atomic bomb is exaggeration, overstatement, hysteria, or panic. But "all the manufactured calm and scorn in the world cannot alter the precise fact that the atomic bomb plus another war equals global disaster."[27] Eighteen years later, in one of the final statements of the Atomic Generation, the bomb's presence again lurked in the background or, perhaps more accurately, rushed madly toward earth. The Port Huron Statement continued the trend of many atomic narratives by proposing specific steps that must be taken immediately, by this generation, to bring sanity back to modern civilization.[28]

"Not only is ours the first generation to live with the possibility of world-wide cataclysm," Tom Hayden declared, "it is the first to experience the actual social preparation for cataclysm, the general militarization of American society." Rather than deterrence and arms control, Hayden called for universal controlled disarmament. He urged the United States to replace world hunger, poverty, disease, ignorance, violence, and exploitation with abundance, reason, love, and international cooperation. The country should demonstrate its commitment to democratic institutions, he said, by "making domestic democracy exemplary." The political process had to be opened to everyone through "participatory democracy," with peaceful dissent actively promoted rather than discouraged, a direct legacy of "education for citizenship" and democratic, action-centered education for democracy introduced in the early 1950s.

Freedom, Hayden warned, was being undermined by the spreading fear and apathy among his generation and particularly among mainstream adult society. "Some would have us believe that Americans feel contentment amidst prosperity," he wrote, "but might it not better be called a glaze above deeply felt anxieties about their role in the new world?" Society's underlying fear of the world's precariousness had led to a fear of change itself, "since change might smash whatever invisible framework seems to hold back chaos for them now." In fact, any crusade or movement had become threatening, even though democracy, Hayden upheld, was supposedly based upon the freedoms of speech, assembly, thought, religion, and the press.

Brotherhood, yet another recurring theme in postwar atomic narratives, was expressed as "a condition of future survival and as the most appropriate form of social relations." The accumulation of atomic weapons had undermined traditional concepts of power relations between nations.

Missiles had "(figuratively) thumbed their nose cones at national bound-aries." Power, Hayden maintained, was now rooted in love, reflection, rea-son, and creativity — all tenets expressed repeatedly by educators during the early postwar years. Belief in the community was mandatory in the Atomic Age. "There are no convincing apologies for the contemporary malaise," he wrote. "While the world tumbles toward the final war, while men in other nations are trying desperately to alter events, while the very future qua future is uncertain — America is without community impulse, without the inner momentum necessary for an age when societies cannot successfully perpetuate themselves by their military weapons...."

The 1960s would present new historical events and social challenges to those youth traversing adolescence. They would confront another war abroad and witness an escalation of racial and civil strife at home. They would participate in a burgeoning subculture aided by the baby-boom explosion, economic affluence, and the mass media's mainstreaming effects on American society. Their personal experiences would be shaded by gen-der, race, class, and social ecology. Yet one universal constant would exist: the lingering threat of the atomic bomb. Speaking for themselves, for their small band of student activists, and, in many respects, for their genera-tion and the one that followed, an impassioned Hayden and his youthful cohorts ended their "manifesto of hope"— their atomic narrative — with the inescapable truth that the world might end at any moment:

> As students for a democratic society, we are committed to stimulating this kind of social movement, this kind of vision and program in campus and community across the country. If we appear to seek the unattainable, as it has been said, then let it be known that we do so to avoid the unimagin-able.

Other generations had experienced dramatic social change and the intensity of technological advancements. None, however, had been faced with the threat of world destruction exploding on television screens and in movie theaters, in books and magazines, and in their everyday experi-ences at home and at school. Nor had any American generation confronted communism as a threat to democracy and civilization itself. None had been indoctrinated to safeguard democracy or face atomic apocalypse. None had sought shelter from hypothetical atomic bombs, nor dealt with survivability in such bleak terms. Finally, none had been inundated with such bifurcated views of the atom: hope for humankind; power of mass destruction. The Atomic Generation, indeed, was forced to be optimistic in an era of prosperity built precariously over a foundation of fear and anxiety.

Epilogue: 1955

We're gonna rock, rock, rock....
— Bill Haley and His Comets

By 1955, more than 30 million families tuned in each evening to watch game shows and situation comedies, original dramas and adaptations, news updates and lighthearted fare for the entire family. Television not only entertained an ever-expanding audience and reflected the country's hopes and fears; it also began to alter the social landscape — to shape a more mainstream society while heightening awareness of America's blemishes.

In May of that year, Americans received the news that the Supreme Court had finally issued its instructions in the *Brown v. Board of Education of Topeka, Kansas*, desegregation case heard the previous year. Justice Earl Warren ordered the district court to take "deliberate speed" in its efforts to implement the landmark ruling on the integration of public schools. That December, Rosa Parks sparked a bus boycott in Birmingham, Alabama, placing the plight of Southern blacks in the national limelight, this time aided by television, and introducing a young minister, Martin Luther King, Jr., to a national audience. The exigency for racial harmony, a theme often encountered in postwar atomic narratives, had been acted upon.[1]

Atomic survival, yet another theme, had become an everyday dimension of American life. Schools and communities conducted civil-defense drills on a regular basis, and the federal government did its part by sponsoring the annual Operation Alert. A girl graduating from high school in 1955 wrote, "[L]iving has been a difficult and insecure thing; at worst, an insurmountable wall of bewilderment and frustration ... we've never lived a minute of our lives without war or the threat of war."[2] A senior boy wrote the same year, "We of today's graduating class are on the threshold of a new world. It is a world of possible destruction. It is also, we hope, a world of peace."[3] Remembers sociologist Todd Gitlin, president of SDS in the early 1960s: "For us, the future was necessarily more salient than the past. The Bomb threatened that future, and therefore undermined the ground on which affluence was built. Rather than feel grateful for the Bomb, we felt menaced. The Bomb was the shadow hanging over all human endeavor. It threatened all the prizes."[4]

Self-reliance became synonymous with self-preservation, as Americans built bomb shelters at an explosive rate. Film historian Andrew Dowdy, nineteen years old in 1955, remembers, "Some of us were going underground, immediately and literally, digging in from bomb shelter instructions available in two-dollar booklets." But the ability to withstand the force of a hydrogen bomb was questionable at best, which led *Time* magazine to ask in June 1955 whether the best defense against the bomb was prayer. Not long after, the prayer was seemingly answered for many youth as the new *Mad* magazine, which had evolved from comic-book status to a 25-cent, bimonthly compendium of social satire, adopted the "What, Me Worry?" kid as its official mascot. Alfred E. Neuman, as the kid would later be known, became America's quintessential fatalistic youth — and future "new man." A poll taken the previous year by the American Institute of Public Opinion, in fact, found that 95 percent of respondents would not move to escape a hydrogen bomb, even though most believed one would be used against the United States. Why worry?[5]

On October 13, 1955, the young stalwarts of the Beat Generation — Gary Snyder, Jack Kerouac, Michael McClure, and Lawrence Ferlinghetti — gathered at San Francisco's Six Gallery to hear poet Allen Ginsberg read his new work, "Howl." Ginsberg, articulating the viewpoint of postwar rebels without a cause, lamented, "I saw the best minds of my generation destroyed by madness, starving hysterical naked,/dragging themselves through the negro streets at dawn looking for an angry fix,/angelheaded hipsters burning for the ancient heavenly connection to the starry dynamo in the machinery of night/ ... who distributed Supercommunist pamphlets in Union Square weeping and undressing while the sirens of Los Alamos wailed them down, and wailed down Wall, and the Staten Island ferry also wailed,...." The voice of youth beat down by the finality of the atomic bomb was being heard.[6]

In 1954, *Cashbox* commented that white high school and college students in the South — largely "youthful hillbilly fans rather than the pop bobbysoxers" — were frantically buying rhythm-and-blues songs. White youth had been listening and dancing to black R&B for several years, assisted by disc jockeys like Cleveland's Alan Freed. But when *Billboard* proclaimed in a banner headline, "1955 — THE YEAR R&B TOOK OVER

POP FIELD," it marked the final explosion of rock 'n' roll — the fusing of black R&B and white rockabilly that crossed geographic, racial, and socio-economic boundaries. This also was the year "(We're Gonna) Rock Around the Clock" by Bill Haley and His Comets became the first rock 'n' roll record to hit number one on *Billboard*'s pop chart.[7] Jerry Lee Lewis, Fats Domino, Buddy Holly, Chuck Berry, Elvis, Little Richard, and many others followed quickly: black and white performers covering the same tunes for the same audiences.

The deaths of actor James Dean and bop jazz improviser Charlie Parker occurred in 1955: one setting the style for white youth; the other setting the tone for African American youth. And R&B singer Johnny Ace took his life just a few days before 1955 began. That year saw the release of *Rebel Without a Cause* and *Blackboard Jungle*, movies that created the young rebel as an icon fighting against a hostile, uncaring society. At the same time, teen-oriented radio and television programs, like Dick Clark's *American Bandstand* in Philadelphia, were being joined by new magazines aimed at the burgeoning youth culture: *Hep Cats, Teenager, Teen-Age Confessions, Teenage Rock and Roll Review, Teen Digest, 'Teen, Dig,* and *Modern Teen.*[8]

By the mid–1950s, youth had solidified its place — its role — in society. "Youth culture," historian W.T. Llamon, Jr., has written, "became largely the main culture; it became the atmosphere of American life."[9] This largely high-school–based, adolescent culture had taken form replete with a unique style and attitude. In the years that followed, this culture ultimately created its own social narrative to be interpreted by those coming of age in the 1960s, a new era of uncertainty.

Appendix A: Atomic Narratives for the Classroom

Teachers charged with the responsibility of educating students for the Atomic Age were greatly assisted by governmental agencies, educational associations, publishing companies, and private corporations, all of which collectively published books, booklets, pamphlets, comic books, films, and filmstrips on the atomic bomb, atomic energy, and (in the early 1950s) civil defense. Many of these materials—available free of charge or for a nominal fee—were used in high school classrooms (including English, science, history, and social studies) across the country. Materials listed below were recommended to teachers, students, and community organizations in the pages of *Senior Scholastic,* and by other governmental and educational agencies and publications. The Federal Civil Defense Administration, for example, published numerous titles readily available to teachers, students, and the general public. In addition, educational publications often recommended articles from mass-circulation magazines, such as *Time, Newsweek, Saturday Review of Literature, Harper's, Atlantic Monthly,* etc., as well as the *Bulletin of the Atomic Scientists,* which are not included.

Although the following narratives stop at 1955, which is the timeframe of this study, government-supported and commercial narratives—written and visual—continued to be available to America's youth throughout the rest of the decade. (Note: Some publishing dates and related information were unavailable.) For additional information on films available to educators, see Frederic Krahn, editor, *Educational Film Guide 1953* (New York: H.W. Wilson Co., 1953) and Josephine Antonini, editor, *Educational Film Guide 1954–1958* (New York: H.W. Wilson Co., 1958); and A. Costandina Titus, "Back to Ground Zero: Old Footage Through New Lenses," *Journal of Popular Film and Television* 20 (1983): 2–11.

Books, Booklets, Pamphlets, Bulletins, Comics

Adventures Inside the Atom. General Electric, 1948.

All Hands — Atomic Bomb Test Extra Issue, July 1, 1946. Washington, D.C.: Government Printing Office, 1946.

American Association for the United Nations, Inc. *A Third World War Can Be Prevented Now!* New York: True Comics, 1946.

The Atom Age Opens. New York: Pocket Books, 1945.

The Atom — New Source of Energy. New York: McGraw-Hill Publishing Co.

The Atomic Bomb. Chicago: The Atomic Scientists of Chicago, 1946.

Atomic Challenge. New York: Foreign Policy Association, 1947.

Atomic Information. National Committee on Atomic Information.

Atomic Peace or Atomic War. Washington, D.C.: National Institute of Social Relations, 1947. Series G-122.

Baruch, Bernard. *Proposals for an International Atomic Development Authority.* No. 2560. Washington, D.C.: Government Printing Office, 1946.

Bethe, H.A. *H-Bomb and World Order.* New York: Foreign Policy Association, 1950.

Bradley, David. *No Place to Hide.* New York: Little, Brown, 1948.

Brookhaven National Laboratory. *ABC's of Radiation.* Hamilton, Ohio: Champion Paper and Fibre Co., 1949.

Brown, Harrison. *Must Destruction Be Our Destiny?* New York: Simon & Schuster, 1946.

Bulletin of the Atomic Scientists. *Civilian Defense Against Atomic Attack.* Chicago: University of Chicago Press, August–September 1950.

Bulletin of the Atomic Scientists. *International Control of Atomic Energy.* Chicago: University of Chicago Press, 1947.

Burnett, R. Will. *Atomic Energy — Double Edged Sword of Science.* Columbus, Ohio: Charles Merrill, Inc., 1949.

Campbell, John. *The Atomic Story.* New York: Henry Holt & Co., 1947.

Chubb, L.W.. *The World Within the Atom.* Pittsburgh, Pa.: Westinghouse Electric Corp.

Civil Defense Supplement to the American Red Cross First Aid Textbook. Philadelphia: The Blakiston Co., 1951.

Clearing House. Oak Ridge's Youth Council on the Atomic Crisis, May 1947.

Control of Atomic Energy — International Conciliation No. 430. April 1947.

Cousins, Norman. *Modern Man is Obsolete.* New York: Viking, 1945.

Crary, Ryland; Evans, Hubert; Gotlieb, Albert; and Light, Israel. *The Challenge of Atomic Energy.* New York: Bureau of Publications, Teachers College, Columbia University, 1948.

Dietz, H. *Atomic Energy in the Coming Era.* New York: Dodd, 1945.

Eidinoff, M.L. and R. Hyman. *Atomics for the Millions.* New York: McGraw-Hill, 1947.

The Effects of Atomic Weapons. Washington, D.C.: GPO, 1950.

Evans, Hubert; Crary, Ryland; and Hass, Glenn. *Operation Atomic Vision.* Washington, D.C., National Association of Secondary School Principals, 1948.

Federal Civil Defense Administration. *Civil Defense Against Atomic Warfare.* Washington, D.C., Government Printing Office, 1950.

_____. *Civil Defense Against Biological Warfare.* Washington, D.C.: GPO, 1953.

_____. *Civil Defense in Industry and Institutions.* Washington, D.C.: G.O.P., 1951.

_____. *Civil Defense in Outline: Study Guide for Civil Defense.* Washington, D.C.: GPO, 1951.

_____. *Civil Defense in Schools.* Washington, D.C.: GPO, 1952.

_____. *Civil Defense Nursing Needs.* Washington, D.C.: GPO, 1952.

_____. *Emergency Action to Save Lives.* Washington, D.C.: GPO, 1951.

_____. *Emergency Medical Treatment.* Washington, D.C.: GPO, 1953.

_____. *Emergency Welfare Services.* Washington, D.C.: GPO, 1952.

_____. *Fire Effects of Bombing Attacks.* Washington, D.C.: GPO, 1952.

_____. *Fire Fighting for Householders.* Washington, D.C.: GPO, 1951.

_____. *Fire Services.* Washington, D.C.: GPO, 1951.

_____. *Ground Observer Corps, Guard Our Country, Air Defense.* Washington, D.C.: GPO, 1953.

_____. *Health Services and Special Weapons Defense.* Washington, D.C.: GPO, 1950.

_____. *Home Shelters for Family Protection in An Atomic Attack.* Washington, D.C.: GPO, 1953.

_____. *In Case of Attack! Tune Your AM Radio Dial [to] 640 [or] 1240 For Official Information, CONRELRAD.* Washington, D.C.: GPO, 1953.

_____. *Interim Civil-Defense Instructions for Schools and Colleges.* Washington, D.C.: GPO, 1951.

_____. *The Nurse in Civil Defense.* Washington, D.C.: GPO, 1952.

_____. *Organization and Operation of Civil Defense Casualty Services.* Washington, D.C.: GPO, 1952.

_____. *Outdoor Warning Device Systems.* Washington, D.C.: GPO, 1951.

_____. *Planning and Organizing for Civil Defense Traffic Operations.* Washington, D.C., GPO, 1955.

_____. *Police Services.* Washington, D.C.: GPO, 1951.

_____. *Principles of Civil-Defense Operations.* Washington, D.C.: GPO, 1951.

_____. *Procedure for Evacuation Traffic Movement Studies.* Washington, D.C.: GPO, 1952.

_____. *Radiological Decontamination in Civil Defense.* Washington, D.C.: GPO, 1952.

_____. *The Rescue Service.* Washington, D.C.: GPO, 1951.

_____. *Rescue Techniques and Operations.* Washington, D.C.: GPO, 1953.

_____. *Safe Because Some American Looked to the Sky! [as Ground Observer in G.O.C.].* Washington, D.C.: GPO, 1953.

_____. *Shelter from Atomic Attack in Existing Buildings.* Washington, D.C.: GPO, 1952.

_____. *Survival Under Atomic Attack.* Washington, D.C.: GPO, 1950.

_____. *This Is Civil Defense.* Washington, D.C.: GPO, 1951.

_____. *Time for Air Defense Is Now! Here's How You Can Help [Defend America as Member of Ground Observer Corps].* Washington, D.C.: GPO, 1953.

_____. *Training Courses for Civil Defense.* Washington, D.C.: GPO, 1954.

_____. *The Warden Service.* Washington, D.C.: GPO, 1951.

_____. *The Warden's Handbook.* Washington, D.C.: GPO, 1951.

_____. *Water Supplies for Wartime Fire Fighting.* Washington, D.C.: GPO, 1951.

_____. *What You Should Know About Biological Warfare*. Washington, D.C.: GPO, 1951.

Fox, William. *The Struggle for Atomic Control*. New York, Public Affairs Committee, 1947.

Gamow, George. *Atomic Energy in Cosmic and Human Life*. New York: Macmillan, 1946.

_____. *Mr. Tompkins Explores the Atom*. New York: Macmillan Co., 1944.

Gerstell, Richard. *How to Survive an Atom Bomb*. Lancaster, Pa.: Bantam Books, 1950.

Glasstone, Samuel. *Sourcebook on Atomic Energy*. New York: D. Van Nostrand Co., 1950.

Gotlieb, Albert. *Achieving International Control of Atomic Energy — Critical Thinking for a New Age*. New York: Bureau of Publications, Teachers College, Columbia University, 1947.

Hawley, Gessner and Sigmund Leifson. *Atomic Energy in War and Peace*. New York: Reinhold Publishing Corp., 1945.

Hecht, Selig. *Explaining the Atom*. New York, Viking Press, 1947.

Hersey, John. *Hiroshima*. New York: Viking Press, 1946.

Higinbotham, W.A., and Lindley, Ernest. *Atomic Challenge*. New York: Foreign Policy Association, 1947.

Inside the Atom. General Electric.

John Citizen's Bible on Atomic Attack Protection. National Security Resources Board, 1950.

Johnsen, Julia, comp. *The Atomic Bomb*. New York: H.W. Wilson Co., 1946.

Lang, Daniel. *Early Tales of the Atomic Age*. New York: Doubleday & Co., 1948.

Laurence, William. *Dawn Over Ground Zero — The Story of the Atomic Bomb*, second edition. New York: Knopf, 1947.

_____. *Hell Bomb*. New York: Knopf, 1947.

Lewellen, John. *Exploring Atomic Energy*. Chicago: Science Research Associates, 1952.

_____. *Primer of Atomic Energy*. Chicago: Science Research Associates, 1952.

Los Alamos Scientists. *The Effects of Atomic Weapons*. Washington, D.C.: Government Printing Office, 1950 (revised).

Man vs. the Atom — Year 1. Washington, D.C.: National Commission on Atomic Information, 1946.

Masters, Dexter and Way, Katherine. *One World or None*. New York: McGraw-Hill Book Co., 1946.

McMahon, Brien and W.F. Knowland. *Atomic Peace*. Washington, D.C.: Ransdell, Inc., 1950.

Meyer, Cord, Jr. *Peace or Anarchy*. New York: Little, Brown, and Co., 1948.

Moore, Harry. *Survival or Suicide*. New York: Harper, 1948.

Musial, Joe. *How Dagwood Split the Atom*. New York: King Features Syndicate, 1949.

Miller, M. and A. Spitzer. *We Dropped the A-Bomb*. New York: Crowell, 1946.

National Red Cross. *What to Do in an Atomic Attack*.

Newman, James and Miller, Byron. *The Control of Atomic Energy: A Study of Its Social, Economic, and Political Implications*. New York: Whittlesey House, 1948.

Nucleonics. Washington, D.C.: Progress Press.

Nucleonics Issue — Monsanto Issue, Vol. 24, No. 6. St. Louis: Monsanto Chemical Co.
Nucleonics — What Everybody Should Know About Atomic Physics. Washington, D.C.: U.S. Navy and Public Affairs Press, 1946.
Our Atom World. Albuquerque, N.M.: University of New Mexico Press.
Potter, Robert D. *Young People's Book of Atomic Energy.* New York: Robert McBride & Co., 1946.
Power of the Atom. General Electric.
A Report on the International Control of Atomic Energy. No. 2498. Washington, D.C.: Government Printing Office.
Rothmann, Charles. *Constructive Uses of Atomic Energy.* New York: Harper, 1949.
Sacks, Jacob. *The Atom At Work.* New York: Ronald Press, 1951.
The Seventh (Atomic Energy and the Physical Sciences) and *Eleventh (Some Applications of Atomic Energy in Plant Science) Semiannual Reports of the Atomic Energy Commission to the Congress.* Washington, D.C.: Government Printing Office.
Smyth, H.D. *Atomic Energy for Military Purposes.* Princeton, N.J.: Princeton University Press, 1946.
_____. *A General Account of the Development of Methods of Using Atomic Energy for Military Purposes Under the Auspices of the U.S. Government 1940–1945.* Washington, D.C., 1945.
Stokley, James. *Electrons in Action.* New York: McGraw-Hill Book Co., 1946.
Stout, Wesley. *Secret.* Chrysler Corporation, 1947.
Supervisor of Science, High School Division, Board of Education of New York City and the Atomic Energy Commission, eds. *Laboratory Experiments with Radioisotopes for High School Science Demonstrations.* Washington, D.C., 1953. *Tools for Atomic Education.* Washington, D.C.: National Commission for Atomic Information, 1947.
U.S. Atomic Energy Commission. *Atomic Energy and the Life Sciences.* Washington, D.C.: Government Printing Office, 1949.
Where Will We Hide?
The World Within the Atom. The Westinghouse Co.
Yates, Raymond F. *Atom Smashers.* 1945.

Plays

Corwin, Norman. "Set Your Clock at U-235." In *Untitled and Other Radio Dramas.* New York: Henry Holt and Co., 1947.
Davis, Hallie Flanagan. "Dawn Over Zero." New York: Samuel French, 1947.
Hagedorn, Herman. "The Bomb That Fell On America."

Bibliographies

Annotated Civil Defense Bibliography for Teachers. Washington, D.C.: Federal Civil Defense Administration, 1951.
Light, Israel. *Annotated Bibliography on Atomic Energy.* New York: Bureau of Publications, Teachers College, Columbia University, 1947.

Selected Readings on Atomic Energy. Washington, D.C.: Atomic Energy Commission, 1951.

Films

A Is for Atom. General Electric Co., 1951.
A.A.F. Special Delivery. United States Air Force, 1946.
The Atom and Agriculture. Encyclopedia Britannica Films, 1953.
The Atom and Biological Science. Encyclopedia Britannica Films, 1953.
The Atom and Industry. Encyclopedia Britannica Films, 1952.
The Atom and You. Paramount News, Inc.
Atom Bomb — Right or Wrong? Film Forum Foundation, 1948.
The Atom Strikes. U.S. Army, 1946.
Atomic Alert. Encyclopedia Britannica Films, 1951.
Atomic Atoll. U.S. Army, 1953.
Atomic Bomb — Its Effects and How to Meet Them. British Information Service, 1953.
Atomic Bomb Injuries to the Bikini Animals. U.S. Navy, 1947.
Atomic Bomb Test — Bikini Island. U.S. Navy, 1946.
Atomic Energy. Encyclopedia Britannica Films, 1947.
Atomic Energy As a Force For Good. Christophers, Inc., 1954.
Atomic Energy Can Be A Blessing. Christophers, Inc., 1952.
Atomic Physics. J. Arthur Rank Organization Ltd. Released in the United States by United World Films, Inc., 1948.
Atomic Power. March of Time, 1946.
Atomic Survival. Federal Civil Defense Administration, 1951.
Atomic Tests in Nevada. United States Air Force and Atomic Energy Commission, 1955.
Atoms At Work. British Ministry of Supply, 1952.
Atoms for Peace. U.S. Information Agency and Warner News, 1955.
Beginning or the End. MGM, 1947.
Bikini, The Atomic Island. MGM and U.S. Navy, 1946.
Bikini — Radiological Laboratory. Atomic Energy Commission, 1949; United World-Government, 1951.
Church in the Atomic Age. Film Program Services.
Dawn's Early Light. Westinghouse, 1955.
Debris Clearance. British Information Service, 1953.
Duck and Cover — With Bert the Turtle. Federal Civil Defense Administration and Archer Productions, 1951.
Effects of an Atomic Bomb Explosion. U.S. Government, 1951.
Everybody's Business. U.S. Army, 1950.
First Atomic Pile. MGM, 1947.
Fire Fighting for Householders. United World Films, 1951.
Five Stages of Rescue. British Information Service, 1953.
God of the Atom. Moody Bible Institute, 1947.

H Bomb. World in Color, 1953.

Homeless Ones. Canadian National Film Board, 1954.

House in the Middle. Federal Civil Defense Administration and McGreary-Smith Laboratories, 1954.

How We Get Our Power. Young America, 1949.

The Injured Can't Wait. Health Education Service, 1953.

Inside the Atom. Canadian Atomic Research Center, 1948.

An Introduction to Radiation Detection Devices. Armed Forces Special Weapons Project, 1951.

The Magic of the Atom Series. Handel Film Corp., 1954–55. (This series reinforced the positive aspects of atomic energy, with titles including *Atomic Goldrush, Atomic Cities, Atomic Furnaces, Atomic Detective, Atomic Greenhouse, Atomic Metallurgy, Atomic Pharmacy, Atomic Zoo, Atoms for Health, Atomic Biology for Medicine, Atomic Alchemist, Atomic Age Farmer, Atom Smashers, Atom in Industry, Atom and the Weather, Atom and the Doctor, Industrial Atom, Jobs in Atomic Energy, Security,* and *Power Unlimited.*)

Making Atomic Energy A Blessing. United World-Government, 1952.

Medical Aspects of Nuclear Radiation. U.S. Government, 1952.

Medical Effects of the Atomic Bomb. U.S. Army, 1950.

Nature of Energy. Coronet, 1949.

One World or None. Film Publishers, 1946.

Operation A-Bomb. Atomic Energy Commission, 1952.

Operation Crossroads. U.S. Navy, 1946; United World-Government, 1949.

Operation Doorstep. Byron, Inc., 1953.

Operation Greenhouse. U.S. Air Force, 1952.

Operation Hurricane. British Information Service, 1953.

Operation Ivy. United States Air Force, 1954.

Operation Sandstone. United States Air Force, 1951.

Our Atomic Development. McGraw-Hill, 1953.

Our Cities Must Fight.

Pattern for Survival.

Radioactive Contamination. U.S. Department of Defense, 1952.

Radioactivity: Lab Demonstrations. U.S. Army, 1949.

Radioisotopes Series. U.S. Army, 1952. (The series included *Fundamentals of Radioactivity, Properties of Radiation, Practical Procedures of Measurement, The Radioisotope Methodology, The Practice of Radiological Safety,* and *Radioisotopes in General Science.*)

Radiological Safety at Operation Crossroads. U.S. Navy, 1946.

Radiological Survey. U.S. Department of Defense, 1952.

Report on the Atom. March of Time Forum Films, 1950.

Self-Preservation in Atomic Bomb Attack. Armed Forces Special Weapons Project, 1951.

Survival City. Federal Civil Defense Administration and Twentieth Century Fox, 1955.

Survival Under Atomic Attack. Federal Civil Defense Administration and United World Films, 1951.

A Tale of Two Cities. U.S. Army, 1946.
Target Nevada. Nu-Art Films, 1952.
Target Nevada. United States Air Force, 1953.
Unlocking the Atom. United World-Education, 1951.
What You Should Know About Biological Warfare. United World Films, 1951.
You Can Beat the A-Bomb. McGraw-Hill Text Films, 1951.

Filmstrips

The Atom. Life Filmstrips.
Atom At Work. Society for Visual Education.
Atomic Energy. The New York Times.
Atomic Energy and the United Nations: Problems of International Control. United
   Nations.
Atomic Physics. J. Arthur Rank Organization. Released in the United States by
   United World Films.
How to Live with the Atom. Film Publishers, Inc.
Let's Look at the Atom. Society for Visual Education.
Making Atomic Energy Help Mankind. Popular Science Publishing Co., Audio
   Visual Division.
One World or None.
Up and Atom. Film Publishers.
World Control of Atomic Energy. Film Publishers.
You and the Atom.
You and the Atomic Bomb.
Your Atomic World. The Council on Atomic Implications. Distributed by Society
   for Visual Education.

Records, Transcriptions, Radio Scripts, and Broadcasts

The Atomic Bomb. Chicago: Lewellen's Club Production. Two 12-inch, 78 rpm
   records, for sale with filmstrips.
The Atomic Bomb — Civilian or Military Control. Radio broadcast, *The American
   Forum of the Air*, March 26, 1946. Reprinted as pamphlet.
"Deadline for Living." National Education Association.
Does the Atomic Bomb Make World Government Essential Now? Radio broadcast,
   The Town Hall, November 29, 1945. Reprinted as pamphlet.
Does Atomic Warfare Make Military Training Obsolete? Radio broadcast, *The Amer-
   ican Forum of the Air*, February 12, 1946. Reprinted as pamphlet.
"Hydrogen, The Explosive." Reprinted in *School Activities* 23 (December 1951).
The Implications of Atomic Energy. Radio broadcast, *University of Chicago Round
   Table*, May 5, 1946. Reprinted as pamphlet.
Peacetime Uses of Atomic Energy. Chicago: Lewellen's Club Productions. Two 12-
   inch, 78 rpm records.

Ridenour, Louis. "Pilot Lights of the Apocalypse." Originally in *Fortune*, January 1946.

Should the Baruch Proposal Be Adopted? Radio broadcast, *The Town Hall*, July 4, 1946. Reprinted as pamphlet.

Should We Internationalize the Atomic Bomb? Radio broadcast, *The American Forum of the Air*, October 16, 1945. Reprinted as pamphlet.

Should We Share the Secret of the Atomic Bomb with Any Other Nation? Radio broadcast, *The Town Hall*, October 25, 1945. Reprinted as pamphlet.

The United Nations and the Bomb. Radio broadcast, *University of Chicago Round Table*, July 23, 1946. Reprinted as pamphlet.

The War That Must Not Come. Radio Script, KOA Denver, March 19, 1946.

Who Should Control the Atomic Bomb? Radio broadcast, *The Town Hall*, September 20, 1945. Reprinted as pamphlet.

Who Should Control the Production and Use of Atomic Energy? Radio broadcast, *The Town Hall*, March 28, 1946. Reprinted as pamphlet.

Appendix B: "Hydrogen, the Explosive"

In the late 1940s, the following script was written by high school science students in Buffalo, New York, under the direction of their teacher, George Greisen Mallinson. The script was broadcast over a local radio station, and subsequently modified for presentation before a school assembly. A few years later, Mallinson, then on the faculty of Iowa State Teachers College, presented the script to his chemistry class, who again modified it as part of a series of radio programs. In 1950, the script was presented to a group of science teachers in Michigan, which led to numerous requests for copies for use in school assemblies, science clubs, and other similar programs. To encourage teachers nationwide to use the script, *School Activities* published it in its December 1951 issue.

"Hydrogen, the Explosive" represents the type of atomic narrative often adapted for use in high school classrooms. Of particular note, it reveals the scientific knowledge about atomic energy being taught to members of the Atomic Generation, and clearly shows that the destructive powers of the hydrogen bomb were understood by many students long before the United States tested the H-bomb in 1951. Additionally, this script provides evidence of the gender bias during this era. The boys' "masculine brains" are responsible for the successful experiment, as the girls, who appear primarily as cheerleaders and helpmates, appeared enthralled with the boys' achievement.

(The scene opens in a classroom shortly after school has been dismissed for the day. Two girls are talking about a school matter that has arisen.)

GIRL 1: Gosh, I can't understand why the profs can't give us our assignments some time other than over the weekends. Every week it seems to be the same way.

GIRL 2: Yes, last week it was turn in a paper on atomic structure, this week bring in some evidence to show that hydrogen is an explosive.

GIRL 1: Well, I can see Prof's point. He's been harping all year on the fact that air doesn't have any materials in it that burn. Today half the class thought that they get hydrogen for balloons, and for cutting torches, by extracting it from the air. Still everybody seemed to know it burns.

GIRL 2: I guess everybody gets it mixed up with nitrogen.

GIRL 1: Yes, I guess so, too. But the point is how are we going to bring in some proof that it is an explosive? Prof said a statement from a book wasn't enough, because we had read it many times this year and hadn't paid any attention to it.

GIRL 2: Are there any simple experiments we could hatch up?

GIRL 1: I don't know.

(Two boys enter the room.)

BOY 1: Say, what [are] you two hanging around the lab for at this hour?

GIRL 2: Say, yourself! What are you two coming in for at this hour?

BOY 2: Probably for the same reason that you two are. Prof gave us permission to make up some hydrogen to see if we could prove it explodes.

GIRL 1: Are both of you going to do it, or are you going to work separately?

BOY 1: Oh, Prof said we could work in groups. All he wants us to do really is to get it in our heads that hydrogen explodes when it's mixed with air and lighted.

GIRL 2: Hey, how about letting us in on it?

GIRL 1: Yes, how about it?

BOY 2: *(Dubiously.)* I don't know. Prof just said the two of us.

BOY 1: Oh, come on! We might as well. He didn't say we couldn't have more.

BOY 2: Well, O.K. But no fooling around. We want to get this done and get out.

GIRL 1: Good! Let's get on it now.

GIRL 2: What do you want us to do?

BOY 1: First, you can help me get some of the chemicals, while _____ helps _____ get out the apparatus.

BOY 2: We're going to need a stand, a couple of clamps, a flask, a rubber stopper, some glass and rubber tubing, and a candle. Let's get it.

(Boy 2 and Girl 1 move off.)

GIRL 2: *(to Boy 1)* What chemicals do we need?

BOY 1: Some zinc and some sulfuric acid. They're right here in this cabinet. *(Doors open and bottles come out.)*

(Boy 2 and Girl 1 come back.)

GIRL 1: I guess this is all, isn't it?

BOY 2: Yes, this is all we need.

(All four gather.)

GIRL 2: How do you make the hydrogen?

BOY 1: You dilute some of this sulfuric acid, — that's this stuff in the bottle marked H2SO4, and pour it over some zinc chips.

GIRL 1: Say, I know a poem about that stuff. It goes like this:
Here lies the bones
Of Samuel Jones
Who died upon the floor
(All mockingly in chorus)
Cause what he thought was H20
Was H2SO4.

BOY 2: Yes, we've all heard it and don't think it's funny. Go ahead, will you _____.

BOY 1: First, you clamp this ring on the stand, then you put the flask on the ring and attach the neck of the flask to the iron rod with this clamp.

GIRL 2: Oh, I see the ring just supports the flask and the clamp holds it steady.

BOY 2: That's right.

GIRL 2: But I still don't see where the hydrogen comes from.

BOY 2: You just make it in the flask. First you put some zinc chips in the flask. Pass them over will you _____? See, like this. (Dropping down in flask.)

GIRL 1: The next thing is to pour some of that diluted acid down over the zinc, is that right?

BOY 1: That's it and then we collect the hydrogen.

GIRL 2: I follow so far but I don't see how you are going to prove that hydrogen explodes. You can't light it as it comes out or it would blow up the whole apparatus.

GIRL 1: How are you going to do it?

BOY 2: Just stop talking and watch awhile. Now we dilute the acid. Always pour the acid into the water, not the other way around or it will splatter. *(Sound of pouring.)*

BOY 1: Now I'll pour it down over the zinc. *(Pours.)* Hear how it fizzes! *(Fizzing sound.)*

GIRL 2: Well, this is our idea. You see this rubber stopper with the hole in it? Well, we'll put a glass tube through it and put the stopper in the neck of the flask.

BOY 1: That's it, and then all the hydrogen being formed in the flask will be coming out the end of the glass tubing.

BOY 2: And that's where this balloon comes in. *(Removing balloon and string from his pocket.)*

GIRL 1: Oh, I see now. You're going to fill the balloon with the hydrogen by putting it over the glass tubing and then you're going to tie it up.

GIRL 2: Well, then you have a balloon full of hydrogen, but how does that prove that hydrogen explodes?

BOY 1: You're still right, but when it is full we'll put a lighted candle up to the balloon and if it goes as it should, she'll really blow up.

BOY 2: Now, what do you think of the idea?

GIRL 1: Say fellow, that's O.K.

GIRL 2: How did you ever figure that out?

BOY 1: Just masculine brains, that's all.

BOY 2: Well, let's get going. Have you got the glass tubing in the stopper, _____?

BOY 1: Yes, here it is.

GIRL 1: How about my pouring more acid on the zinc in the flask?

GIRL 2: Sure, let us get in on it.

BOY 1: All right, go ahead. Pour it in slowly. *(Pouring and fizzing.)*

BOY 2: All right. Now here's the stopper with the tube. Plug it up fast. *(Plugging noise.)*

BOY 1: Now to put the balloon over the tubing. Here goes.

GIRL 1: Gosh, that's filling fast.

GIRL 2: There really must be some pressure there.

BOY 2: There is. It's almost time now to tie off the balloon. Here's the string.

BOY 1: O.K. I'll hold it while you tie it. That's it. Quick. Is it tied?

BOY 2: Let go now. I have it tied.

GIRL 1: This is the part I want to see. Let's light it quick!

GIRL 2: Yes, come on!

BOY 1: Not yet! We've got to fill this flask with water and get it out of the way when we light the balloon or that may start to burn too. Remember hydrogen burns!

(Move apparatus — water running.)

BOY 2: Well, let's try it. Tie the balloon to this yardstick and hold it away from you. O.K. Now, light the candle and set it on the desk.

BOY 1: All set? Now, hold the balloon over the candle. *(Balloon blows up.)*

GIRL 1: Gosh, I never thought that little bit of hydrogen would explode like that.

GIRL 2: Neither did I. Can you imagine what would happen if there were hydrogen in the air and someone lit a match? The whole mass of air would blow up.

BOY 1: That's right. Well, I guess we've got proof enough now that hydrogen is bad stuff around flames.

GIRL 1: I'll bet no one else had an idea like this one. When we show this on Monday, it should be an A for each of us.

BOY 2: Yes sir! Well, let's clean up and start spending our week-end.

(Fade out.)

Appendix C: Film and Television Chronology

This chronology of science-fiction television programs and films was compiled from *Variety* as well as James Robert Parish and Michael R. Pitts, eds., *The Great Science Fiction Pictures* (Metuchen, N.J.: Scarecrow Press, 1977); Douglas Brode, *The Films of the Fifties: Sunset Boulevard to On the Beach* (Secaucus, N.J.: Carol Publishing Group, 1976); Bill Warren, *Keep Watching the Skies! American Science Fiction Movies of the Fifties, Volume 1* (Jefferson, N.C.: McFarland, 1982); Donald Willis, *Horror and Science Fiction Films: A Checklist* (Metuchen, N.J.: Scarecrow Press, 1972); Raymond Stedman, *The Serials: Suspense and Drama by Installment* (Norman: University of Oklahoma Press, 1977); Harris Lentz III, *Science Fiction, Horror & Fantasy Film and Television Credits* (Jefferson, N.C.: McFarland, 1983); John Brosnan, *Future Tense: The Cinema of Science Fiction* (London: MacDonald and Janes, 1978); Patrick Lucanio, *Them or Us: Archetypal Interpretations of Fifties Alien Invasion Films* (Bloomington: Indiana University Press, 1987); Gary Grossman, *Saturday Morning TV* (New York: Dell Publishing, 1981); *Superman: Serial to Cereal* (New York: Popular Library, 1976); E. Nelson Bridwell, *Superman, from the Thirties to the Eighties* (New York: Crown Publishers, 1983); and Joyce A. Evans, *Celluloid Mushroom Clouds: Hollywood and the Atomic Bomb* (Boulder, Colo.: Westview Press, 1998).

Science-Fiction and Atomic-Theme Movies (including Serials)

1945	*First Yank in Tokyo*	1946	*Rendezvous 24*
	Shadow of Terror	1947	*The Beginning or the End?*
	The House on 92nd Street		*Sombra, the Spider Woman*

1948 *Superman*
1949 *King of the Rocket Men*
      Radar Patrol vs. Sky King
1950 *Atom Man vs. Superman*
      Destination Moon
      Invisible Monster
      Rocketship XM
      The Flying Saucer
      The Perfect Woman
1951 *Captain Video*
      Five
      Flight to Mars
      Flying Disc Man from Mars
      Krakatit (Czechoslovakian)
      Lost Continent
      Mysterious Island
      Radar Men from the Moon
      The Atomic Duck (or Mr. Drake's Duck)
      The Day the Earth Stood Still
      The Man from Planet X
      The Thing
      The Whip Hand
      Unknown World
      When Worlds Collide
1952 *Above and Beyond*
      Captive Women
      Captain Video
      Radar Men from the Moon
      Red Planet Mars
      Retik, the Moon Menace
      Superman and the Mole Men
      The Atomic City
      Zombies of the Stratosphere
1953 *Abbott and Costello Go to Mars*
      Canadian Mounties vs. Atomic Invaders
      Commando Cody, Sky Marshall of the Universe
      Invasion U.S.A.
      Invaders from Mars
      It Came from Outer Space
      Phantom from Space
      Project Moonbase
      Robot Monster
      Run for the Hills

      Spaceways
      The Atomic Monster
      The Beast from 20,000 Fathoms
      The Lost Planet
      The Magnetic Monster
      The Twonky
      The War of the Worlds
1954 *20,000 Leagues Under the Sea*
      Atomic Attack
      Cat-Women of the Moon
      Creature from the Black Lagoon
      Godzilla (Japanese)
      Gog
      Hell and High Water
      Killers from Space
      Living It Up
      Monster from the Ocean Floor
      Riders to the Stars
      Target Earth
      The Atomic Kid
      The Rocket Man
      Them!
      Tobor the Great
1955 *Conquest of Space*
      Creature with the Atomic Brain
      Devil Girl from Mars
      It Came from Beneath the Sea
      Jungle Moon Men
      Kiss Me Deadly
      Revenge of the Creature
      Strategic Air Command
      Tarantula
      The Beast with 1,000,000 Eyes
      This Island Earth
      World Without End
1956 *A Short Vision (atomic short film)*
      Attack of the Crab Monsters
      Bride of the Atom
      Forbidden Planet
      Invasion of the Body Snatchers
      Phantom from 10,000 Leagues
      The Atomic Man
      The Creature Walks Among Us
      The Day the World Ended

Late 1950s

1957 Bombers B-52
Enemy from Space
From Hell It Came
Not of This Earth
The Amazing Colossal Man
The Beginning of the End
The Cyclops
The Deadly Mantis
The Giant Claw
The Incredible Shrinking Man
The Invisible Boy
The Monster That Challenged the
World
Twenty Million Miles to Earth
1958 Attack of the Fifty Foot Woman
Earth vs. the Spider
I Married A Monster from Outer
Space
It! The Terror from Beyond
Space

Terror from the Year 5000
The Astounding She Monster
The Blob
The Cosmic Monsters
The Lost Missile
The Monster from Green Hell
The Space Children
War of the Colossal Beast
War of the Satellites
1959 4-D Man
Alligator People
City of Fear
Invisible Invaders
Island of Lost Women
On the Beach
Teenagers from Outer Space
The Black Scorpion
The Cosmic Man
The Giant Behemoth
The H-Man
The Hideous Sun Demon

Television Chronology (Series and Programs)

1948 Captain Video (1948–1956)
1949 Lights Out (1949–1952)
1950 Buck Rogers
Tom Corbett, Space Cadet
(1950–1956)
1951 Space Patrol (1950–1956)
1952 Out of This World
Tales of Tomorrow
1953 Superman (1953–1957)
Rod Brown of the Rocket
Rangers (1953–1954)
Flash Gordon
The Atom Squad
Johnny Jupiter (1953–1954)
Operation Neptune
1954 Captain Midnight (1954–1958)
Rocky Jones, Space Ranger
(1954–1958)

Inner Sanctum
Stage 7, "The Secret Weapon
of 117"
Studio One, "U.F.O."
Studio One, "It Might Happen
Tomorrow"
Summer Theatre, "Experiment
Perilous"
TV Hour, "Atomic Attack"
1955 Science Fiction Theatre (1955–
1957)
Commando Cody, Sky Marshall
of the Universe
Studio 57, "Ring Once for
Death"
TV Playhouse, "Visit to a Small
Planet"

Notes

Preface

1. Jean Thompson, "The Impact on the Child's Emotional Life, *National Elementary Principal* 30 (June 1951): 31.

2. Peter Schwenger, *Letter Bomb: Nuclear Holocaust and the Exploding Word* (Baltimore: Johns Hopkins University Press, 1992), 15.

3. This is a study of narratives. Therefore, the very essence of this book rests in the words and images contained herein. What should become readily apparent, particularly among those sensitive to gender issues, is that many of these narratives address the masculine (e.g., he, him, his, mankind, Man). It would be cumbersome and, in my opinion, inappropriate, however, to comment upon this bias at each occurrence. It should be pointed out that during this era, the masculine pronoun was deemed correct English in general, non-specific, usage. This study, perhaps, may provide the framework, or the footnote, for additional studies into the language of gender.

4. For a discussion of adolescent culture in colonial times, see Ray Hiner, "Adolescence in Eighteenth-Century America," in *History of Childhood Quarterly* 3 (Fall 1975): 254–280, or Roger Thompson, "Adolescent Culture in Colonial Massachusetts," in *Journal of Family History* 9, 2 (1984): 127–144. For the nineteenth century, see Nancy Cott, "Young Women in the Second Great Awakening," *Feminist Studies* 3 (Fall 1975) 15–29, and Joseph Kett, *Rites of Passage: Adolescence in America, 1790 to the Present* (New York: Basis Books, 1977). Two additional studies, both dissertations, shed light on twentieth-century adolescent culture: Kathleen Clare Hilton, "Growing Up Female: Girlhood Experiences and Social Feminism, 1890–1929 (Carnegie-Mellon University, 1987), and Richard Ugland, "The Adolescent Experience During World War II" (Indiana University, 1977).

5. Kenneth Keniston, *Young Radicals: Notes on Committed Youth* (New York: Harcourt Brace Jovanovich, 1968) 297–342.

6. Timothy Miller, *The Hippies and American Values* (Knoxville: University of Tennessee Press, 1991).

7. General Omar Bradley's comments are cited in J.G. Umstattd, "Contributions of the Secondary Schools in the Present World Situation," *The High School Journal* 34 (May 1951): 147.

8. Philip A. Knowlton, "Great Issues Facing High School Students," *Senior Scholastic*, 22 Sept. 1948, 18.

9. Gunther Kress, "Discourses, Texts, Readers and the Pro-Nuclear Arguments," in *Language and the Nuclear Arms Debate: Nukespeak Today*, ed. Paul Chilton (London: Frances Pinter, 1985) 65–87.

10. Lawrence W. Levine, *The Unpredictable Past: Explorations in American Cultural History* (New York: Oxford University Press, 1993) 313.

11. Hayden White, "The Value of Narrativity in the Representation of Reality," *Critical Inquiry* 7, 1 (Autumn 1980): 5–27.

12. Paul Chilton, "Introduction," in *Language and the Nuclear Arms Debate: Nukespeak Today*, ed. Paul Chilton (London: Frances Pinter, 1985) xv.

Introduction

1. Quoted in David Dowling, *Fictions of Nuclear Disaster* (Iowa City: University of Iowa Press, 1987) vi.

2. For a comprehensive history of the Students for a Democratic Society (SDS) and the complete text of the Port Huron Statement, see James Miller's "*Democracy Is in the Streets*": *From Port Huron to the Siege of Chicago* (New York: Simon and Schuster, 1987). Although Tom Hayden, Al Haber, and Bob Ross formed the drafting committee, Hayden served as the primary writer of the Port Huron Statement, with input from a number of sources, and thus is acknowledged here as such.

3. Norman Ryder, "The Cohort As a Concept in the Study of Social Change," *American Sociological Review* 30 (1965): 843-861.

4. Karl Mannheim, "The Problem of the Generations," *Essays on the Sociology of Knowledge* (New York: Oxford University Press, 1928); Bernie Neugarten and Nancy Datan, "Sociological Perspectives on the Life Cycle," *Life-Span Development Psychology*, eds. P.A. Beales and K.W. Schaie (New York: Academic Press, 1973): 53-69; Glen Elder, "Adolescence in the Life Cycle: An Introduction," *Adolescence in the Life Cycle: Psychological Change and Social Context*, eds. Glen Elder and Sigmund Dragastin (Washington, D.C.: Hemisphere Publishing Corp., 1975), 1-22. Also additional insights into the significance of cohorts, see Elder, *Children of the Great Depression* (Chicago: University of Chicago Press, 1974).

5. Jeff Smith, *Unthinking the Unthinkable: Nuclear Weapons and Western Culture* (Bloomington: Indiana University Press, 1989) 19.

6. Robert Thom, "Self-Analysis," *Senior Scholastic*, 6 Oct. 1947.

7. David McCullough, Truman (New York: Simon & Schuster, 1992), 582. McCullough discusses the origins of the term "cold war."

8. "You Have a Date with Destiny," *Senior Scholastic*, 20 Sept. 1950, 9.

9. For more insight on civil rights, anti-nuclear, and other movements during the late 1940s and 1950s, see Richard Pells, *The Liberal Mind in a Conservative Age: American Intellectuals in the 1940s & 1950s* (New York: Harper & Row, 1985) and Lawrence Wittner, *Rebels Against War: The American Peace Movement, 1933-1983* (Philadelphia: Temple University Press, 1984).

10. Jerome Rodnitzky, "The Evolution of the American Protest Song," in Timothy E. Scheurer, editor, *The Age of Rock* (Bowling Green, Ohio: Bowling Green State University Popular Press, 1989) 118.

11. "The Times They Are A-Changin," copyright 1963 Warner Bros., Inc., and renewed 1991 by Special Rider Music; "Blowin' in the Wind" copyright 1962 Warner Bros., Inc., and renewed 1990 by Special Rider Music.

12. Edward Reuter, "Sociological Research in Adolescence: The Adolescent World," *American Journal of Sociology* 42 (July 1936): 81-83. Reuter argued that the degree of "unity and organization and solidarity" of the youth culture varies inversely with the ease and uniformity with which adolescents are able to participate fully in the adult culture.

Chapter 1

1. Quoted in *The New York Times* 23 June 1946.

2. "V-J Day Celebrations Vary with Students While at Home, Away," *The Southwest Trail* (Kansas City, Missouri) 24 Sept. 1945: 2.

3. William Graebner, *Coming of Age in Buffalo: Youth and Authority in the Postwar Era* (Philadelphia: Temple University Press, 1990).

4. William Reaves, "Organized Extra-Curricular Activities in the High School," *The High School Journal* 34 (May 1951): 130.

5. Gerald Van Pool, "The Student Council Trains for Effective Citizenship," *School Activities* 25 (September 1953): 9; Gordon Dean, "The Atomic Age Moves Forward," *School Life* 35 (1953): 159; "Lyman Graybeal," Democratic Education in a Time of Crisis," *School Activities* 20 (March 1949): 211.

6. Bonaro Overstreet, "Understanding Our Fears," *Journal of the National Education Association* 41 (February 1952): 85–86.

7. Laurence Sears, "Anxiety in the United States of America," in H. Gordon Hullfish, ed., *Educational Freedom in an Age of Anxiety: Yearbook of the John Dewey Society 1953* (New York: Harper & Brothers, 1953) 26.

8. Sears, "Anxiety in the United States of America," 1.

9. H. Gordon Hullfish, "Education in an Age of Anxiety," in H. Gordon Hullfish, ed., *Educational Freedom in an Age of Anxiety: Yearbook of the John Dewey Society 1953* (New York: Harper & Brothers, 1953) 208.

10. "After School Hours," *The Journal of Education* 134 (September 1951(: 159; T. H. Butterworth, "Group Thinking Strengthens Democracy" *The High School Journal* 32 (October 1949): 191–192.

11. "Teen-Age Girls," *Life* 11 Dec. 1944, 91–99; "Teen-Age Boys," *Life* 11 June 1945, 91–97.

12. Richard Ugland, "The Adolescent Experience During World War II," dissertation, Indiana University, 1977; "Centers for Youth," *School Review* 53 (December 1945): 574.

13. "Jam Session," *Senior Scholastic* 22 Oct. 1945, 42, 48; "Jam Session," *Senior Scholastic*, 22 Oct. 1945, 30.

14. "Birth of an Era," *Time* 13 Aug. 1945: 17–18.

15. See Thomas Robinson, "School Newspaper Can Promote Learning," *Journal of the National Education Association* 36 (March 1947): 210–211; S.A. Slater, "Not A Gossip Sheet! High School Newspapers," *Journal of the National Education Association* 40, 7 (1951): 489–490; N.C. Merrick and W.C. Seyfert, "School Publications As a Source of Desirable Group Experience," *School Review* 55 (January 1947): 1–28.

16. "The Significant Year," *The East Echo* 5 Sept. 1945: 1.

17. "Peacetime School Era Challenges Us," *The Southwest Trail* 24 Sept. 1945: 2.

18. "Volunteers Serve by Selling Flowers Made by Veterans," *The Northeast Courier* (Kansas City, Missouri) 28 Sept. 1945: 3; "Planning for Peace," *The Westport Crier* (Kansas City, Missouri) 19 Sept. 1945: 2; "Last Southwest Bond Drive to Begin This Week," *The Southwest Trail* (Kansas City, Missouri) 8 Oct. 1945: 1; "Gift Boxes Ready for War Children; Red Cross Sponsors," *The Southwest Trail* (Kansas City, Missouri) 8 Oct. 1945; 1; "Japanese Concentration Camp Internees Tell Stories of Life Under Jap Rule," *The Paseo Press* (Kansas City, Missouri) 11 Oct. 1945: 1; "Float," *The Paseo Press* (Kansas City, Missouri) 25 Oct. 1945: 1; "Building Invincible Peace," *The Paseo Press* (Kansas City, Missouri) 11 Oct. 1945: 2; "R.O.T.C. Begins Year with New Plans," *The Southwest Trail* (Kansas City, Missouri) 24 Sept. 1945: 1; "You Gain By Giving," *The Manual Craftsman* (Kansas City, Missouri) 21 Sept. 1945: 1; "Junior Red Cross Fills Gift Boxes for Children," *The Manual Craftsman* (Kansas City, Missouri) 5 Oct. 1945: 1; "Give to War Chest Fund Campaign," *The Manual Craftsman* (Kansas City, Missouri) 5 Oct. 1945: 1; "Navy League Announces War Bond Contest," *The Manual Craftsman* (Kansas City, Missouri) 5 Oct. 1945: 1; "World War II Veterans Speak to East Girls," *The East Echo* (Kansas City, Missouri) 27 Sept. 1945: 1; "Cooperative Occupation Education at East," *The East Echo* (Kansas City, Missouri) 27 Sept. 1945: 1; "Memorial Program for Gold Star Knights," *The Southeast Tower* (Kansas City, Missouri) 1 Nov. 1945: 1; "Navy Day Speaker Served in Europe," *The Southeast Tower* (Kansas City, Missouri) 1 Nov. 1945: 1; "Red Cross Gift Boxes to Be Made by Homerooms," *The Northeast Courier* (Kansas City, Missouri) 5 Oct. 1945: 1; "Northeast Asks Help of Students in Victory Drive for Bonds," *The Northeast Courier* (Kansas City, Missouri) 19 Oct.

1945: 1; "Assembly Heard in Celebration of Brotherhood Week," *The Northeast Courier* (Kansas City, Missouri) 1 March 1946: 1; "Jr. Red Cross Inspired By Work for Youth in Europe," *The Central Luminary* (Kansas City, Missouri) 1 March 1946: 1; "Opinion Polls," *The East Echo* (Kansas City, Missouri) 28 March 1946: 2; "All Students Are Asked to Help House Veterans," *The Southeast Tower* (Kansas City, Missouri) 1 March 1946: 2; "Three Ex-Servicemen Visit History Classes," *The Southeast Tower* (Kansas City, Missouri) 12 April 1946: 1; "Students Fill Junior Red Cross Christmas Boxes," *School Activities* 22 (November 1950): 109.

19. "Editorial on Atom Bomb Entry in Contest," *The Southwest Trail* (Kansas City, Missouri) 7 Dec. 1945: 3; "Southwest Broadcasts on National Hookup," *The Southwest Trail* (Kansas City, Missouri) 22 Oct. 1945: 1; *The Central Luminary* (Kansas City, Missouri) 16 Nov. 1945; "High School Poll Taken in Classes," *The Paseo Press* (Kansas City, Missouri) 20 Dec. 1945: 1; "Show Thankful Spirit By Working for Peace," *Southeast Tower* (Kansas City, Missouri) 15 Nov. 1945: 2.

20. *La Loma*, Los Alamos High School, Los Alamos, New Mexico, 1954.

21. W. Ogden, "Ridge Kids Use the Atom," *New York Times Magazine* 2 June 1946: 24–25; W.C. Seyfert, "Youth in the Atomic Age," *School Review* 54 (June 1946): 319–320; Philip Kennedy, "Oak Ridge and the Educational Crossroads," *National Association of Secondary-School Principals Bulletin* 30 (October 1946): 81–83.

22. Sally Cartwright, "Where the Atom Bomb Was Born," *Progressive Education* 24 (October 1946): 4.

23. Ogden, "Ridge Kids Use the Atom," 24–25; Seyfert, "Youth in the Atomic Age," 319–320; Cartwright, "Where the Atom Bomb Was Born," 4; Kennedy, "Oak Ridge and the Educational Crossroads," 81–83.

24. Florence Gelbond, "The Impact of the Atomic Bomb on Education," *The Social Studies* 65 (March 1974): 110.

25. Gerrit Zwart, "How a Small High School Meets the Challenge of the Atomic Age: Suffern High School Atomic Energy Club," *School Life* 35 (September 1953): 147+.

26. Margaret March-Mount, "Atom-Agers Look to the Future," *Progressive Education* 27,6 (1950): 165–171.

27. "Pupils Advertise American Education Week," *The Manual Craftsman* (Kansas City, Missouri) 1 Nov. 1946: 1; "Cans of Milk for Needy to Y-Teen Party," *The Southeast Tower* (Kansas City, Missouri) 6 Nov. 1946: 3; "'Atomic Power, Peace' Discussed by R. Riley," *The Southeast Tower* (Kansas City, Missouri) 22 Nov. 1946: 2; "Speech on Atomic Age," *The Manual Craftsman* (Kansas City, Missouri) 27 Nov. 1946: 1.

28. "The Atomic Challenges Education," *The Central Luminary* (Kansas City, Missouri) 1 Nov. 1946: 3; "A Challenge to Education," *The East Echo* (Kansas City, Missouri) 14 Nov. 1946: 1.

29. *The Paseon*, Paseo High School (Kansas City, Missouri) 1946; *Nor-easter*, Northeast High School (Kansas City, Missouri) 1948, 29.

30. See Graebner, "Outlawing Teenage Populism: The Campaign Against Secret Societies in the American High School, 1900–1960," *The Journal of American History* 74 (September 1987): 411–435.

31. Edward Olds, "How Do Young People Use Their Leisure Time?" *Recreation* 42 (January 1949): 458–463; Irene Grubick, "School Forums and Student Responsibility," *School Activities* 20 (April 1949): 247–248; "Pan American Club Activities," *School Life* 28 (October 1945): 20–23; Janet Bassett Johnson Baker, "U.N. Youth Develop Global Consciousness," *School Activities* 23 (May 1952): 285–287; Virginia Hardin Stearns, "Denver's International Relations Club," *The Journal of Education* 133 (May 1950): 138–140; "Junior Hi Forum Stresses Intercultural Education," *School Activities* 20 (January 1949): 167; "World Affairs Clubs Still Too Few," *The Journal of Education* 133 (May 1950): 155; S. L. Counselbaum, "Building Democracy Through Extra-Curricular Clubs," *Education* 68 (November 1947): 162–166; Graebner, *Coming of Age in Buffalo: Youth and Authority in the Postwar Era*.

32. "Youth Meets the Challenge," *The Manual Craftsman* (Kansas City, Missouri) 2 Nov. 1951: 2. High school newspapers in Kansas City published articles virtually each week on student activities to help veterans and other relief efforts. For a sampling, see "Volunteers Serve By Selling Flowers Made By Veterans," *The Northeast Courier* 28 Sept. 1945: 3; "Homerooms to Fill Red Cross Boxes," *The Southwest Trail* 23 Oct. 1947: 1; "Community Drive Starts," *The Northeast Courier* 19 Oct. 1945: 1; "Junior Red Cross Fills Gift Boxes for Children," *The Manual Craftsman* 5 Oct. 1945: 1.

33. *Sachem*, Southwest High School (Kansas City, Missouri) 1949; *Lincolnite*, Lincoln High School (Kansas City, Missouri) 1947; *The Centralian*, Central High School (Kansas City, Missouri) 1952; "Homerooms to Nominate Service Society Members," *The Manual Craftsman* (Kansas City, Missouri) 20 April 1951: 1; *Eastonian*, East High School (Kansas City, Missouri) 1945; *Sumnerian*, Sumner High School (Kansas City, Kansas) 1952. Also see A.J. Orrico, "School Club Gives Preview of Nursing," *Occupations* 24 (December 1945): 156–157.

34. For a discussion of adolescent clubs outside of school and gangs, see Graebner, *Coming of Age in Buffalo: Youth and Authority in the Postwar Era*, and James Gilbert, *A Cycle of Outrage: America's Reaction to the Juvenile Delinquent in the 1950s* (New York: Oxford University Press, 1986).

35. Mary Laxson and Berenice Mallory, "Education for Homemaking in Today's High School," *School Life* 32 (June 1950): 134–135, 138; E. Mundt, "Home Economics Clubs in High School." *Journal of Home Economics* 38 (April 1946): 213–215; H.S. Zucker, "Charm Club; Extra-Curricular Activity Conducted on a Voluntary Basis," *Senior Scholastic* (Teacher Edition) 9 Dec. 1946: 5T+.

36. Organized activities within the school and the community, particularly team sports, had been used as social-control mechanisms long before the atomic age. This was readily apparent at the turn of the century, as progressive educators and other activists promoted public school attendance and activities like the organized playground movement. For more discussion on schools, sports, and play as social-control devices, see Paul Boyer, *Urban Masses and Moral Order in America, 1820–1920* (Cambridge, Mass.: Harvard University Press, 1978); Dom Cavallo, "Social Reform and the Movement to Organize Children's Play During the Progressive Era," *History of Childhood Quarterly* 3 (Spring 1976); and Joel Spring, "Education as a Form of Social Control," in Clarence Karies, Paul Violas, and Joel Spring, eds., *Roots of Crisis: American Education in the Twentieth Century* (Chicago: Rand McNally College Publishing Co., 1973): 30–39.

37 Charles McCloy, editor, *The Organization and Administration of Physical Education* (New York: Appleton-Century-Crofts, 1958) 13, 70.

38. McCloy, *The Organization and Administration of Physical Education*, 13, 66–67, 70.

39. McCloy, *The Organization and Administration of Physical Education*, 74–75.

40. For a look at girls' sports activities, see *The Nor'easter*, Northeast High School (Kansas City, Missouri) 1947–49; *The Centralian*, Central High School (Kansas City, Missouri) 1945; *The Paseon*, Paseo High School (Kansas City, Missouri) 1945–49; and *Sachem*, Southwest High School (Kansas City, Missouri) 1946–49.

41. Elaine Tyler May, *Homeward Bound: American Families in the Cold War Era* (New York: Basic Books, 1988) 20, 113.

42. *Nor'easter*, Northeast High School (Kansas City, Missouri) 1949; Marion Nowak, "'How to Be a Woman': Theories of Female Education in the 1950s," *Journal of Popular Culture* 9 (Summer 1975): 77.

43. William H. Whyte, Jr., *The Organization Man* (New York: Simon and Schuster, 1956) 63–78; Kenneth Keniston, *The Uncommitted: Alienated Youth in American Society* (1960; New York: Dell, 1965).

44. *Historical Statistics of the United States: Colonial Times to 1970* (Washington, D.C.: U.S. Department of Commerce, 1975) 20.

45. Lynn White, Jr., *Educating Our Daughters* (New York: Harper & Row, 1950).

46. White, *Educating Our Daughters*, 19.

47. Laxson and Mallory, "Education for Homemaking in Today's High School," 134.

48. *The Paseon*, Paseo High School, Kansas City, Missouri, 1948; *Historical Statistics of the United States*, 378.

49. "Family Living Classes Study Family Finance," *The Northeast Courier* (Kansas City, Missouri) 10 Dec. 1948: 1; *The Centralian*, Central High School (Kansas City, Missouri) 1950; *The Eastonian*, East High School (Kansas City, Missouri) 1952. 1955; JoAnne Brown, "'A' Is for 'Atom'; 'B' Is for 'Bomb': Civil Defense in American Public Education, 1948–1963," *Journal of American History* 75 (June 1988): 84; Federal Civil Defense Administration, *Civil Defense Educational Practices and References for Homemaking Classes, Classroom Practices* (Washington, D.C.: GPO, 1957).

50. "N.R.O.T.C. and N.A.C.P. Program Offered to Senior Boys," *The Northeast Courier* (Kansas City, Missouri) 27 Nov. 1946: 1; *The Eastonian*, East High School (Kansas City, Missouri) 1954.

51. "ROTC Adopts New Training Program," *The Westport Crier* (Kansas City, Missouri) 19 Sept. 1945: 3; *Sachem*, Southwest High School (Kansas City, Missouri) 1946–1952; "Marines Land at Southeast to Interest Boys in Training," *The Southeast Tower* (Kansas City, Missouri) 3 Oct. 1947: 1; "Municipal Auditorium Scene of R.O.T.C. Circus," *The Northeast Courier* (Kansas City, Missouri) 3 May 1946: 1; "Army Men Speak to Boys," *The Northeast Courier* (Kansas City, Missouri) 24 March 1950: 1; "Students Are Orderly," *The Southwest Trail* (Kansas City, Missouri) 21 Feb. 1951: 1; "R.O.T.C. Field Day Held at Gillham Park," *The Northeast Courier* (Kansas City, Missouri) 23 May 1952: 1; "R.O.T.C. Notes," *The Northeast Courier* (Kansas City, Missouri) 23 May 1952: 3; "R.O.T.C. Summer Camp in Kansas," *The Northeast Courier* (Kansas City, Missouri) 5 Oct. 1951: 1; "Draft Discussions at 'Y,'" *The Northeast Courier* 8 (Kansas City, Missouri) Feb. 1952: 1; *The Nor'easter*, Northeast High School (Kansas City, Missouri) 1947; *The Centralian*, Central High School (Kansas City, Missouri) 1952; *The Eastonian*, East High School (Kansas City, Missouri) 1954; "An Essential for World Brotherhood, ROTC Colonel Stresses Teamwork," *The East Echo* (Kansas City, Missouri) 13 Feb. 1947: 1; John Swomley, Jr., "Is the Military Invading the Boy Scouts?" *Progressive Education* 26, 3 (1949): 93–95; Boy Scouts of America (www.scouting.org). For more on draft laws, see George Q. Flynn, *The Draft, 1940–1973* (Lawrence: University Press of Kansas, 1993).

52. Stuart Little, "The Friendship Train: Citizenship and Postwar Culture, 1946–1949," *American Studies* 34 (Spring 1993): 35–67; "Hundreds Come to See Friendship Train Loaded with Sacks of Grain for Europe," *The Paseo Press* 5 Dec. 1947: 1; "Jam Session," *Senior Scholastic* 29 Sept. 1948: 35.

53. Paul Boyer, *By the Bomb's Early Light: American Thought and Culture at the Dawn of the Atomic Age* (New York: Pantheon Books, 1985) 296–297; Richard Robin, "Power and the Atom," *The Journal of Educational Sociology* 22 (January 1949): 350–352; Richard Hitchcock, "Westinghouse Theater of Atoms," *The Journal of Educational Sociology* 22 (January 1949): 353–355; Lillian Wald Key, "Public Opinion and the Atom," *The Journal of Educational Psychology* 22 (January 1949): 356–362; Louis Heil and Joe Musial, "'Splitting the Atom'—Starring Dagwood and Blondie: How It Developed," *The Journal of Educational Psychology* 22 (January 1949): 331–336; "Atomic Energy Book Exhibit for New York's Golden Jubilee," *Publishers Weekly*, 10 July 1948, 140; "Atomic Energy Book Exhibit Touring the Country," *Publishers Weekly*, 27 November 1948, 204.

54. Mattie Pinette, "School and Community Face the Atomic Age," *School Life* 35 (September 1953): 155; "Oak Ridge on Wheels," *The Journal of the National Education Association* 40 (December 1951): 606.

55. Boyer, *By the Bomb's Early Light*, 296–297.

56. "'In Our Hands' Was Subject of Films Shown Assembly," *The Northeast Courier* (Kansas City, Missouri) 19 Oct. 1951: 1; "Assembly Programs for December," *School Activities* 22 (November 1950): 101–102; "Loyalty Day Assembly," *The Manual Craftsman* (Kansas City, Missouri) 6 Nov. 1953: 1; *The Eastonian*, East High School (Kansas City, Missouri) 1951; "Atomic Age Is Subject Presented in Assembly," *The Manual Craftsman* (Kansas City, Missouri) 22 Oct. 1948: 1; "The 'One World Ensemble' Performs at Music Hall," *The Lin-*

coln Callotype (Kansas City, Missouri) 25 March 1949: 1; "Pan-American Assembly Stresses United World," *The Central Luminary* (Kansas City, Missouri) 6 May 1949: 1.

57. Allan Winkler, *Life Under a Cloud: American Anxiety About the Atom* (New York: Oxford University Press) 114; "Students Attend 'Alert America,'" *The Manual Craftsman* (Kansas City, Missouri) 10 April 1952: 3.

58. Helen Heffernan, "The School Curriculum in American Education," in Edgar Fuller and Jim Pearson, eds., *Education in the States: Nationwide Development Since 1900* (Washington, D.C.: National Education Association, 1969) 215–285; "More Scripts for High School Radio Workshops," *Senior Scholastic*, Teacher Edition 26 Sept. 1951: 27T.

59. "Southwest Broadcasts On National Hookup," *The Southwest Trail* (Kansas City, Missouri) 22 Oct. 1945: 1; "Local High School Radio Forum," *School Activities* 22 (December 1950): 137; "Students Aid Freedom," *The East Echo* (Kansas City, Missouri) 4 March 1954: 1; *Senior Scholastic*, Teacher Edition 7 March 1951: 23T; Elizabeth Drake and Lillian Carmen, "A Broadcast for Brotherhood," *School Activities* 21 (October 1949): 56–58, 68; "Six Pupils Give Radio Talks on Europe's Food Problem," *The Westport Crier* (Kansas City, Missouri) 24 Sept. 1947: 1; "TV Show Spotlights Teenagers; Larry Ray Acts as Moderator," *The Southwest Trail* (Kansas City, Missouri) 25 Feb. 1954: 1; Martha Gable, "Philadelphia Classroom Television," *The Journal of Education* 134 (February 1951): 50–52.

60. Interview with Maureen W. (November 8, 1993), who participated in both the Civil Air Patrol and the Ground Observer Corps in her home state of Iowa during the early 1950s. For more on the G.O.C. and CONELRAD, see the following publications issued by the Federal Civil Defense Administration: *Time for Air Defense Is Now! Here's How You Can Help [Defend America as Member of Ground Observer Corps]* (1953); *Safe Because Some American Looked to the Sky! [as Ground Observer in G.O.C.]* (1953); *Ground Observer Corps, Guard Our Country, Air Defense* (1953); *In Case of Attack! Tune Your AM Radio Dial [to] 640 [or] 1240 for Official Information, CONELRAD* (1953).

61. "National Defense: Ducking for Cover," *Newsweek* 30 July 1956: 28; Spencer Weart, *Nuclear Fear: A History of Images* (Cambridge, Mass.: Harvard University Press, 1988): 131; Winkler, *Life Under a Cloud*, 117–118, 122.

62. "Play Depicts Terror When H-Bomb Drops on the Plaza," *The Southeast Tower* (Kansas City, Missouri) 26 Jan. 1955: 1, 3.

Chapter 2

1. 1946 routine featuring humorist's Frank Sullivan's fictional "cliche expert" Mr. Arbuthnot. Quoted in Spencer Weart, *Nuclear Fear: A History of Images* (Cambridge, Mass.: Harvard University Press, 1988) 105.

2. David Lilienthal, "Youth in the Atomic Age," *Journal of the National Education Association* 37 (September 1948): 370-371.

3. *The Sumnerian*, Sumner High School (Kansas City, Kansas) 1949.

4. John S. Perkins, "Where Is the Social Sciences' Atomic Bomb?," *School and Society* 17 Nov. 1945: 315-317.

5. "Psychologists Advise on the Atomic-Bomb Peril," *School and Society*, 8 June 1946: 405-406.

6. Excerpt of Fordham University address quoted in "Education for the Atomic Age," *The Educational Digest* 12 (October 1946): cover 4.

7. Benjamin Fine, "'A Better World' Courses in New York City Schools," *The Education Digest* 12 (September 1946): 10-11. (A reprint from *The New York Times*, 19 May 1949.)

8. Dorothy McClure and Philip Johnson, "Where the School Takes Hold," *School Life* Supplement 31 (March 1949): 7.

9. McClure and Johnson, "Where the School Takes Hold," 7.

10. "Colleges Chosen for Atom Study," *The Journal of Education* 131 (May 1948): 165; "Pupils Beat Teachers on Atom Knowledge," *The Journal of Education* 133 (May 1950): 155;

Hubert Evans and Ryland Crary, "Atomic Education: A Continuing Challenge," 515-520; "Learning Experiences in Atomic Energy Education," *School Life* Supplement 32 (March 1949): 10; Glasheen, "What Schools Are Doing in Atomic Energy Education," 152-154+.

11. *Atomic Education: Chicago's Challenge. Report on the Atomic Energy Institute for Teachers, Chicago, Illinois, 1949-1950.*

12. Josephine Antonini, editor, *Educational Film Guide 1954-1958* (New York: H.W. Wilson Co., 1958) 72.

13. For a description of this series as well as the other films discussed, see Frederic Krahn, editor, *Educational Film Guide*, 11th edition (New York: H.W. Wilson Co., 1953); Antonini, *Educational Film Guide 1954-1958*; and A. Costandina Titus, "Back to Ground Zero: Old Footage Through New Lenses," *Journal of Popular Film and Television* 20 (1983): 2-11.

14. Jack Shaheen and Richard Taylor, "The Beginning or the End," *Nuclear War Films*, ed. Jack Shaheen (Cardondale: Southern Illinois Press, 1978) 8.

15. Lisle A. Rose, *The Cold War Comes to Main Street* (Lawrence, Kan.: University Press of Kansas, 1999): 3-4.

16. R. Will Burnett, Ryland Crary, and Hubert Evans, "The Minds of Men," *School Life* 31 (March 1949): 11-13.

17. "What Is Operation Atomic Vision?" *National Association of Secondary-School Principals Bulletin* 32 (April 1948): 198-204; Hubert Evans, Ryland Crary, and Glenn Hass, "Operation Atomic Vision," *Journal of the National Education Association* 37 (October 1948): 439-442; Paul Boyer, *By the Bomb's Early Light: American Thought and Culture at the Dawn of the Atomic Age* (New York: Pantheon Books, 1985) 281-297.

18. Evans, Crary, and Hass, "Operation Atomic Vision," 442. Emphasis in original text.

19. Quoted in Boyer, *By the Bomb's Early Light*, 298.

20. Evans, Crary, and Hass, "Operation Atomic Vision," 440.

21. Hubert Evans and Ryland Crary, "Atomic Education: A Continuing Challenge," *Teachers College Record* 50 (1949) 519.

22. Benjamin Starr and Abraham Leavitt, "Social Studies and 'Operation Atomic Vision,'" *High Points* 31 (April 1949): 22-32.

23. Starr and Leavitt, "Social Studies and 'Operation Atomic Vision,'" 24.

24. *Eastonian*, East High School (Kansas City, Missouri) 1949. For a sampling of some schools' activities, see George Glasheen, "What Schools Are Doing in Atomic Energy Education," *School Life* 35 (September 1953): 152-154+; McClure and Johnson, "Where the School Takes Hold," 7-9+; "Mouse Traps for Chain Reaction," *School Life* 32 (November 1949): 21-22; Gerrit Zwart, "How a Small High School Meets the Challenge of the Atomic Age," *School Life* Supplement 35 (September 1953): 147, 160; *The Lincoln Callotype* (Kansas City, Missouri) 28 April 1954: 1; Audrey Lindsey, "I Taught Atomic Energy: With Statements By Thirteen Members of the Class," Education 71, 7 (1951): 451-469; Rosalie Kirshen, "A Unit on Atomic Energy in the Experience Curriculum," *High Points* 33 (February 1951): 27-31; David Hilton and Mary Jeffries, "Atomic Energy in the Classroom and Community," *Journal of Education* 131 (March 1948): 88-89; Bryan Swan and Generose Dunn, "Unit on Atomic Energy for Junior High School," *The School Review* 62 (April 1954): 231-236; "Schools Facing Reality in Preparing for an Attack," *The Southeast Tower* (Kansas City, Missouri) 16 March 1951: 1; Hubert Evans and Ryland Crary, "Atomic Education: A Continuing Challenge," *Teachers College Record* 50 (1949): 515-520; "Make and Show," *School Life* Supplement 31 (March 1949): 6.

25. Swan and Generose Dunn, "Unit on Atomic Energy for Junior High School," 231-236.

26. Swan and Generose Dunn, "Unit on Atomic Energy for Junior High School," 232.

27. For descriptions of similar programs, see Hilton and Jeffries, "Atomic Energy in the Classroom and Community," and Leo Weitz, "A Social Studies on Atomic Energy," *High Points* 31 (February 1949): 14-26.

28. "What Are We Fighting For," *The Southeast Tower* (Kansas City, Missouri) 10 March 1952: 2.

29. George Gallup, *The Gallup Poll: Public Opinion 1935-1971* (New York: Random House, 1972) 675, 916; Rose, *The Cold War Comes to America*, p. 4.

30. Edwin Miner, "National Conference on Zeal for American Democracy," *School Life* 30 (May 1948): 3-5; Ward Keesecker, "Duty of Teachers to Promote Ideals and Principles of American Democracy," *School Life* 30 (February 1948): 31-33.

31. Charles Peters, *Teaching High School History and Social Studies for Citizenship Training* (Coral Gables, Fla.: University of Miami Press, 1948).

32. Peters, *Teaching High School History and Social Studies for Citizenship Training*, 38-40.

33. Peters, *Teaching High School History and Social Studies for Citizenship Training*, 19-20.

34. Ron Davis, "Laboratory Practice in Protective Skills," *School Life* 35 (1953): 158-159; "Another Citizenship Program," *The Journal of Education* 133 (May 1950): 135; "For Citizenship and Moral Training," *Senior Scholastic*, 7 Nov. 1951: 12-13.

35. "Dix's Students Discuss Current World Topics," *The East Echo* (Kansas City, Missouri) 13 March 1952: 1; Hazel Torrens, "Current Events in the Ninth Grade," *The Education Digest* 12 (December 1946): 22-23; Barbara York, "Quincy High School's P.D. Course," *The Journal of Education* 13 (September 1948): 218-219; "Kansas Will Train Youth As Citizens," *The Journal of Education* 133 (September 1950): 189; *Senior Scholastic* (Teacher Edition) 15 April 1946, 5T.

36. This so-called "experience curriculum" was proposed in 1933 by the National Council of Teachers of English. The aim was to provide a series of guided experiences that paralleled real-life situations. For more discussion, see Edward Krug, *The Shaping of the American High School, 1920-1941* (Madison: University of Wisconsin Press, 1972) 267-268.

37. Kirshen, "A Unit on Atomic Energy in the Experience Curriculum," 27-31.

38. Lindsey, "I Taught Atomic Energy: With Statements By Thirteen Members of the Class," 451-469. When the unit was first offered, in 1949-50, it was titled "Implications of Atomic Energy"; the second year, it was retitled "What It Means to Live in the World with Atomic Energy" because of the availability of more articles and the rapidly changing world situation.

39. Lindsey, "I Taught Atomic Energy: With Statements By Thirteen Members of the Class," 451.

40. Lindsey, "I Taught Atomic Energy: With Statements By Thirteen Members of the Class," 460-461.

41. Lindsey, "I Taught Atomic Energy: With Statements By Thirteen Members of the Class," 469.

42. Dorothy McClure, "Social Studies Textbooks and Atomic Energy," *The School Review* 57 (December 1949): 540-546.

43. "National Governments," *Journal of Education* 131 (January 1948): 6.

Chapter 3

1. Beltrame, student president, was quoted in "What Are the Teen-agers Thinking? Summary of an Unrehearsed Exchange of Views in San Francisco," *Rotarian* 74 (January 1949): 14.

2. "The Significant Year," *The East Echo* (Kansas City, Missouri) 5 September 1945: 1.

3. *Eastonian*, East High School (Kansas City, Missouri), 1946.

4. "Building Invisible Peace," *The Paseo Press* (Kansas City, Missouri) 11 October 1945: 2; "The Generation Hopes for Peace, Growth," *The Southwest Trail* (Kansas City, Missouri) 11 April 1946: 2; "Planning for Peace," *The Westport Crier* (Kansas City, Missouri) 19 September 1945: 2; *The Herald*, Westport High School, 1947.

5. Tracy Mygatt, "World Government Is Common Sense," *Progressive Education* 24 (October 1946): 10-11.

6. William Fisher, "Let's Look at Secondary Education," *Progressive Education* 24 (April 1947): 200-201.

7. Gladys Wiggin, "Teaching Peace Is Not Enough," *School Life* 28 (July 1946): 17-18; William Drake, *The American School in Transition* (New York: Prentice-Hall, 1955) 478; "The World Federation Summer School in Geneva, Switzerland," *School and Society* 26 July 1947: 54.

8. See Paul Boyer, *By the Bomb's Early Light: American Thought and Culture At the Dawn of the Atomic Age* (New York: Pantheon Books, 1985). He has written that between 1945 and 1947, world government was "an enormously important culture motif, symbolizing for many the need to revise policy responses equal to the magnitude of the atomic threat" (p. 38).

9. "U.N. Day Broadcast Heard in Auditorium," *The Central Luminary* (Kansas City, Missouri) 3 Nov. 1950: 1; "United Nations Week to Be Observed By East Pupils," *The East Echo* (Kansas City, Missouri) 16 Oct. 1952: 1; "Teaching the U.N. in Crisis," *The Journal of Education* 134 (January 1951): 11-12; "Gettysburg Address Fits Our Problems," *The Southeast Tower* (Kansas City, Missouri) 15 Feb. 1946: 2.

10. Carey, "The Schools and Civil Defense: The Fifties Revisited," 120.

11. "Anniversary of V-E Day," *The Paseo Press* (Kansas City, Missouri) 8 May 1947: 2.

12. "Civilization," *The Lincoln Callotype* (Kansas City, Missouri) 20 Feb. 1948: 2.

13. "Youth Speaks for Democracy," *School Life* 30 (February 1948): 20-23; "Winning with the American Way," *School Life* 31 (April 1949): 2-3+; "Theme of Democracy to Encourage Youth," *The Westport Crier* (Kansas City, Missouri) 11 Dec. 1952, 5.

14. "Youth Speaks for Democracy," 22.

15. Earl James McGrath, *Education: The Wellspring of Democracy* (University, Alabama: University of Alabama Press, 1951) 70, 127-129.

16. James Bryant Conant, *Education in a Divided World* (Cambridge, Massachusetts: Harvard University Press, 1948) 18.

17. Conant, *Education in a Divided World*, 232.

18. "'Democracy Beats Communism' Is Theme of School Week," *The Southeast Tower* (Kansas City, Missouri) 24 Sept. 1948: 1; "Youth Must Decide Between Democracy and Totalitarianism," *The Southeast Tower* 5 Nov. 1948: 1; Jackie Janney and Beverly Cohen, "American Youth Must Have Education to Meet Challenges," *The Southeast Tower* 19 Nov. 1948: 3; "Speaker for Our Democracy," *The Southeast Tower* 8 Oct. 1948: 3; "Democracy, Pep Are Themes of S.W. Assemblies," *The Southwest Trail* (Kansas City, Missouri) 7 Oct. 1948: 1.

19. C.W. Dawson, "Teen-Agers Help Stage Democracy Program," *School Activities* 21 (September 1949): 15-16; "Democracy vs. Communism Is Theme of Assembly," *The Northeast Courier* (Kansas City, Missouri) 24 Sept. 1948: 1.

20. "Democracy," *The Manual Craftsman* (Kansas City, Missouri) 15 Feb. 1952: 2; "What Will Christmas Bring You?" *The East Echo* (Kansas City, Missouri) 20 Dec. 1951: 2; "Truth and Freedom Must Be Weapon Against Another War," *The Southeast Tower* (Kansas City, Missouri) 7 Dec. 1951: 1; "Ingredients of Democracy," *The Southeast Tower* (Kansas City, Missouri) 16 Nov. 1951: 2; "Voice of Democracy Open to East Students," *The East Echo* 18 Oct. 1951: 1; "How Safe Are You?," *The Northeast Courier* (Kansas City, Missouri) 19 Oct. 1951: 2; "N.E. Joins to Fight Communism By Signing 'Crusade for Freedom,'" *The Northeast Courier* 5 Oct. 1951: 1.

21. "A Decade of War: When Comes Quiet?," *The Northeast Courier* (Kansas City, Missouri) 7 Dec. 1951: 2.

22. Albert Lerch, "We Taught the Meaning of Democracy," *School Activities* 25 (January 1954): 151-153.

23. "Educational Progress in American Schools," *Northeast Courier* (Kansas City, Missouri) 21 May 1946: 2; Stanley Dimond, "Keys to Good Citizenship," *National Parent-Teacher* 49 (February 1955): 20.

24. "Atomic Age Is Subject Presented in Assembly," *The Manual Craftsman* (Kansas City, Missouri) 22 Oct. 1948: 1; "This Is Our America," *The Manual Craftsman* 10 Dec. 1948: 2; "And Then Comes Tomorrow," *The Paseo Press* (Kansas City, Missouri) 22 April

1949: 2; "Learn About the Atom," *The Manual Craftsman* 14 April 1949: 4; "Dr. Arthur H. Compton Discusses Atomic Energy," *The Manual Craftsman* 25 March 1949: 1; "Compton Tells of Goals, Atoms," *The Southwest Trail* (Kansas City, Missouri) 24 March 1949: 1; "Interview Atomic Scientist," *The Northeast Courier* (Kansas City, Missouri) 1 April 1949: 1; "Irwin A. Moon Gives World Peace Formula for the Atomic Age," *The Southeast Tower* (Kansas City, Missouri) 11 Feb. 1949; 1.

25. "Westport Graduate Dies in Korea Fighting," *The Westport Crier* (Kansas City, Missouri) 28 Sept, 1950: 4; "Marines Call Kramer to Active Service," *The Westport Crier* 28 Sept. 1950: 4; "Ex-Manualite A Hero in Korea," *The Manual Craftsman* (Kansas City, Missouri) 20 Oct. 1950: 1; "Navy to Test High School Seniors," *The Manual Craftsman* 20 Oct. 1950: 1; "Southeast Knights Join Crusade for Freedom," *The Southeast Tower* (Kansas City, Missouri) 6 Oct. 1950: 1; "Freedoms Are Theme," *The Southeast Tower* 20 Oct. 1950: 1; "Former Student Wounded in Korea," *The Manual Craftsman* 6 April 1951: 1; "Manual Alumnus to Korea," *The Manual Craftsman* 6 April 1951: 1; "Home Nursing in Human Sciences," *The Manual Craftsman* 6 April 1951: 1.

26. For an analysis of textbook content, see Frances FitzGerald, *America Revised: History Schoolbooks in the Twentieth Century* (Boston: Little, Brown, 1979) 56-57, 117, 122.

27. Brown, "'A' Is for 'Atom'; 'B' Is for 'Bomb': Civil Defense in American Public Education, 1948-1963," *Journal of American History* 75 (June 1988): 77.

28. R.J. Blakely, "Living Without Fear In a Century of Continuing Crisis," *School Life* 35 (September 1953): 145-146; Ryland Crary, "Curriculum Adaptation to Changing Needs," *School Life* 35 (1953): 160.

29. Fleege, "The Teacher and Civil Defense," 542-543.

30. James Ridgway, "Education's Policy for Planning and Action in Civil Defense," *American School Board Journal* 120 (March 1950): 24-25; Earl James McGrath, "Education and the National Defense," *School Life* 33 (November 1950): 18-23.

31. JoAnne Brown, "'A' Is for 'Atom'; 'B' Is for 'Bomb': Civil Defense in American Public Education, 1948-1963," 68-90; Mary Meade, "What Programs of Civil Defense Are Needed in Our Schools?" *Bulletin of the National Association of Secondary-School Principals* 36 (April 1952): 180-184; William Lamars, "Identification for School Children," *Journal of the National Education Association* 41 (February 1952): 99; W. Gayle Starnes,, "Schools and Civil Defense," *American School Board Journal* 135 (August 1957): 21-22; Earl Peckham, "The Place of Civil Defense in Education," *School and Society* 9 August 1952: 87-90; Federal Civil Defense Administration, *Civil Defense in Schools* (Washington, D.C.: GPO, 1952) 9; and Allan Winkler, *Life Under a Cloud: American Anxiety About the Atom* (New York: Oxford University Press, 1993) 112. Also see Winkler, "A Forty-Year History of Civil Defense," *Bulletin of the Atomic Scientists* 40 (June/July 1984): 16-22.

32. John Sternig, "For Adults Only," *Nation's Schools* 47 (March 1951): 31-32; "Civil Defense for Our Schools," *The Journal of Education* 134 (March/April 1951): 112.

33. "Civil Defense Plan Rolls Into Action," *The East Echo* (Kansas City, Missouri) 19 April 1951: 1; Civil Defense Office, *Survival Under Atomic Attack* (Washington, D.C: GPO, 1950). For a discussion of government materials distributed to schools, including *Survival Under Atomic Attack*, see JoAnne Brown, "'A' Is for 'Atom'; 'B' Is for 'Bomb'" and Spencer Weart, *Nuclear Fear: A History of Images* (Cambridge, Mass.: Harvard University Press, 1988) 130-133.

34. Richard Gerstell, *How to Survive an Atomic Bomb* (New York: Bantam Books, 1950) 84.

35. Gerstell, *How to Survive an Atomic Bomb*, 5, 7, 11, 16-18, 21-23.

36. Gerstell, *How to Survive an Atomic Bomb*, 39, 60-63, 103, 138-139.

37. *Civil Defense in Schools*, 8.

38. Michael Carey, "The Schools and Civil Defense: The Fifties Revisited," *Teachers College Record* 84, 1 (1982): 115-127; D.B. Roblee, "What Schools Are Doing About Civil Defense," *School Life* 35 (September 1953): 154.

39. Meade, "What Programs of Civil Defense Are Needed in Our Schools?" 180-184;

Paul Rankin and John Pritchard, "More Than a Place to Hide," *Journal of the National Education Association* 40 (December 1951): 604-605; Urban Fleege, "The Teacher and Civil Defense," *Journal of the National Education Association* 40 (November 1951): 542-543; "Schools Alert for Air Raid," *The Southeast Tower* 13 March 1953: 1; "PTA Warned to Prepare Youth for Atomic Attacks," *The Journal of Education* 134 (September 1951): 177; L.W. Huber, "What Programs of Civil Defense Are Needed in Our Schools" *Bulletin of the National Association of Secondary-School Principals* 36 (April 1952): 184-188.

40. "Sgt. Halverson to Direct Fire, Air-Raid Drills," *The Southwest Trail* (Kansas City, Missouri) 4 Jan. 1951: 1; "The Great Rehearsal," *The Southwest Trail* 4 Jan. 1951: 2.

41. "East Drills for Attack," *The East Echo* (Kansas City, Missouri) 15 Feb. 1951: 1; "Hungate Gives Precautions for Atomic Attack," *The Southwest Trail* (Kansas City, Missouri) 8 Feb. 1951: 1; "Civil Defense Committee Is Organized at Manual," *The Manual Craftsman* (Kansas City, Missouri) 19 Jan. 1951): 2; "Students Are Orderly in First Air Raid Drill," *The Southwest Trail* 21 Feb. 1951: 1; Buddy Beeman, "A-Bomb Assembly Alerts Paseo to Blast Effects," *The Paseo Press* (Kansas City, Missouri) 11 Jan. 1951, 1.

42. "News Students View Shelter," *The Southeast Tower* (Kansas City, Missouri) 2 March 1951: 1.

43. "Practice Drill Points Up Do's and Don'ts of Air Raid," *The Paseo Press* (Kansas City, Missouri) 24 Jan. 1951: 1; "Students Are Orderly in First Air Raid Drill," *The Southwest Trail* (Kansas City, Missouri) 21 Feb. 1951: 1; "Radio Program Brought to Life," *The Southeast Tower* (Kansas City, Missouri) 2 March 1951: 1; "First Aid Classes Organized in K.C. High Schools," *The Southwest Trail* 22 March 1951: 1.

44. "School Facing Reality in Preparing for an Attack," *The Southeast Tower* (Kansas City, Missouri) 16 March 1951: 1; "'The Bomb That Fell on America' Presented in Exchange Assembly," *The Central Luminary* (Kansas City, Missouri) 13 April 1951: 1; "Atomic Tests, Theme of Col. Lincoln's Talk," *The Southwest Trail* (Kansas City, Missouri) 3 May 1951: 3.

45. "Schools Alert for Air Raid," 1.

46. R.J. Blakely, "Living Without Fear in a Century of Continuing Crisis," *School Life* 35 (1953): 145-146; Jack Johnson, "Protective Citizenship — Its Educational Implications," *School Life* 35 (1953): 150-151.

47. D.B. Roblee, "What Schools Are Doing About Civil Defense," *School Life* 35 (1953): 152, 154.

48. JoAnne Brown, "'A' Is for 'Atom'; 'B' Is for 'Bomb': Civil Defense in American Public Education, 1948-1963," 76, 80; Paul Rankin and John Pritchard, "More Than a Place to Hide," *Journal of the National Education Association* 40 (December 1951): 604-605; Urban Fleege, "The Teacher and Civil Defense," *Journal of the National Education Association* 40 (November 1951): 542-543.

49. "PTA Warned to Prepare Youth for Atomic Attacks," *The Journal of Education* 134 (September 1951): 177.

50. D.B. Roblee, "What Schools Are Doing About Civil Defense," *School Life* 35 (September 1953): 152-154+; William Shunck, "Daily Routine Sets Emergency Pattern," *Nation's Schools* 47 (March 1951): 33.

51. For more on civil-defense films, see Frederic Krahn, editor, *Educational Film Guide*, 11th edition (New York: H.W. Wilson Co., 1953); Antonini, *Educational Film Guide 1954-1958* (New York: H.W. Wilson Co., 1958); and A. Constandina Titus, "Back to Ground Zero: Old Footage Through New Lenses," *Journal of Popular Film and Television* 20 (1983): 2-11.

52 "In Case of Attack," *The Manual Craftsman* (Kansas City, Missouri) 10 April 1952: 3.

53 "Civil Defense Committee Is Organized at Manual," *The Manual Craftsman* (Kansas City, Missouri) 19 Jan. 1951: 2; *The Paseon*, Paseo High School (Kansas City, Missouri) 1951.

54 "How About Civil Defense," *The East Echo* (Kansas City, Missouri) 20 Jan. 1955: 2.

55 Laxson and Mallory, "Education for Homemaking in Today's High School," 134; "Girl Scouts Take Part in Civil Defense," *The Southwest Trail* (Kansas City, Missouri) 6 Nov. 1953: 2; *The Paseon*, Paseo High School (Kansas City, Missouri) 1948.

Chapter 4

1. Quoted in Josette Frank, "Chills and Thrills in Radio, Movies and Comics," *Child Study* 25 (Spring 1948): 44.

2. The magazine's circulation increased 16.4 percent between 1945 and 1950 (going from 265,568 to 309,187), even though high school enrollments increased less than one percent during the same period. From 1950 to 1955, however, the magazine's circulation increased more than 120 percent, reaching an annual circulation of 681,790. This far outpaced the 14.1 percent increase in the number of high school students over the same six-year span. In 1951, Scholastic Magazines Inc. announced that one million copies of its three publications (*Senior Scholastic, Junior Scholastic*, and *World Week*) were being read each week.

3. John W. Studebaker, "Avowed Objectives," *Senior Scholastic*, Teacher Edition, 12 April 1952, 11T; John W. Studebaker, "Not 'Should' But 'How,'" *Senior Scholastic* Teacher Edition, 3 Nov. 1948, 2-T.

4. E.H. Gombrich, *The Image and the Eye* (Ithaca, N.Y.: Cornell University Press, 1982).

5. Edmund Burke Feldman, *Varieties of Visual Experiences: Art as Image and Idea* (New York: Harry N. Abrams Inc., 1972) 50.

6. *Senior Scholastic*, 13 May 1953, 18.

7. These conclusions are based on an analysis of 90 short stories appearing between the school years 1945–46 and 1954–55. The intent was to select a story from the first issue of each month; however, occasionally an issue did not contain a short story; in other cases, a story was published in two parts, forcing the selection of a short story from a prior or subsequent issue, whichever was appropriate. The analysis focused on the relationship between the themes of brotherhood and self-reliance and two possible outcomes: favorable or unfavorable. The central question was how these stories projected attitudes or themes congruent with the magazine's editorial platform and the larger social themes of the late 1940s and early 1950s. In other words, the objective was to determine whether these stories reflected a shift from brotherhood, teamwork, or cooperation leading to a favorable outcome or positive resolution, to these themes leading to an unfavorable outcome or negative resolution; conversely, whether themes of self-reliance, self-preservation, or survival were linked to a positive resolution or favorable outcome, or to a negative resolution or unfavorable outcome.

This type of study admittedly is problematic. First of all, each story is subject to conflicting interpretations. What may appear to be an emphasis on self-reliance to one may be viewed by another as a willingness to sacrifice one's self for the benefit of the group. Moreover, the terms brotherhood and self-reliance must be clearly defined. For simplicity, brotherhood in the context of this study is a sense of fellowship, alliance, teamwork, or interdependency with a larger group; self-reliance is the reliance upon one's own abilities or efforts. Finally, not all stories fit neatly into a brotherhood/self-reliance dichotomy; therefore, thematic conclusions may be considered questionable if not incorrect. Despite these drawbacks in what is essentially a qualitative analysis incorporating attributes of a quantitative methodology, some general conclusions can be reached concerning the nature of short stories appearing in *Senior Scholastic* between 1945 and 1955.

8. "Editorial," *Senior Scholastic*, 17 Sept. 1945, 3–4.

9. "Atomic Revolution," *Senior Scholastic*, 17 Sept. 1945, 13–14.

10. "It Is Later Than We Think! Atomic," *Senior Scholastic*, 17 Sept. 1945, 8.

11. *Senior Scholastic* (Teacher Edition), 17 Sept. 1945, 1T.

12. *Senior Scholastic* (Teacher Edition), 12 Nov. 1945, 1T. Emphasis in original text.

13. Part One of Stephen Vincent Benét's "William Riley and the Fates appeared in *Senior Scholastic*, 17 Sept. 1945, 28–30+. Part Two appeared in the next issue, 24 Sept. 1945, 25–26+.

14. Stephen Vincent Benét, "William Riley and the Fates, Part 1," 36.

15. Stephen Vincent Benét, "William Riley and the Fates, Part 2," 38.

16 "A Forum Discussion on Atomic Bomb Control," *Senior Scholastic*, 12 Nov. 1945, 3–5.

17. "Does the UNO Go Far Enough?" *Senior Scholastic*, 4 Feb. 1946, 15–16.

18. "Living with the Atom," *Senior Scholastic*, 3 March 1947, 10–11.

19. The intent here is to suggest that atomic narratives, as discussed throughout this study, emphasized such themes as fear, violence, self-reliance, survival, and so forth. The short stories analyzed over this decade not only contained similar themes, but, as noted above, these themes continually reflected those contained in the magazine's more overt factual and fictional atomic narratives. As Milton Stewart has pointed out [see "Importance in Content Analysis: A Validity Problem," *Journalism Quarterly* 20 (September 1943: 286–293], the frequency of a specific symbol is only one indication of the communicator's anxiousness or intent that the symbol's message (e.g., the ability to confront an atomic threat) be understood. Moreover, Ole Holsti [*Content Analysis for the Social Sciences and Humanities* (Reading, Mass.: Addison-Wesley Publishing, 1969] has suggested that qualititative content analysis is an appropriate methodology in the drawing of inferences from the text on the basis of the appearance or nonappearance of specified attributes or messages. For more on the assumption made in all content analysis that inferences can, indeed, be made about the relationship between intent and content, see Bernard Berelson, *Content Analysis in Communication Research* (New York: Hafner Press, 1952).

20. Dr. Louis Ridenour, "Pilot Lights of the Apocalypse," *Senior Scholastic*, 29 April 1946, 17–20.

21. James Atlee Phillips, "The Delegate from Everywhere," *Senior Scholastic*, 6 May 1946, 25–29.

22. James Atlee Phillips, "The Delegate from Everywhere," 29.

23. Sam Burger, "I Saw the Bombs Go Off," *Senior Scholastic*, 16 Sept, 1946, 10–11; "The Atom Bomb and the Teacher's Obligations," *Senior Scholastic* Teacher Edition, 30 Sept. 1946, 3T–4T; "Atomic Power...for Progress or Destruction," *Senior Scholastic*, 30 Sept. 1946, 5–7.

24. "Keepers of the Secret: The Atomic Energy Commission," *Senior Scholastic*, 20 Oct. 1947, 16–17.

25. Rosa Kohler Eichelberger, "Learning Democracy in School," *Senior Scholastic*, 1 Dec. 1947, 14–15.

26. "You and America's Future," *Senior Scholastic*, 17 May 1948, 23.

27. David Lilienthal, "Atomic Energy...and You," *Senior Scholastic*, 12 April 1946, 3.

28. "Atomic Energy in Overalls," *Senior Scholastic*, 12 April 1946, 8–9, 11.

29. Theodore Sturgeon, "The Purple Light," *Senior Scholastic*, 12 April 1946, 25–29; "Teaching Aids for Senior Scholastic," *Senior Scholastic* Teacher Edition, 12 April 1946, 1T; "Citizenship Quiz," *Senior Scholastic*, 12 April 1946, 11–12.

30. Philip Knowlton, "Great Issues Facing High School Students: Building a Philosophy," *Senior Scholastic*, 22 Sept. 1948, 19–20.

31. Philip Knowlton, "Civilization's Race with Death," *Senior Scholastic*, 5 Jan. 1949, 16.

32. Philip Knowlton, "Is Science Man's Greatest Enemy?," *Senior Scholastic*, 2 Feb. 1949, 17.

33. Kenneth Gould, "You Are America," *Senior Scholastic*, 3 Feb. 1947, 3.

34. "One World...or None," *Senior Scholastic*, 20 Oct. 1948, 5.

35. "The World's Still on a Tightrope," *Senior Scholastic*, 30 Nov. 1949, 5–7.

36. "Non-United Navy," *Senior Scholastic*, 10 Oct. 1949, 14; "Breeding Atomic Fuel," *Senior Scholastic*, 7 Dec. 1949, 12.

37. Knowlton, "Great Issues Facing High School Students: Building a Philosophy," 18; "Atomic Energy in Overalls," *Senior Scholastic*, 12 April 1948, 8; "Non-United Navy," *Senior Scholastic*, 10 Oct. 1949, 14; "The World's Still on a Tightrope," *Senior Scholastic*, 30 Nov. 1949, 5–7; "Breeding Atomic Fuel," *Senior Scholastic*, 7 Dec. 1949, 12; "What High-Schoolers Think," *Senior Scholastic*, 5 April 1950, 5.

38. Phyllis Bottome, "Caesar's Wife's Ear," *Senior Scholastic*, 4 Jan. 1950, 19–20+.

39. Michael Armine, "What the Atom Age Has Done to Us," *New York Times Magazine*, 6 Aug. 1950, 26.

40. "Must We Build the Hydrogen Bomb?," *Senior Scholastic*, 8 Feb. 1950, 8.

41. "If...the Bomb Falls," *Senior Scholastic*, 8 Nov. 1950, 6.

42. Harold Rogers, "Smoke Jumper," *Senior Scholastic*, 20 Sept. 1950, 25–26+.

43. Clement Wood, "Tzagan," *Senior Scholastic*, 11 Oct. 1950, 23–24+.

44. Hal Everts, "Conquest," *Senior Scholastic*, 6 Dec. 1950, 19–20+.

45. See "Atomic Energy in Our Time," "Atomic-Powered Planes and Submarines," "Brookhaven: Atomic Pioneers at Work," "Isotopes at Work," "How the Bomb Works," and "The Devil in the Atom," in *Senior Scholastic*'s special issue on atomic energy, *Senior Scholastic*, 7 March 1951. Also see "Atoms Aloft and A-Sea," *Senior Scholastic*, 26 Sept. 1951, 14. This article described the awarding of contracts to build an atomic-powered plane for the U.S. Air Force and a hull for the first atomic-powered submarine for the U.S. Navy; and the Navy's announcement that A-bombs had been developed that were small enough to be delivered by planes launched from aircraft carriers.

46. "A Strong Defense Against the A-Bomb — Dispersal," *Senior Scholastic*, 26 Sept. 1951, 17–19; "Matador Guided Missile," *Senior Scholastic*, 3 Oct. 1951, 16; "Stalin and the Atom," *Senior Scholastic*, 17 Oct. 1951, 16.

47. "U.S. Defense Girdles the Globe," *Senior Scholastic*, 31 Oct. 1951, 10–12; "The Atom in a Divided World," *Senior Scholastic*, 31 Oct. 1951, 14–15.

48. "Say What You Please," *Senior Scholastic*, 5 Dec. 1951, 5.

49. "Our Expanding Atom," *Senior Scholastic*, 17 Sept. 1952, 20; "Atoms for Peace," *Senior Scholastic*, 9 Dec. 1953, 13; *Senior Scholastic* Teacher Edition, 9 Dec. 1953, 1T.

50. "Do We Have the H-Bomb?," *Senior Scholastic*, 3 Dec. 1952, 18; "Year One — Hydrogen Time," *Senior Scholastic*, 11 Feb. 1953, 10.

51. "Year One — Hydrogen Time," 12.

52. "Year One — Hydrogen Time," 12.

53. "Top Secret or Top Mistake?," *Senior Scholastic*, 4 Nov. 1953, 7–9; "Atoms for Peace," *Senior Scholastic*, 9 Dec. 1953, 13–15; *Senior Scholastic* Teacher Edition, 9 Dec. 1953, 1T.

54. "Pooling Atomic Power for Peace," *Senior Scholastic*, 6 Jan. 1954, 10–11.

55. "Biggest Manmade Explosion," *Senior Scholastic*, 7 April 1954, 17; "H-Bomb: Cities in Danger," *Senior Scholastic*, 14 April 1954, 17; "Arm of Disarm for Peace?," *Senior Scholastic*, 5 May 1954, 7.

56. "Can We Win Freedom from Fear," *Senior Scholastic*, 5 May 1954, 13–14.

57. Hal Evarts, "Killer in the Pass," *Senior Scholastic*, 2 April 1952, 21–22+.

58. Bob Dooling, "A Matter of Time," *Senior Scholastic*, 30 April 1952, 16–17.

59. Manual Komroff, "Death of an Eagle," *Senior Scholastic*, 6 April 1955, 20, 28.

60. John Kruse, "Alone in Shark Waters," *Senior Scholastic*, 4 May 1955, 40–41, 53.

61. "The Split Atom: For Peace, for War," *Senior Scholastic*, 13 Oct. 1954, 9–10.

62. "NATO: From Straw Man to Superman," *Senior Scholastic*, 4 May 1955, 11.

63. For a discussion of the relationship of juvenile delinquency to the rising youth culture, the mass media, and the Atomic Age, see James Gilbert, *A Cycle of Outrage: America's Reaction to the Juvenile Delinquent in the 1950s* (New York: Oxford University Press, 1986) and William Graebner, *Coming of Age in Buffalo: Youth and Authority in the Postwar Era* (Philadelphia: Temple University Press, 1990).

Chapter 5

1. *The Day the Earth Stood Still*. Dir. Robert Wise. Perf. Michael Rennie and Patricia Neal. Twentieth Century Fox. 1951.

2. *Variety,* 27 Nov. 1946: 14.

3. For more discussion on trends in the movie industry, see Robert Ray, *A Certain*

Tendency of the Hollywood Cinema, 1930–1980 (Princeton, N.J.: Princeton University Press, 1985).

4. Jackie Byars, *All That Hollywood Allows: Re-reading Gender in 1950s Melodrama* (Chapel Hill: The University of North Carolina Press, 1991) 113; Andrew Dowdy, *"Movies Are Better Than Ever": Wide Screen Memories of the Fifties* (New York: W. Morrow, 1973) 63.

5. *Historical Statistics of the United States: Colonial Times to 1970* (Washington, D.C.: Bureau of the Census, 1975) 400; Dowdy, *"Movies Are Better Than Ever,"* 6.

6. Lawrence W. Levine, *The Unpredictable Past: Explorations in American Cultural History* (New York: Oxford University Press, 1993) 313.

7. Leo Handel, *Hollywood Looks At Its Audience* (Urbana: University of Illinois Press, 1950) 102–103.

8. Kerry Segrave, *Drive-in Theaters: A History from Their Inception in 1933* (Jefferson, N.C.: McFarland & Co., 1992) 144.

9. Thomas Doherty, *Teenagers & Teenpics: The Juvenilization of American Movies in the 1950s* (Boston: Unwin Hyman, 1988) 8–14, 65.

10. Dowdy, *"Movies Are Better Than Ever,"* 160.

11. Susan Sontag, "The Imagination of Disaster," *Against Interpretation and Other Essays* (New York: Farrar, Straus & Giroux, 1965) 220–225; Joyce A. Evans, *Celluloid Mushroom Clouds: Hollywood and the Atomic Bomb* (Boulder, Colo.: Westview Press, 1998) 8.

12. Thomas Leitch, *What Stories Are: Narrative Theory and Interpretation* (University Park: Pennsylvania State University Press, 1986) 188.

13. David Freedberg, *The Power of Images: Studies in the History and Theory of Response* (Chicago: University of Chicago Press, 1989) 23, 235, 438.

14. For the changing views toward children, see Kathy Merlock Jackson, *Images of Children in American Film* (Metuchen, N.J.: The Scarecrow Press, 1986).

15. For background information on documentaries during this era, see Richard Barsam, "'This Is America': Documentaries for Theaters, 1942–1951," *Cinema Journal* 12 (Spring 1973): 22; Evans, *Celluloid Mushroom Clouds*, 41, 95–96.

16. Evans, *Celluloid Mushroom Cloud*, 32.

17. Jack Shaheen and Richard Taylor, "The Beginning or the End?," *Nuclear War Films*, ed. Jack Shaheen (Cardondale: Southern Illinois Press, 1978) 8; Michael Yavenditti, "John Hersey and the American Conscience: The Reception of *Hiroshima*," *Pacific Historical Review* 43 (February 1974): 45; "Following the Films," *Senior Scholastic*, 31 March 1947, 30; "Jam Session," *Senior Scholastic*, 3 Nov. 1947, 32.

18. Brode, *The Films of the Fifties*, 51; Hodgens, "A Brief, Tragical History of the Science Fiction Film," 82–83; *Variety* 4 April 1951: 6; Chris Steinbrunner and Burt Goldblatt, *Cinema of the Fantastic* (New York: Saturday Review Press, 1972) 230–232; Stuart Kaminsky, *American Film Genres: Approaches to a Critical Theory of Popular Film* (New York: Dell Publishing Co., 1974) 110.

19. Kaminsky, *American Film Genres*, 112; John Brosnan, *Future Tense: The Cinema of Science Fiction* (London: MacDonald and Janes, 1978) 84; *Variety* 5 Sept. 1951: 6; H. Bruce Franklin, *War Stars: The Superweapon and the American Imagination* (New York: Oxford University Press, 1988) 182; Pierre Kast, "Don't Play with Fire," *Focus on the Science Fiction Film* (Englewood Cliffs, N.J.: Prentice-Hall, 1972) 69–70.

20. *Variety*, 29 Aug. 1951: 6; "Worlds in Collison," *Senior Scholastic*, 1 March 1950, 13–14; "When Worlds Collide," *Senior Scholastic*, 28 Nov. 1951, 22.

21. Evans, *Celluloid Mushroom Clouds*, 130–131.

22. Spencer Weart, *Nuclear Fear: A History of Images* (Cambridge, Mass.: Harvard University Press, 1988) 192. For additional discussions about science-fiction themes, see Martha Bartter, "Nuclear Holocaust as Urban Renewal," *Science-Fiction Studies* 13 (July 1986): 148–158; Bartter, *The Way to Ground Zero: The Atomic Bomb in American Science Fiction* (New York: Greenwood Press, 1988); Albert Berger, "Love, Death, and the Atomic Bomb: Sexuality and Community in Science Fiction, 1935–1955," *Science Fiction Studies* 8 (Novem-

ber 1981): 279–290; Berger, "Science Fiction Fans in Socio-Economic Perspective: Factors in the Social Consciousness of a Genre," *Science-Fiction Studies* 4 (1977): 232–246; Richard Hodgens, "A Brief, Tragical History of the Science Fiction Film" *Focus on the Science Fiction Film*, ed. William Johnson (Englewood Cliffs, N.J.: Prentice-Hall, 1972) 78–90; Patrick Lucanio, *Them or Us: Archetypal Interpretations of Fifties Alien Invasion Films* (Bloomington: Indiana University Press, 1987); Brian Murphy, "Monster Movies: They Came from Beneath the Fifties," *Journal of Popular Film* 1 (Winter 1972): 31–44; Jacqueline Smetak, "Sex and Death in Nuclear Holocaust Literature of the 1950s," *The Nightmare Considered: Critical Essays on Nuclear War Literature*, ed. Nancy Anisfield (Bowling Green, Ohio: Bowling Green State University Popular Press, 1991): 15–26; and Margaret Tarratt, "Monsters from the Id," *Films and Filming* 17 (December 1970): 38–42, (January 1971): 40–42.

23. William Graebner, *The Age of Doubt: American Thought and Culture in the 1940s* (Boston: Twayne Publishers, 1991).

24. *Variety*, 14 May 1952: 20.

25. *Variety*, 10 Dec. 1952: 6; Bill Warren, *Keep Watching the Skies! American Science Fiction Movies of the Fifties*, Volume 1 (Jefferson, N.C.: McFarland & Co., 1982) 214–217.

26. *Variety*, 8 April 195: 6; Brosnan, *Future Tense*, 93.

27. *Variety*, 30 March 1955: 9; James Robert Parish and Michael R. Pitts, eds., *The Great Science Fiction Pictures* (Metuchen, N.J.: The Scarecrow Press, 1977) 323; Brode, *The Films of the Fifties*, 173; *Variety*, 29 Feb. 1956: 6.

28. *Variety*, 4 March 1953: 18; Warren, *Keep Watching the Skies!*, 157.

29. *Variety*, 27 Jan. 1954: 6; Thomas Doherty, *Teenagers & Teenpics: The Juvenilization of American Movies in the 1950s* (Boston: Unwin Hyman, 1988) 144; Warren, *Keep Watching the Skies!*, 178.

30. Brosnan, *Future Tense*, 95; *Variety*, 17 June 1953: 6; Lucanio, *Them or Us*, 40–41; *Variety*, 9 June 1954: 6; *Variety*, 22 June 1955: 6; *Variety*, 11 Jan. 1956: 6; *Variety*, 14 April 1954: 6; Murphy, "Monster Movies: They from Beneath the Fifties," 42; Michael Rogin, *Ronald Reagan, the Movie and Other Episodes in Political Demonology* (Berkeley: University of California Press, 1987) 263–266.

31. Jeff Smith, *Unthinking the Unthinkable: Nuclear Weapons and Western Culture* (Bloomington: Indiana University Press, 1989) 43.

32. Robert Hatch, "The Garden of Atom," *New Republic*, 14 May 1951, 23; David Dowling, *Fictions of Nuclear Disaster* (Iowa City: University of Iowa Press, 1987) 219; Brosnan, *Future Tense*, 82; *Variety* 25 April 1951: 6; Ernest Martin, "Five," *Nuclear War Films*, ed. Jack Shaheen (Carbondale: Southern Illinois Press, 1978) 11–16.

33. *Variety*, 8 Dec. 1954: 6; Warren, *Keep Watching the Skies!*, 166, 448; Raymond Stedman, *The Serials: Suspense and Drama by Installment* (Norman: University of Oklahoma Press, 1977) 139–140; E. Nelson Bridwell, *Superman, from the Thirties to the Eighties* (New York: Crown, 1983) 9–16; Parish and Pitts, *The Great Science Fiction Pictures*, 57–66, 200–201, 306; *Variety* 30 March 1955: 9; Donald Willis, *Horror and Science Fiction Films: A Checklist* (Metuchen, N.J.: Scarecrow Press, 1972) 30.

34. Raymond Fielding, *The March of Time, 1935–1951* (New York, 1978) 291–296.

35. *Variety*, 28 June 1950: 6; "Destination Moon," *Senior Scholastic*, 20 Sept. 1950, 38.

36. *Variety*, 9 April 1952: 6; A. Costandina Titus, *Bombs in the Backyard: Atomic Testing and American Politics* (Las Vegas: University of Nevada Press, 1986) 90.

37. Franklin, *War Stars*, 182; Dowdy, *"Movies Are Better Than Ever,"* 160; Brode, *The Films of the Fifties*, 111.

38. Warren Susman and Edward Griffin, "Did Success Spoil the United States? Dual Representations in Postwar America," *Recasting America: Culture and Politics in the Age of Cold War*, ed. Lary May (Chicago: University of Chicago Press, 1989) 30; Lary May, "Introduction," *Recasting America: Culture and Politics in the Age of Cold War*, 7. Also see Brode, *The Films of the Fifties*, and Dowdy, *"Movies Are Better Than Ever."*

39. Dowdy, *"Movies Are Better Than Ever,"* 130–159; Brode, *The Films of the Fifties: Sunset Boulevard to On the Beach* (Secaucus, N.J.: Carol Publishing Group, 1976) 87.

40. Peter Biskind, "Pods, Blobs, and Ideology in American Films of the Fifties," *Shadows of the Magic Lamp: Fantasy and Science Fiction in Film*, eds. George Slusser and Eric S. Rabkin (Carbondale: Southern Illinois Press, 1985) 200.

41. Douglas Brode, *The Films of the Fifties: Sunset Boulevard to On the Beach* (Secaucus, N.J.: Carol Publishing Group, 1976) 165.

42. Sam Astrachan, "New Lost Generation," *New Republic*, 4 Feb., 1957: 17; *Variety* 26 Oct. 1955: 6.

43. Brode, *The Films of the Fifties*, 65, 153–155; Kathy Merlock Jackson, *Images of Children in American Film* (Metuchen, N.J.: The Scarecrow Press, 1986) 106.

44. Brode, *The Films of the Fifties*, 45–46, 60–79, 87; Dowdy, "*Movies Are Better Than Ever,*" 20–21, 74, 130–158. A good discussion of underlying themes in 1940s movies is contained in Barbara Deming, *Running Away from Myself: A Dream Portrait of America Drawn from the Films of the Forties* (New York: Grossman, 1969).

45. Kaminsky, *American Film Genres*, 112.

46. Chester Eisinger, ed. *The 1940s: Profile of a Nation in Crisis, Documents in American Civilization Series* (New York: Anchor Books, 1969) xiv–xv. A number of historical works on the 1940s and 1950s deal with the underlying themes of anxiety, fear, apathy, and similar disquieting attitudes, such as Paul Boyer, *By the Bomb's Early Light: American Thought and Culture at the Dawn of the Atomic Age* (New York: Pantheon Books, 1985); Peter Hales, "The Atomic Sublime," *American Studies* 32 (Spring 1991): 5–31; Robert Lifton, *The Broken Connection: On Death and the Continuity of Life* (New York: Simon & Schuster, 1979); Michael Yavenditti, "The American People and the Use of Atomic Bombs on Japan: The 1940s," *Historian* 36 (February 1974): 224; Weart, *Nuclear Fear: A History of Images*; and W.T. Lhamon, Jr., *Deliberate Speed: The Origins of a Cultural Style in the American 1950s* (Washington, D.C.: Smithsonian Institution Press, 1990). An excellent overview of the mood during these years, including themes prevalent in literature and movies, is provided by Gaile McGregor, "Domestic Blitz: A Revisionist History of the Fifties," *American Studies* 34 (Spring 1993): 5–33.

47. Lucanio, *Them or Us*, 76–77.

48. Evans, *Celluloid Mushroom Clouds*, 68.

Chapter 6

1. Edward Olds, "How Do Young People Use Their Leisure Time?" *Recreation* 42 (January 1949): 458–463; F.C. Gruber, "Out-of-School Radio-Listening Habits of High School Students," *English Journal* 39 (June 1950): 325.

2. Sam Astrachan, "New Lost Generation," *New Republic*, 4 Feb. 1957: 17; Bureau of the Census, *Historical Statistics of the United States: Colonial Times to 1970* (Washington, D.C., U.S. Department of Commerce, 1975) 796; P. Witty, "Television and the High School Student," *Education* 72 (December 1951): 246.

3. "Who Reads the Comics," *Senior Scholastic*, 17 May 1948, 3; Paul Witty and Harry Bricker, *Your Child and Radio, TV, Comics and Movies* (Chicago: Science Research Associates, 1952); Albert I. Berger, "Love, Death, and the Atomic Bomb: Sexuality and Community in Science Fiction, 1935–1955," *Science-Fiction Studies* 8 (November 1981): 281; Mike Benton, *The Comic Book in America: An Illustrated History* (Dallas: Taylor Publishing Co., 1989) 53.

4. A. Shatter, "A Survey of Student Reading," *English Journal* 40 (May 1951): 271–273; John Lamb McIntire, "Dream World or Reality?" *Progressive Education* 24,1 (1946): 18–19+.

5. Mark Gayn, "Terror in Japan," *Collier's*, 16 June 1945: 11.

6. "Birth of an Era," *Time*, 13 Aug. 1945, 17–18; "Atomic Age," *Time*, 20 Aug. 1945, 29.

7. "The War Ends: Burst of Atomic Bomb Brings Swift Surrender of Japanese," *Life*, 20 Aug. 1945, 25–31; "The Atomic Age," *Life*, 20 Aug. 1945, 32; Hanson Baldwin, "*Life's* Reports: The Atom Bomb and Future War," *Life*, 20 Aug. 1945, 18.

8. Norman Cousins, "Modern Man Is Obsolete," *Saturday Review of Literature*, 18 Aug. 1945, 5–7.

9. "The 36-Hour War," *Life*, 19 Nov. 1945, 27–35.

10. Michael Yavenditti, "John Hersey and the American Conscience: The Reception of Hiroshima," *Pacific Historian Review* 43 (February 1974): 31.

11. "World War III Preview," *Time*, 25 March 1946, 90; "What Ended the War," *Life*, 17 Sept. 1945, 37.

12. John Hersey, *Hiroshima* (New York: Alfred A. Knopf, 1946) 59–60, 67–69.

13. David Bradley, *No Place to Hide* (1946; London: University Press of New England, 1983) 165; *Senior Scholastic*, Teachers Edition, 2 March 1949, 15-T.

14. Dexter Masters, *The Accident* (1955; New York: Penguin Books, 1985) 305.

15. Rob Paarlberg, "Forgetting About the Unthinkable," *Foreign Policy* 10 (Spring 1973): 132; Paul Boyer, *By the Bomb's Early Light: American Thought and Culture at the Dawn of the Atomic Age* (New York: Pantheon Books, 1985); Michael Yavenditti, "The American People and the Use of Atomic Bombs on Japan: The 1940s," *Historian* 36 (February 1974): 224–246.

16. Styles Bridges, "Where Do You Stand on the Greatest Question of Our Time," *Collier's*, 8 Jan. 1954, 36.

17. Donald Day, ed. *Index to the Science Fiction Magazines, 1926–1950* (Boston: G.K. Hall & Co., 1952); H.W. Hall, *Science Fiction and Fantasy Reference Guide, 1878–1985* (Detroit: Gale Research Co., 1987).

18. Paul Brians, *Nuclear Holocausts: Atomic War in Fiction, 1895–1984* (Kent, Ohio: Kent State University Press, 1987) 11–15; Martha Bartter, *The Way to Ground Zero* (New York: Greenwood Press, 1988) 119–120; H. Bruce Franklin, *War Stars: The Superweapon and the American Imagination* (New York: Oxford University Press, 1988) 158–159.

19. Franklin, *War Stars*, 174–175; Bartter, *The Way to Ground Zero*, 125–127.

20. H. Bruce Franklin, *Robert A. Heinlein: America As Science Fiction* (New York: Oxford University Press, 1978) 101–102.

21. David Dowling, *Fictions of Nuclear Disaster* (Iowa City: University of Iowa Press, 1987) 33, 105, 143; Jack Finney, *Invasion of the Body Snatchers* (1955; New York: Fireside, 1989).

22. E. Nelson Bridwell, Introduction, *Superman, from the Thirties to the Eighties* (New York: Crown Publishers, 1983) 189–200; Mike Benton, *The Comic Book in America: An Illustrated History* (Dallas: Taylor Publishing Co., 1989) 11, 47–55, 145, 172–174; Katherine M. Wolf and Marjorie Fiske, "The Children Talk About Comics," in *Communication Research, 1948–1949*, eds. Paul Lazarsfeld and Frank Stanton (New York: Harper & Brothers, 1949): 3–50.

23. Les Daniels, *Marvel: Five Fabulous Decades of the World's Greatest Comics* (New York: Harry N. Abrams, 1991) 64, 68–72.

24. George Orwell, *Nineteen Eighty-Four* (New York: Harcourt, Brace and Co., 1949) 29, 137, 300.

25. Ray Bradbury, *Fahrenheit 451* (1953; New York: Ballantine Books, 1984) 178–179.

26. Berger, "Love, Death, and the Atomic Bomb: Sexuality and Community in Science Fiction, 1935–1955," 290.

27. Dowling, *Fictions of Nuclear Disaster*, 51, 133–134; Jacqueline Smetak, "Sex and Death in Nuclear Holocaust Literature of the 1950s," in *The Nightmare Considered: Critical Essays on Nuclear War Literature*, ed. Nancy Anisfield (Bowling Green, Ohio: Bowling Green University Popular Press, 1991) 15–26.

28. Dowling, *Fictions of Nuclear Disaster*, 59, 106; Franklin, *War Stars*, 177–179.

29. Lynn Spigel, *Make Room for TV: Television and the Family Ideal in Postwar America* (Chicago: The University of Chicago Press, 1992) Chapter 2; Franklin Dunham, "Effect of Television on School Achievement of Children," *School Life* 34 (March 1952): 88–89+; H.H. Remmers, R.H. Horton, and R.E. Mainer, *Attitudes of High School Students Toward Certain Aspects of Television* (Indiana: Purdue University Press, 1953).

30. Robert Lewis Shayon, "Television and Children's Reading," *Horn Book* 29 (April 1953): 91–100.

31. "Ninety-Three Murders a Week," *National Education Association Journal* 42 (May 1953): 266.

32. Conrad Phillip Kottak, *Prime-Time Society: An Anthropological Analysis of Television and Culture* (Belmont, California: Wadsworth Publishing Co., 1990) 139.

33. George Gerbner, Larry Gross, Michael Morgan, and Nancy Signorielli, "The 'Mainstreaming' of America: Violence Profile No. 11," *Journal of Communication* 30,3 (1980): 10–29.

34. For more on science-fiction television shows, see John Javna, *The Best from Science Fiction TV: The Critics' Choice from Captain Video to Star Trek, from The Jetsons to Robotech* (New York: Harmony Books, 1987); Harris Lentz III, *Science Fiction, Horror & Fantasy Film and Television Credits* (Jefferson, N.C.: McFarland, 1983); Gary Grossman, *Saturday Morning TV* (New York: Dell Publishing, 1981) 331–332; Brosnan, *Future Tense,* 291–304; Allan Winkler, *Life Under a Cloud: American Anxiety About the Atom* (New York: Oxford University Press, 1993) 114.

35. "History Is Made: Telecast of an Atomic Explosion," *Time,* 5 May 1952: 86+; A. Constandina Titus, *Bombs in the Backyard: Atomic Testing and American Politics* (Reno: University of Nevada Press, 1986) 65, 95.

36. Quoted in Boyer, *By the Bomb's Early Light,* 5.

37. Spencer Weart, *Nuclear Fear: A History of Images* (Cambridge, Mass.: Harvard University Press, 1988) 116, 131, 172; Irving Gitlin, "Radio and Atomic Energy, *Education* 22 (January 1949), 327–330; *Senior Scholastic,* 24 Sept. 1945, 31; *Senior Scholastic,* Teachers Edition, 23 Sept, 1946, 16-T; *Senior Scholastic,* 8 Oct. 1945, 45. Recommended radio and television programs were discussed and listed in numerous issues of *Senior Scholastic* and the magazine's Teachers Edition, including 19 Nov. 1945, 7-T; 8 Oct. 1945, 45; 7 Jan. 1946, 37; 13 Jan. 1947, 18-T; 3 Jan. 1947, 37; 3 Feb. 1954, 12-T; 3 March 1954, 59; 22 Sept. 1954, 3-T. For more on radio, see J. Fred MacDonald, *Don't Touch That Dial: Radio Programming in American Life, 1920–1960* (Chicago: Nelson-Hall, 1980).

38. Charles Wolfe, "Nuclear Country: The Atomic Bomb in Country Music," *Journal of Country Music,* 7 (January 1978): 7–21. Also see A. Costandina Titus and Jerry Simich, "From 'Atomic Bomb Baby' to 'Nuclear Funeral': Atomic Music Comes of Age, 1945–1990," *Popular Music and Society,* 14,4 (1990): 11–37.

39. See in Elaine Tyler May, *Homeward Bound: American Families in the Cold War Era* (New York: Basic Books, 1988) 92.

40. Quoted in Raymond Stedman, *The Serials: Suspense and Drama by Installment* (Norman: University of Oklahoma Press, 1977) 189–190.

41. Javna, *The Best from Science Fiction TV: The Critics' Choice from Captain Video to Star Trek, from The Jetsons to Robotech*; Lentz, *Science Fiction, Horror & Fantasy Film and Television Credits*; Brosnan, *Future Tense: The Cinema of Science Fiction,* 291–304; Gary Grossman, *Saturday Morning TV* (New York: Dell Publishing, 1981).

42. John Campbell, Jr., "The Place of Science Fiction," *Modern Science Fiction: Its Meanings and Its Future,* second edition, ed. Reginald Bretnor (Chicago: Advent, 1979) 12; Michael Riffaterre, *Fictional Truth* (Baltimore: The Johns Hopkins University Press, 1990) 86.

Chapter 7

1. Quoted in Erick Kahler, "The Reality of Utopia," *American Scholar,* 15 (Spring 1946): 179.

2. Lawrence W. Levine, *The Unpredictable Past: Explorations in American Cultural History* (New York: Oxford University Press, 1993) 304.

3. Levine, *The Unpredictable Past,* 312–313.

4. Norman Ryder, "The Cohort As a Concept in the Study of Social Change," *American Sociological Review,* 30 (1965): 843–861.

5. "Peacetime School Era Challenges Us," *The Southwest Trail* (Kansas City, Missouri), 24 Sept. 1945.

6. "Smashed Atom Holds World Future," *The Southwest Trail* (Kansas City, Missouri), 7 Dec. 1945.

7. "New Year Brings Light Into War-Ravaged World," *The Southwest Trail* (Kansas City, Missouri),16 Jan. 1946.

8. "Achievements of 1945 Challenge Future," *The Southwest Trail* (Kansas City, Missouri), 16 Jan. 1946.

9. "The Port Huron Statement," reprinted in James Miller's *"Democracy Is in the Streets": From Port Huron to the Siege of Chicago* (New York: Simon and Schuster, 1987) 330.

10. *Sachem*, Southwest High School, Kansas City, Missouri.

11. Dorothy Shearer, "Undying Youth," *The Central Luminary* (Kansas City, Missouri), 10 May 1946.

12. "And Then Comes Tomorrow," *The Paseo Press* (Kansas City, Missouri), 22 April 1949.

13. Joachim Ries, "A Bicycle Without Wheels," *Senior Scholastic*, 17 Feb. 1947.

14. Yoshio Kishi, "What It Means to Me to be Growing Up with Nuclear Energy, *The Journal of Educational Sociology*, 22 (January 1949): 336–337.

15. "I Am a Part of All That I Have Met," *The Westport Crier* (Kansas City, Missouri), 10 Oct. 1945.

16. "Editorial Objectivity in a World of Crisis," *Senior Scholastic*, 26 April 1948, 3-T.

17. "A Challenge to Mankind," *The Central Luminary* (Kansas City, Missouri), 23 Feb. 1951.

18. Joyce Dominie Sloane, "Brothers," *Senior Scholastic*, 23 Feb. 1948.

19. "The World at Peace," *The East Echo* (Kansas City, Missouri), 10 Jan. 1946.

20. "World Government" *The East Echo* (Kansas City, Missouri), 28 Feb. 1946.

21. Martha Ann Nichols, "Transition," *The East Echo* (Kansas City, Missouri), 9 May 1946.

22. Hampton Stevens, "Humanity Versus Nationalism," *Sachem*, 1947.

23. William Melvin, "The Bitter Apple," *Senior Scholastic*, 20 May 1946.

24. Robert Blackwell, "What Will Tomorrow Bring?" *The Lincoln Callotype* (Kansas City, Missouri), 23 Jan. 1948.

25. Robert Alan Levine, "Youth Explores the Requirements of World Order," *Progressive Education* 25, 6 (1948): 99–100.

26. Eleanor Gibson, "It Waits for Peace," *The Central Luminary* (Kansas City, Missouri), 10 May 1948.

27. Dolores Ross, "Freedom," *The Northeast Courier* (Kansas City, Missouri), 7 May 1948.

28. "Youth Must Stop Communism," *The Southeast Tower* (Kansas City, Missouri), 28 May 1953.

29. "Democracy," *The Manual Craftsman* (Kansas City, Missouri), 15 Feb. 1952.

30. Carrie Lee Bates, letter to the editor, *Senior Scholastic*, 28 March 1951.

31. Katie Shattuck, letter to the editor, *Senior Scholastic*, 2 Feb. 1955.

32. Susan Vanderlyn Kohler, letter to the editor, *Senior Scholastic*, 2 March 1955.

33. Miller, *"Democracy Is in the Streets": From Port Huron to the Siege of Chicago*, 332, 345; Kenneth Keniston, *The Uncommitted: Alienated Youth in America* (New York: Dell Publishing Co., 1960).

34. Robert B. Kwit, "I Am Going Away," *Senior Scholastic*, 5 Jan. 1949.

35. David Dignwell, "Solar Things," *Senior Scholastic*, 5 May 1947.

36. Sharon Southworth, "Atomic Theory," *Senior Scholastic*, 19 May 1947.

37. Carol Van Alstine, "Heartbeat," *Senior Scholastic*, 17 Nov. 1948.

38. Jay Gellens, "Fall Thralldom," *Senior Scholastic*, 9 Dec., 1946.

39. Bruce McIntyre, "To Those That Shall Be Born," *Senior Scholastic*, 17 Feb. 1947.

40. Don Richardson, "Cornerstone," *Senior Scholastic*, 4 May 1949.

41. Sheila Crofut, "Seasons," *Senior Scholastic*, 3 Nov. 1948.

42. Mary Cahn, "Nature and Man," *Senior Scholastic*, 26 Oct. 1949.

43. Dorothy Finnel, "Peace," *The Southeast Tower* (Kansas City, Missouri), 1 Nov. 1945.

44. Reprinted from *School Activities* 22 (April 1951): 252.

45. "Easter Then and Now," *The Lincoln Callotype* (Kansas City, Missouri), 7 April 1955.

Chapter 8

1. Todd Gitlin, *The Sixties: Years of Hope, Days of Rage,* 34–35.

2. Joseph Lantagne, "Health Interests of 10,000 Secondary School Students," *The Research Quarterly,* 23 (October 1952): 330–346; H.A. Anderson, "High-School Seniors Tell Their Story," *The School Review,* 57 (September 1949): 334–335; "More Maladjusted Boys Found Than Girls in High School Survey," *Personnel & Guidance Journal* 31 (November 1952): 130; "Where Youth Stands," *America,* 26 March 1955: 667.

3. Edward Wynne, "Adolescent Alienation and Youth Policy," *Teachers College Record* 78, 1 (1976): 23–40; "Mental Health and Atomic Energy," *Science,* 17 Jan. 1958, 140; James Carey, "Changing Courtship Patterns in the Popular Songs," *American Journal of Sociology,* 74 (May 1969): 720–731.

4. Robert Lifton, *The Broken Connection,* 365; "The Younger Generation," *Time* 5 Nov. 1951, 46–48+; H.H. Remmers and D.H. Radler, *The American Teenager* (New York: Bobbs-Merrill, 1957) 182–192.

5. David Riesman (with Nathan Glazer and Reuel Denney), *The Lonely Crowd* (c. 1950; New Haven: Conn.: Yale University Press, 1961).

6. William Whyte, Jr., *The Organization Man* (New York: Simon and Schuster, 1956) 221.

7. Elaine Tyler May, *Homeward Bound: American Families in the Cold War Era* (New York: Basic Books, 1988).

8. Howard Becker, "Notes on the Concept of Commitment," *American Journal of Sociology,* 66 (July 1960): 32–40.

9. Howard McCluskey, "The Status of Youth in Our Culture," *Education* ,76 (December 1955) 208.

10. S.E. Eisenstadt, "Archetypal Patterns of Youth," *Daedalus,* 91 (Winter 1962): 28–46.

11. James Coleman, *The Adolescent Society* (New York: The Free Press, 1961) 42–43.

12. Coleman, et al. *Transition to Adulthood* (Chicago: University of Chicago Press, 1974).

13. Bruno Bettelheim, "The Problem of Generations," *Youth: Change and Challenge,* ed. Erik Erikson (New York: Basic Books, 1963); Edgar Friedenberg, *The Vanishing Adolescent* (Boston: Beacon Press, 1959).

14. Hans Sebald, *Adolescence: A Sociological Analysis* (New York: Appleton-Century-Crofts, 1968), 207–208.

15. Among Kenneth Keniston's writings on youth are *The Uncommitted: Alienated Youth in American Society* (c. 1960; New York: Dell Publishing, 1965); "Social Change and Youth in America," in Erik Erikson, ed., *Youth: Change and Challenge* (New York: Basic Books, 1963); "Youth, A (New) Stage of Life," *American Scholar* 39 (Fall 1970): 631–654; *Youth and Dissent* (c. 1960; New York: Harcourt Brace Johanovich, 1971); and *Young Radicals* (New York: Harcourt Brace Johanovich, 1968).

16. Keniston, *The Uncommitted: Alienated Youth in America,* 4.

17. David Woodbury, "The Peacetime Atom," *Look,* 9 August 1955: 26.

18. "The Younger Generation," *Time,* 5 Nov. 1951: 47.

19. "Rebel or Psychopaths?" *Time,* 6 Dec. 1954: 64.

20. Oscar Handlin, "Yearning for Security," *Atlantic,* 187 (January 1951): 25–27; "The Younger Generation," *Time,* 5 Nov. 1951, 46–48+.

21. Otto Butz, *The Unsilent Generation: An Anonymous Symposium in Which Eleven College Seniors Look at Themselves and Their World* (New York: Rinehart & Co., 1958) 106–107, 126, 130.

22. J. Ronald Oakley, *God's Country: America in the Fifties* (1986; New York: Dembner Books, 1990) 435.

23. Gaile McGregor, "Domestic Blitz: A Revisionist History of the Fifties," *American Studies,* 34,1 (Spring 1993): 5–33.

24. May, *Homeward Bound,* 113.

25. James Gilbert, *Another Chance: Postwar America, 1945–1968* (New York: Alfred A. Knopf, 1981); Paul Carter, *Another Part of the Fifties* (New York: Columbia University Press, 1983); Joseph Goulden, *The Best Years: 1945–1950* (New York: Atheneum, 1976); Llamon, *Deliberate Speed: The Origins of a Cultural Style in the American 1950s;* Fred Powledge, *Free at Last? The Civil Rights Movement and the people Who Made It* (New York: Little, Brown and Co., 1991); and Jeffrey Hart, *When the Going Was Good: American Life in the Fifties* (New York: Crown Publishers, 1982). For a general analysis, see David Halberstam, *The Fifties* (New York: Villard Books, 1993).

26. Gilbert, *Another Chance: Postwar America, 1945–1968,* 254.

27. Norman Cousins, *Modern Man Is Obsolete* (New York: The Viking Press, 1946) 48.

28. The complete text of the Port Huron Statement appears in James Miller, *"Democracy Is in the Streets": From Port Huron to the Siege of Chicago* (New York: Simon & Schuster, 1987).

Epilogue

1. W. T. Lhamon, Jr., *Deliberate Speed: The Origins of a Cultural Style in the American 1950s* (Washington, D.C.: Smithsonian Institution Press, 1990) 32–33; Fred Powledge, *Free at Last? The Civil Rights Movement and the People Who Made It* (New York: Little, Brown and Co., 1991).

2. Elizabeth Evans, "In Defense of My Generation," *Journal of the National Education Association* 44 (March 1955): 140.

3. Robert Piper, "Where Do We Go from Here?," *American Mercury* 81 (August 1955): 82–84.

4. Todd Gitlin, *The Sixties: Years of Hope, Days of Rage* (New York: Bantam Books, 1987) 22–23.

5. Andrew Dowdy, *The Films of the Fifties: The American State of Mind* (New York: William Morrow and Co., 1975) 60; "Civil Defense: Best Defense? Prayer," *Time,* 27 June 1955: 17; Maria Reidelbach, *Completely Mad: A History of the Comic Book and Magazine* (Boston: Little, Brown and Co., 1991) 32, 136–140; Allan Winkler, *Life Under a Cloud* (New York: Oxford University Press, 1993) 5.

6. Barry Miles, *Ginsberg* (New York: Simon and Schuster, 1989) 195–197; Allen Ginsberg, *Howl and Other Poems* (San Francisco: City Light Books, 1956).

7. Rock 'n' roll did not magically appear in 1955, far from it. As Nick Tosches has discussed in his book, *Unsung Heroes of Rock 'n' Roll: The Birth of Rock in the Wild Years Before Elvis* (New York: Harmony Books, 1984), white and black teenagers were listening to the sounds of rock 'n' roll in the early 1950s, primarily on the jukebox and records. But it was not until 1955, with the emergence of Top 40 radio, transistors, 45-rpm records, a well-defined youth culture, and the recognition of the youth consumer market, that this music began to cross white and black boundaries. Also see Tom McCourt, "Bright Lights, Big City: A Brief History of Rhythm and Blues 1945–1957," in Timothy E. Scheurer, editor, *The Age of Rock* (Bowling Green, Ohio: Bowling Green State University Popular Press, 1989) 46–62; Michael Bane, *White Boy Singin' the Blues: The Black Roots of White Rock* (New York: Da Capo Press, 1982); N.K. Cohn, *Rock: From the Beginning* (New York: Stein & Day, 1969); and Charlie Gillett, *The Sound of the City: The Rise of Rock and Roll* (New York: Outerbridge and Dienstfrey, 1970).

8. *New Serial Titles 1950–1970* (Washington, D.C.: R.R. Bowker Co., 1973). For more on media and youth, see James Gilbert, *A Cycle of Outrage: America's Reaction to the Juvenile Delinquent in the 1950s* (New York: Oxford University Press, 1986).

9. Lhamon, *Deliberate Speed,* 8.

Bibliography

Abraham, Herbert. "A World Organization for Peace." *School Life,* 28 (October 1945): 3–4.
"The A-Bomb: Moral or Not?" *Senior Scholastic,* 1 Nov. 1950: 9.
"A-Bomb's Children. *Life,* 12 Dec. 1949: 59–60+.
Abrams, Philip. *Historical Sociology.* Shepton Mallet, England: Open Books, 1982.
"After School Hours." *The Journal of Education,* 134 (September 1951): 159.
Albrecht, Milton. "Does Literature Reflect Common Values?" *American Sociological Review,* 21 (December 1956): 722–729.
_____. "The Relationship of Literature and Society." *American Journal of Sociology,* 59 (March 1954): 425–436.
"All Our Children: Nationwide Survey." *Newsweek,* 9 Nov. 1953: 28–30.
Allhoff, Fred. "Lightning in the Night." *Liberty,* 24 Aug., 31 Aug., 7 Sept., 14 Sept., 21 Sept., 28 Sept., 5 Oct., 12 Oct., 19 Oct., 26 Oct., 2 Nov. 9, Nov., 16 Nov., 1940.
Alsop, Joseph and Stewart Alsop. "Your Flesh *Should* Creep: Did Our National Safety Die at Hiroshima? *Saturday Evening Post,* 13 July 1946: 9+.
Amatora, S. Mary. "Emotional Stability of Children in the Atomic Age." *Education,* 67 (March 1951): 446–450.
Anderson, H.A. "High-School Seniors Tell Their Story." *The School Review,* 57 (September 1949): 334–335.
Anderson, Poul, and Waldrop, F.N. "Tomorrow's Children." *Astounding Science-Fiction* (March 1947): 56–79.
Anderson, Walt Anderson, ed. *The Age of Protest.* Pacific Palisades, Calif.: Goodyear Publishing Co., 1969.
Anisfield, Nancy, ed. *The Nightmare Considered.* Bowling Green, Ohio: Bowling Green State University Popular Press, 1991.
"Another Citizenship Program." *The Journal of Education,* 133 (May 1950): 135.
Antonini, Josephine, ed. *Educational Film Guide 1954–1958.* New York: H.W. Wilson Co., 1958.
"Arm of Disarm for Peace?" *Senior Scholastic,* 5 May 1954: 7–9.
Armine, Michael. "What the Atom Age Has Done to Us." *New York Times Magazine,* 6 Aug. 1950: 12+.
Ashby, Lyle. "Operation Crossroads." *Journal of the National Education Association,* 35 (1946): 292.
Asklund, G., and D. Taylor, eds. "Teen-Agers and Music! Analysis of Week-end with Music Interviews." *Etude,* 67 (April 1949); 226+.
Astrachan, Sam. "New Lost Generation." *New Republic,* 4 Feb. 1957: 17–18.
"Atom Aftermath." *Newsweek* 10 Sept. 1945: 31–32.
"The Atom Bomb and the Teacher's Obligations." *Senior Scholastic* (Teacher Edition), 30 Sept. 1946: 3T–4T.

"The Atom in a Divided World." *Senior Scholastic*, 31 Oct. 1951: 14–15.
"The Atomic Age." *Life*, 20 Aug. 1945: 32.
"Atomic Age." *Time*, 20 Aug. 1945: 29–36.
"The Atomic Age Opens." *The Journal of Education*, 128 (November 1945) 258.
"Atomic Energy Education." *School Life* Supplement, 31 (March 1949): 4–7.
"Atomic Energy Here to Stay." *School Life* Supplement, 31 (March 1949): 2.
"Atomic Energy in Overalls." *Senior Scholastic*, 12 April 1946: 8–9, 11.
"Atomic Power...for Progress or Destruction." *Senior Scholastic*, 30 Sept. 1946: 5–7.
"Atomic Revolution," *Senior Scholastic*, 17 Sept. 1945: 13–14.
"Atoms Aloft and A-Sea." *Senior Scholastic* ,26 Sept. 1951: 14.
"Atoms for Peace." *Senior Scholastic*, 9 Dec. 1953: 13–15.
"Atoms for Peace or Death?" *America*, 24 Dec. 1955: 348.
Atomic Education: Chicago's Challenge. Report on the Atomic Energy Institute for Teachers, Chicago, Illinois, 1949–1950.
Austin, Warren. "Atomic Weapons and World Peace." *Education*, 71,7 (1951): 414–419.
"B-29s Almost Finished the Job." *Life*, 20 Aug. 1945: 28–29.
Bailey, Beth. *From Front Porch to Back Seat: Courtship in Twentieth-Century America.* Baltimore: Johns Hopkins University Press, 1988.
Baker, Janet Bassett Johnson. "U.N. Youth Develop Global Consciousness." *School Activities*, 23 (May 1952): 285–287.
Baldwin, Hanson. "*Life*'s Reports: The Atom Bomb and Future War." *Life*, 20 Aug. 1945: 17–20.
Balsay, Gene. "The Hot-Rod Culture." *American Quarterly* 2 (Winter 1959) 353–358.
Bane, Michael. *White Boy Singin' the Blues: The Black Roots of White Rock.* New York: Da Capo Press, 1982.
Barnouw, Erik. *Documentary: A History of the Non-Fiction Film.* New York: Oxford University Press, 1983.
Barsam, Richard. "'This Is America': Documentaries for Theaters, 1942–1951." *Cinema Journal* 12 (Spring 1973): 22.
Barthes, Roland. *Camera Lucida: Reflections on Photography.* Trans. Richard Howard. New York: Hill and Wang, 1981.
Bartter, Martha. "Nuclear Holocaust as Urban Renewal." *Science-Fiction Studies*, 13 (July 1986): 148–158.
_____. *The Way to Ground Zero: The Atomic Bomb in American Science Fiction.* New York: Greenwood Press, 1988.
Beach, Goodwin. "Liberal Education and Leisure in the Atomic Age." *Education*, 67 (June 1947): 595–602.
Becker, Howard. "Notes on the Concept of Commitment." *American Journal of Sociology*, 66 (July 1960): 32–40.
Benét, Stephen Vincent. "William Riley and the Fates." *Senior Scholastic*, 17 Sept. 1945: 28–30+; 24 Sept. 1945: 25–26+.
Benjamin, H. "Place of the Secondary School in American Society." *School Review*, 56 (November 1948): 510–518.
Benne, Kenneth. "Democratic Ethics in Social Engineering." *Progressive Education*, 26,7 (1949): 201–207.
Benton, Mike. *The Comic Book in America: An Illustrated History.* Dallas: Taylor Publishing Co., 1989.
Berelson, Bernard. *Content Analysis in Communication Research.* New York: Hafner Press, 1952.
Berger, Albert. "Love, Death, and the Atomic Bomb: Sexuality and Community in Science Fiction, 1935–1955." *Science Fiction Studies*, 8 (November 1981): 279–290.
_____. "Science Fiction Fans in Socio-Economic Perspective: Factors in the Social Consciousness of a Genre." *Science-Fiction Studies*, 4 (1977): 232–246.
Berger, Bennett. *Looking for America: Essays on Youth, Suburbia, and Other Obsessions.* Englewood Cliffs, N.J.: Prentice-Hall, 1971.

Berger, Peter, and Thomas Luckmann. *The Social Construction of Reality*. Garden City, N.Y.: Doubleday, 1966.

Bernard, Jesse. "Teen-Age Culture: An Overview." *Middle-Class Juvenile Delinquency*. Ed. Edmund Vax. New York: Harper & Row, 1967. 23–38.

Besse, Janet, and Harold Lusswell. "Our Columnists on the A-Bomb." *World Politics*, 3 (October 1950): 72–87.

Bester, Alfred. "The Push of a Finger." *Astounding Science-Fiction* (May 1942). Reprinted in *Isaac Asimov Presents the Great Science Fiction Stories, Volume 4, 1942*. Ed. Isaac Asimov and Martin H. Greenberg. New York: DAW, 1980. 110–149.

Bettelheim, Bruno. "The Problem of Generations." Ed. Erik Erikson. *Youth: Change and Challenge*. New York: Basic Books, 1963.

"Biggest Manmade Explosion." *Senior Scholastic*, 7 April 1954: 17.

"Birth of an Era" *Time*, 13 Aug. 1945: 17–18.

Biskind, Peter. "Pods, Blobs, and Ideology in American Films of the Fifties." *Shadows of the Magic Lamp: Fantasy and Science Fiction in Film*. Eds. George Slusser and Eric S. Rabkin. Carbondale: Southern Illinois Press, 1985. 58–72.

_____. *Seeing Is Believing*. New York: Pantheon, 1983.

Blackett, P.M.S. *Fear, War, and the Bomb: Military and Political Consequences of Atomic Energy*. New York: McGraw-Hill, 1948.

Blakely, R. J. "Living Without Fear in a Century of Continuing Crisis." *School Life*, 35 (September 1953): 145–146.

Bliven, Bruce. "The Bomb and the Future." *The New Republic*, 20 Aug. 1945: 210–212.

Block, J. "Ego Identity, Role Variability, and Adjustment." *Journal of Consulting Psychology* 25 (October 1961): 392–397.

"The Bomb." *Time*, 20 Aug. 1945: 19.

Booth, Wayne. *The Rhetoric of Fiction*, second edition. Chicago: University of Chicago Press, 1983.

Bordwell, David. *Narration in the Fiction Film*. Madison: University of Wisconsin Press, 1985.

_____, and Kristin Thompson. *Film Art*. Reading, Mass: Addison-Wesley, 1979.

Bottome, Phyllis. "Caesar's Wife's Ear." *Senior Scholastic*, 4 Jan. 1950: 19–20+.

Boyer, Paul. *By the Bombs Early Light: American Thought and Culture at the Dawn of the Atomic Age*. New York: Pantheon Books, 1985.

Brackett, Leigh. *The Long Tomorrow*. New York: Ace, 1955.

Bradbury, Ray. *Fahrenheit 451*. 1953. New York: Ballantine Books, 1979.

_____. "The Million-Year Panic." *Planet Stories* (Summer 1946). Reprinted in *The Martian Chronicles*. Garden City, N.Y.: Doubleday, 1950.

_____. "There Will Come Soft Rains." *Collier's*, 6 May 1950. Reprinted in *The Martian Chronicles*. Garden City, N.Y.: Doubleday, 1950.

Bradley, David. *No Place to Hide*. 1946. London: University Press of New England, 1983.

"Breeding Atomic Fuel." *Senior Scholastic* 7 Dec. 1949: 12.

Breines, Wini. "Domineering Mothers in the 1950s: Image and Reality." *Women's Studies International Forum* 8,6 (1985): 601–608.

Brians, Paul. *Nuclear Holocausts: Atomic War in Fiction, 1895–1984*. Kent, Ohio: Kent State University Press, 1987.

Bridges, Styles. "Where Do You Stand on the Greatest Question of Our Time." *Collier's*, 8 Jan. 1954: 36.

Bridwell, E. Nelson. Introduction. *Superman, from the Thirties to the Eighties*. New York: Crown Publishers, 1983. 189–200.

Briskind, Peter. "Pods, Blobs, and Ideology in American Films of the Fifties." *Shadows of the Magic Lamp: Fantasy and Science Fiction in Film*. Eds. George Slusser and Eric Rabkin. Carbondale: Southern Illinois Press, 1985. 58–72.

Brode, Douglas. *The Films of the Fifties: Sunset Boulevard to On the Beach*. Secaucus, N.J.: Carol Publishing Group, 1976.

Broder, Dorothy Elizabeth. "Life Adjustment Education: An Historical Study of a Program of the United States Office of Education, 1945–1954." Dissertation. Teachers College, Columbia University, 1976.

Brody, Paula. "Adults' Memories of Growing Up in the Atomic Age." Dissertation. Boston University, 1987.

Bronson, G.W. "Identity Diffusion in Late Adolescence." *Journal of Abnormal and Social Psychology,* 59 (November 1959): 414–417.

Brooks, John. "Ends and Means in Teaching a World Order." *Progressive Education,* 30,3 (1953): 72–74.

Brosnan, John. *Future Tense: The Cinema of Science Fiction.* London: MacDonald and Janes, 1978.

Brown, JoAnnne. "'A' Is for 'Atom'; 'B' Is for 'Bomb': Civil Defense in American Public Education, 1948–1963." *Journal of American History,* 75 (June 1988): 68–90.

Bucher, Charles. "The Atomic Age Strikes Youth." *Education,* 71 (December 1955): 203–205.

Bullough, William. *Cities and Schools in the Guilded Age: The Revolution of an Urban Education.* Port Washington, N.W.: Kennikat Press, 1974.

Bunche, Ralph. "Democracy: A World Issue." *Journal of Negro Education,* 19 (1950: 431–438.

Burger, Sam. "I Saw the Bombs Go Off." *Senior Scholastic,* 16 Sept, 1946: 10–11.

Burnett, R. Will. "The Teacher and Atomic Energy." *Education,* 68 (1948): 545.

_____, Ryland Crary, and Hubert Evans. "The Minds of Men." *School Life,* 31 (March 1949): 11–13.

_____, and Harold Hand. "Educational Implications of the Atomic Age, *Education,* 71,7 (1951): 429–445.

Bush, Merril. "World Organization or Atomic Destruction?" *School and Society,* 23 Nov. 1946: 353–355.

Butterworth, T. H. "Group Thinking Strengthens Democracy." *The High School Journal,* 32 (October 1949): 191–192.

Butz, Otto. *The Unsilent Generation: An Anonymous Symposium in Which Eleven College Seniors Look at Themselves and Their World.* New York: Rinehart & Co., 1958.

Campbell, D'Ann. *Women At Work with America: Private Lives in a Patriotic Era.* Cambridge, Mass.: Harvard University Press, 1984.

Campbell, John, Jr. *The Atomic Story.* New York: Henry Holt, 1947.

_____. "The Place of Science Fiction." *Modern Science Fiction: Its Meanings and Its Future,* Second Edition. ed. Reginald Bretnor. Chicago: Advent, 1979.

"Can We Win Freedom from Fear?" *Senior Scholastic,* 5 May 1954: 13–14.

Capen, Samuel. "The Truth Will Prevail." *School and Society,* 9 Sept. 1947: 177–182.

Carey, James. "Changing Courtship Patterns in the Popular Songs." *American Journal of Sociology,* 74 (May 1969): 720–731.

Carey, Michael. "The Schools and Civil Defense: The Fifties Revisited." *Teachers College Record,* 84, 1 (1982): 115–127.

Carr, William. "On the Waging of Peace." *Journal of the National Education Association* ,36 (1947): 495–500.

Carter, Paul. *Another Part of the Fifties.* New York: Columbia University Press, 1983.

Cartwright, Sally. "Where the Atom Bomb Was Born." *Progressive Education,* 24 (October 1946): 4–6+.

Caute, David. *The Great Fear: The Anti-Communist Purge Under Truman and Eisenhower.* New York: Simon and Schuster, 1978.

Chafe, William. *The American Woman: Her Changing Social, Economic, and Political Roles, 1920–1970.* New York: Oxford University Press, 1972.

Chatman, Seymour. *Coming to Terms: The Rhetoric of Narrative in Fiction and Film.* Ithaca, N.Y.: Cornell University Press, 1990.

Christ, Henry. "The Atom Bomb Shakes the Classroom." *Journal of the National Education Association,* 35 (1946): 296.

"Citizenship Quiz." *Senior Scholastic,* 12 April 1946: 11–12.

"Civil Defense: Best Defense? Prayer." *Time,* 27 June 1955: 17.

"Civil Defense: So Much to Be Done." *Newsweek,* 27 June 1955: 21–22.

"Civil Defense for Our Schools." *The Journal of Education,* 134 (March/April 1951): 112.

Clarke, Arthur C. *Childhood's End.* 1954.

_____. "When Worlds Collide." *Focus on the Science Fiction Film.* Ed. William Johnson. Englewood Cliffs, N.J.: Prentice-Hall, 1972. 66–67.

"The Class of '49." *Fortune,* 39 (June 1949): 84–87+.

Cloete, Stuart. "The Blast." *Collier's* 12 and 19 April 1947.

Cohen, Mitchell, and Dennis Hale, eds. *The New Student Left.* Boston: Beacon Press, 1967.

Cohn, N.K. *Rock: From the Beginning.* New York: Stein & Day, 1969.

Coleman, John. *The Adolescent Society.* New York: The Free Press, 1961.

_____. "The Adolescent Subculture and Academic Achievement." *American Journal of Sociology,* 65 (January 1960): 337–347.

"Colleges Chosen for Atom Study." *The Journal of Education,* 131 (May 1948): 165.

Conant, James Bryant. *Education and Liberty: The Role of the Schools in a Modern Democracy.* Cambridge, Mass.: Harvard University Press, 1953.

_____. *Education in a Divided World.* Cambridge, Massachusetts: Harvard University Press, 1948.

Conlin, Joseph. *The Troubles: A Jaundiced Glance Back at the Movement of the 60s.* New York: Franklin Watts 1982.

Considine, David. *The Cinema of Adolescence.* Jefferson, N.C.: McFarland, 1985.

Conversations with the New Reality. San Francisco: Canfield Press, 1971.

Cook, Bruce. *The Beat Generation.* New York: Charles Scribner's Sons, 1971.

Counselbaum, S. L. "Building Democracy Through Extra-Curricular Clubs." *Education,* 68 (November 1947): 162–166.

Cousins, Norman. *Modern Man Is Obsolete.* New York: The Viking Press, 1946. Originally published under the same title in *Saturday Review of Literature,* 18 August 1945: 5–9.

Crary, Ryland. "Curriculum Adaptation to Changing Needs." *School Life,* 35 (September 1953): 157–160.

Cremin, Lawrence. *American Education, The Metropolitan Experience, 1876–1980.* New York: Harper & Row, 1988.

_____. *Transformation of the School: Progressivism in American Education, 1896–1957.* New York: Alfred A. Knopf, 1961.

Cromie, Robert. *The Crack of Doom.* London: Digby, 1895.

Cuban, Larry. *How Teachers Taught: Constancy and Change in American Classrooms, 1890–1980.* New York: Longman, 1984.

Daniels, Les. *Marvel: Five Fabulous Decades of the World's Greatest Comics.* New York: Harry N. Abrams, 1991.

Davis, Ron. "Laboratory Practice in Protective Skills." *School Life,* 35 (1953): 158–159.

Dawson, C.W. "Teen-Agers Help Stage Democracy Program." *School Activities,* 21 (September 1949): 15–16.

Day, Donald, ed. *Index to the Science Fiction Magazines, 1926–1950.* Boston: G.K. Hall & Co., 1952.

Day, Edmund. "Educational Mobilization in a Free Society." *The Educational Forum* 11 (November 1946): 5–10.

Dean, Gordon. "The Atomic Age Moves Forward." *School Life,* 35 (1953): 148–149+.

"Delirium Over Dead Star." *Life,* 24 Sept. 1956: 75–80.

Deming, Barbara. *Running Away from Myself: A Dream Portrait of American Drawn from the Films of the Forties.* New York: Grossman, 1969.

Derrida, Jacques. "No Apocalypse, Not Now (full speed ahead, seven missles, seven missives)." *Diacritics,* 14 (1984): 20–31.

"Destination Moon." *Senior Scholastic,* 20 Sept. 1950: 38.

"The Devil in the Atom." *Senior Scholastic,* 7 March 1951: 10–11.

Diettert, Chester. "To Keep Democracy at Its Best." *School Activities,* 21 (March 1950): 212–213.

Dimond, Stanley. "Keys to Good Citizenship." *National Parent-Teacher,* 49 (February 1955): 19–21.

"Do We Have the H-Bomb?" *Senior Scholastic,* 3 Dec. 1952: 18.

"Does the UNO Go Far Enough?" *Senior Scholastic,* 4 Feb. 1946: 15–16.

Doherty, Thomas. *Teenagers & Teenpics: The Juvenilization of American Movies in the 1950s.* Boston: Unwin Hyman, 1988.

"Don't Share the Bomb Say High School Student Votes." *Senior Scholastic,* 21 Jan. 1946: 29.

Dooling, Bob. "A Matter of Time." *Senior Scholastic,* 30 April 1952: 16–17.

Douglass, Harl. *Education for Life Adjustment: Its Meaning and Implication.* New York: Ronald Press, 1950.

Dowdy, Andrew. *The Films of the Fifties: The American State of Mind.* New York: William Morrow and Co., 1975.

_____. *"Movies Are Better Than Ever": Wide Screen Memories of the Fifties.* New York: W. Morrow, 1973.

Dowling, David. *Fictions of Nuclear Disaster.* Iowa City: University of Iowa Press, 1987.

Drake, William. *The American School in Transition.* New York: Prentice-Hall, 1955.

Drake, Elizabeth, and Lillian Carmen. "A Broadcast for Brotherhood." *School Activities* 21 (October 1949): 56–58, 68.

Eagleton, Terry. *Literary Theory: An Introduction.* Oxford: Basil Blackwell, 1983.

"Editorial," *Senior Scholastic,* 17 Sept. 1945: 3–4.

"Editorial." *Progressive Education,* 24, 1 (1946): 16.

"Education and National Security." *Journal of the National Education Association,* 41 (January 1952): 21–22.

Ehlers, Henry, ed., *Crucial Issues in Education: An Anthology.* New York: Holt & Co., 1955.

Eichelberger, Rosa Kohler. "Learning Democracy in School." *Senior Scholastic,* 1 Dec. 1947: 14–15.

Eisenstadt, S.E. "Archetypal Patterns of Youth." *Daedulus* 91 (Winter 1962): 28–46.

Eisinger, Chester, ed. *The 1940s: Profile of a Nation in Crisis, Documents in American Civilization Series.* New York: Anchor Books, 1969.

Elder, Glen. "Adolescence in the Life Cycle: An Introduction." Eds. Glen Elder and Sigmund Dragastin. *Adolescence in the Life Cycle: Psychological Change and Social Context.* Washington, D.C.: Hemisphere Publishing Corp., 1975. 1–22.

_____. *Children of the Great Depression.* Chicago: University of Chicago Press, 1974.

Elie, R. "High School Set's New High Style." *Life,* 36 25 Jan. 1954: 133–134+.

Elliott, L.H. "Understanding the Serio-Comic Teens." *Home Economics,* 33 (September 1954): 82–86.

Engel, Leonard, and Emanuel A. Piller. *World Aflame: The Russian-American War of 1950.* New York: Dial, 1947.

Erenberg, Lewis. "Things to Come: Swing Bands, Bebop, and the Rise of a Postwar Jazz Scene." *Recasting America: Culture and Politics in the Age of Cold War.* Ed. Larry May. Chicago: University of Chicago Press, 1989. 221–245.

Erikson, Erik. *Childhood and Society.* New York: W.W. Norton, 1950.

_____. *Dimensions of a New Identity.* New York: W.W. Norton, 1974.

_____. *Identity: Youth and Crisis.* New York: W.W. Norton, 1968.

_____. "Youth: Fidelity and Diversity." *The Challenge of Youth.* Ed. Erik Erikson. Garden City, N.Y: Anchor Books, 1965. 1–23.

Erikson, Kai. "Sociology and the Historical Perspective." *The American Sociologist,* 5 (1970): 331–338.

Erskine, Hazel Gaudet. "The Polls: Atomic Weapons and Nuclear Energy." *Public Opinion Quarterly,* 27 (Summer 1963): 155–190.

Evans, Elizabeth. "In Defense of My Generation." *Journal of the National Education Association* 44 (March 1955): 139–140.

Evans, Hubert, and Ryland Crary. "Atomic Education: A Continuing Challenge." *Teachers College Record,* 50 (1949): 515–520.

_____, _____, and Glenn Hass. "Operation Atomic Vision." *Journal of the National Educa-tion Association*, 37 (October 1948): 439–442.

Evans, Joyce A. *Celluloid Mushroom Clouds: Hollywood and the Atomic Bomb*. Boulder, Colo.: Westview Press, 1998.

Everts, Hal. "Conquest." *Senior Scholastic*, 6 Dec. 1950: 19–20+.

_____. "Killer in the Pass." *Senior Scholastic*, 2 April 1952: 21–22+.

Favel, William. "Noel at Madame Rolland's." *Senior Scholastic*, 7 Dec. 1949: 22.

Fearing, Franklin. "Influence of the Movies on Attitude and Behavior." *Annals of the Amer-ican Academy of Political and Social Sciences*, 254 (November 1947): 70–79.

Federal Civil Defense Administration. *Civil Defense Educational Practices and References for Homemaking Classes, Classroom Practices*. Washington, D.C.: GPO, 1957.

Felding, Raymond. *The March of Time, 1935–1951*. New York, 1978.

_____. "Time Flickers Out: Notes on the Passing of the March of Time." *Quarterly of Film, Radio, and Television* 11 (Summer 1957): 354–361.

Feldman, Edmund Burke. *Varieties of Visual Experience: Art as Image and Idea*. New York: Harry N. Abrams Inc., 1972.

Fine, Benjamin. "'A Better World' Courses in New York City Schools." *The Education Digest*, 12 (September 1946): 10–11.

Finney, Jack. "The Body Snatchers." *Collier's*, 26 Nov. 1954: 26, 90–99; 10 Dec. 1954: 114, 116–125; 24 Dec. 1954: 62–73. Later published as *Invasion of the Body Snatchers*. 1955. New York: Fireside, 1989.

Fisher, William. "Let's Look at Secondary Education." *Progressive Education*, 24 (April 1947): 200–201+.

FitzGerald, Frances. *America Revised: History Schoolbooks in the Twentieth Century*. Boston: Little, Brown, 1979.

Fleege, Urban. "The Teacher and Civil Defense." *Journal of the National Education Associ-ation*, 40 (November 1951): 542–543.

Fletcher, Marilyn, ed. *Science Fiction Story Index (1950–1979)*. Chicago: American Library Association, 1981.

"Focus on the New Look Defense Progrom." *Senior Scholastic*, 14 April 1954: 14–16.

"Following the Films." *Senior Scholastic*, 31 March 1947: 30.

"For Citizenship and Moral Training." *Senior Scholastic*, 7 Nov. 1951: 12–13.

"Fortune Survey: Use of Atomic Bomb." *Fortune*, 33 (December 1945): 305–306+.

"Fortune Survey: Young People of the U.S." *Fortune*, 36 (December 1948): 40+.

"A Forum Discussion on Atomic Bomb Control." Senior Scholastic, 12 Nov. 1945: 3–5.

Foulkes, William. "The Atom: Death — or Life Abundant?" *Vital Speeches of the Day* 14, 11 (1948): 345.

Frank, Josette. "Chills and Thrills in Radio, Movies and Comics." *Child Study*, 25 (Spring 1948): 42–46+.

Franklin, H. Bruce. "Fatal Fiction: A Weapon to End All Wars." *The Nightmare Considered: Critical Essays on Nuclear War Literature*. Ed. Nancy Anisfield. Bowling Green, Ohio: Bowling Green State University Popular Press, 1991. 5–14.

_____. *Robert A. Heinlein: America As Science Fiction*. New York: Oxford University Press, 1978.

_____. *War Stars: The Superweapon and the American Imagination*. New York: Oxford Uni-versity Press, 1988.

Franklin, Vincent. *The Education of Black Philadelphia: The Social and Educational History of a Minority Community, 1900–1950*. Philadelphia: University of Pennsylvania Press, 1979.

Freedberg, David. *The Power of Images: Studies in the History and Theory of Response*. Chicago: University of Chicago Press, 1989.

Friedan, Betty. *The Feminine Mystique*. Boston: Dell Publishing Co., 1963.

Friedenberg, Edgar. *The Vanishing Adolescent*. Boston: Beacon Press, 1959.

Gable, Martha. "Philadelphia Classroom Television." *The Journal of Education*, 134 (Feb-ruary 1951): 50–52.

Gail, Harry. "Atomic Energy and Education." *Progressive Education*, 24,4 (1947): 116–199+.
_____. "Some Educational Implications of Atomic Energy." *Education*, 67 (1947): 463–472.
Gallup, George. *The Gallup Poll: Public Opinion 1935–1971*. New York: Random House, 1972.
Gayn, Mark. "Terror in Japan." *Collier's* 16 June 1945: 11–12, 59.
Gelbond, Florence. "The Impact of the Atomic Bomb on Education." *The Social Studies*, 65 (March 1974): 109–114.
Genet, Nancy. "Harnessing Atomic Power for Peace." *Senior Scholastic*, 7 Jan. 1946: 5.
Gerbner, G., L. Gross, M. Morgan, N. Signorielli. "The 'Mainstreaming' of America: Violence Profile No. 11." *Journal of Communication*, 30,3 (1980): 10–29.
Gerstell, Richard. *How to Survive an Atomic Bomb*. New York: Bantam Books, 1950.
Gerzon, Mark. *A Young Man Looks at Youth's Dissent*. New York: The Viking Press, 1969.
Gifford, Denis. *Science Fiction Film*. London: Studio Vista Ltd., 1971.
Gilbert, James. *Another Chance: Postwar America, 1945–1968*. New York: Alfred A. Knopf, 1981.
_____. *A Cycle of Outrage: America's Reaction to the Juvenile Delinquent in the 1950s*. New York: Oxford University Press, 1986.
Gillett, Charlie. *The Sound of the City: The Rise of Rock and Roll*. New York: Outerbridge and Dienstfrey, 1970.
Gilman, Mildred. "Why They Can't Wait to Wed," *Parents' Magazine*, 33 (November 1958): 46+.
Ginsberg, Allen. *Howl and Other Poems*. San Francisco: City Light Books, 1956.
Gitlin, Irving. "Radio and Atomic Energy. *Education*, 22 (January 1949): 327–330.
Gitlin, Todd. *The Sixties: Years of Hope, Days of Rage*. New York: Bantam Books, 1987.
Glasheen, George. "What Schools Are Doing in Atomic Energy Education." *School Life* ,35 (September 1953): 152–154+.
Gleason, Philip. "Identifying Identity: A Semantic History." *Journal of American History* 69 (March 1983): 910–931.
Godfrey, Hollis. *The Man Who Ended War*. Boston: Little, Brown, 1908.
Goldstein, Ruth, and Edith Zornos. *The Screen Image of Youth: Movies About Children and Adolescents*. Metuchen, N.J.: Scarecrow Press, 1980.
Gombrich, E.H. *The Image and the Eye*. Ithaca, N.Y.: Cornell University Press, 1982.
Gordon, C. Wayne. *The Social System of the High School*. New York: Free Press of Glencoe, 1957.
Gordon, Kelly. "Literature and the Historian." *American Quarterly*, 26,2 (1974): 154–155.
Goslin, Willard. "A Task for Administrators." *School Life* Supplement 31 (March 1949): 1.
Gould, Kenneth. "You Are America." *Senior Scholastic*, 3 Feb. 1947: 3.
Goulden, Joseph C. *The Best Years 1945–1950*. New York: Antheneum, 1976.
Graebner, William. *The Age of Doubt: American Thought and Culture in the 1940s*. Boston: Twyane Publishers, 1991.
_____. *Coming of Age in Buffalo, Youth and Authority in the Postwar Era*. Philadelphia:Temple University Press, 1990.
_____. "The 'Containment' of Juvenile Delinquency: Social Engineering and American Youth Culture in the Postwar Era." *American Studies*, 27 (Spring 1986): 81–97.
_____. "Outlawing Teenage Populism: The Campaign Against Secret Societies in the American High School, 1900–1960." *The Journal of American History*, 74 (September 1987): 411–435.
Graybeal, Lyman. "Democratic Education in a Time of Crisis." *School Activities*, 20 (1949): 211–212, 215, 218.
Grendon, Edward. "The Figure." Reprinted in *A Treasury of Science Fiction*. Ed. Groff Conklin. New York: Crown, 1948.
Grossman, Gary. *Saturday Morning TV*. New York: Dell Publishing, 1981.
_____. *Superman: Serial to Cereal*. New York: Popular Library, 1976.
Gruber, F.C. "Out-of-School Radio-Listening Habits of High School Students," *English Journal*, 39 (June 1950): 325–327.

Grubick, Irene. "School Forums and Student Responsibility." *School Activities,* 20 (April 1949): 247–248.

Gunn, James. *Alternate Worlds: The Illustrated History of Science Fiction.* Englewood Cliffs, N.J.: Prentice-Hall, 1975.

Halberstam, David. *The Fifties.* New York: Villard Books, 1993.

Hales, Peter. "The Atomic Sublime." *American Studies,* 32 (Spring 1992): 5–31.

Hall, H.W., ed. *Science Fiction and Fantasy Reference Index, 1878–1985.* Detroit: Gale Research Co., 1987.

_____. *Science Fiction Book Review Index, 1923–1973.* Detroit: Gale Research Co., 1975.

Hampel, Robert. *The Last Little Citadel: American High Schools Since 1940.* Boston: Houghton Mifflin, 1986.

Handel, Leo. *Hollywood Looks at Its Audience: A Report of Film Audience Research.* Urbana: University of Illinois Press, 1950.

Handlin, Oscar. "Yearning for Security." *Atlantic,* 187 (January 1951): 25–27.

Hanff, Helene. *The Movies and Shakers: Young Activists of the Sixties.* New York: S.G. Phillips, 1970.

Hart, Jeffrey. *When the Going Was Good: American Life in the Fifties.* New York: Crown Publishers, 1982.

Hartmann, Susan. *The Home Front and Beyond: American in the 1940s.* Boston: Twayne Publishers, 1982.

Haskell, Molly. *From Reverence to Rape: The Treatment of Women in the Movies,* 2nd edition. 1974. Chicago: 1987.

Hatch, Robert. "The Garden of Atom." *New Republic,* 14 May 1951, 23.

"H-Bomb: Cities in Danger." *Senior Scholastic,* 14 April 1954: 17.

Heffernan, Helen. "The School Curriculum in American Education." *Education in the States: Nationwide Development Since 1900.* Edgar Fuller and Jim Pearson, eds. Washington, D.C.: National Education Association, 1969. 215–285.

Heil, Louis, and Joe Musial. "'Splitting the Atom'— Starring Dagwood and Blondie: How It Developed." *The Journal of Educational Psychology,* 22 (January 1949): 331–336.

Heinlein, Robert. "Project Nightmare." *Amazing Stories* (April 1953). Reprinted in *The Menace from Earth.* 1959. New York: Signet, 1963. 158–178.

_____. *The Puppet Masters.* Garden City, New York: Doubleday, 1951.

_____ (as Anson MacDonald). "Solution Unnsatisfactory." *Astounding Science-Fiction* (May 1941). Reprinted in *Expanded Universe: The New Worlds of Robert A. Heinlein.* New York: Ace, 1980. 92–144.

_____. "The Year of the Jackpot." *Galaxy Science Fiction* (March 1952). Reprinted in *The Menace from Earth.* New York: Signet, 1959. 7–38.

Herken, Gregg. *The Winning Weapon: The Atomic Bomb in the Cold War 1945–1950.* New York: Vintage, 1982.

Hersey, John. *Hiroshima.* 1946. New York: Vintage Books, 1989. Originally published as "Hiroshima: Terrible Implications of the Atomic Bomb." *The New Yorker* 31 Aug. 1946: 15–26+.

"Hiding from the Atom." *Senior Scholastic,* 18 March 1953: 35–36.

Higbee, Homer. "The Social, Economic, and Political Implications of Atomic Energy." *Education* 71, 7 (1951): 420–428.

"High-School Fads." *Life,* 17 Nov. 1947: 119–123.

Hightower, Howard. "On War and Peace." *Progressive Education,* 29,7 (1952): 252–253.

Hill, Trent. "The Enemy Within: Censorship in Rock Music in the 1950s." *Present Tense: Rock & Roll and Culture.* Ed. Anthony DeCurtis. Durham, N.C.: Duke University Press, 1972. 39–71.

Hilton, David, and Mary Jeffries. "Atomic Energy in the Classroom and Community." *Journal of Education* 131 (March 1948): 88–89.

Hilton, Kathleen Clare. "Growing Up Female: Girlhood Experiences and Social Feminism, 1890–1929." Dissertation. Carnegie-Mellon University, 1987.

"History Is Made: Telecast of an Atomic Explosion." *Time,* 5 May 1952: 86+.

Hitchcock, Richard. "Westinghouse Theater of Atoms." *The Journal of Educational Sociology,* 22 (January 1949): 353–355.

Hodgens, Richard. "A Brief, Tragical History of the Science Fiction Film." *Focus on the Science Fiction Film.* Ed. William Johnson. Englewood Cliffs, N.J.: Prentice-Hall, 1972. 78–90.

Hogan, David. "Education and the Making of the Chicago Working Class, 1880–1930." *History of Education Quarterly,* 18 (Fall 1978): 231–242.

Hogan, Dennis. *Transitions and Social Change: The Early Lives of American Men.* New York: Academic Press, 1981.

Holland, Norman. *The Dynamics of Literary Response.* Oxford: Oxford University Press, 1963.

_____. "Unity Identity Text Self," *Reader-Response Criticism: From Formalism to Post-Structuralism.* Ed. Jane Tompkins. Baltimore: Johns Hopkins University Press, 1980. 118–133.

Holsti, Ole. *Content Analysis for the Social Sciences and Humanities.* Reading, Mass.: Addison-Wesley Publishing, 1969.

Hopkins, George. "Bombing and the American Conscience During World War II." *Historian,* 28 (May 1966): 451–473.

Huber, L.W. "What Programs of Civil Defense Are Needed in Our Schools?" *Bulletin of the National Association of Secondary-School Principals,* 36 (April 1952): 184–188.

Hullfish, H. Gordon. "Education in an Age of Anxiety." *Educational Freedom in an Age of Anxiety: Yearbook of the John Dewey Society 1953.* H. Gordon Hullfish, ed., *Educational Freedom in an Age of Anxiety: Yearbook of the John Dewey Society 1953.* New York: Harper & Brothers, 1953. 208.

Hutchins, Robert. "The Atomic Bomb Versus Civilization." *Today's Education,* 35 (March 1946): 114–117.

_____. "The Issues in Education: 1946." *The Educational Record* 27 (1946): 365–375.

Hyman, Herbert H., and Paul B. Sheatsley, "Attitudes Towards Desegregation." *Scientific American,* 195 (December 1956): 35–39.

"If...the Bomb Falls." *Senior Scholastic,* 8 Nov. 1950: 6.

Inglis, Ruth. "An Objective Approach to the Relationship Between Fiction and Society." *American Sociological Review* 3 (August 1938): 526–531.

Inkeles, Alex, and Daniel Levinson. "National Character: The Study of Modal Personality and Sociocultural Systems." Eds. Gardner Lindzey and Elliot Aronson. *The Handbook of Social Psychology,* 2nd edition. Reading, Mass.: Addison-Wesley Publishing Co., 1954. 418–506.

Iser, Wolfgang. *The Act of Reading.* Baltimore: Johns Hopkins University Press, 1980.

_____. *The Implied Reader.* Baltimore: Johns Hopkins University Press, 1978.

_____. "The Reading Process: A Phenomenological Approach." *Reader-Response Criticism: From Formalism to Post-Structuralism.* Ed. Jane Tompkins. Baltimore: Johns Hopkins University Press, 1980. 50–69.

"It Is Later Than We Think!" *Senior Scholastic,* 17 Sept. 1945: 8.

Jackson, Kathy Merlock. *Images of Children in American Film.* Metuchen, N.J.: The Scarecrow Press, 1986.

"Jam Session." *Senior Scholastic,* 29 Sept. 1948: 35.

"Jam Session." *Senior Scholastic,* 3 Nov. 1947: 32.

Jameson, Malcolm. "The Giant Atom." *Startling Stories* (Winter 1944). Reprinted as *Atomic Bomb.* Hollywood: Bond-Charteris, 1945.

Javna, John. *The Best from Science Fiction TV: The Critics' Choice from Captain Video to Star Trek, from The Jetsons to Robotech.* New York: Harmony Books, 1987.

Jenkins, David. "Social Engineering in Educational Change: An Outline of Method." *Progressive Education,* 26,7 (1949): 193–197.

Jenkins, Will. *The Murder of the U.S.A.* New York: Crown, 1946.

Johnson, Gerald. "The Liberal of 1946." *The American Scholar,* 15 (1946): 154–159.

Johnson, J. Clyde. "Teaching Democratic Skills and Attitudes." *The High School Journal,* 35 (February 1952): 137–142.

Johnson, Jack. "Protective Citizenship — Its Educational Implications." *School Life,* 35 (1953): 150–151.

Johns-Heine, Patricke, and Hans Gerth. "Values in Mass Periodical Fiction, 1921–1940." *Mass Culture: The Popular Arts in America.* Eds. Bernard Rosenberg and David Manning. Glencoe, Ill." The Falcon's Wing Press, 1957. 226–234,

"Junior Hi Forum Stresses Intercultural Education." *School Activities,* 20 (January 1949): 167.

Kahler, Erich. "The Reality of Utopia." *The American Scholar,* 15 (1946): 167–179.

Kaiser, Charles. *1968 in America.* New York: Weidenfeld & Nicholson, 1988.

Kaminsky, Stuart. *American Film Genres: Approaches to a Critical Theory of Popular Film.* New York: Dell Publishing Co., 1974.

"Kansas Will Train Youth As Citizens." *The Journal of Education,* 133 (September 1950): 189.

Kaplan, Louis. "The Need for Creative Education." *The Journal of Education,* 131 (November 1948): 241–242.

Kast, Pierre. "Don't Play with Fire." *Focus on the Science Fiction Film.* Ed. William Johnson. Englewood Cliffs, N.J.: Prentice-Hall, 1972. 68–70.

Katznelson, Ira, Kathleen Gille, and Margaret Weir, "Public Schooling and Working Class Formation: The Case of the United States." *American Journal of Education* (February 1982): 111–143.

Kay, Lillian Wald. "Public Opinion and the Atom." *The Journal of Educational Sociology* 22 (January 1949): 356–362.

"Keepers of the Secret: The Atomic Energy Commission." *Senior Scholastic,* 20 Oct. 1947: 16–17.

Keesecker, Ward. "Duty of Teachers to Promote Ideals and Principles of American Democracy." *School Life,* 30 (February 1948): 31–33.

Kelly, R. Gordon. "Literature and the Historian," *American Quarterly* 26,2 (1974): 141–159.

Keniston, Kenneth. "Psychological Development and Historical Change." *Journal of Interdisciplinary History,* 2 (Autumn 1971): 329–345.

_____. "Social Change and Youth in America." Ed. Erik Erikson. *Youth: Change and Challenge.* New York: Basic Books, 1963.

_____. *The Uncommitted: Alienated Youth in America.* New York: Dell Publishing Co., 1960.

_____. *Young Radicals: Notes on Committed Youth.* New York: Harcourt Brace Jovanovich, 1968.

_____. "Youth, A (New) Stage of Life." *American Scholar,* 39 (Fall 1970): 631–654.

_____. *Youth and Dissent.* New York: Harcourt Brace Jovanovich, 1971.

Kennedy, Philip. "Oak Ridge and the Educational Crossroads." *National Association of Secondary-School Principals Bulletin,* 30 (October 1946): 81–83.

_____. "Youth, Hope, and the Atomic Paradox." *Journal of the National Education Association,* 35 (October 1946): 392–393.

Kesey, Ken. *One Flew Over the Cuckoo's Nest.* 1962. New York: Penguin Books, 1976.

Kett, Joseph. *Rites of Passage: Adolescence in America, 1790 to the Present.* New York: Basic Books, 1977.

Key, Lillian Wald. "Public Opinion and the Atom." *The Journal of Educational Psychology* 22 (January 1949): 356–362.

Kirshen, Rosalie. "A Unit on Atomic Energy in the Experience Curriculum." *High Points,* 33 (February 1951): 27–31.

Kishi, Yoshio. "What It Means to Me to Be Growing Up with Nuclear Energy." *The Journal of Educational Sociology,* 22 (January 1949): 336–337.

Knowlton, Philip. "Civilization's Race with Death." *Senior Scholastic,* 5 Jan. 1949: 16.

_____. "Great Issues Facing High School Students: Building a Philosophy." *Senior Scholastic,* 22 Sept. 1948: 19–20.

_____. "Is Science Man's Greatest Enemy?" *Senior Scholastic,* 2 Feb. 1949: 17.

Komroff, Manual. "Death of an Eagle." *Senior Scholastic,* 6 April 1955: 20, 28.

Krahn, Frederic, ed. *Educational Film Guide,* 11th edition. New York: H.W. Wilson Co., 1953.

Kramer, Dale, and Madeline Karr. *Teen-Age Gangs.* New York: Henry Holt & Co., 1953.

Krug, Edward. *The Shaping of the American High School, 1920–1941.* Madison: University of Wisconsin Press, 1972.

Kruse, John. "Alone in Shark Waters." *Senior Scholastic,* 4 May 1955: 40–41, 53.

Lamars, William. "Identification for School Children." *Journal of the National Education Association,* 41 (February 1952): 99.

Lang, Daniel. *From Hiroshima to the Moon: Chronicles of Life in the Atomic Age.* New York: Simon and Schuster, 1959.

Lantagne, Joseph. "Health Interests of 10,000 Secondary School Students." *The Research Quarterly,* 23 (October 1952): 330–346.

Lasch, Christopher. *Haven in a Heartless World: The Family Besieged.* New York: Basic Books, 1977.

Laxson, Mary, and Berenice Mallory. "Education for Homemaking in Today's High School." *School Life,* 32 (June 1950): 134–135, 138.

Leamer, Laurence. *The Paper Revolutionaries: The Rise of the Underground Press.* New York: Simon and Schuster, 1972.

"Learning Experiences in Atomic Energy Education." *School Life,* Supplement 31 (March 1949): 10.

Leitch, Thomas. *What Stories Are: Narrative Theory and Interpretation.* University Park: Penn State University Press, 1986.

Lentz, Harris, III. *Science Fiction, Horror & Fantasy Film and Television Credits.* Jefferson, N.C.: McFarland & Co., 1983.

Lerch, Albert. "We Taught the Meaning of Democracy." *School Activities,* 25 (January 1954): 151–153.

"Lesson of Hiroshima." *Time,* 17 Feb. 1947: 29.

Levine, Robert Alan. "Youth Explores the Requirements of World Order." *Progressive Education* 25,6 (1948): 99–100.

Lhamon, W.T. Jr., *Deliberate Speed: The Origins of a Cultural Style in the American 1950s.* Washington, D.C.: Smithsonian Institution Press, 1990.

Lifton, Robert. *The Broken Connection: On Death and the Continuity of Life.* New York: Simon and Schuster, 1979.

Lilienthal, David. "Atomic Energy...and You." *Senior Scholastic,* 12 April 1946, 3.

_____. "Democracy and the Atom." *Progressive Education,* 25,3 (1948): 2–5+.

_____. "Education's Responsibilities." *School Life,* Supplement 31 (March 1949): 1–2.

_____. "Youth in the Atomic Age." *Journal of the National Education Association* 37 (September 1948): 370–371.

Lindsey, Audrey. "I Taught Atomic Energy: With Statements By Thirteen Members of the Class." *Education,* 71, 7 (1951): 451–469.

Lipton, Lawrence. *The Holy Barbarians.* New York: Julian Messner, 1959.

Little, Stuart. "The Friendship Train: Citizenship and Postwar Culture, 1946–1949." *American Studies,* 34 (Spring 1993): 35–67.

"Living with the Atom." *Senior Scholastic,* 3 March 1947: 10–11.

Llamon, W.T., Jr. *Deliberate Speed: The Origins of a Cultural Style in the American 1950s.* Washington, D.C.: Smithsonian Institution Press, 1990.

"Local High School Radio Forum." *School Activities,* 22 (December 1950): 137.

Long, Elizabeth. *The American Dream and the Popular Novel.* Boston, 1985.

Lora, Ronald. "Education: Schools as Crucible in Cold War America." *Reshaping America.* Ed. Robert Bremner and Gary Reichard. Columbus, Ohio: Ohio State University, 1982. 223–260.

Lucanio, Patrick. *Them or Us: Archetypal Interpretations of Fifties Alien Invasion Films.* Bloomington: Indiana University Press, 1987.

McCloy, Charles, ed. *The Organization and Administration of Physical Education.* New York: Appleton-Century-Crofts, 1958.

McClure, Dorothy. "Social-Studies Textbooks and Atomic Energy." *The School Review,* 57 (December 1949): 540–546.

_____, and Philip Johnson, "Where the School Takes Hold." *School Life,* Supplement 31 (March 1949): 7–9+.

McConnell, Frank. "Song of Innocence: *The Creature from the Black Lagoon." Journal of Popular Film,* 2 (1973): 15–28.

McCourt, Tom. "Bright Lights, Big City: A Brief History of Rhythm and Blues 1945–1957." *The Age of Rock.* Timothy E. Scheurer, ed. Bowling Green, Ohio: Bowling Green State University Popular Press, 1989. 46–62.

McFarland, W.H. "World Unity in the Classroom." *The Journal of Education,* 129 (March 1946): 96–97.

McGrath, Earl James. *Education: The Wellspring of Democracy.* University, Alabama: University of Alabama Press, 1951.

_____. "Education and the National Defense." *School Life,* 33 (November 1950): 18–23.

McGregor, Gaile. "Domestic Blitz: A Revisionist History of the Fifties." *American Studies,* 34 (Spring 1993): 5–33.

McIntire, John Lamb. "Dream World or Reality?" *Progressive Education,* 24,1 (1946): 18–19+.

MacDonald, J. Fred. *Don't Touch That Dial: Radio Programming in American Life, 1920–1960.* Chicago: Nelson-Hall, 1980.

MacDougall, Curtis. "Language and Human Welfare." *Progressive Education,* 25,1 (1947): 269.

MacFarlane, Robert. "Prelude to Hiroshima." *The Educational Forum,* 10 (March 1946): 331–339.

Mailer, Norman. *Armies of the Night.* New York: Signet, 1968.

"Make and Show." *School Life,* Supplement 31 (March 1949): 6.

Mannheim, Karl. "The Problem of the Generations." *Essays on the Sociology of Knowledge.* New York: Oxford University Press, 1928.

Marchand, Roland. "Visions of Classlessness, Quests for Dominion: American Popular Culture, 1945–1960." *Reshaping America.* Eds. Robert Bremner and Gary Reichard. Columbus, Ohio: Ohio State University Press, 1982. 163–192.

March-Mount, Margaret. "Atom-Agers Look to the Future." *Progressive Education,* 27,6 (1950): 165–171.

Marsh, Margaret. "From Separation to Togetherness: The Social Construction of Domestic Space in American Suburbs." *Journal of American History,* 76,2 (September 1989): 506–527.

Marshall, Kendric. "Teachers and the International Crisis." *School Life,* 30 (June 1948): 2–3.

Martin, Ernest. "Five." *Nuclear War Films.* Ed. Jack Shaheen. Carbondale: Southern Illinois Press, 1978. 11–16.

Martin, Wallace. *Recent Theories of Narrative.* Ithaca, N.Y.: Cornell University Press, 1986.

Masters, Dexter. *The Accident.* 1955. New York: Penguin Books, 1985.

_____, and Katharine Way, eds. *One World or None.* New York: McGraw-Hill, 1946.

"Matador Guided Missile." *Senior Scholastic,* 3 Oct. 1951: 16.

May, Alonzo. "Atomic Energy and the Liberal Arts." *School and Society* 24 Aug. 1946: 131–133.

May, Elaine Tyler. *Homeward Bound: American Families in the Cold War Era.* New York: Basic Books, 1988.

May, Lary. Introduction. *Recasting America: Culture and Politics in the Age of the Cold War.* Ed. Lary May. Chicago: University of Chicago Press, 1989.

Meade, Mary. "What Programs of Civil Defense Are Needed in Our Schools?" *Bulletin of the National Association of Secondary-School Principals,* 36 (April 1952): 180–184.

"Mental Health and Atomic Energy." *Science,* 17 Jan. 1958, 140.

Merrick, N.C., and W.C. Seyfert. "School Publications As a Source of Desirable Group Experience." *School Review,* 55 (January 1947): 1–28.

Merril, Judith. *Shadow of the Hearth.* Garden City, N.Y.: Doubleday, 1950.

_____. "That Only a Mother." *Astounding Science-Fiction* (June 1948). Reprinted in *The Road to Science Fiction, Volume 3.* Ed. James Gunn (New York: Mentor/NAL, 1979. 143–152.

Miles, Barry. *Ginsberg.* New York: Simon and Schuster, 1989.

Miller, James. *"Democracy Is in the Streets": From Port Huron to the Siege of Chicago.* New York: Simon and Schuster, 1987.

Miller, Timothy. *The Hippies and American Values.* Knoxville: University of Tennessee Press, 1991.

Miner, Claudia Ann. "What About the Children? Americans' Attitudes Toward Children and Childhood During the 1950s." Dissertation. Washington State University, 1986.

Miner, Edwin. "National Conference on Zeal for American Democracy." *School Life* 30 (May 1948): 3–5.

Modell, John. *Into One's Own.* Berkeley: University of California Press, 1989.

Moore, Ward. "Lot." *Fantasy and Science Fiction* (May 1953). Reprinted in *Best from Fantasy and Science Fiction, Third Series.* Ed. Anthony Boucher and J. Francis McComas. Garden City, New York: Doubleday, 1954. 100–130.

_____. "Lot's Daughter." *Fantasy and Science Fiction* (October 1954): 3–27.

"More Maladjusted Boys Found Than Girls in High School Survey." *Personnel & Guidance Journal* 31 (November 1952): 130.

"More Scripts for High School Radio Workshops." *Senior Scholastic* (Teacher Edition) 26 Sept. 1951: 27T.

"Mouse Traps for Chain Reaction." *School Life,* 32 (November 1949): 21–22.

Mumford, Lewis. "Gentlemen: You Are Mad." *Saturday Review of Literature,* 2 March 1946: 5–6.

Mundt, E. "Home Economics Clubs in High School." *Journal of Home Economics,* 38 (April 1946): 213–215.

Murphy, Brian. "Monster Movies: They Came from Beneath the Fifties." *Journal of Popular Film,* 1 (Winter 1972): 31–44.

"Must We Build the Hydrogen Bomb?" *Senior Scholastic,* 8 Feb. 1950: 8.

Muuss, Rudolf. *Theories of Adolescence.* 1962. New York: Random House, 1975.

Mygatt, Tracy."World Government Is Common Sense." *Progressive Education,* 24 (October 1946): 10–11+.

"National Defense: Ducking for Cover." *Newsweek,* 30 July 1956: 28.

"National Governments." *Journal of Education,* 131 (January 1948): 6.

"NATO: From Straw Man to Superman." *Senior Scholastic,* 4 May 1955: 11.

Nelson, R. "Citizenship Laboratory; School Community Projects." *School Review,* 56 (March 1948): 156–162.

Neugarten, Bernie, and Nancy Datan. "Sociological Perspectives on the Life Cycle." Eds. P.A. Beales and K.W. Schaie. *Life-Span Development Psychology.* New York: Academic Press, 1973): 53–69.

New Serial Titles 1950–1970. Washington, D.C.: R.R. Bowker Co., 1973.

"New Way to Use the Atom for Power." *Senior Scholastic,* 10 Feb. 1954: 31.

Newspapers and Periodicals, 1946 through 1956. Philadelphia: N.W. Ayers & Sons, Inc., 1956.

Nixon, R.E. "An Approach to the Dynamics of Growth in Adolescence." *Psychiatry,* 24 (1961): 18–31.

"Non-United Navy." *Senior Scholastic,* 10 Oct. 1949: 14.

Norton, Roy. *The Vanishing Fleets.* New York: D. Appleton, 1908.

Norvell, George. *The Reading Interests of Young People.* Boston: Heath, 1950.

Nowak, Marion. "'How to Be a Woman': Theories of Female Education in the 1950s." *Journal of Popular Culture,* 9 (Summer 1975): 77–83.

Noyes, Richard. "The Teacher and the Atom Bomb." *Journal of the National Education Association,* 35,6 (1946): 296–297.

"Oak Ridge On Wheels." *The Journal of the National Education Association,* 40 (December 1951): 606.

Oakley, J. Ronald. *God's Country: America in the Fifties.* 1986. New York: Dembner Books, 1990.

O'Brien, Tim. *The Nuclear Age.* New York: Alfred A. Knopf, 1985.

Ogden, Annegret. *The Great American Housewife: From Helpmate to Wage Earner, 1776–1986.* Westport, Conn.: Greenwood Press, 1986.

Ogden, W. "Ridge Kids Use the Atom." *New York Times Magazine,* 2 June 1946: 24–25.

Olson, Keith. *The G.I. Bill, the Veterans, and the Colleges*. Lexington: University of Kentucky Press, 1974.

"One World and the Teaching of History." *School and Society*, 23 Aug. 1947: 132.

"One World...or None." *Senior Scholastic*, 20 Oct. 1948: 5.

O'Neill, William. *Coming Apart*. New York: Quadrangle, 1975.

Orrico, A.J. "School Club Gives Preview of Nursing." *Occupations*, 24 (December 1945): 156–157.

Orwell, George. *Ninety Eighty-Four*. New York: Harcourt, Brace and Co., 1949.

"Our Expanding Atom." *Senior Scholastic*, 17 Sept. 1952: 19–21.

Overstreet, Bonaro. "Understanding Our Fears." *Journal of the National Education Association*, 41 (February 1952): 85–86.

Paarlberg, Rob. "Forgetting About the Unthinkable." *Foreign Policy* 10 (Spring 1973): 132.

Palmer, E.L. "What Next? Education for the Atomic Age." *Nature Magazine*, 40 (January 1947): 45.

"Pan American Club Activities." *School Life*, 28 (October 1945): 20–23.

Parish, James Robert, and Michael R. Pitts, eds. *The Great Science Fiction Pictures*. Metuchen, N.J.: The Scarecrow Press, 1977.

Peckham, Earl. "The Place of Civil Defense in Education." *School and Society*, 9 August 1952: 87–90.

Peffer, Nathaniel. "Politics Is Peace." *The American Scholar*, 15 (1946): 160–166.

Pells, Richard. *The Liberal Mind in a Conservative Age*. New York: Harper & Row, 1985.

Perkins, John S. "Where Is the Social Sciences' Atomic Bomb?" *School and Society*, 17 Nov. 1945: 315–317.

Perry, Arnold. "Fundamental Education and the Defense of Democracy." *The High School Journal*, 38 (January 1955): 117–123.

Peters, Charles. *Teaching High School History and Social Studies for Citizenship Training*. Coral Gables, Fla.: University of Miami Press, 1948.

Phillips, James Atlee. "The Delegate from Everywhere." *Senior Scholastic*, 6 May 1946: 25–29.

Phillips, Rog. (As Symmes Chadwick Oliver.) "Atom War." *Amazing Stories*, May 1946: 74–91.

_____. "So Shall Ye Reap!" *Amazing Stories* (August 1947): 8–43, 101–155.

Pike, Sumner. "The Promise of Atomic Energy." *Education*, 71,7 (1951): 407–413.

Pinette, Mattie. "School and Community Face the Atomic Age." *School Life*, 35 (September 1953): 155.

Piper, H. Beam. "Day of the Moron." *The Worlds of H. Beam Piper*. Ed. John Carr. New York: Ace Books, 1983. 199–231.

Piper, Robert. "Where Do We Go from Here?" *American Mercury*, 81 (August 1955): 82–84.

"Pooling Atomic Power for Peace." *Senior Scholastic*, 6 Jan. 1954: 10–11.

Powledge, Fred. *Free at Last? The Civil Rights Movement and the People Who Made It*. New York: Little, Brown and Co., 1991.

Prince, Gerald. *Narratology: The Form and Functioning of Narrative*. New York: Mouton, 1982.

"Psychologists Advise on the Atomic-Bomb Peril." *School and Society*, 8 June 1946: 405–406.

"PTA Warned to Prepare Youth for Atomic Attacks." *The Journal of Education*, 134 (September 1951): 177.

"Public Schools Urged to Stress Citizenship and United Nations." *The Journal of Education*, 133 (November 1950): 239.

"Pupils Beat Teachers on Atom Knowledge." *The Journal of Education*, 133 (May 1950): 155.

Rankin, Paul, and John Pritchard. "More Than a Place to Hide." *Journal of the National Education Association*, 40 (December 1951): 604–605.

Ravitch, Diane. *The Troubled Crusade: American Education, 1945–1980*. New York: Basic Books, 1983.

Rayburn, Sam. "That Civilization May Survive." *School Life*, 28 (October 1945): 9–10.

"Reactions of 150,000,000: Average American and the Russian Bomb." *Newsweek*, 3 Oct. 1949: 25–26.

Reaves, William. "Organized Extra-Curricular Activities in the High School." *The High School Journal,* 34 (May 1951): 130–133.

Reidelbach, Maria. *Completely Mad: A History of the Comic Book and Magazine.* Boston: Little, Brown and Co., 1991.

Remmers, H.H., and D.H. Radler. *The American Teenager.* New York: Bobbs-Merrill Co., 1957.

Reuter, Edward. "Sociological Research in Adolescence: The Adolescent World." *American Journal of Sociology,* 42 (July 1936): 81–83.

"Review of Seventy-Five, A Study of a Generation in Transition." *Time,* 9 Feb. 1953: 66+.

Rhodes, Richard. *The Making of the Atomic Bomb.* New York: Simon and Schuster, 1986.

Ridenour, Dr. Louis. "Pilot Lights of the Apocalypse," *Senior Scholastic,* 29 April 1946: 17–20.

_____. "Science and Secrecy." *The American Scholar,* 15 (1946): 147–153.

Ridgway, James. "Education's Policy for Planning and Action in Civil Defense." *American School Board Journal,* 120 (March 1950): 24–25.

Riesman, David. *The Lonely Crowd.* 1950. New Haven: Conn.: Yale University Press, 1961.

Riffaterre, Michael. *Fictional Truth.* Baltimore: Johns Hopkins University Press, 1990.

Robin, Richard. "Power and the Atom." *The Journal of Educational Sociology,* 22 (January 1949): 350–352.

Robinson, Thomas. "School Newspaper Can Promote Learning." *Journal of the National Education Association,* 36 (March 1947): 210–211.

Roblee, D.B. "What Schools Are Doing About Civil Defense." *School Life* 35 (September 1953): 154.

Rockwell, Joan. *Fact in Fiction: The Use of Literature in the Systematic Study of Society.* London: Routledge and Kegan Paul, 1974.

Rodnitzky, Jerome. "The Evolution of the American Protest Song." *The Age of Rock.* Ed. Timothy E. Scheurer. Bowling Green, Ohio: Bowling Green State University Popular Press, 1989. 118.

Rogers, Harold. "Smoke Jumper." *Senior Scholastic,* 20 Sept. 1950: 25–26+.

Rogin, Michael. "Kiss Me Deadly: Communism, Motherhood and Cold War Movies." *Representations,* 6 (Spring 1984): 1–36.

_____. *Ronald Reagan, the Movie and Other Episodes in Political Demonology.* Berkeley: University of California Press, 1987.

Rose, Mark. *Alien Encounters: Anatomy of Science Fiction.* Cambridge, Mass.: Harvard University Press, 1981.

Rosen, Marjorie. *Popcorn Venus: Women, Movies, and the American Dream.* New York: Coward, McCann, and Geohegan, 1973.

Rothman, Sheila. *Woman's Proper Place: A History of Changing Ideals and Practice, 1870 to the Present.* New York: Basic Books, 1978.

Rovin, Jeff. *A Pictorial History of Science Fiction Films.* Secaucus, N.J.: The Citadel Press, 1975.

Roznak, Theodore. *The Making of a Counter Culture.* New York: Pantheon, 1969.

Rubin, Nancy. *The New Surburban Woman: Beyond Myth and Motherhood.* New York: Coward, McCann & Geohegan, 1983.

Rudy, Willis. *Schools in the Age of Mass Culture.* Englewood, New Jersey: Prentice Hall, 1965.

Rugg, Harold. "Progressive Education — Which Way?" *Progressive Education,* 25,4 (1948): 35–37, 45.

Ryder, Norman. "The Cohort As a Concept in the Study of Social Change." *American Sociological Review,* 30 (1965): 843–861.

Scandrett, Nancy. "The Atom Goes to Sea." *Senior Scholastic,* 3 Feb. 1954: 18.

Saleh, Dennis. *Science Fiction Gold: Film Classics of the Fifties.* New York: Comma Books, 1979.

Salisbury, Harrison. *The Shook-Up Generation.* New York: Harper & Row, 1958.

"Say What You Please." *Senior Scholastic,* 5 Dec. 1951: 5.

Schwenger, Peter. *Letter Bomb: Nuclear Holocaust and the Exploding Word.* Baltimore: Johns Hopkins University Press, 1992.

Schultz, Robert. "Celluloid History: Postwar Society in Postwar Popular Culture." *American Studies,* 31 (Spring 1990): 46–63.

Sears, Laurence. "Anxiety in the United States of America." *Educational Freedom in an Age of Anxiety: Yearbook of the John Dewey Society 1953.* H. Gordon Hullfish, ed. New York: Harper & Brothers, 1953. 1–26.

Sebald, Hans. *Adolescence: A Sociological Analysis.* New York: Appleton-Century-Crofts, 1968.

Segrave, Kerry. *Drive-In Theaters: A History from Their Inception in 1933.* Jefferson, N.C.: McFarland & Co., 1992.

Seyfert, W.C. "Youth in the Atomic Age." *School Review,* 54 (June 1946): 319–320.

Shaheen, Jack, and Richard Taylor. "The Beginning or the End." Ed. Jack Shaheen. *Nuclear War Films.* Carbondale: Southern Illinois Press, 1978. 3–10.

"Shall We Share the Atomic Secret?" *Senior Scholastic,* 12 Nov. 1945: 3–5.

Shatter, A. "A Survey of Student Reading." *English Journal,* 40 (May 1951): 271–273.

Shunck, William. "Daily Routine Sets Emergency Patter." *Nation's Schools,* 47 (March 1951): 33.

"Sighted Navy, Sank Same." *Senior Scholastic,* 25 Feb. 1946: 3.

Silvens, G.H. "International Relations and the Secondary Curriculum." *Education,* 68 (May 1948): 526–531.

Slater, S.A. "Not A Gossip Sheet! High School Newspapers." *Journal of the National Education Association,* 40, 7 (1951): 489–490.

Smetak, Jacqueline. "Sex and Death in Nuclear Holocaust Literature of the 1950s." *The Nightmare Considered: Critical Essays on Nuclear War Literature.* Ed. Nancy Anisfield. Bowling Green, Ohio: Bowling Green State University Popular Press, 1991. 15–26.

Smith, Tom. "Nuclear Anxiety." *Public Opinion Quarterly,* 52 (1988): 557–575.

Sobchack, Vivian Carol. "The Alien Landscapes of the Planet Earth." *Science-Fiction Films.* Ed. Thomas Atkins. New York: Monarch Press, 1976. 49–61.

Sontag, Susan. "The Imagination of Disaster." *Against Interpretation and Other Essays.* New York: Farrar, Straus & Giroux, 1965. 220–225.

Sorrentino, Gilbert. "Remembrance of Bop in New York, 1945–1950." *Things in the Driver's Seat: Readings in Popular Culture.* Ed. Henry Russell. Chicago: Rand McNally, 1972. 124–136.

"The Split Atom: For Peace, for War." *Senior Scholastic,* 13 Oct. 1954: 9–10.

Spring, Joel. "Education as a Form of Social Control." *Roots of Crisis: American Education in the Twentieth Century.* Clarence Karies, Paul Violas, and Joel Spring, eds. Chicago: Rand McNally College Publishing Co., 1973). 30–39.

_____. *The Sorting Machine: National Educational Policy Since 1945.* New York: David McKay, 1976.

"Stalin and the Atom." *Senior Scholastic* 17 Oct. 1951: 16.

Stanley, William O., Jr. "The Sword and the Shield." *Progressive Education,* 25 (March 1948): 61–64+.

Starie, John. "Schools and the Atom." *Education,* 66 (1946): 501–502.

Starnes, W. Gayle. "Schools and Civil Defense." *American School Board Journal,* 135 (August 1957): 21–22.

Starr, Benjamin, and Abraham Leavitt. "Social Studies and 'Operation Atomic Vision.'" *High Points* 31 (April 1949): 22–32.

Stearns, Virginia Hardin. "Denver's International Relations Club." *The Journal of Education,* 133 (May 1950): 138–140.

Stedman, Raymond. *The Serials: Suspense and Drama by Installment.* Norman: University of Oklahoma Press, 1977.

Stein, David Lewis. *Living the Revolution: The Yippies in Chicago.* New York: Bobbs-Merrill, 1969.

Steinbrunner, Chris, and Burt Goldblatt, *Cinema of the Fantastic.* New York: Saturday Review Press, 1972.

Sternig, John. "For Adults Only." *Nation's Schools,* 47 (March 1951): 31–32.

Stewart, Milton. "Importance in Content Analysis: A Validity Problem." *Journalism Quarterly*, 20 (September 1943: 286–293.

Stone, I.F. "Atomic Pie in the Sky." *The Nation*, 6 April 1946: 390–391.

The Storm Before the Calm. Chicago: The Playboy Press, 1971.

Strang, Ruth. "Students Interpret the School to the Community." *The High School Journal* 34 (March 1951): 66–68.

"A Strong Defense Against the A-Bomb — Dispersal." *Senior Scholastic*, 26 Sept. 1951: 17–19.

Stubebaker, Mabel. "The Teacher and the Atom." *School Life*, Supplement 31 (March 1949): 1.

Studebaker, John W. "Avowed Objectives." *Senior Scholastic*, (Teacher Edition) 12 April 1952: 11T.

_____. "Communism's Challenge to American Education." *School Life*, 30 (February 1948): 1–7.

_____. *Education and the Fate of Democracy*. Los Angeles: University of California Press, 1948.

_____. "The High Schools of the Future." *School Life*, 29 (April 1947): 306.

_____. "Not 'Should' But 'How.'" *Senior Scholastic* (Teacher Edition), 3 Nov. 1948: 2-T.

_____. "Secondary Education for a New World." *School Life*, 29 (October 1946): 3–8.

"Students Favor World Government As Eventual Outgrowth of UNO." *Senior Scholastic*, 8 April 1946: 28.

"Students Fill Junior Red Cross Christmas Boxes." *School Activities*, 22 (November 1950): 109.

Sturgeon, Theodore. "Memorial." *Astounding Science-Fiction* (April 1946): 158–169. Reprinted in *The Worlds of Theodore Sturgeon*. New York: Ace, 1972. 380–398.

_____. "The Purple Light." *Senior Scholastic*, 12 April 1946: 25–29.

_____. "Thunder and Roses." *Astounding Science-Fiction* (November 1947): 76–98. Reprinted in *The Astounding Science-Fiction Anthology*. Ed. John W. Campbell. New York: Simon & Schuster, 1952. 351–370.

Susman, Warren, and Edward Griffin. "Did Success Spoil the United States? Dual Representations in Postwar America." *Recasting America: Culture and Politics in the Age of Cold War*. Ed. Lary May. Chicago: University of Chicago Press, 1989. 19–37.

Swan, Bryan, and Generose Dunn. "Unit on Atomic Energy for Junior High School." *The School Review*, 62 (April 1954): 231–236.

Swomley, John, Jr. "Is the Military Invading the Boy Scouts?" *Progressive Education*, 26, 3 (1949): 93–95.

Tarratt, Margaret. "Monsters from the Id." *Films and Filming*, 17 (December 1970): 38–42; and 17 (January 1971): 40–42.

"Task for Education." *The School Review*, 53 (1945): 503.

"Teaching Aids for Senior Scholastic." *Senior Scholastic* (Teacher Edition), 12 April 1946: 1T.

"Teaching the U.N. in Crisis." *The Journal of Education*, 134 (January 1951): 11–12.

"Teen-agers." *Life*, 20 Dec. 1948: 67–75.

"The 36-Hour War." *Life*, 19 Nov. 1945: 27–35.

Thomas, Frances. "Teaching the U.N. in Crisis." *The Journal of Education*, 134 (January 1951): 11–12.

Thompson, Jean. "The Impact on the Child's Emotional Life." *National Elementary Principal*, 30 (June 1951): 31.

Titus, A. Costandina. "Back to Ground Zero: Old Footage Through New Lenses." *Journal of Popular Film and Television* 20 (1983): 2–11.

_____. *Bombs in the Backyard: Atomic Testing and American Politics*. Reno: University of Nevada Press, 1986.

Todd, Lewis. "Atomic Energy and the Coming Revolution in Education." *School and Society*, 62 (1945): 251–257.

"Top Secret or Top Mistake?" *Senior Scholastic*, 4 Nov. 1953: 7–9.

Torrens, Hazel. "Current Events in the Ninth Grade." *The Education Digest*, 12 (December 1946): 22–23.

Tosches, Nick. *Unsung Heroes of Rock 'n' Roll: The Birth of Rock in the Wild Years Before Elvis*. New York: Harmony Books, 1984.

Train, Arthur Cheney, and Robert Williams Wood. *The Man Who Rocked the Earth*. Garden City, N.Y.: Doubleday, Page, 1915.

Troen, Samuel. "The Discovery of the Adolescent by American Educational Reformers, 1900–1920: An Economic Perspective." *Schooling and Society: Studies in the History of Education*. Lawrence Stone, ed. Baltimore: Johns Hopkins University Press, 1976). 239–250.

Tucheman, Gaye, Arlene Kaplan Daniels, and James Benet, eds. *Hearth and Home: Images of Women in the Mass Media*. New York: Oxford University Press, 1987.

Tugwell, Rexford Guy. "Atomic Anxieties." *The New Republic*, 20 Aug. 1945: 222.

"'Two to Five Years.'" *The Journal of Education*, 128 (December 1945): 297.

Ugland, Richard. "The Adolescent Experience During World War II." Dissertation. Indiana University, 1977.

Umstattd, J.G. "Contributions of the Secondary Schools in the Present World Situation." *The High School Journal*, 34 (May 1951): 145–152.

"U.N.: End or Beginning." *Senior Scholastic*, 20 Oct. 1947: 3.

"Uncertain Youth." *Time* 8 May 1950: 43.

United States. Bureau of the Census. *Historical Statistics of the United States: Colonial Times to 1970*. Washington, D.C., U.S. Department of Commerce, 1975.

_____. Office of Civil Defense. *Survival Under Atomic Attack*. Washington, D.C.: GPO, 1950.

Unruh, Adolph. "Life Adjustment Education — A Definition." *Progressive Education*, 29,4 (1952): 137–141.

Urey, Harold. "The Paramount Problem: A Plea for World Government." *The Atomic Age: Scientists in National and World Affairs*. Eds. Morton Grodzins and Eugene Rabinowitch. 1949. New York: Basic Books, 1963. 107–120.

"U.S. Defense Girdles the Globe." *Senior Scholastic*, 31 Oct. 1951: 10–12.

Van Pool, Gerald. "The Student Council Trains for Effective Citizenship." *School Activities*, 25 (September 1953): 7–9.

Viorst, Milton. *Fire in the Streets: America in the 1960s*. New York: Simon and Schuster, 1979.

"The War Ends: Burst of Atomic Bomb Brings Swift Surrender of Japanese." *Life* 20 Aug. 1945: 25–31.

Warner, W. Lloyd, and William E. Henry. "The Radio Daytime Serial: A Symbolic Analysis." *Genetic Psychological Monographs*, 37 (February 1948): 3–73.

Warren, Bill. *Keep Watching the Skies! American Science Fiction Movies of the Fifties, Volume 1*. Jefferson, N.C.: McFarland & Co., 1982.

Weart, Spencer. *Nuclear Fear: A History of Images*. Cambridge, Mass.: Harvard University Press, 1988.

"Week of Shock and Decision." *Life*, 13 Feb. 1950: 36–37.

Weibel, Kathryn. *Mirror Images: Images of Women Reflected in Popular Culture*. Garden City, N.Y.: Anchor, 1977.

Weitz, Leo. "A Social Studies Unit on Atomic Energy." *High Points*, 31 (February 1949): 14–26.

Wells, H.G. *The World Set Free*. New York: E. P. Dutton, 1914.

Welles, Sumner. "One Practical Chance — the UNO." *The American Scholar*, 15 (1946): 141–143.

Westley, William, and Frederick Elkin. "The Protective Environment and Adolescent Socialization." *Social Forces*, 35 (March 1957): 243–249.

"What Are the Teen-agers Thinking? Summary of an Unrehearsed Exchange of Views in San Francisco." *Rotarian*, 74 (January 1949): 14–16.

"What Ended the War." *Life*, 17 Sept. 1945: 37.

"What High-Schoolers Think." *Senior Scholastic*, 5 April 1950: 5.

"What Is Operation Atomic Vision?" *National Association of Secondary-School Principals Bulletin*, 32 (April 1948): 198–204.

Wheelis, Allen. *The Quest for Identity*. New York: W.W. Norton & Co., 1958.

"When Worlds Collide." *Senior Scholastic*, 28 Nov. 1951: 22.

"Where You Goin', But?" *Time*, 3 Oct. 1949: 36–37.

White, Ralph. "Ultimate and New: Ultimate Democratic Values." *Progressive Education,* 27,6 (1950): 165–171.

White, Lynn, Jr. *Educating Our Daughters.* New York: Harper & Row, 1950.

"Who Reads the Comics," *Senior Scholastic,* 17 May 1948: 3.

Whyte, William, Jr. *The Organization Man.* New York: Simon and Schuster, 1956.

Widmer, Kingsley. "American Apocalypse: Notes on the Bomb and the Failure of Imagination." *The Forties: Fiction, Poetry, Drama.* Ed. Warren French. Deland, Florida, 1969.

Wiggin, Gladys. "Teaching Peace Is Not Enough." *School Life,* 28 (July 1946): 17–18.

Williams, Carol Traynor. *The Dream Beside Me: The Movies and the Children of the Forties.* Rutherford, N.J.: Farleigh Dickinson University Press, 1980.

Williams, Nick Boddie. "Important to a Man." *Senior Scholastic,* 22 Sept. 1948: 31–32+.

Willis, Donald. *Horror and Science Fiction Films: A Checklist.* Metuchen, N.J.: Scarecrow Press, 1972.

Winkler, Allan. "A Forty-Year History of Civil Defense." *Bulletin of the Atomic Scientists,* 40 (June/July 1984): 16–22.

_____. *Life Under A Cloud: American Anxiety About the Atom.* New York: Oxford University Press, 1993.

Winne, Harry. "Atomic Energy in Our Time." *Senior Scholastic* ,7 March 1951: 5–7.

"Winning with the American Way," *School Life,* 31 (April 1949): 2–3+.

Wittner, Lawrence. *Rebels Against War: The American Peace Movement, 1933–1983.* Philadelphia: Temple University Press, 1984.

Witty, Paul. "Television and the High School Student." *Education,* 72 (December 1951): 246.

_____, and Harry Bricker. *Your Child and Radio, TV, Comics and Movies.* Chicago: Science Research Associates, 1952.

Wolfe, Charles. "Nuclear Country: The Atomic Bomb in Country Music." *Journal of Country Music* 7 (January 1978): 7–21.

Wolfe, Tom. *The Electric Kool-Aid Acid Test.* New York: Bantam Books, 1968.

"Wonderful to Play In." *Time* 5 Feb. 1951: 12.

Wood, Clement. "Tzagan." *Senior Scholastic,* 11 Oct. 1950: 23–24+.

"World Affairs Clubs Still Too Few." *The Journal of Education,* 133 (May 1950): 155.

"The World Blew Up." *Newsweek,* 19 Feb. 1951: 25.

"The World Federation Summer School in Geneva, Switzerland." *School and Society,* 26 July 1947: 54.

"World War III Preview." *Time,* 25 March 1946: 90.

"Worlds in Collison." *Senior Scholastic,* 1 March 1950: 13–14.

"The World's Still on a Tightrope." *Senior Scholastic,* 30 Nov. 1949: 5–7.

Wright, Quincy. "Barriers to World Peace." *School Review,* 54 (1946): 576–583.

Wylie, Philip. "Blunder." *Collier's,* 12 Feb. 1946. Reprinted in *Strange Ports of Call.* August Derleth, ed. New York: Pelligrini and Cudahy, 1948. 145–162.

_____. *Tomorrow!* New York: Rinehart, 1954.

Wyndham, John. *Re-Birth.* New York: Ballantine, 1955.

Wynne, Edward. "Adolescent Alienation and Youth Policy." *Teachers College Record* 78, 1 (1976): 23–40.

Yavenditti, Michael. "The American People and the Use of Atomic Bombs on Japan: The 1940s." *Historian,* 36 (February 1974): 224–246.

_____. "American Reactions to the Use of Atomic Bombs on Japan, 1945–1947." Dissertation. University of California, Berkeley, 1970.

_____. "John Hersey and the American Conscience: The Reception of Hiroshima." *Pacific Historical Review,* 43 (February 1974): 24–49.

"Year One — Hydrogen Time." *Senior Scholastic* ,11 Feb. 1953: 10–12.

York, Barbara. "Quincy High School's P.D. Course." *The Journal of Education,* 13 (September 1948): 218–219.

"You and America's Future." *Senior Scholastic,* 17 May 1948: 23.

"You Have a Date with Destiny." *Senior Scholastic*, 20 Sept. 1950: 9.

Young, Florence. "Psychological Effects of War on Young Children." *American Journal of Orthopsychiatry*, 17 (July 1947): 500–510.

"The Younger Generation," *Time*, 5 Nov. 1951: 46–48+.

"Youth in a Violent Age." *Commonweal*, 10 Sept. 1954: 550.

"Youth Speaks for Democracy." *School Life*, 30 (February 1948): 20–23.

Zeran, Franklin, ed. *Life Adjustment Education in Action*. New York: Chartwell House, 1953.

Zilliacus, Laurin. "World-Wide Union of Educators." *Progressive Education*, 24,2 (1946): 54–57.

Zwart, Gerrit. "How a Small High School Meets the Challenge of the Atomic Age: Suffern High School Atomic Energy Club." *School Life* Supplement 35 (September 1953): 147+.

Zucker, H.S. "Charm Club; Extra-Curricular Activity Conducted on a Voluntary Basis." *Senior Scholastic* (Teacher Edition) 9 Dec. 1946: 5T+.

Index